AOI HOUSE
in Love!

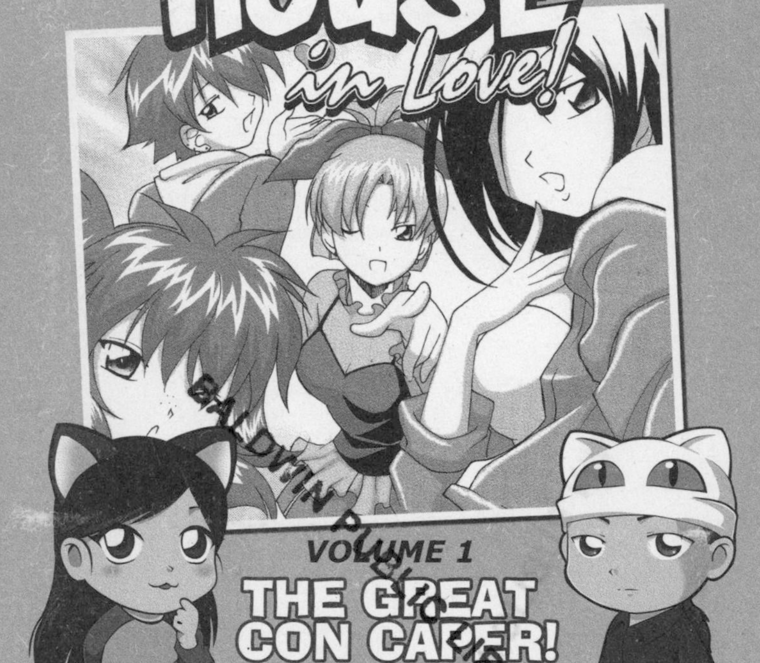

VOLUME 1

THE GREAT CON CAPER!

art by
SHIEI

story by
ADAM ARNOLD

AOI HOUSE in Love!

VOLUME 1

story by Adam Arnold art by Carmela "Shiei" Doneza

STAFF CREDITS

toning	**Armand Roy Canlas**
lettering	**Jon Zamar, Cheese**
graphic design	**Jon Zamar**
cover design	**Nicky Lim**
copy editor	**Randall Hendren**
assistant editor	**Adam Arnold**
editor	**Jason DeAngelis**
publisher	**Seven Seas Entertainment**

Visit us online at www.gomanga.com.

ISBN 978-1-933164-51-9

Printed in Canada

First printing: June, 2007

10 9 8 7 6 5 4 3 2 1

CONTENTS

The Great Con Caper!

EXTRAS

AOI HOUSE *in Love!*

LAST SEASON ON AOI HOUSE

A semester ago, Alex and Sandy were in rough shape. They had just started college and were already sitting in front of the dean of Mooreland State University looking to be kicked out of their dorms. Mr. Perkins is a good guy, though. He knows what college life is like and was more than willing to let the boys off the hook. That is, until Sandy's troublemaking pet hamster decided to call Mr. Perkins' toupee home... so out the boys went!

With nowhere to stay on campus, the boys were ready to quit college when they saw a flyer for a live-in anime club called Aoi House. It was like a beacon of hope in their time of need. But what a nightmare it turned out to be!

Yes, it technically was an anime club... but one that ended up being run by a bunch of crazed yaoi fangirls, who sure put Alex and Sandy through the ringer over the course of that semester. From their all-night yaoi marathons with Alex and Sandy strapped in *A Clockwork Orange*-style to Morgan's panty raids with the "ecchi-cam," things were never exactly what you'd call normal.

Everything really came to a head during that first trip to the mall, though. It started like any other girl-run shopping trip with the boys carrying everything the girls bought and ended up a full-on *DDR* tournament with control of Aoi House riding on the outcome. The boys ended up losing and Alex was forced to go on a date with club founder and resident transvestite Carlo.

Well, Alex and Sandy have somehow managed to survive their Fall Semester of college and warmed up to the girls in the process.

THE MEMBERS OF AOI HOUSE

THE BOYS

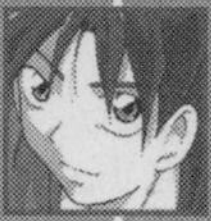

Alexis "Alex" Robert is the everyman. In most cases, Alex is the voice of reason that just gets dragged along by everyone else's wild antics.

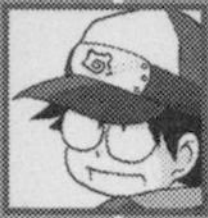

Sandy Grayson is Alex's best friend and a complete otaku. He's the "id" to Alex's "ego." If there's trouble, Sandy always takes the blame..

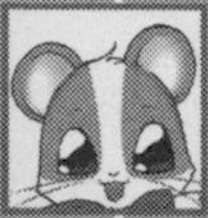

Echiboo is Sandy's pet hamster that has a serious thing for women's panties.

THE GIRLS

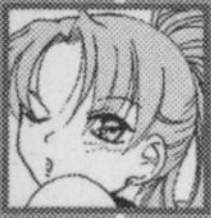

Elle Mathers is this psycho, super-controlling rich girl that always has to have things her way.

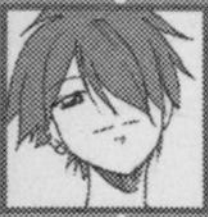

Nina Parker is the exact opposite. She's totally laid back and just likes to go with the flow.

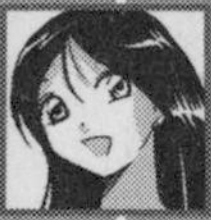

Jessica Kim iis the motherly type that's drop dead gorgeous and sometimes a complete flirt. She's training to be a nurse.

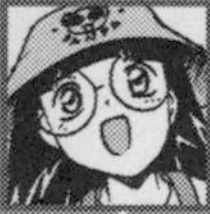

Maria Ortega is the shy and insecure type that tends to keep to herself a lot. She's really sweet if you get to know her, though.

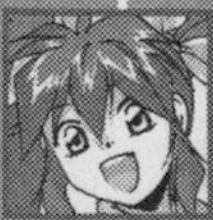

Morgan McKnight cannot be summed up easily. It's like she's on a nonstop sugar high all the time. And the things she says... Oh well, at least her heart is in the right place.

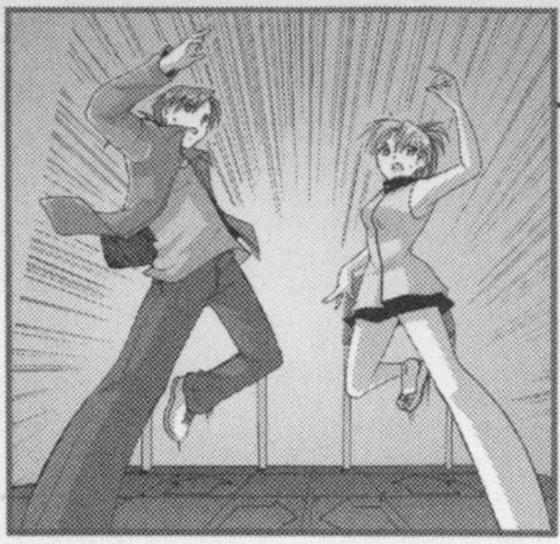

Sure, everyone had a tough time at the end of the semester with everyone being stuck at Aoi House for Christmas, but they stuck together and really become a cohesive club.

There is something more, though. Love is definitely in the air. And with Hatsu-Con—the convention they've waited all semester for—finally upon them, romance is sure to blossom!

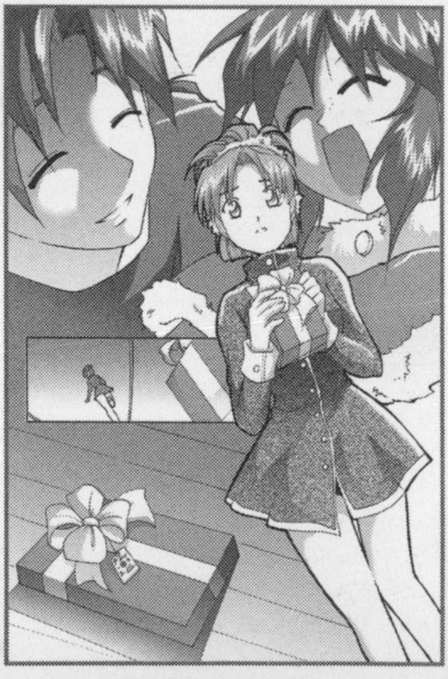

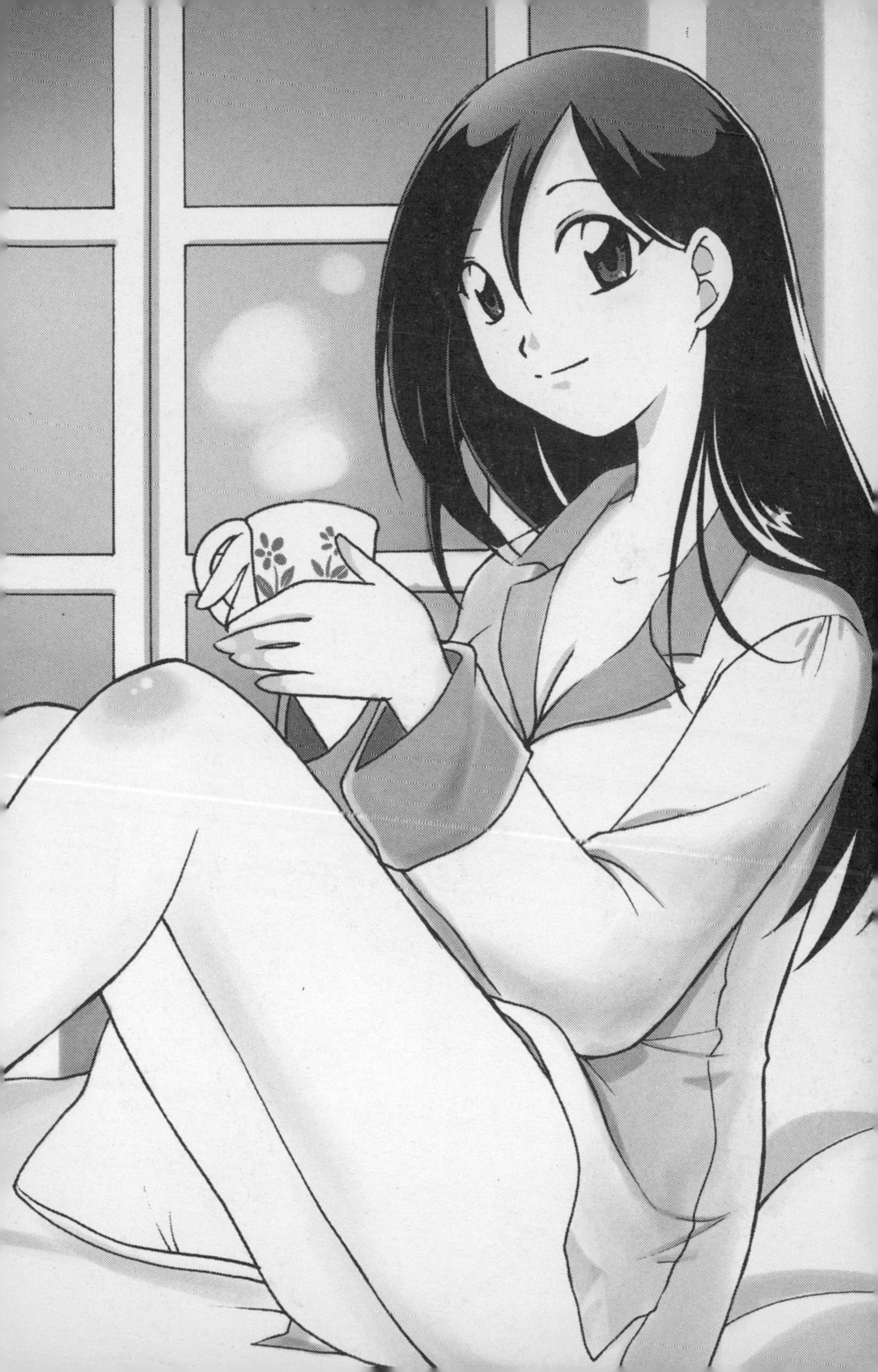

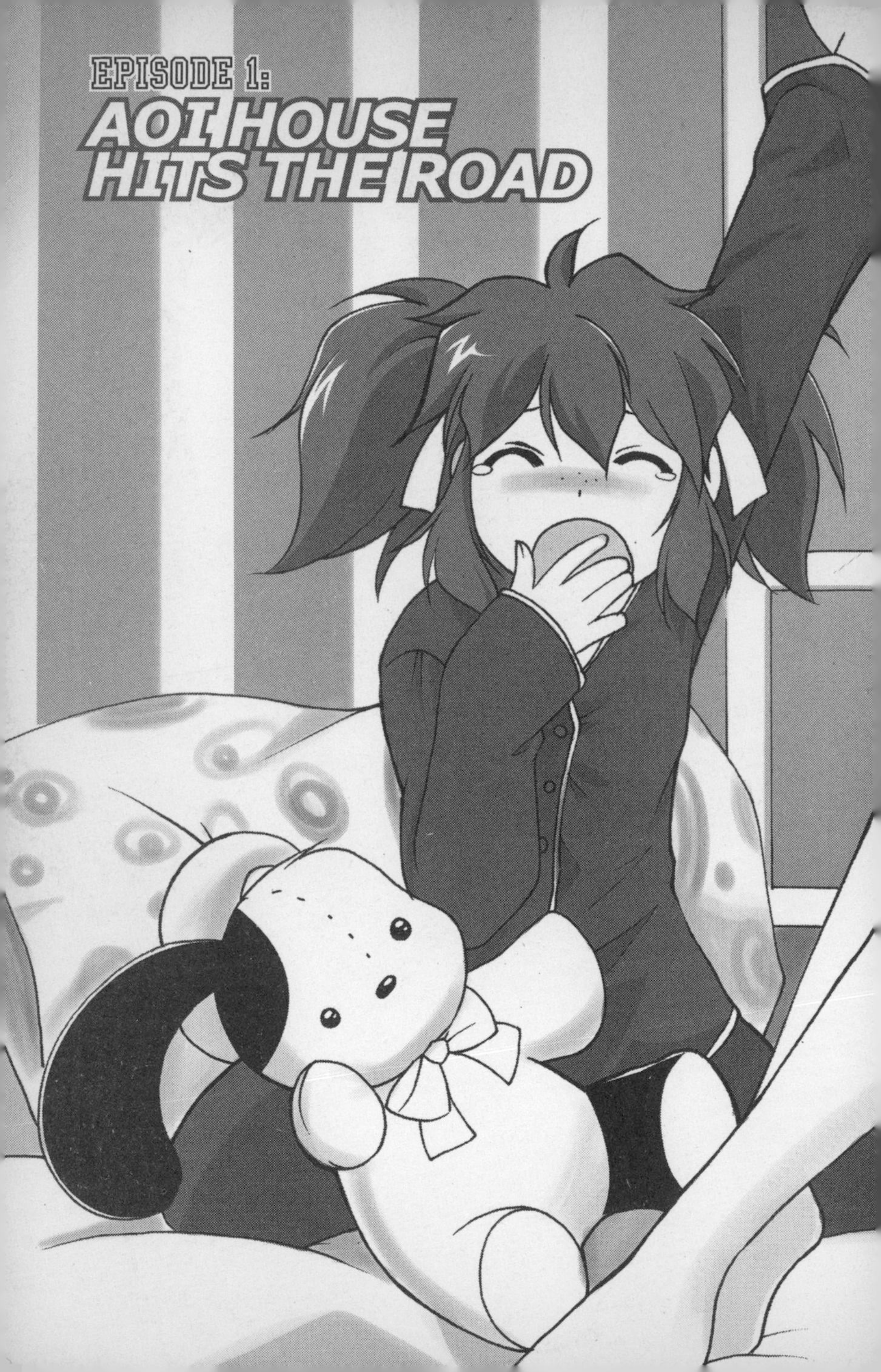
EPISODE 1:
AOI HOUSE
HITS THE ROAD

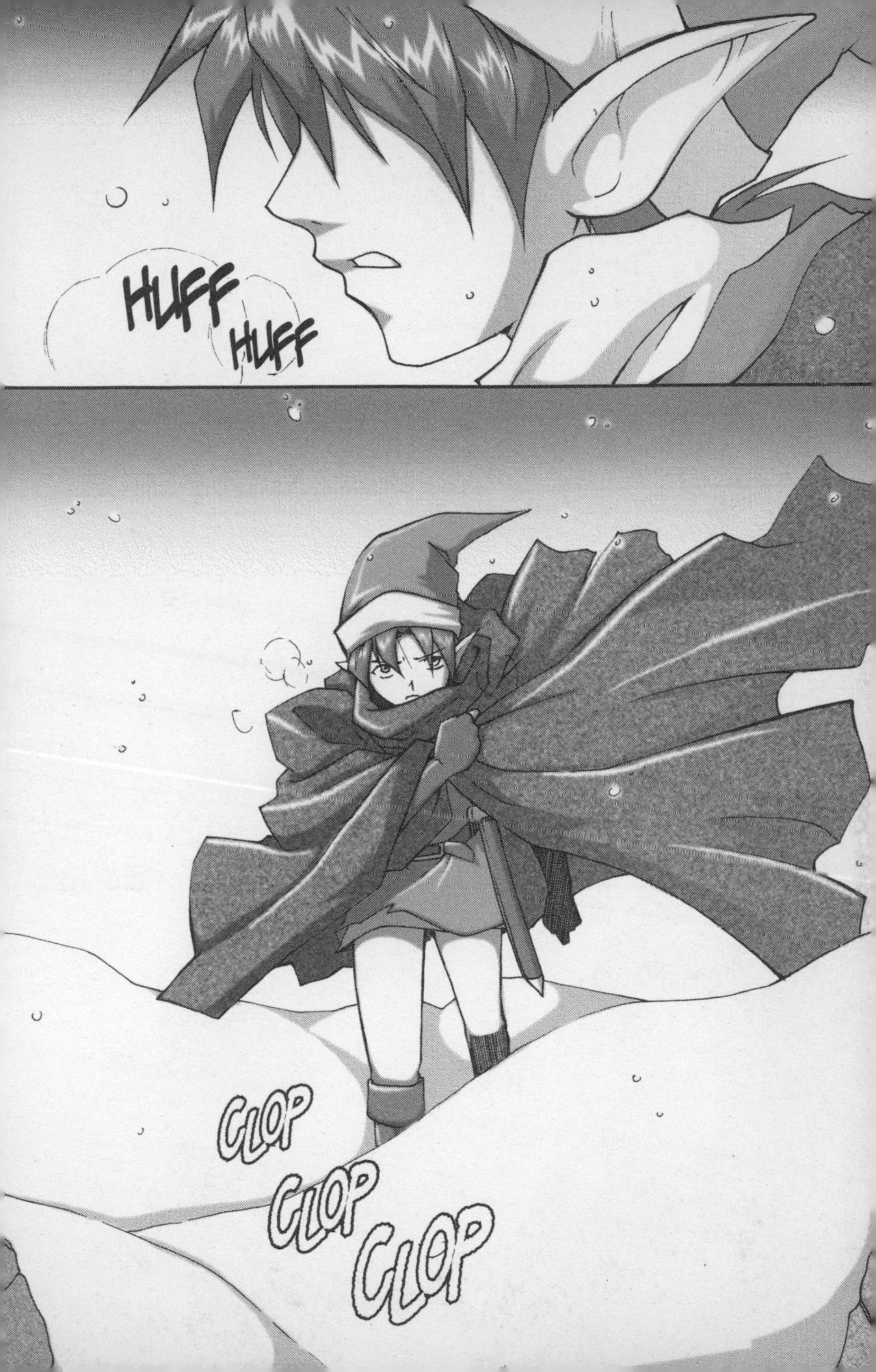
HUFF
HUFF
CLOP
CLOP
CLOP

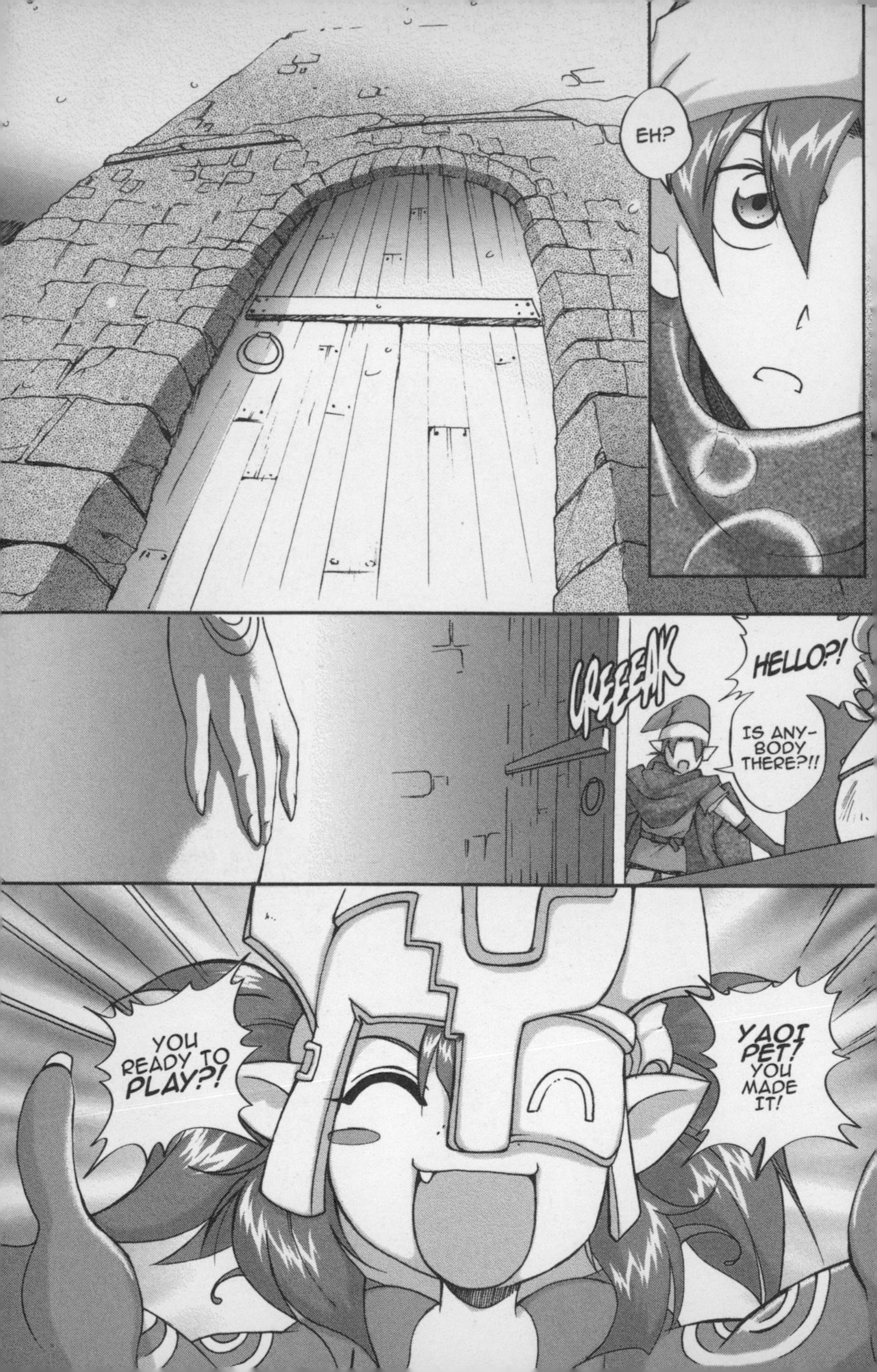
EH?
CREEEAK
HELLO?!
IS ANY-BODY THERE?!!
YAOI PET! YOU MADE IT!
YOU READY TO PLAY?!

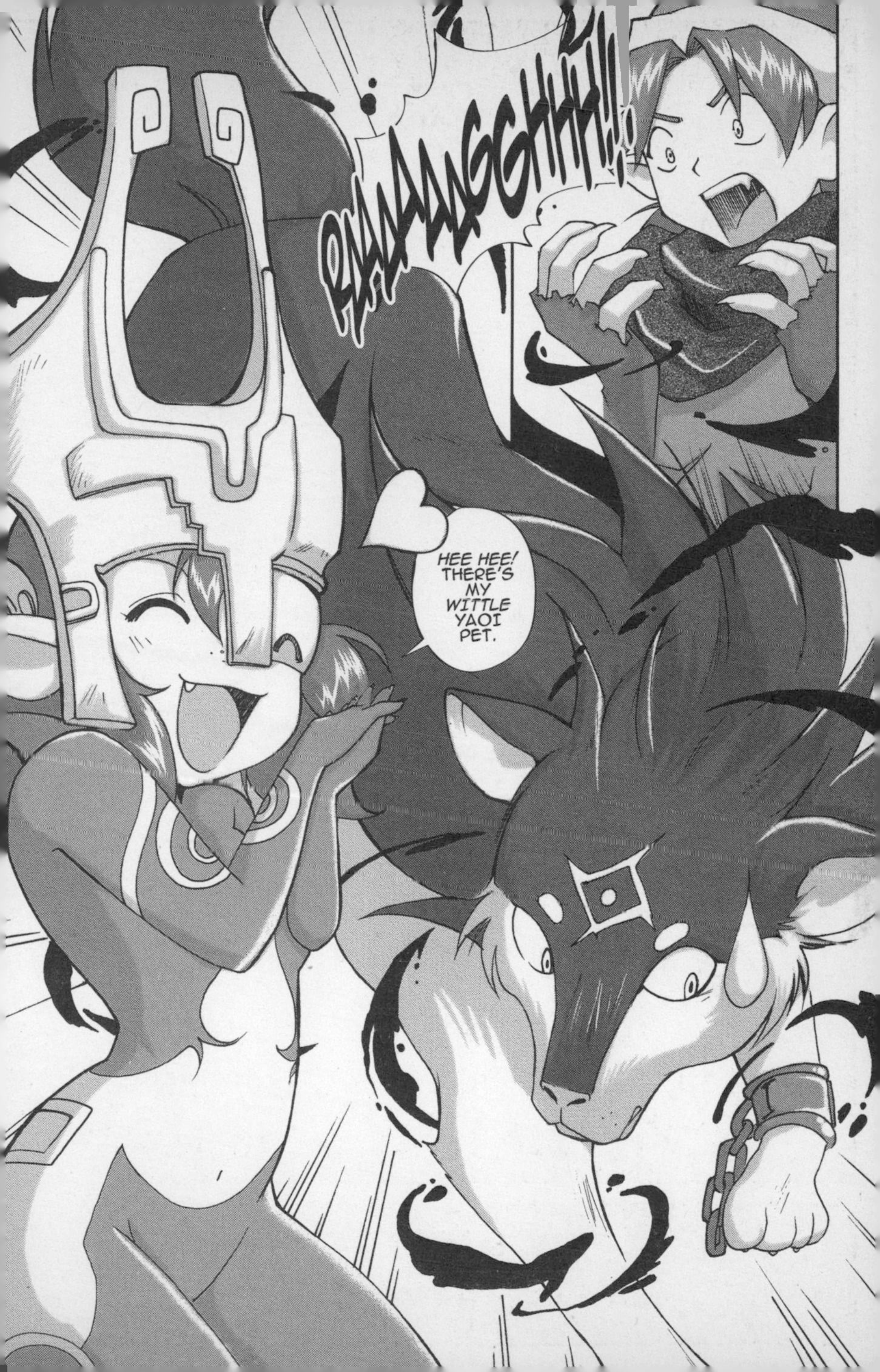
RAAAAGHHH!!!
HEE HEE! THERE'S MY WITTLE YAOI PET.

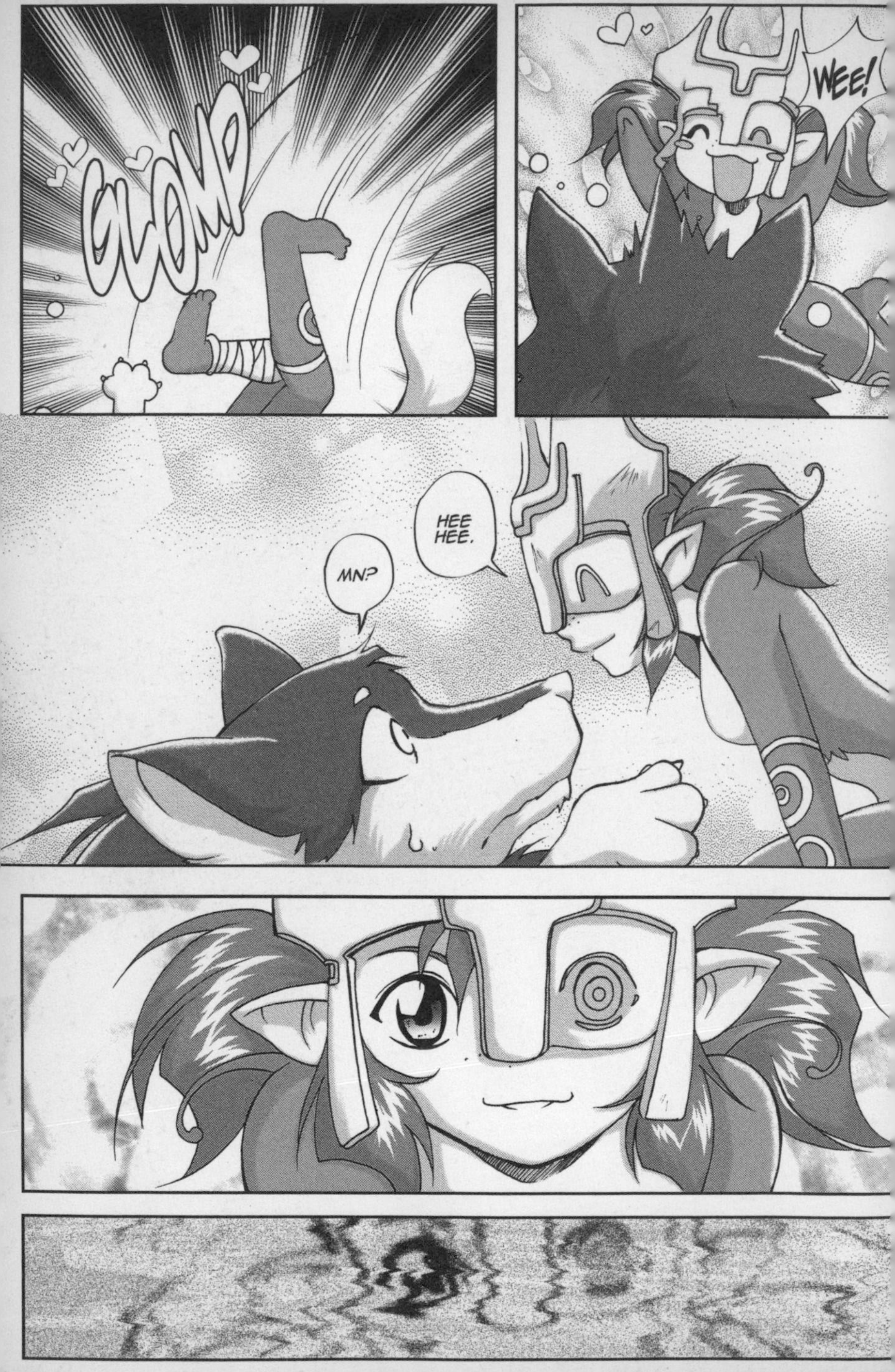
WEE!
GLOMP
HEE HEE.
MN?

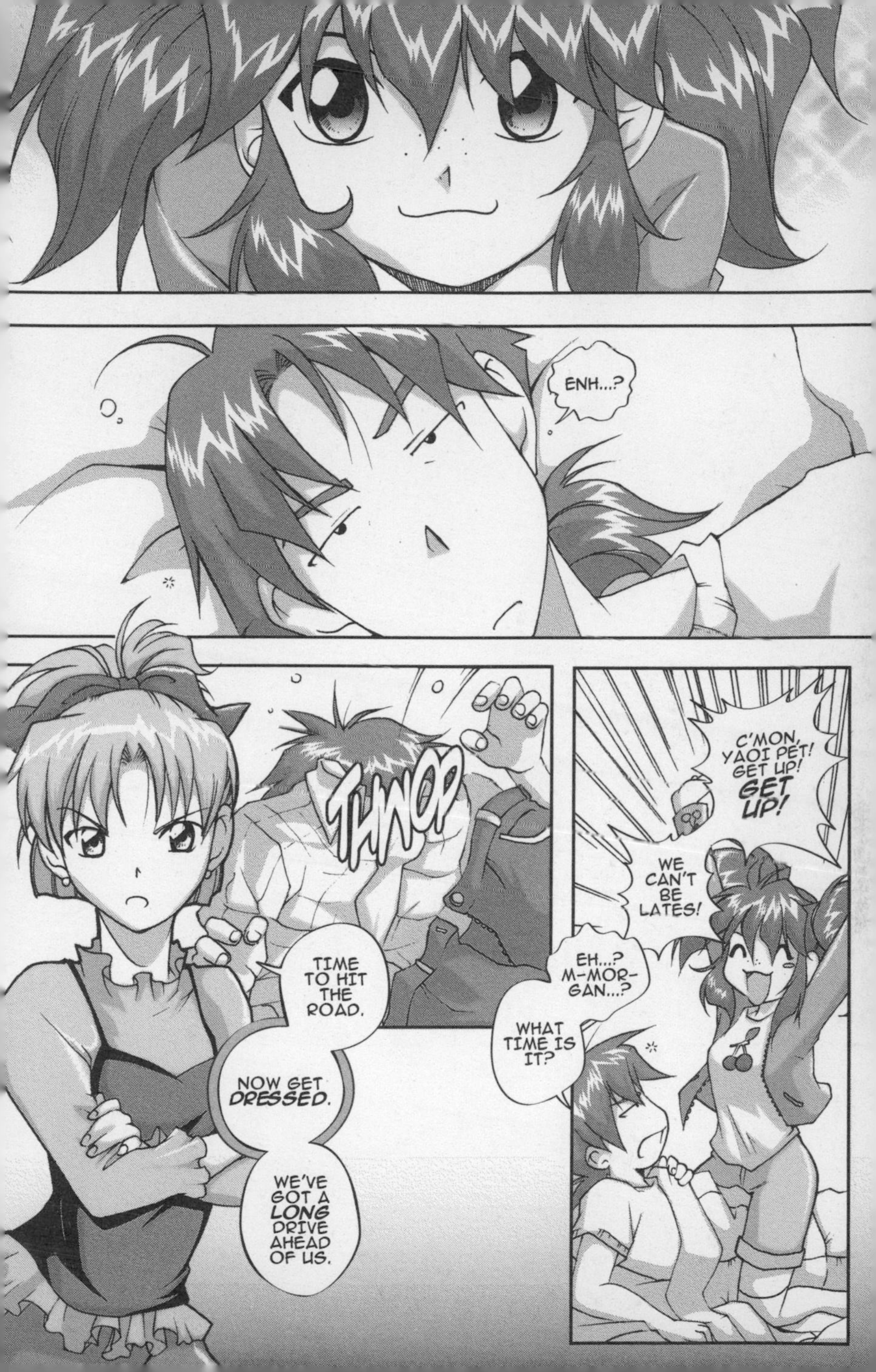
ENH...?
C'MON, YAOI PET! GET UP! GET UP!
WE CAN'T BE LATES!
EH...? M-MORGAN...?
WHAT TIME IS IT?
THWOP
TIME TO HIT THE ROAD.
NOW GET DRESSED.
WE'VE GOT A LONG DRIVE AHEAD OF US.

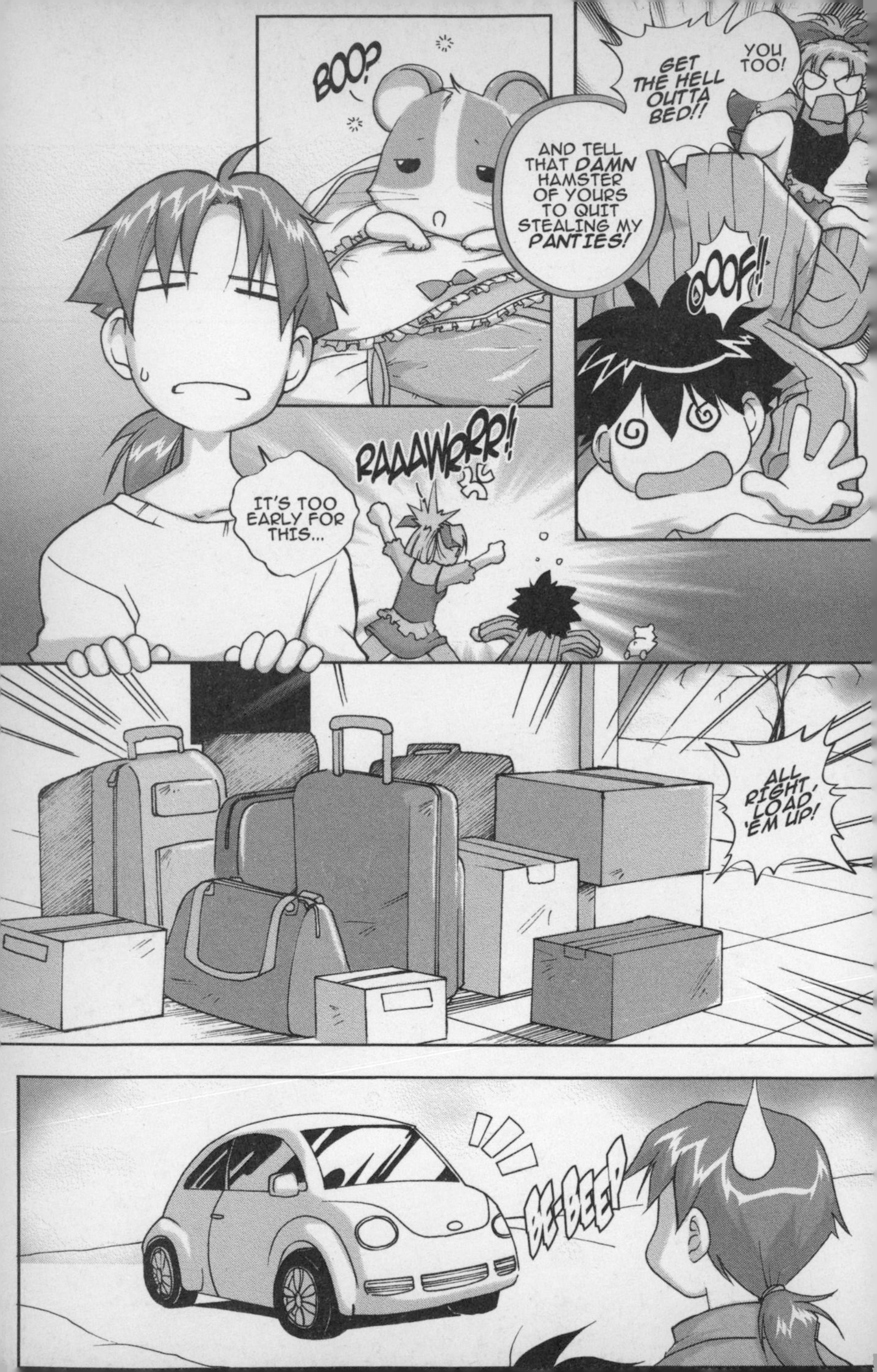
YOU TOO!
GET THE HELL OUTTA BED!!
AND TELL THAT DAMN HAMSTER OF YOURS TO QUIT STEALING MY PANTIES!
OOOF!!
BOOP
RAAAWRRR!!
IT'S TOO EARLY FOR THIS...
ALL RIGHT, LOAD 'EM UP!
BE-BEEP

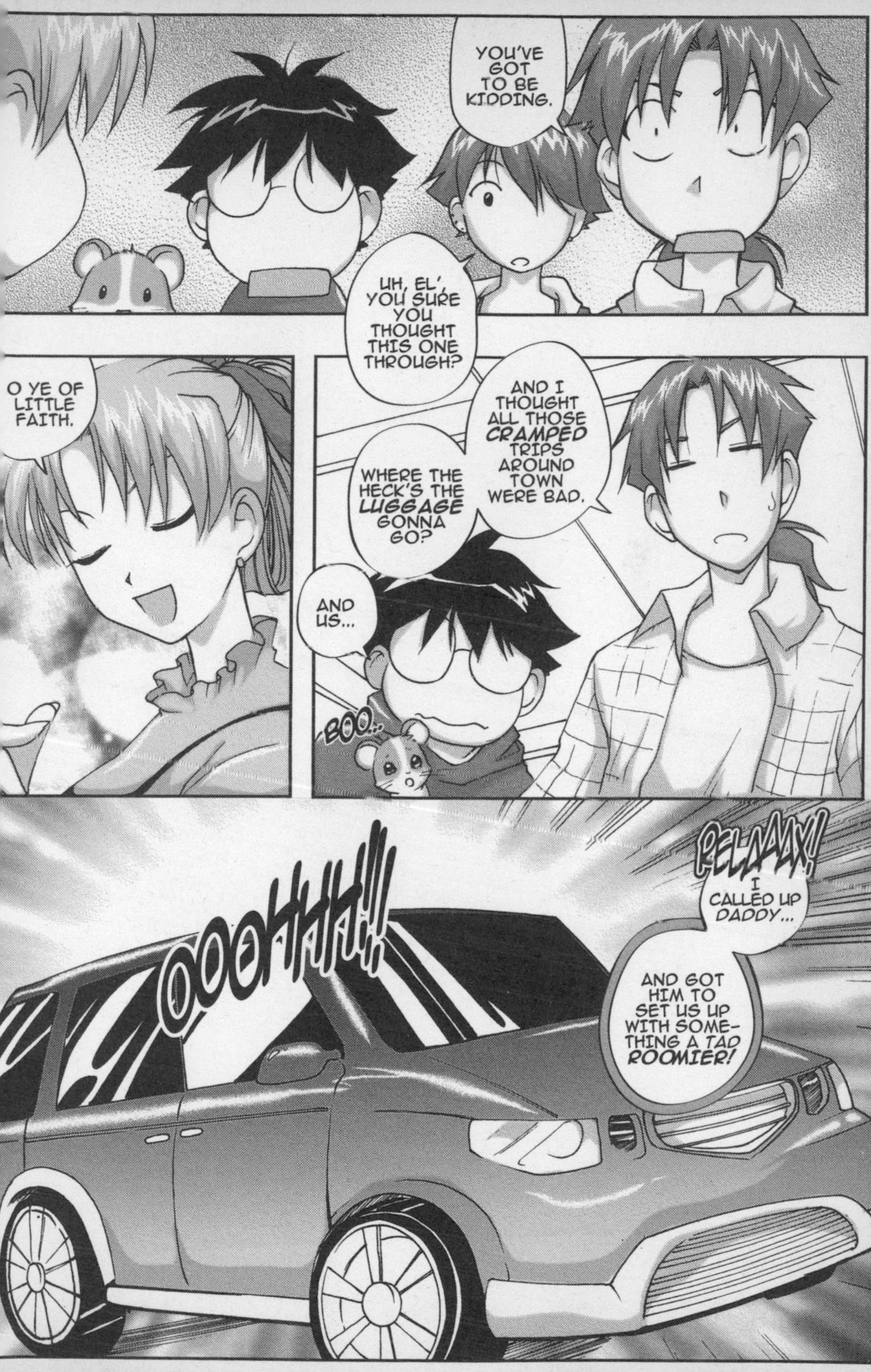
YOU'VE GOT TO BE KIDDING.
UH, EL', YOU SURE YOU THOUGHT THIS ONE THROUGH?
AND I THOUGHT ALL THOSE CRAMPED TRIPS AROUND TOWN WERE BAD.
WHERE THE HECK'S THE LUGGAGE GONNA GO?
AND US...
BOO...
O YE OF LITTLE FAITH.
RELAAAX!
I CALLED UP DADDY...
AND GOT HIM TO SET US UP WITH SOME-THING A TAD ROOMIER!
VOOOHHH!!

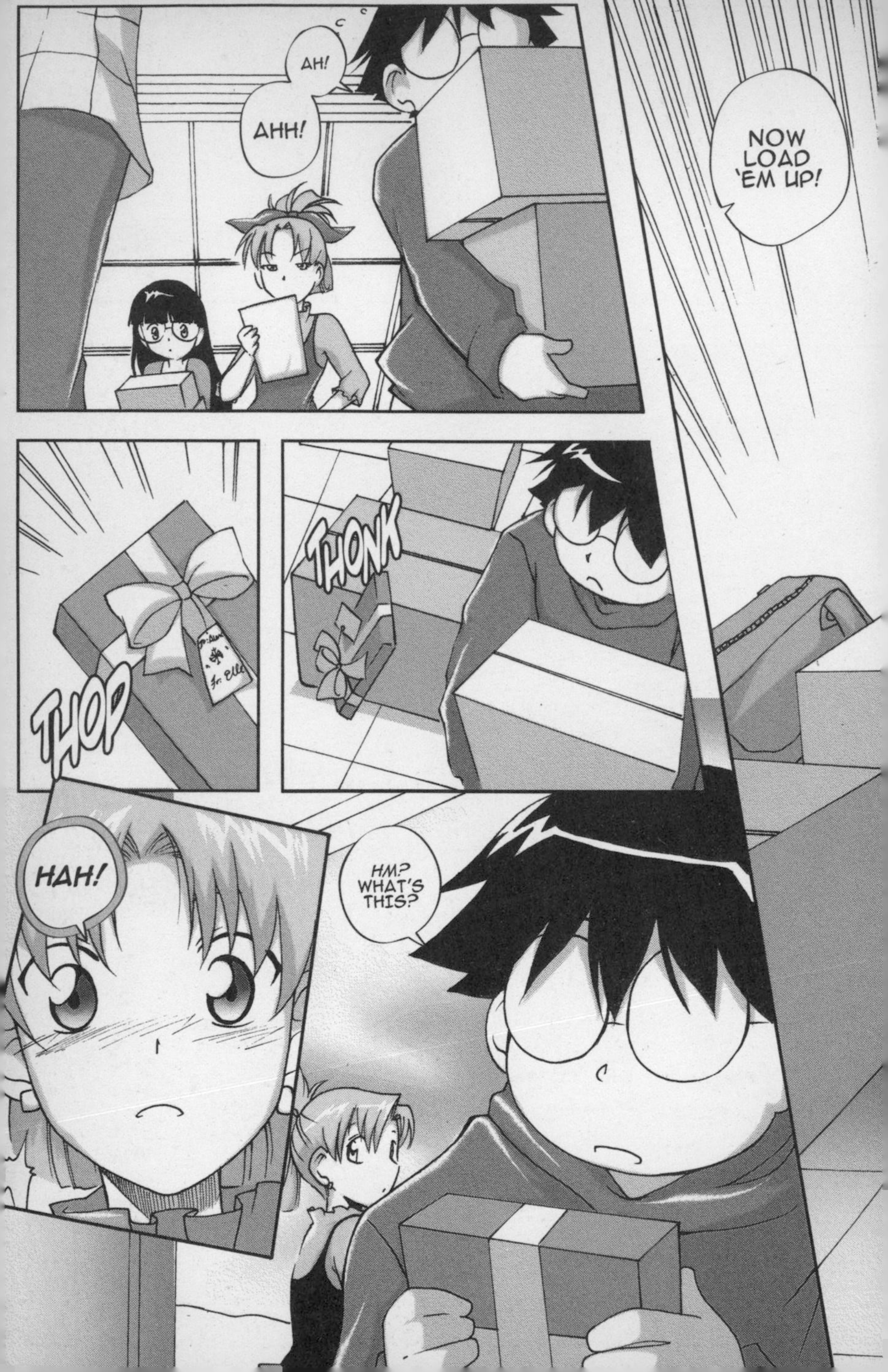
NOW LOAD 'EM UP!
AH!
AHH!
THONK
THOP
HM? WHAT'S THIS?
HAH!

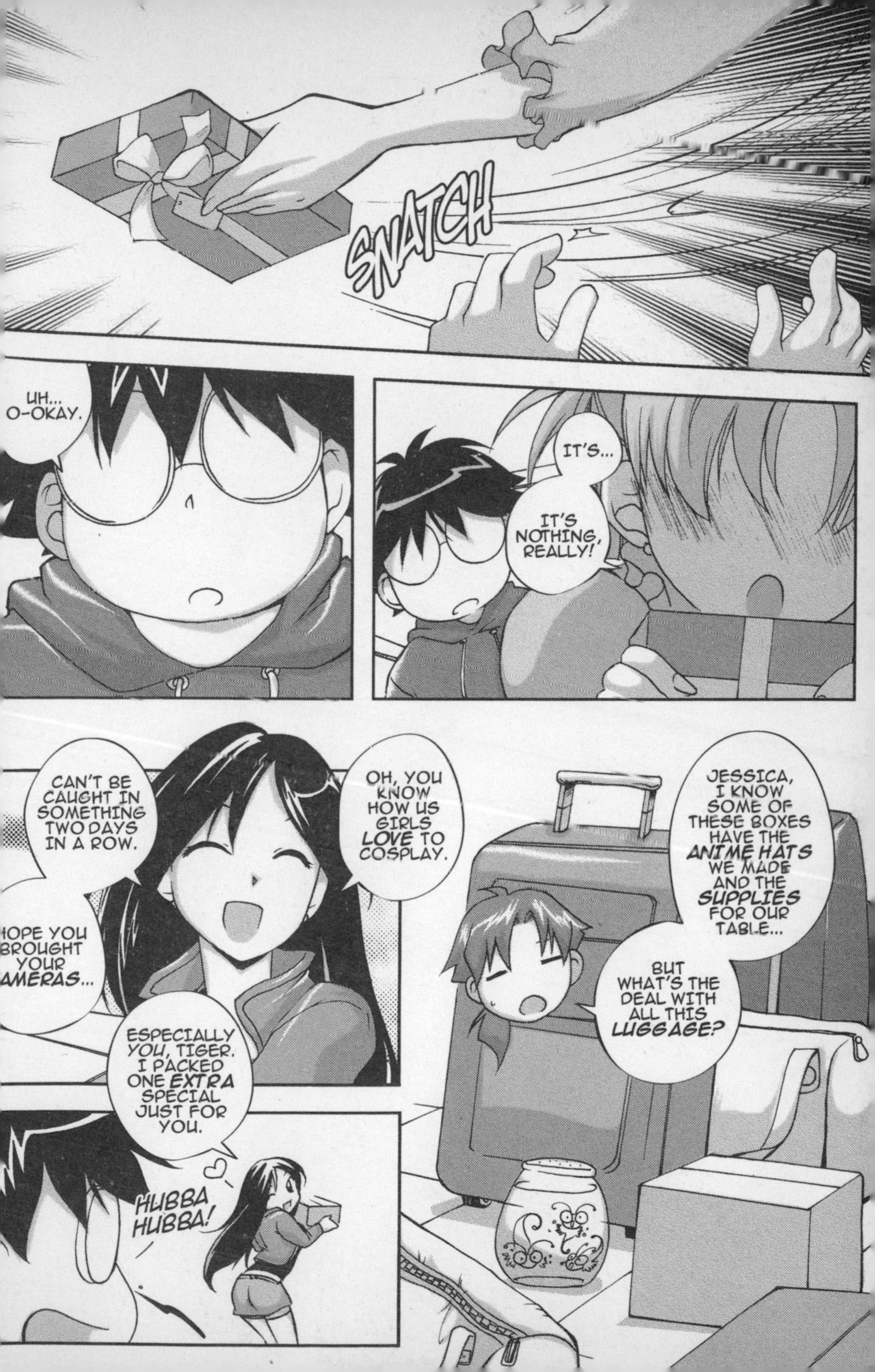
SNATCH
IT'S...
IT'S NOTHING, REALLY!
UH... O-OKAY.
JESSICA, I KNOW SOME OF THESE BOXES HAVE THE ANIME HATS WE MADE AND THE SUPPLIES FOR OUR TABLE...
BUT WHAT'S THE DEAL WITH ALL THIS LUGGAGE?
OH, YOU KNOW HOW US GIRLS LOVE TO COSPLAY.
CAN'T BE CAUGHT IN SOMETHING TWO DAYS IN A ROW.
OPE YOU BROUGHT YOUR AMERAS...
ESPECIALLY YOU, TIGER. I PACKED ONE EXTRA SPECIAL JUST FOR YOU.
HUBBA HUBBA!

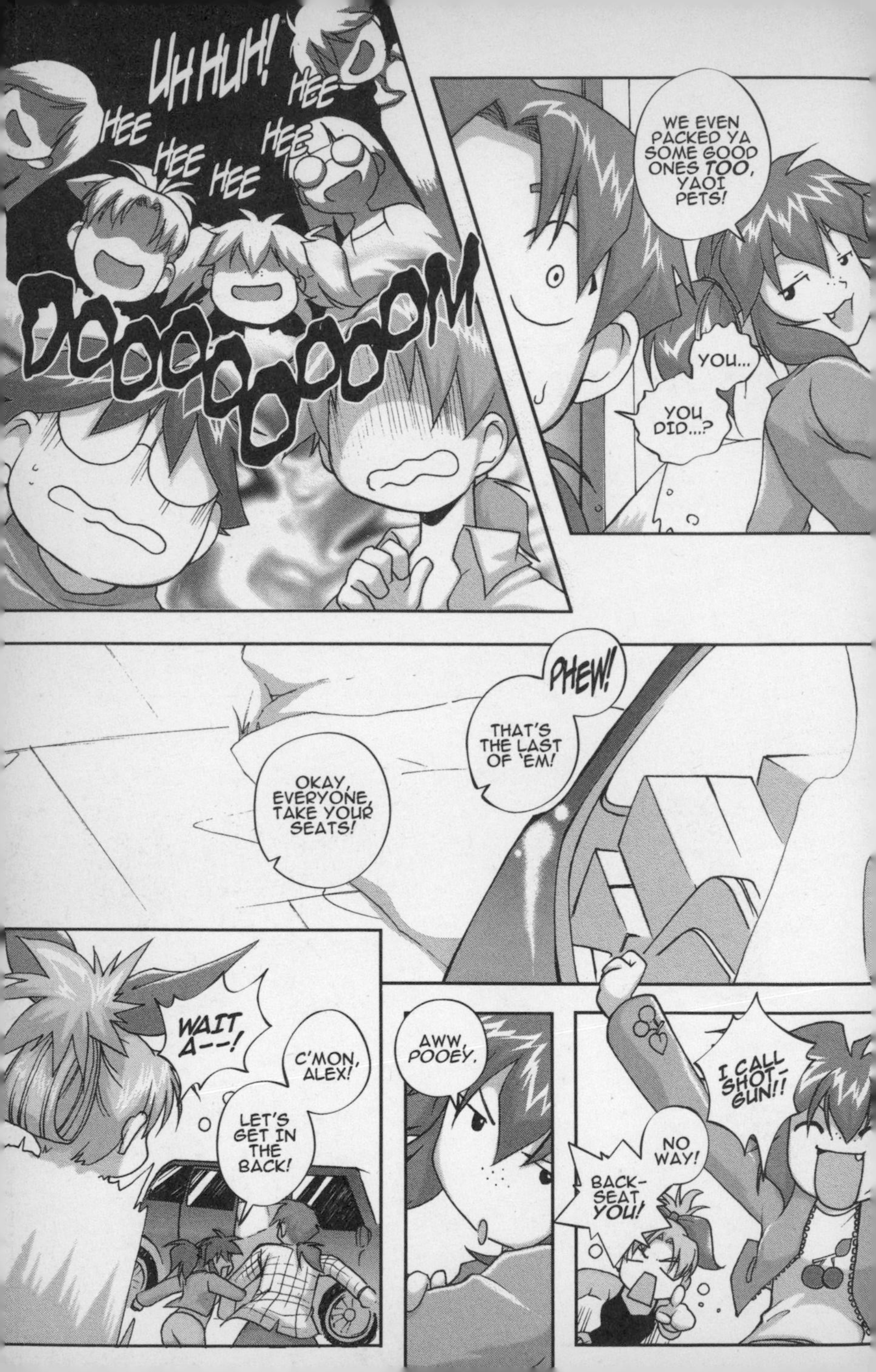
WE EVEN PACKED YA SOME GOOD ONES *TOO*, YAOI PETS!
YOU...
YOU DID...?
UH HUH!
HEE HEE HEE HEE HEE
DOOOOOOOOOM
PHEW!
THAT'S THE LAST OF 'EM!
OKAY, EVERYONE, TAKE YOUR SEATS!
I CALL SHOT-GUN!!
NO WAY!
BACK-SEAT, *YOU!*
AWW, *POOEY.*
WAIT A--!
C'MON, ALEX!
LET'S GET IN THE BACK!

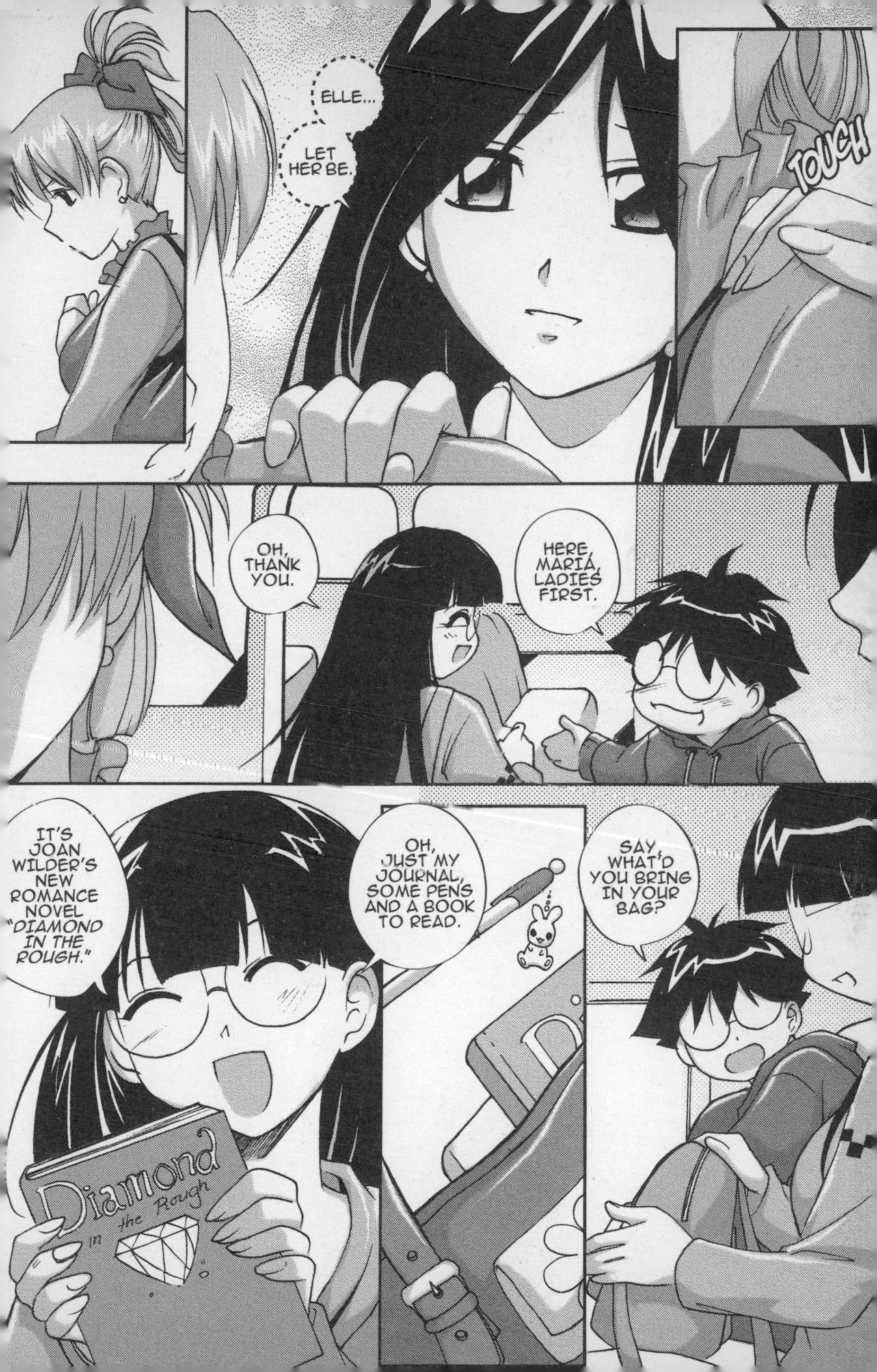
TOUCH
ELLE...
LET HER BE.
HERE, MARIA, LADIES FIRST.
OH, THANK YOU.
SAY, WHAT'D YOU BRING IN YOUR BAG?
OH, JUST MY JOURNAL, SOME PENS AND A BOOK TO READ.
IT'S JOAN WILDER'S NEW ROMANCE NOVEL "DIAMOND IN THE ROUGH."
Diamond in the Rough

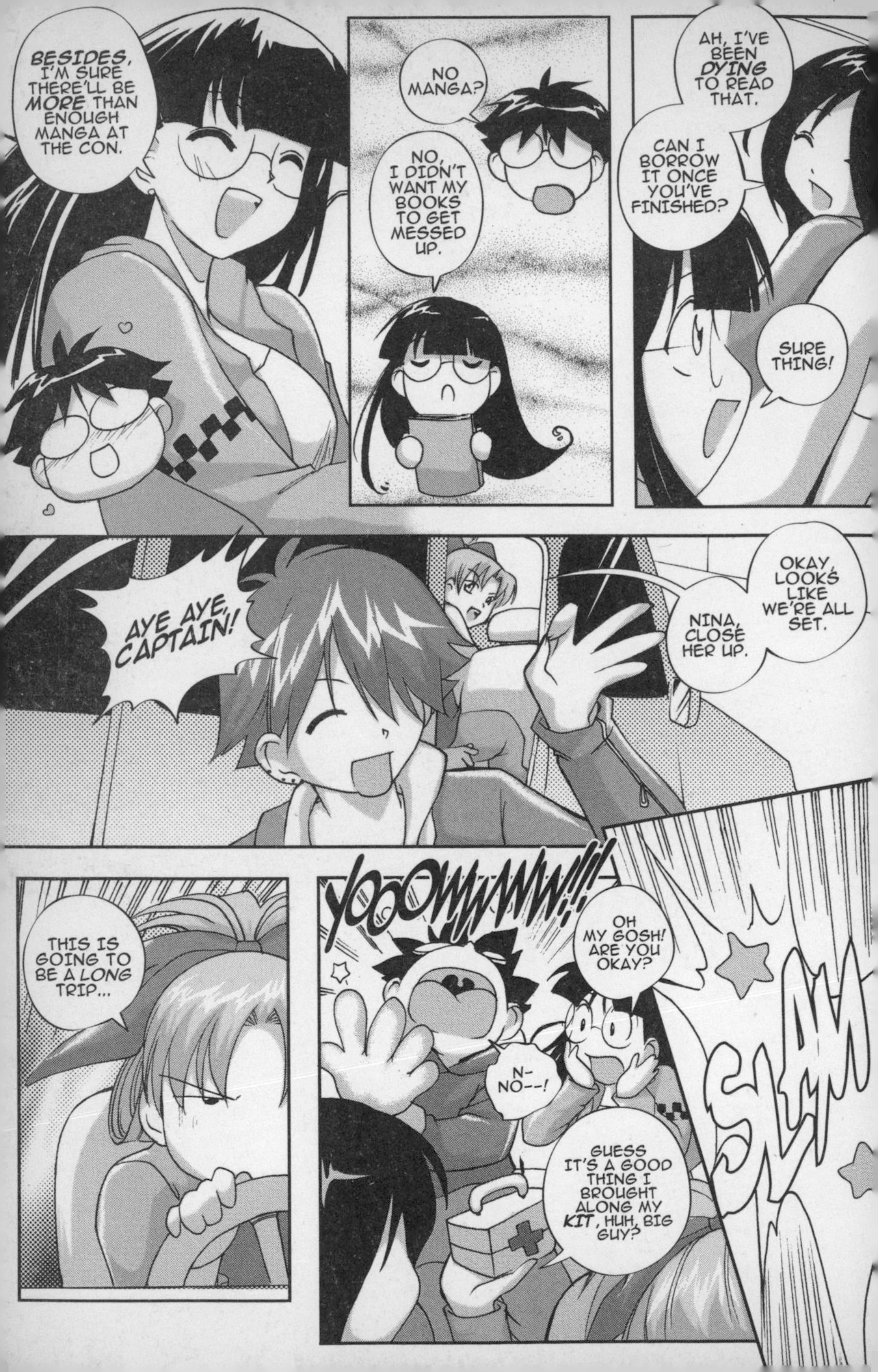
AH, I'VE BEEN DYING TO READ THAT.
CAN I BORROW IT ONCE YOU'VE FINISHED?
SURE THING!
NO MANGA?
NO, I DIDN'T WANT MY BOOKS TO GET MESSED UP.
BESIDES, I'M SURE THERE'LL BE MORE THAN ENOUGH MANGA AT THE CON.
OKAY, LOOKS LIKE WE'RE ALL SET.
NINA, CLOSE HER UP.
AYE AYE, CAPTAIN!
SLAM
YOOOWWWW!!!
OH MY GOSH! ARE YOU OKAY?
N-NO--!
GUESS IT'S A GOOD THING I BROUGHT ALONG MY KIT, HUH, BIG GUY?
THIS IS GOING TO BE A LONG TRIP...

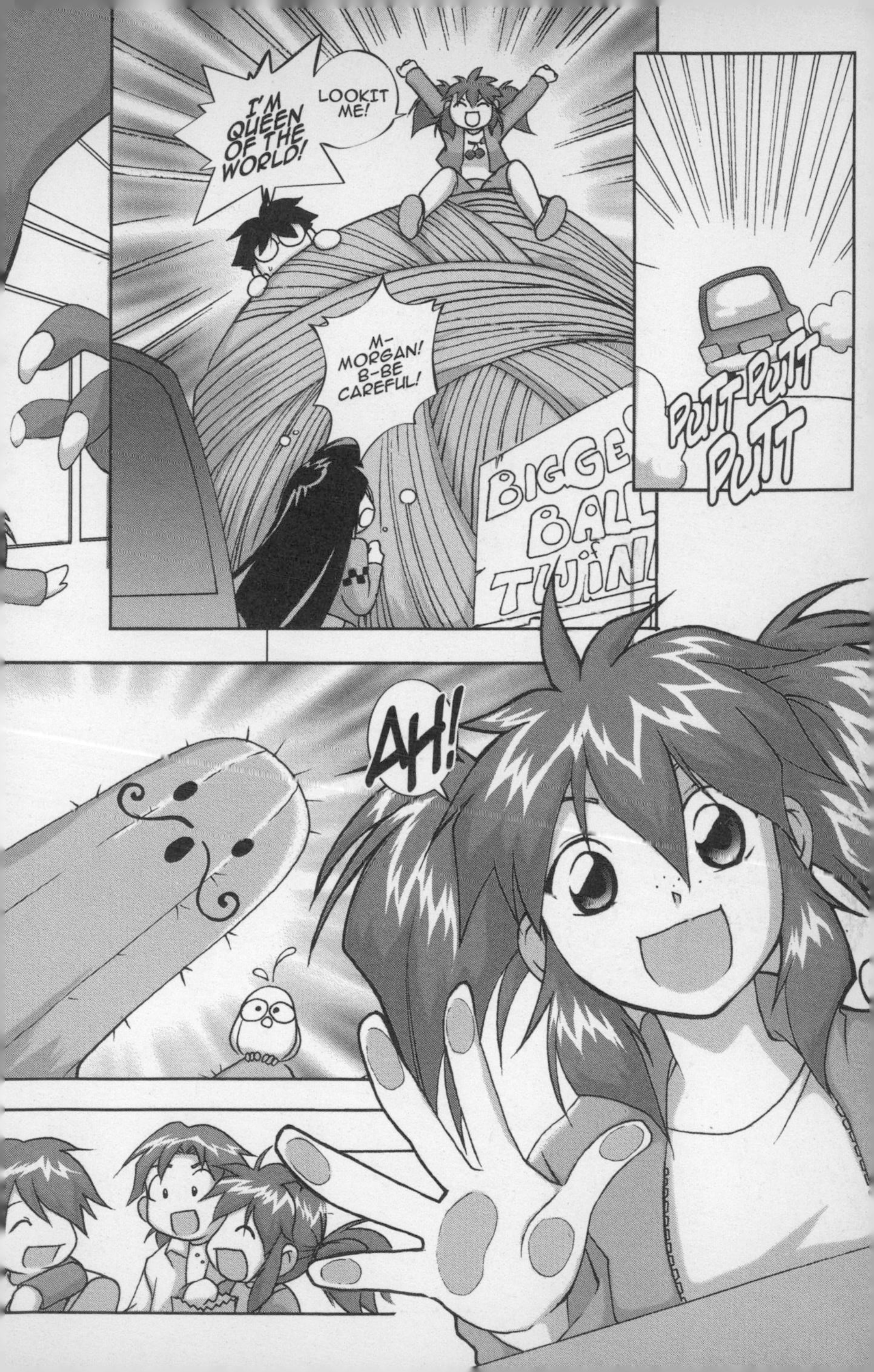
PUTT PUTT PUTT
PUTT
LOOKIT ME!
I'M QUEEN OF THE WORLD!
M-MORGAN! B-BE CAREFUL!
AH!

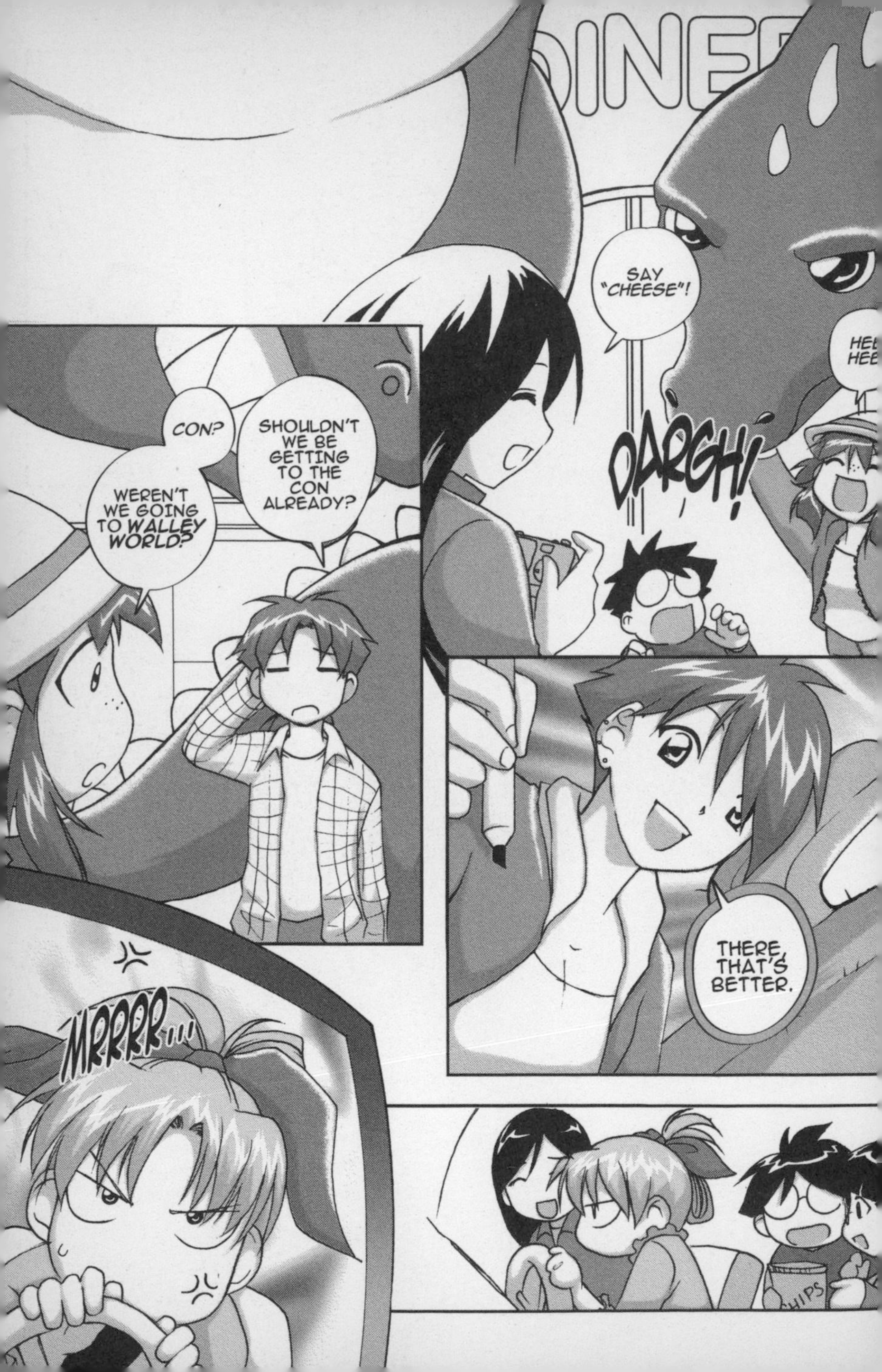
SAY "CHEESE"!
DARGH!
SHOULDN'T WE BE GETTING TO THE CON ALREADY?
CON?
WEREN'T WE GOING TO *WALLEY WORLD?*
THERE, THAT'S BETTER.
MRRRR...

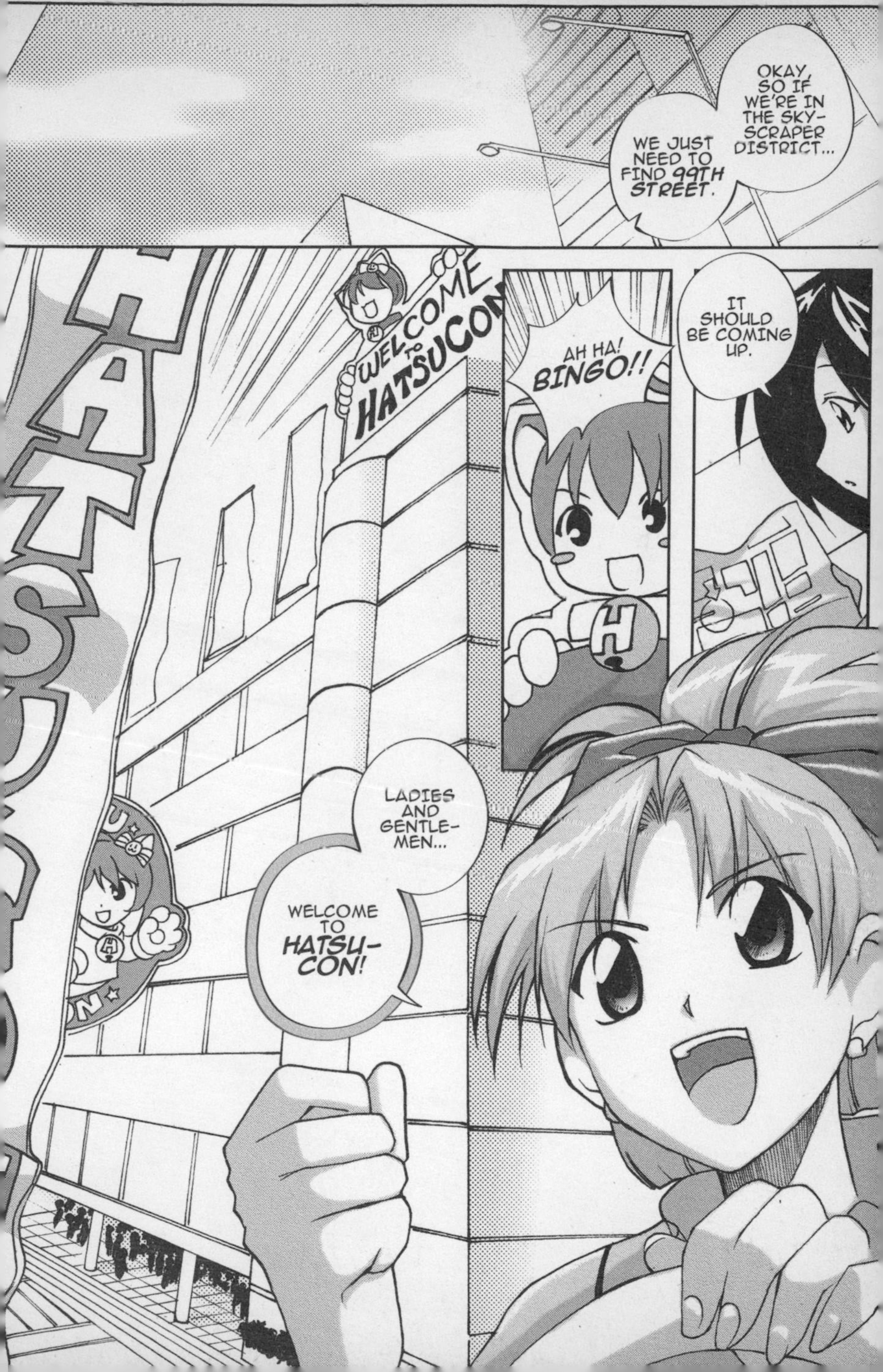
OKAY, SO IF WE'RE IN THE SKY-SCRAPER DISTRICT...
WE JUST NEED TO FIND 99TH STREET.
IT SHOULD BE COMING UP.
AH HA! BINGO!!
WELCOME to HATSUCON
LADIES AND GENTLE-MEN...
WELCOME TO HATSU-CON!

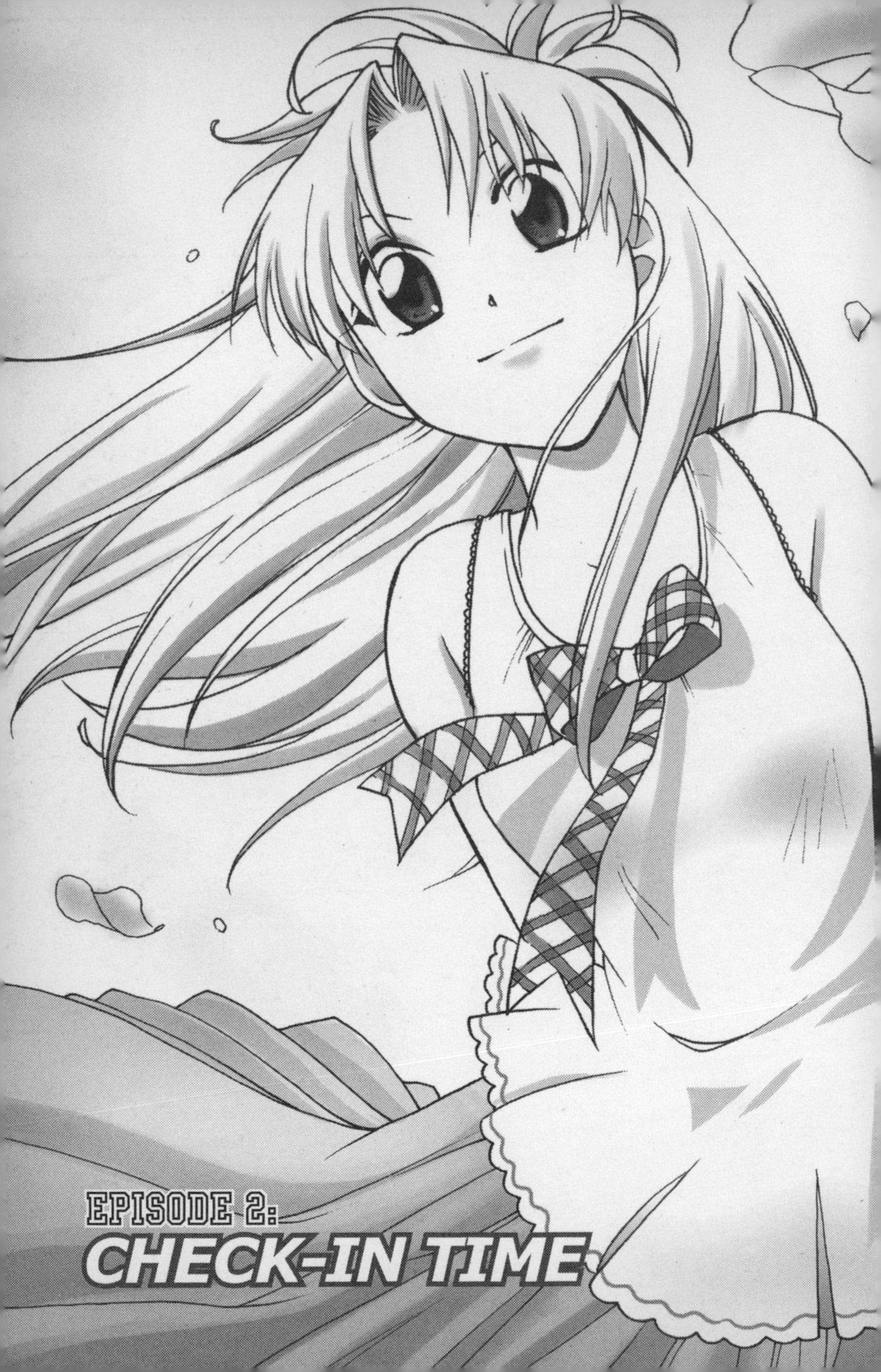
EPISODE 2:
CHECK-IN TIME

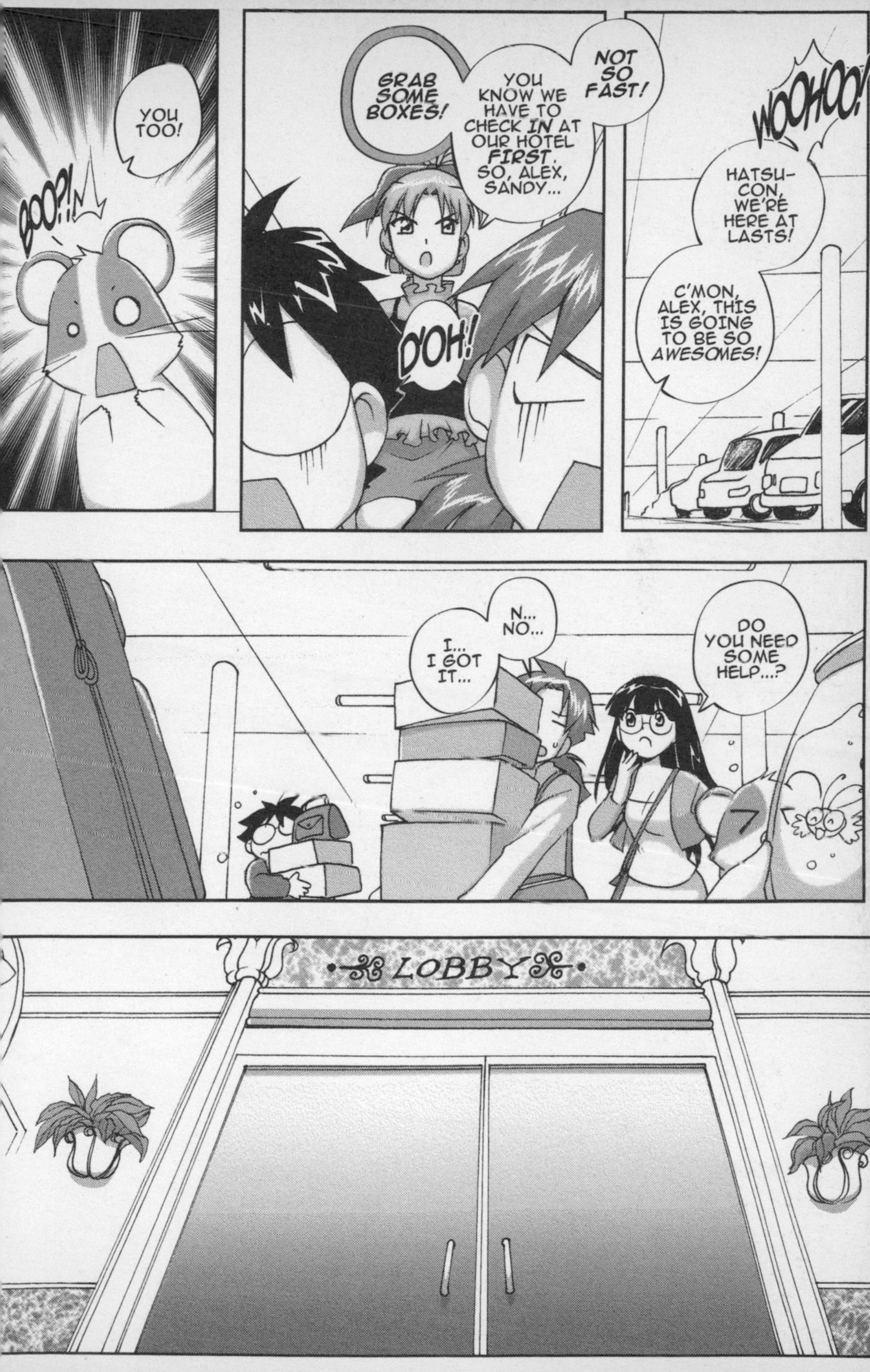
WOOHOO!
HATSU-CON, WE'RE HERE AT LASTS!
C'MON, ALEX, THIS IS GOING TO BE SO AWESOMES!
NOT SO FAST!
YOU KNOW WE HAVE TO CHECK IN AT OUR HOTEL FIRST. SO, ALEX, SANDY...
GRAB SOME BOXES!
D'OH!
YOU TOO!
BOO?!
DO YOU NEED SOME HELP...?
N... NO...
I... I GOT IT...
LOBBY

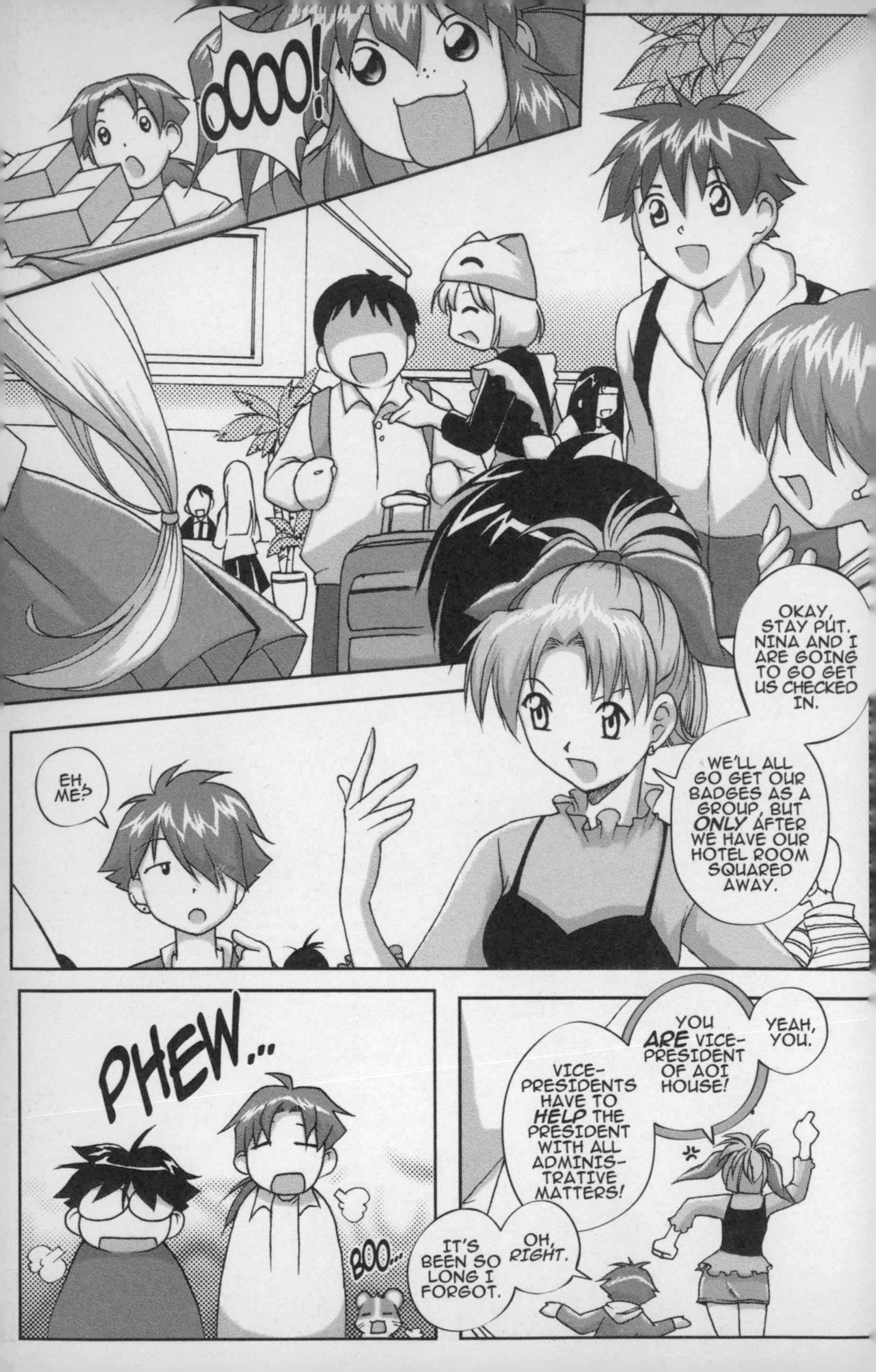
OOOO!
OKAY, STAY PUT. NINA AND I ARE GOING TO GO GET US CHECKED IN.
WE'LL ALL GO GET OUR BADGES AS A GROUP, BUT ONLY AFTER WE HAVE OUR HOTEL ROOM SQUARED AWAY.
EH, ME?
YEAH, YOU.
YOU ARE VICE-PRESIDENT OF AOI HOUSE!
VICE-PRESIDENTS HAVE TO HELP THE PRESIDENT WITH ALL ADMINISTRATIVE MATTERS!
OH, RIGHT.
IT'S BEEN SO LONG I FORGOT.
PHEW...
BOO...

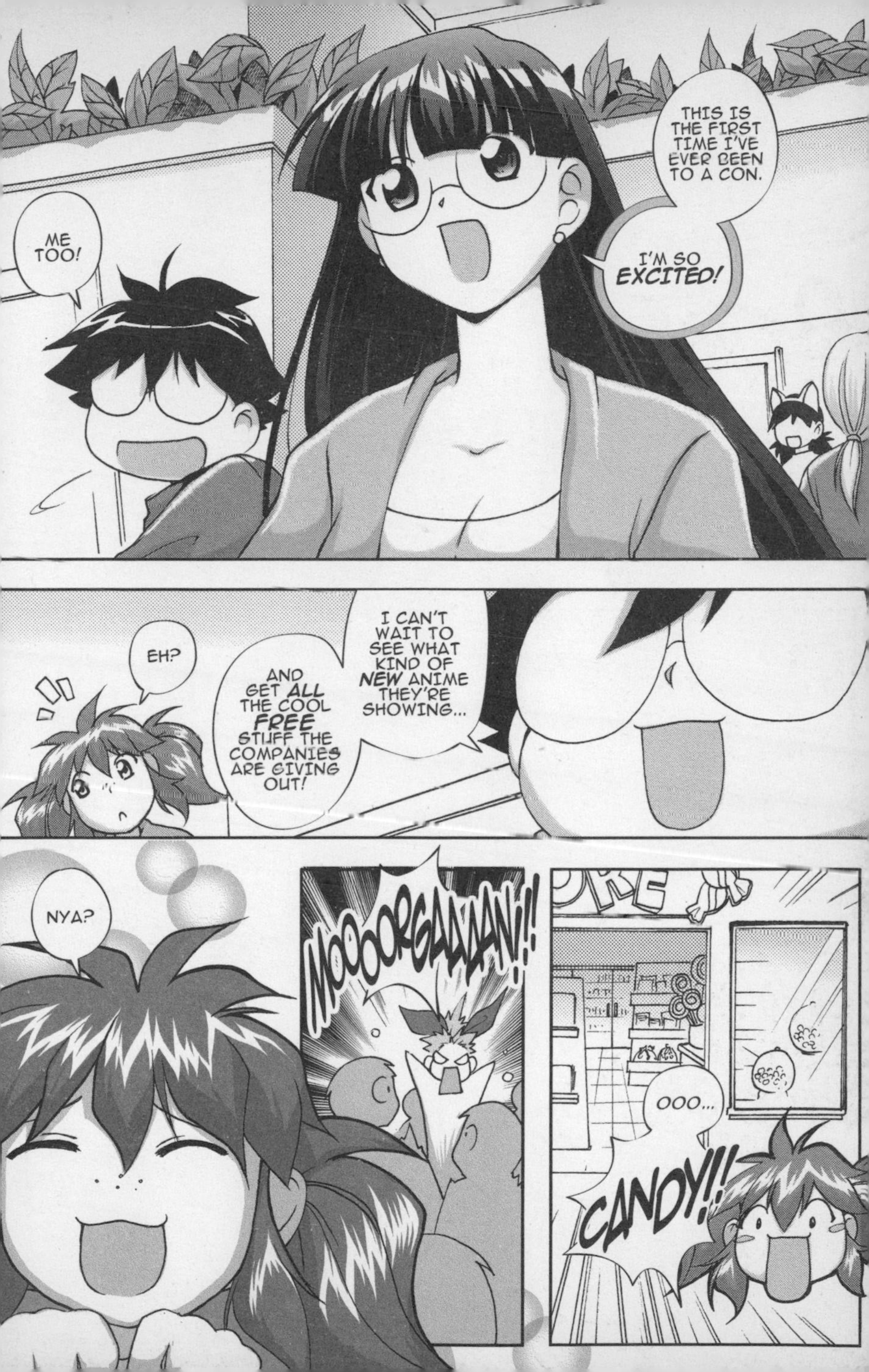
THIS IS THE FIRST TIME I'VE EVER BEEN TO A CON.
I'M SO EXCITED!
ME TOO!
I CAN'T WAIT TO SEE WHAT KIND OF NEW ANIME THEY'RE SHOWING...
AND GET ALL THE COOL FREE STUFF THE COMPANIES ARE GIVING OUT!
EH?
OOO...
CANDY!!
MOOOORGAAAAN!!
NYA?

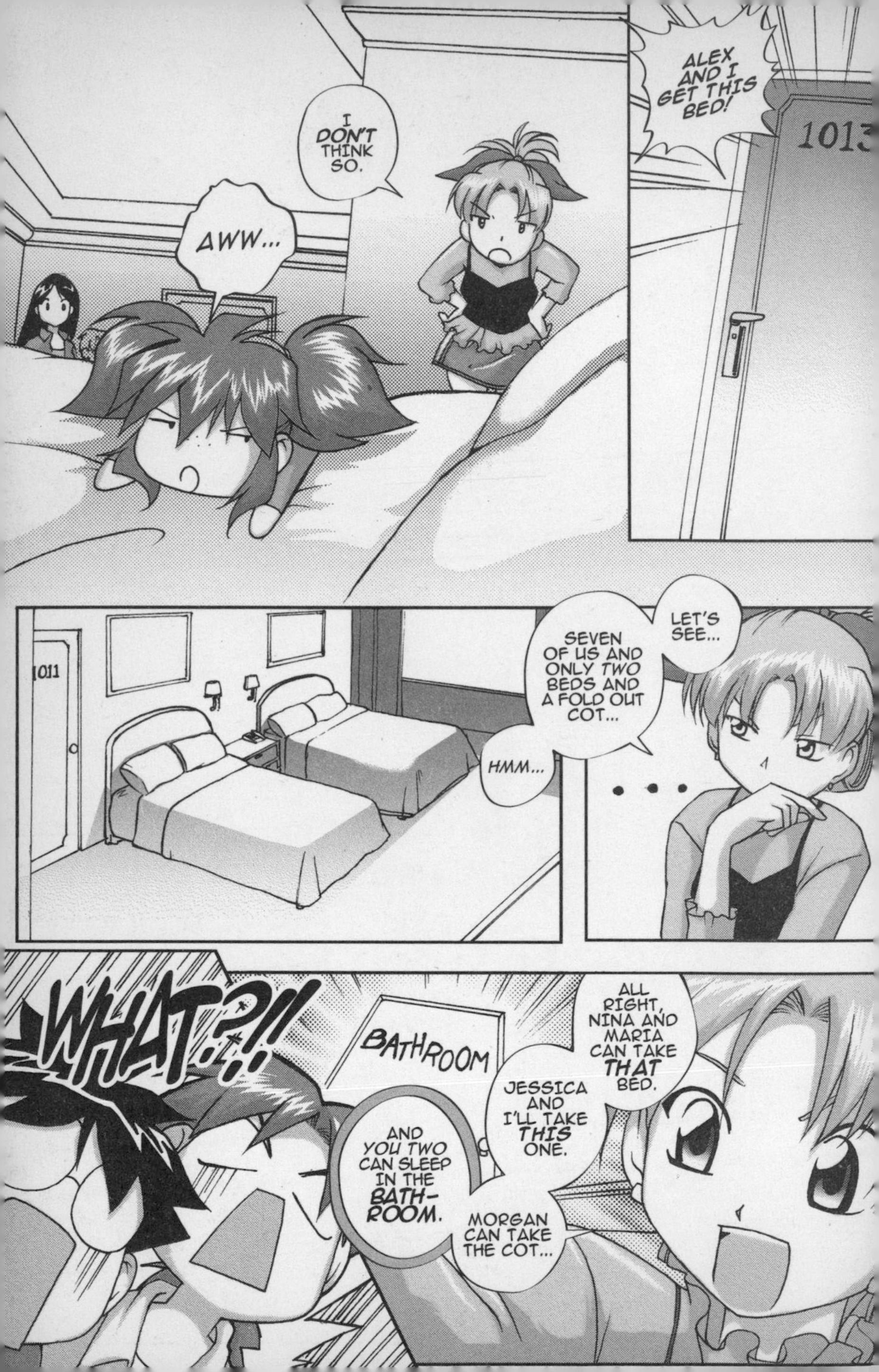

ALEX AND I GET THIS BED!
1013
I DON'T THINK SO.
AWW...
LET'S SEE...
SEVEN OF US AND ONLY TWO BEDS AND A FOLD OUT COT...
1011
HMM...
ALL RIGHT, NINA AND MARIA CAN TAKE THAT BED.
JESSICA AND I'LL TAKE THIS ONE.
MORGAN CAN TAKE THE COT...
AND YOU TWO CAN SLEEP IN THE BATHROOM.
BATHROOM
WHAT?!!

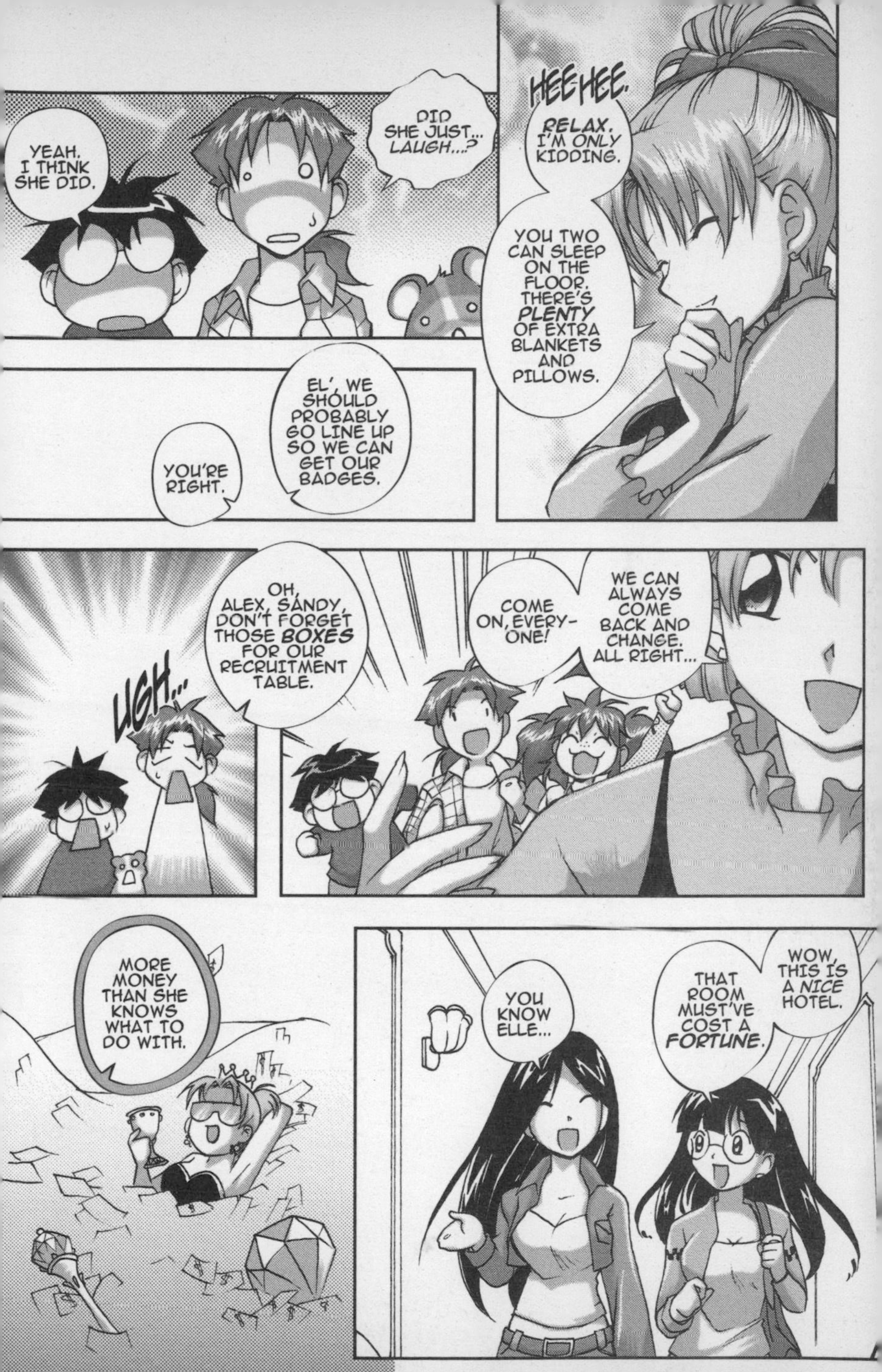
HEE-HEE.
RELAX, I'M ONLY KIDDING.
YOU TWO CAN SLEEP ON THE FLOOR. THERE'S PLENTY OF EXTRA BLANKETS AND PILLOWS.
DID SHE JUST... LAUGH...?
YEAH. I THINK SHE DID.
EL', WE SHOULD PROBABLY GO LINE UP SO WE CAN GET OUR BADGES.
YOU'RE RIGHT.
WE CAN ALWAYS COME BACK AND CHANGE. ALL RIGHT...
COME ON, EVERY-ONE!
OH, ALEX, SANDY, DON'T FORGET THOSE BOXES FOR OUR RECRUITMENT TABLE.
UGH...
WOW, THIS IS A NICE HOTEL.
THAT ROOM MUST'VE COST A FORTUNE.
YOU KNOW ELLE...
MORE MONEY THAN SHE KNOWS WHAT TO DO WITH.

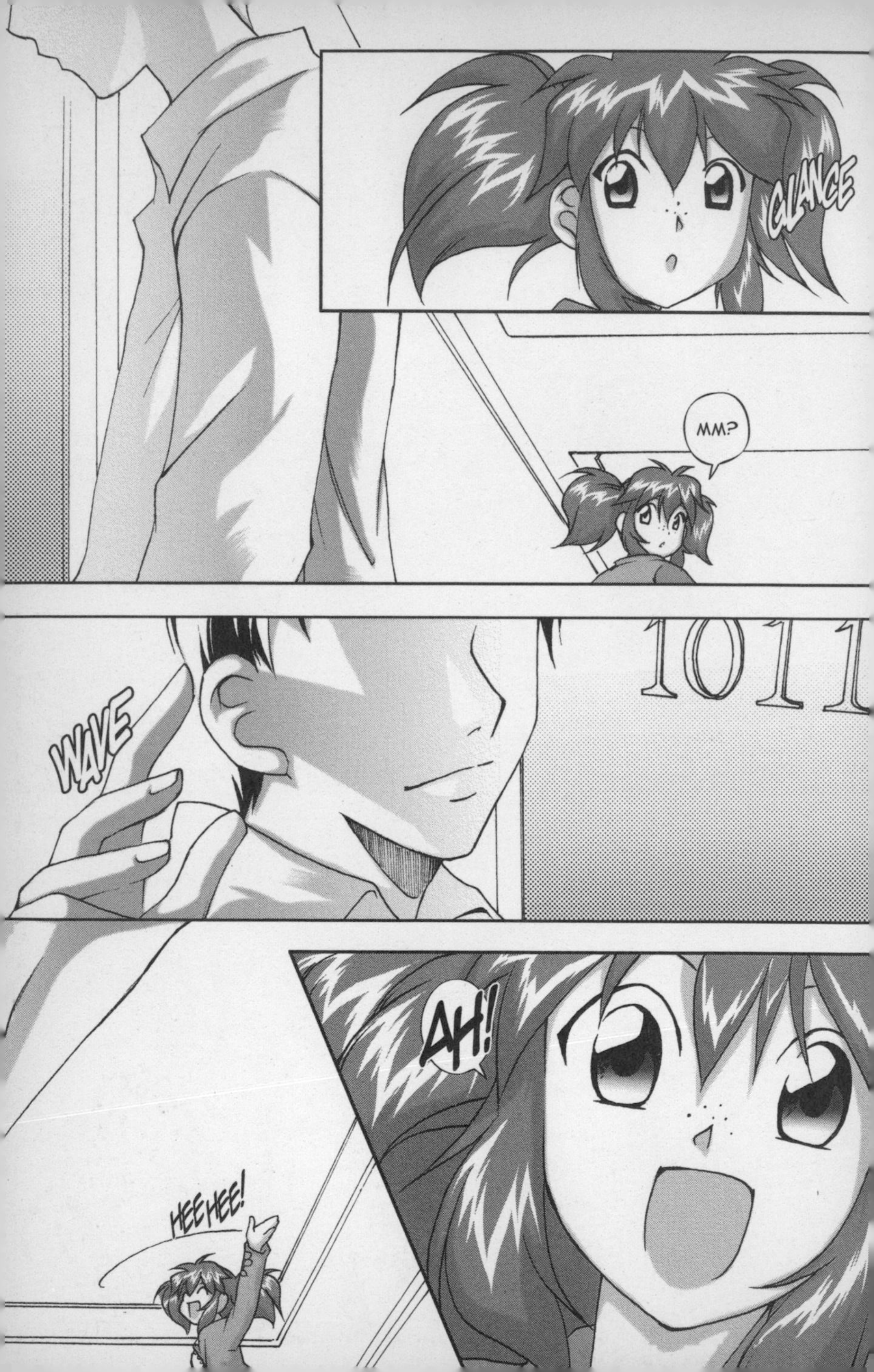
GLANCE
MM?
1011
WAVE
AH!
HEEHEE!

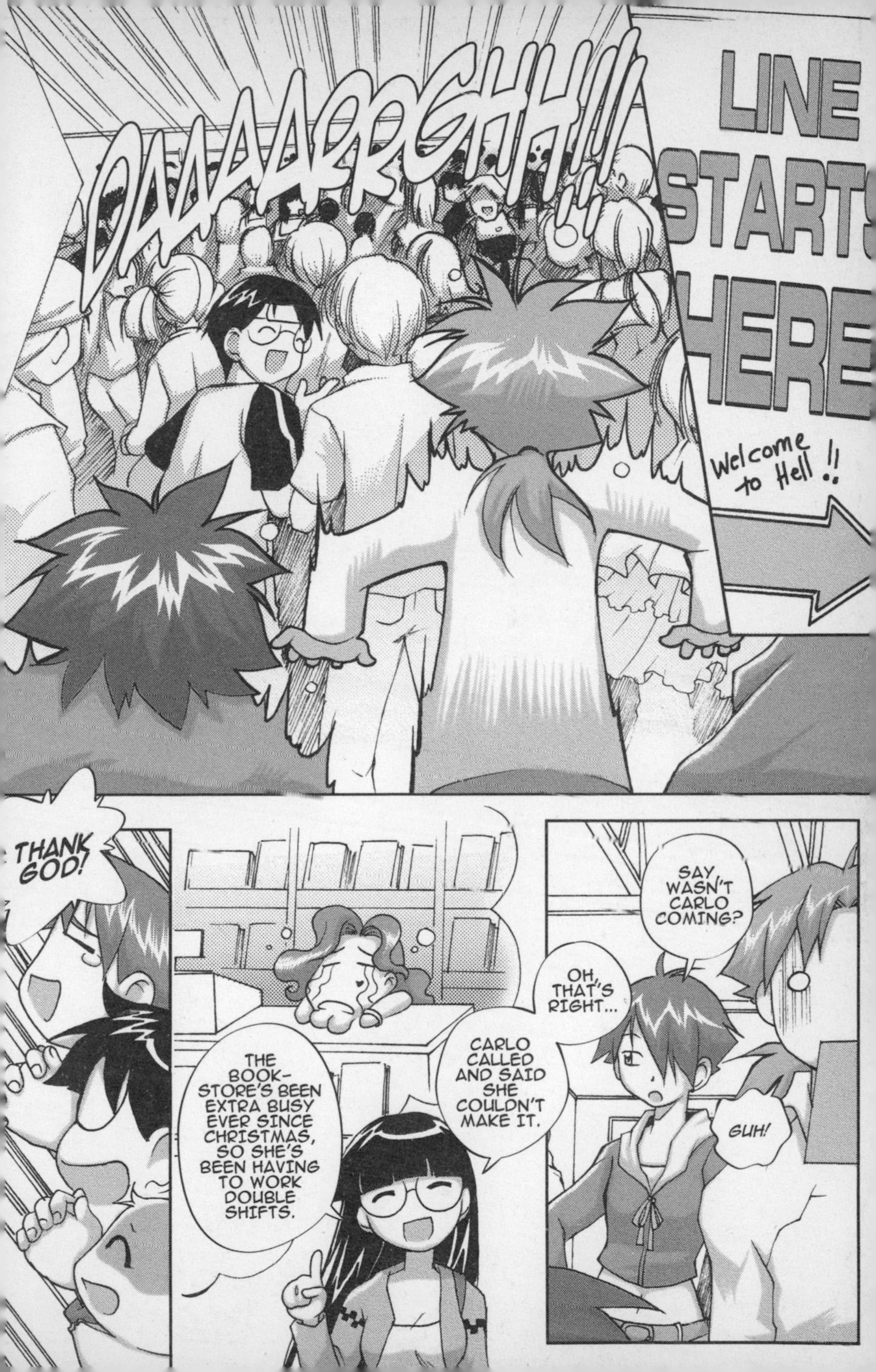
OAAAARRGH!!!
LINE STARTS HERE
Welcome to Hell !!
SAY WASN'T CARLO COMING?
OH, THAT'S RIGHT...
GUH!
CARLO CALLED AND SAID SHE COULDN'T MAKE IT.
THE BOOK-STORE'S BEEN EXTRA BUSY EVER SINCE CHRISTMAS, SO SHE'S BEEN HAVING TO WORK DOUBLE SHIFTS.
THANK GOD!

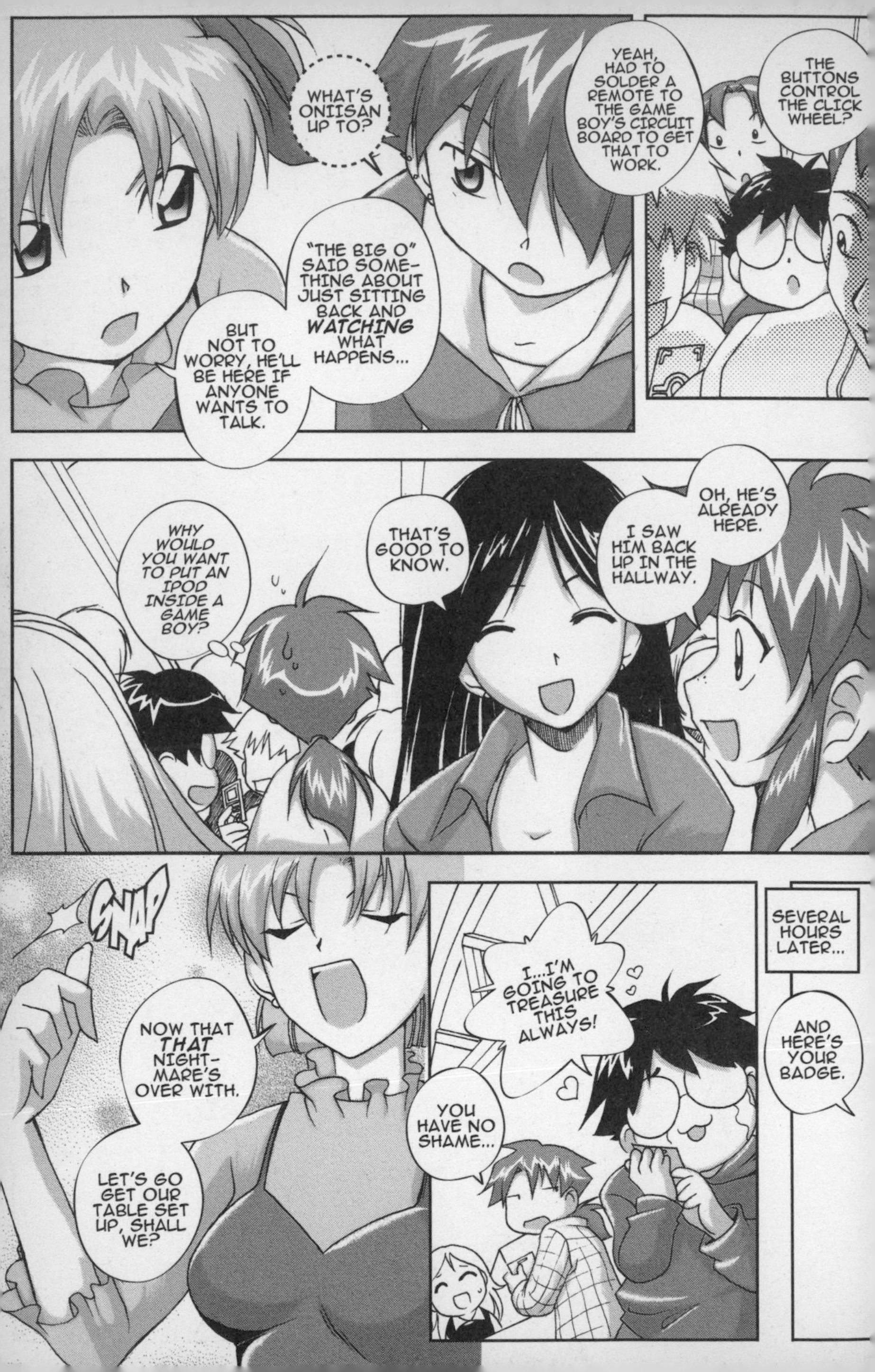
THE BUTTONS CONTROL THE CLICK WHEEL?
YEAH, HAD TO SOLDER A REMOTE TO THE GAME BOY'S CIRCUIT BOARD TO GET THAT TO WORK.
WHAT'S ONIISAN UP TO?
"THE BIG O" SAID SOMETHING ABOUT JUST SITTING BACK AND *WATCHING* WHAT HAPPENS...
BUT NOT TO WORRY, HE'LL BE HERE IF ANYONE WANTS TO TALK.
OH, HE'S ALREADY HERE.
I SAW HIM BACK UP IN THE HALLWAY.
THAT'S GOOD TO KNOW.
WHY WOULD YOU WANT TO PUT AN IPOD INSIDE A GAME BOY?
SEVERAL HOURS LATER...
AND HERE'S YOUR BADGE.
I...I'M GOING TO TREASURE THIS ALWAYS!
YOU HAVE NO SHAME...
SNAP
NOW THAT *THAT* NIGHTMARE'S OVER WITH.
LET'S GO GET OUR TABLE SET UP, SHALL WE?

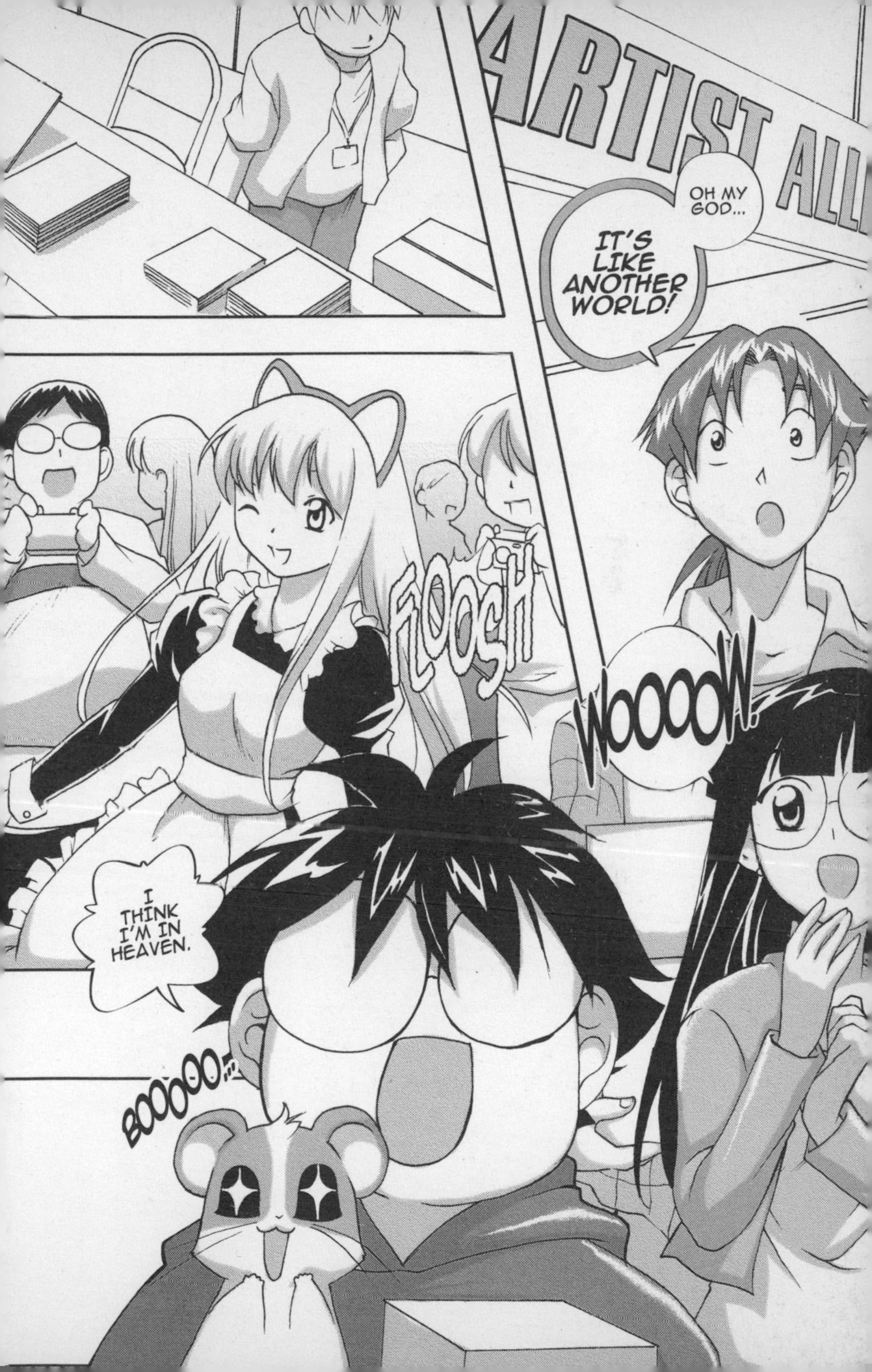
ARTIST ALL
OH MY GOD...
IT'S LIKE ANOTHER WORLD!
WOOOOW!
FLOOSH
I THINK I'M IN HEAVEN.
BOOOOO...

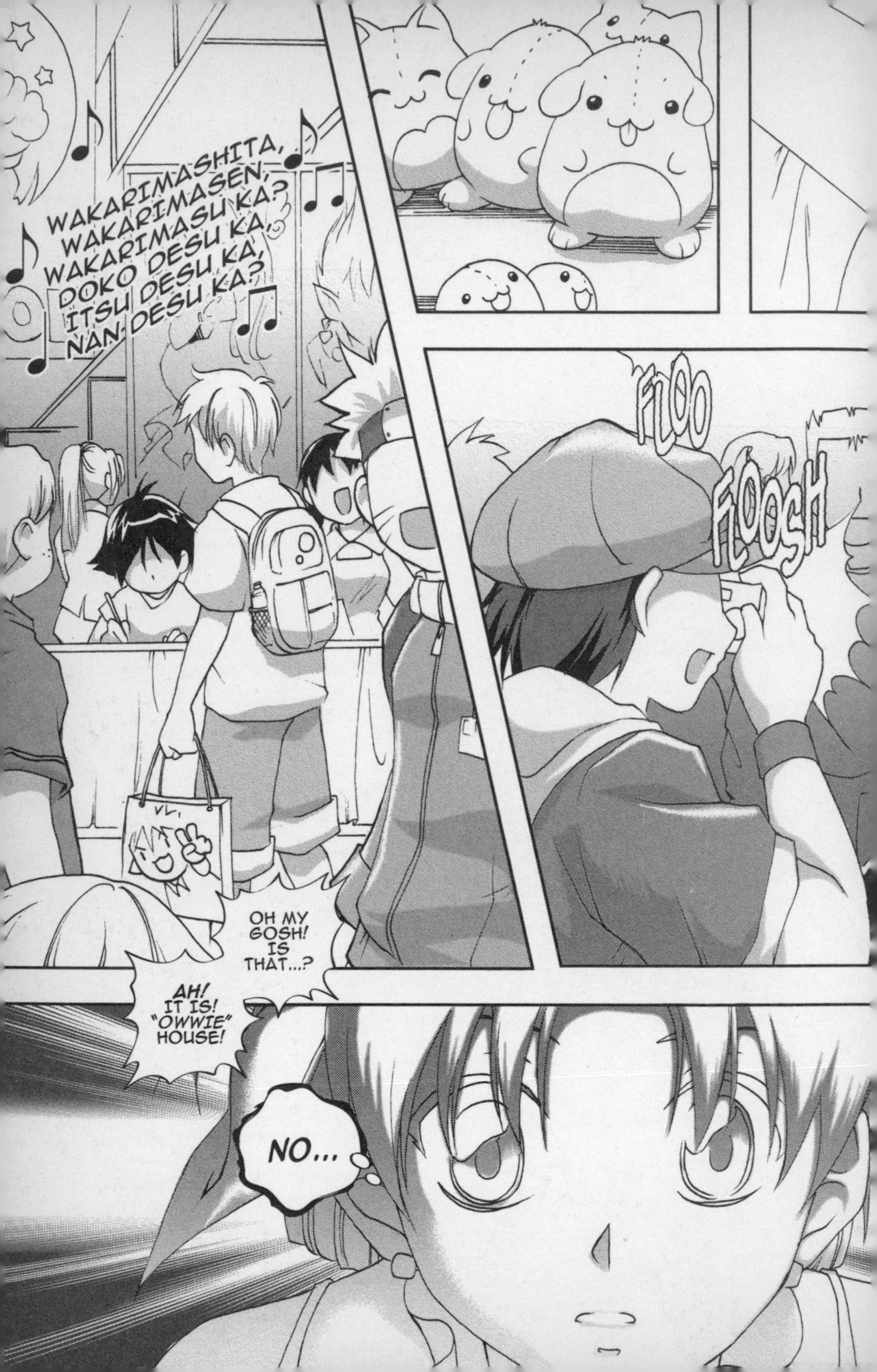
FLOO
FLOOSH
WAKARIMASHITA, WAKARIMASEN, WAKARIMASU KA? DOKO DESU KA, ITSU DESU KA, NAN DESU KA?
OH MY GOSH! IS THAT...?
AH! IT IS! "OWWIE" HOUSE!
NO...

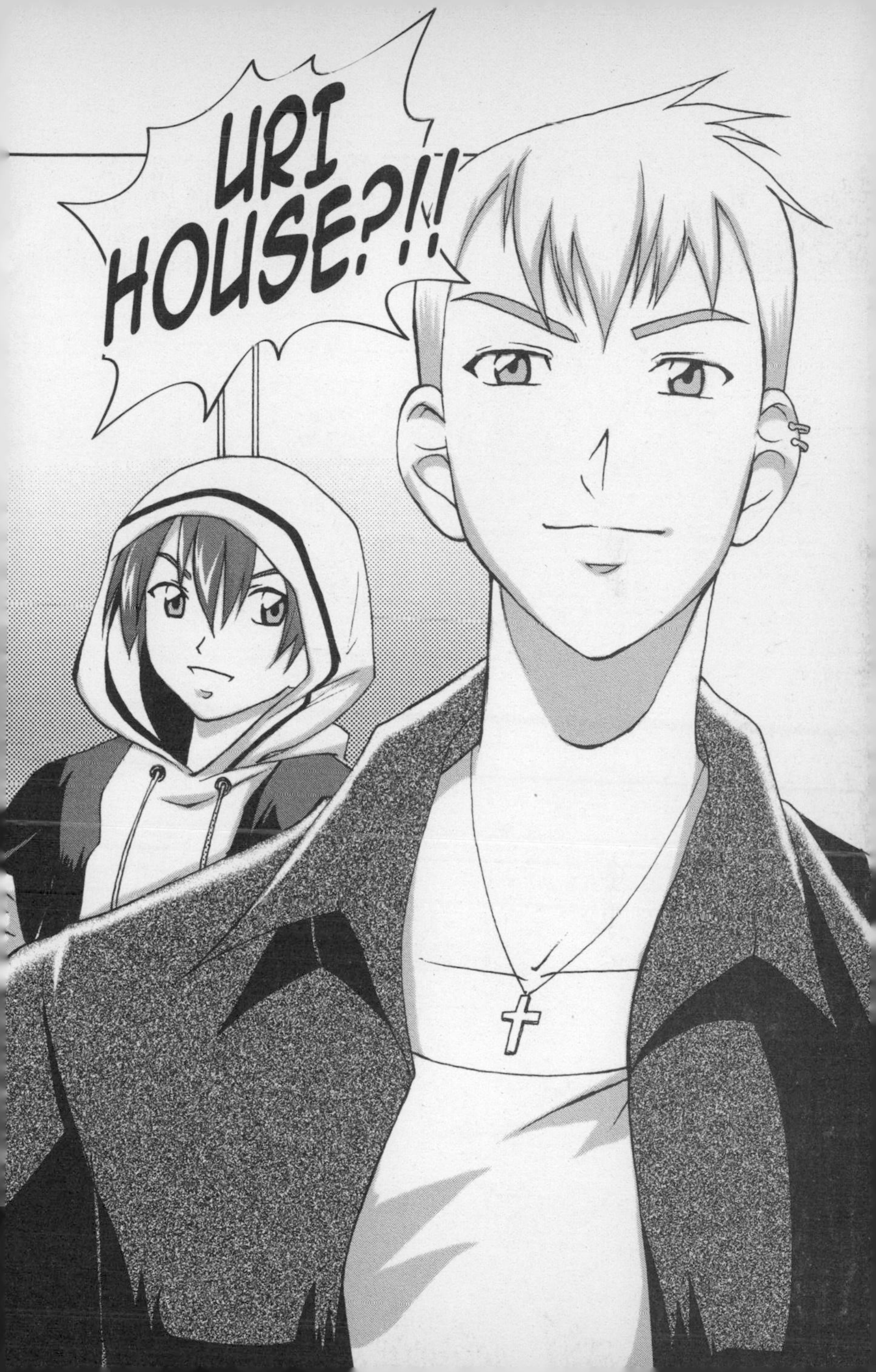
URI HOUSE?!!

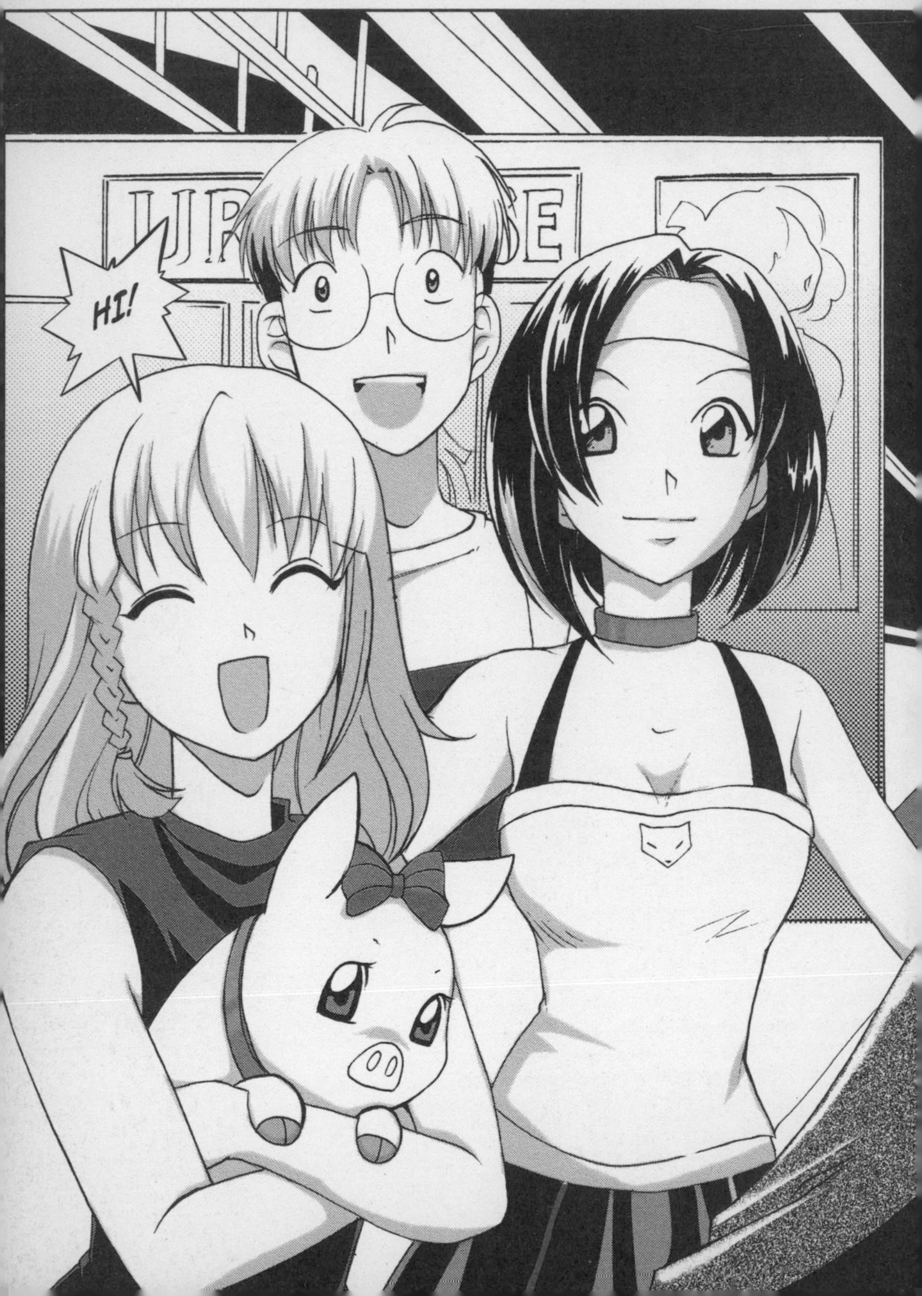
HI!

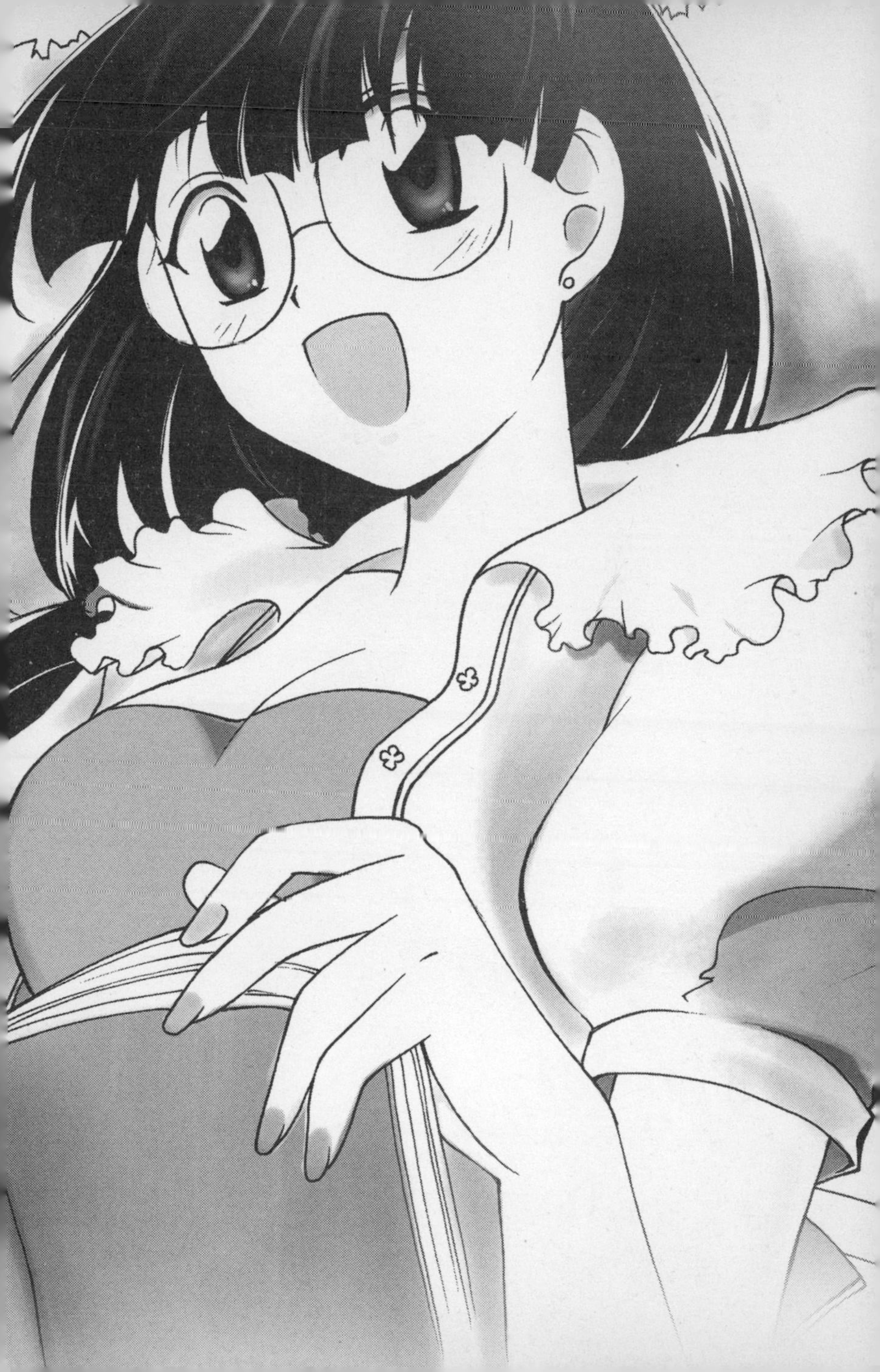

EPISODE 3: RIVAL SCHOOLS

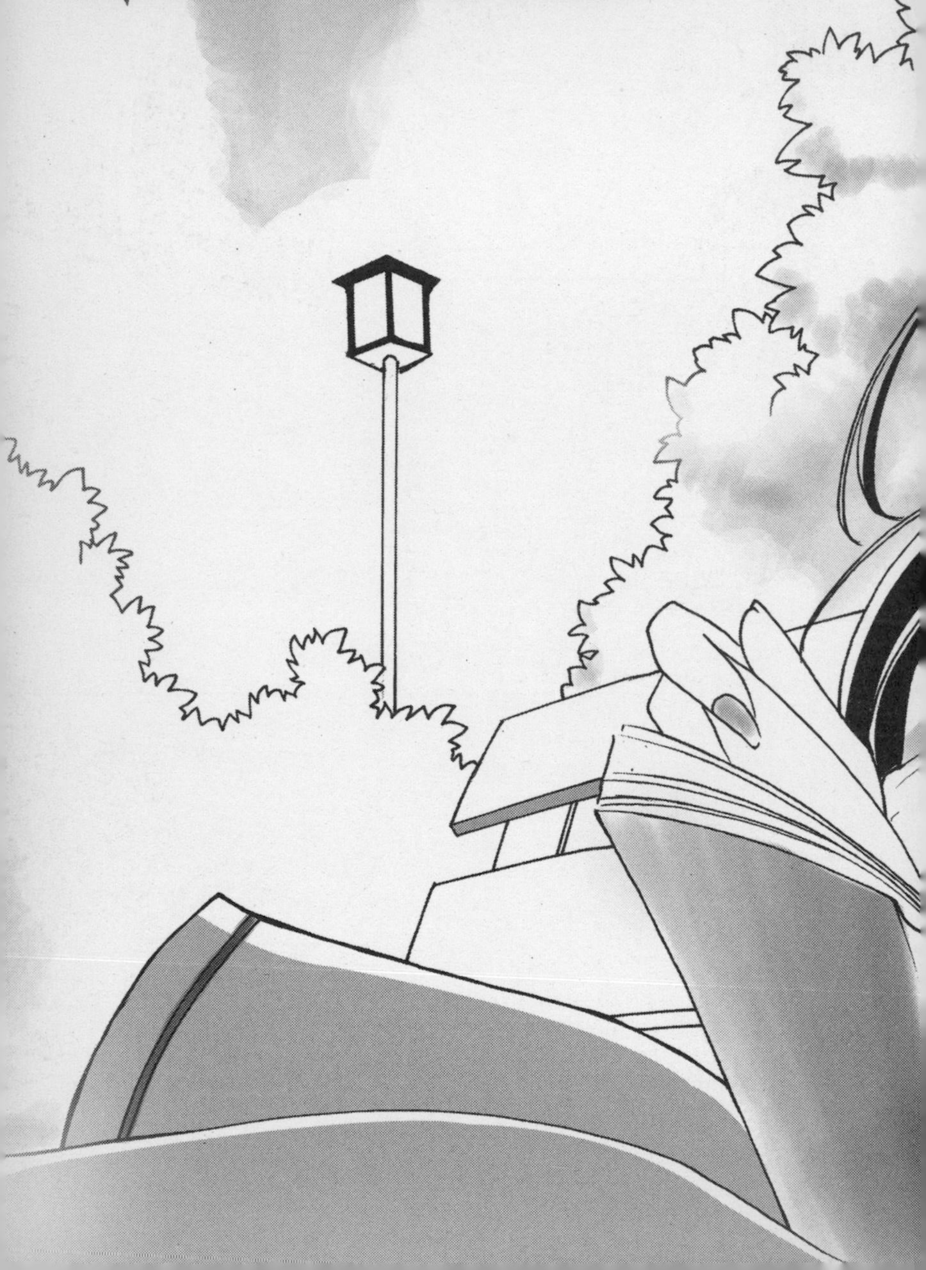

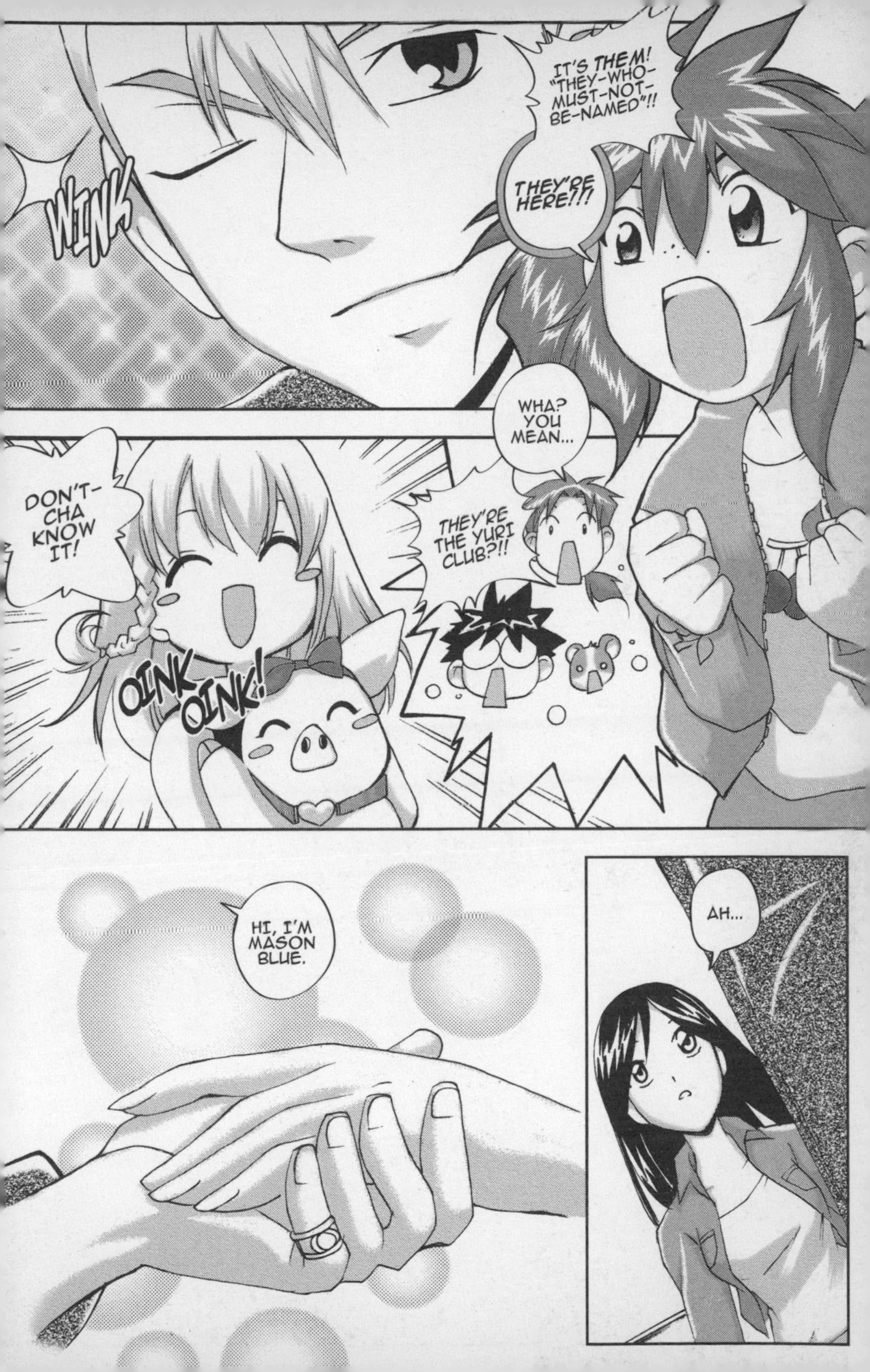
IT'S THEM! "THEY-WHO-MUST-NOT-BE-NAMED"!!
THEY'RE HERE!!!
WINK
WHA? YOU MEAN...
THEY'RE THE YURI CLUB?!!
DON'T-CHA KNOW IT!
OINK OINK!
AH...
HI, I'M MASON BLUE.

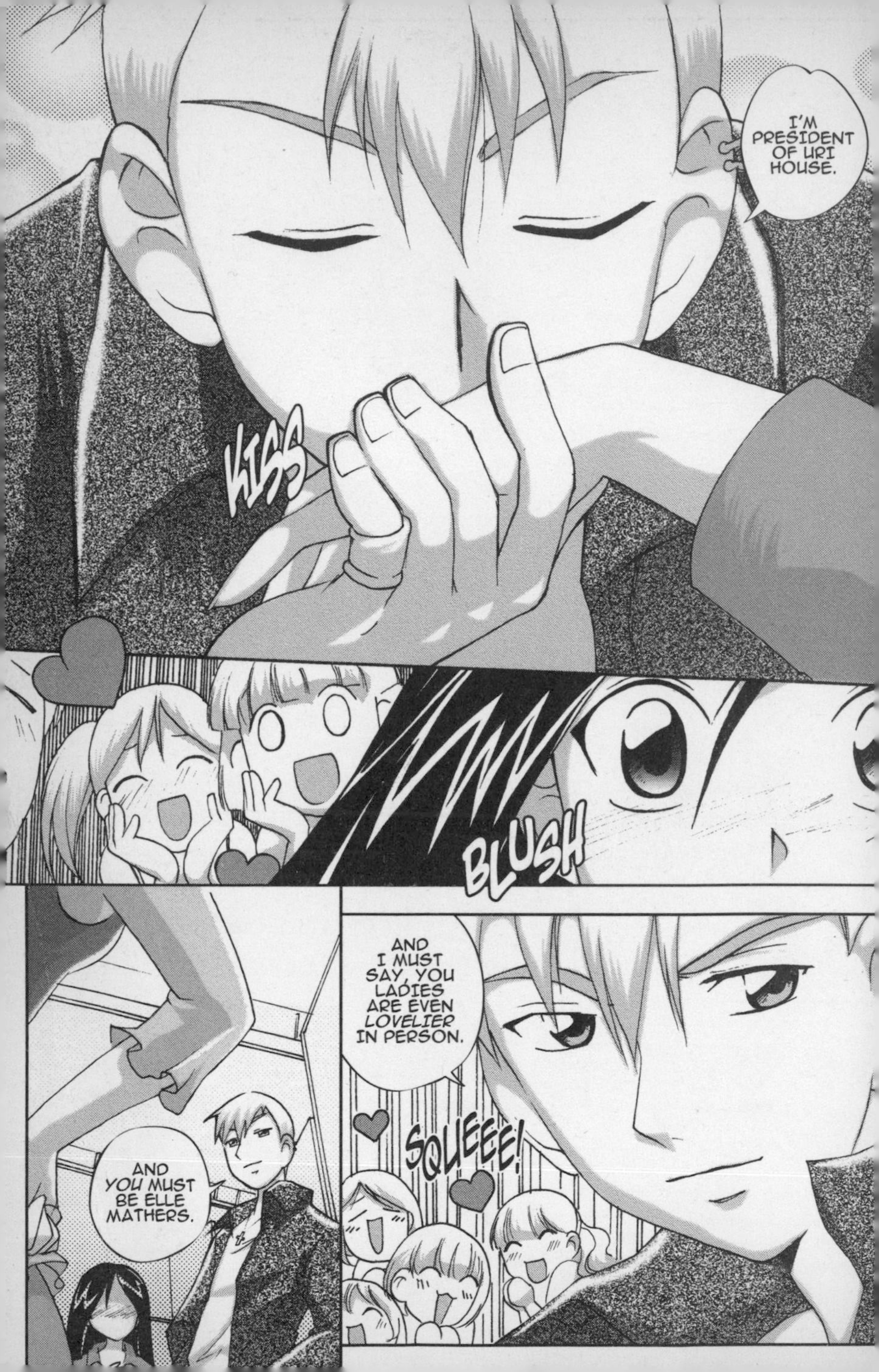
I'M PRESIDENT OF URI HOUSE.
KISS
BLUSH
AND I MUST SAY, YOU LADIES ARE EVEN LOVELIER IN PERSON.
SQUEEE!
AND YOU MUST BE ELLE MATHERS.

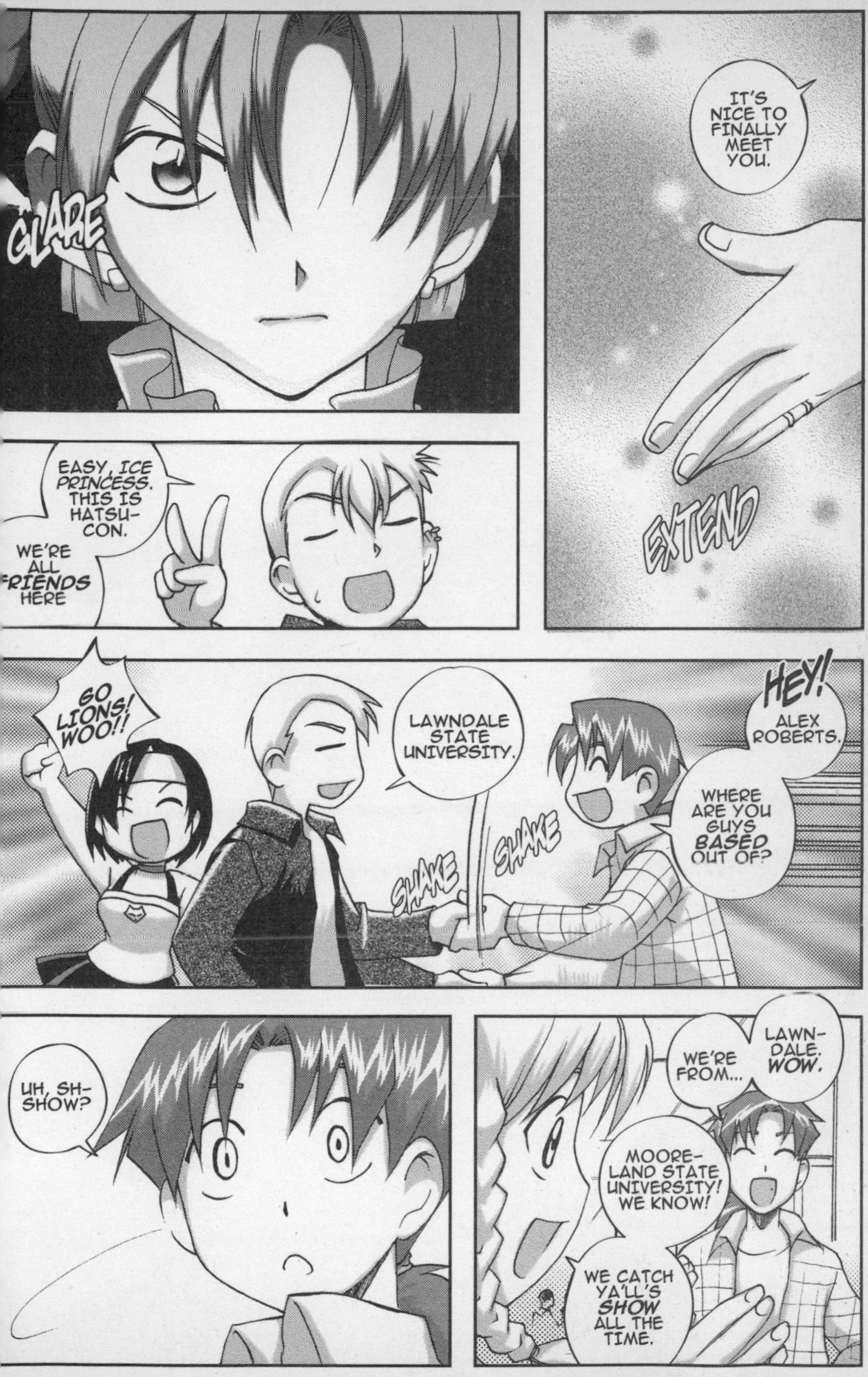
IT'S NICE TO FINALLY MEET YOU.
EXTEND
GLARE
EASY, ICE PRINCESS. THIS IS HATSU-CON.
WE'RE ALL FRIENDS HERE
HEY!
ALEX ROBERTS.
WHERE ARE YOU GUYS BASED OUT OF?
SHAKE
SHAKE
LAWNDALE STATE UNIVERSITY.
GO LIONS! WOO!!
LAWN-DALE. WOW.
WE'RE FROM...
MOORE-LAND STATE UNIVERSITY! WE KNOW!
WE CATCH YA'LL'S SHOW ALL THE TIME.
UH, SH-SHOW?

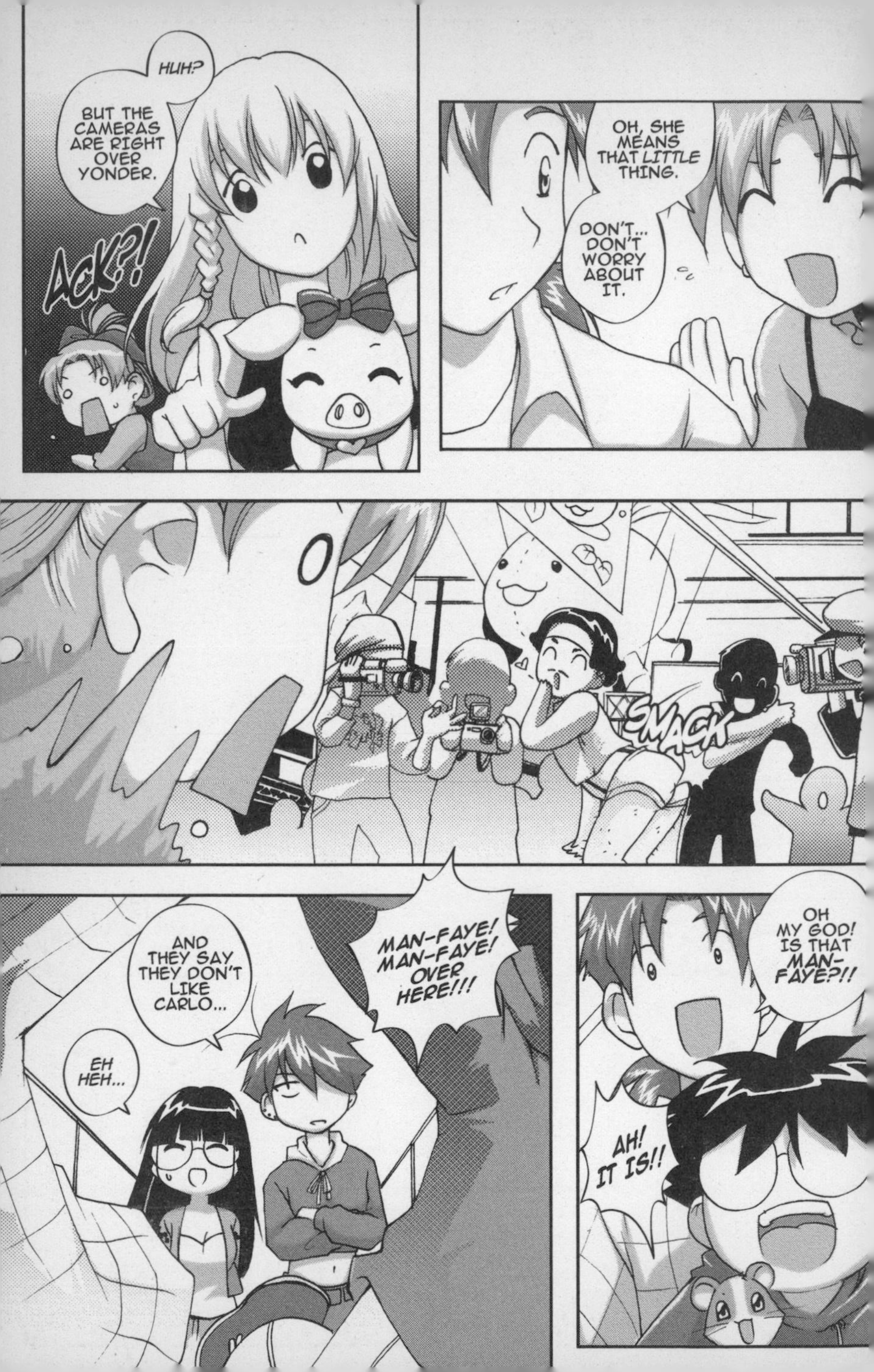
OH, SHE MEANS THAT LITTLE THING.
DON'T... DON'T WORRY ABOUT IT.
HUH?
BUT THE CAMERAS ARE RIGHT OVER YONDER.
ACK?!
SMACK
OH MY GOD! IS THAT MAN-FAYE?!!
AH! IT IS!!
MAN-FAYE! MAN-FAYE! OVER HERE!!!
AND THEY SAY THEY DON'T LIKE CARLO...
EH HEH...

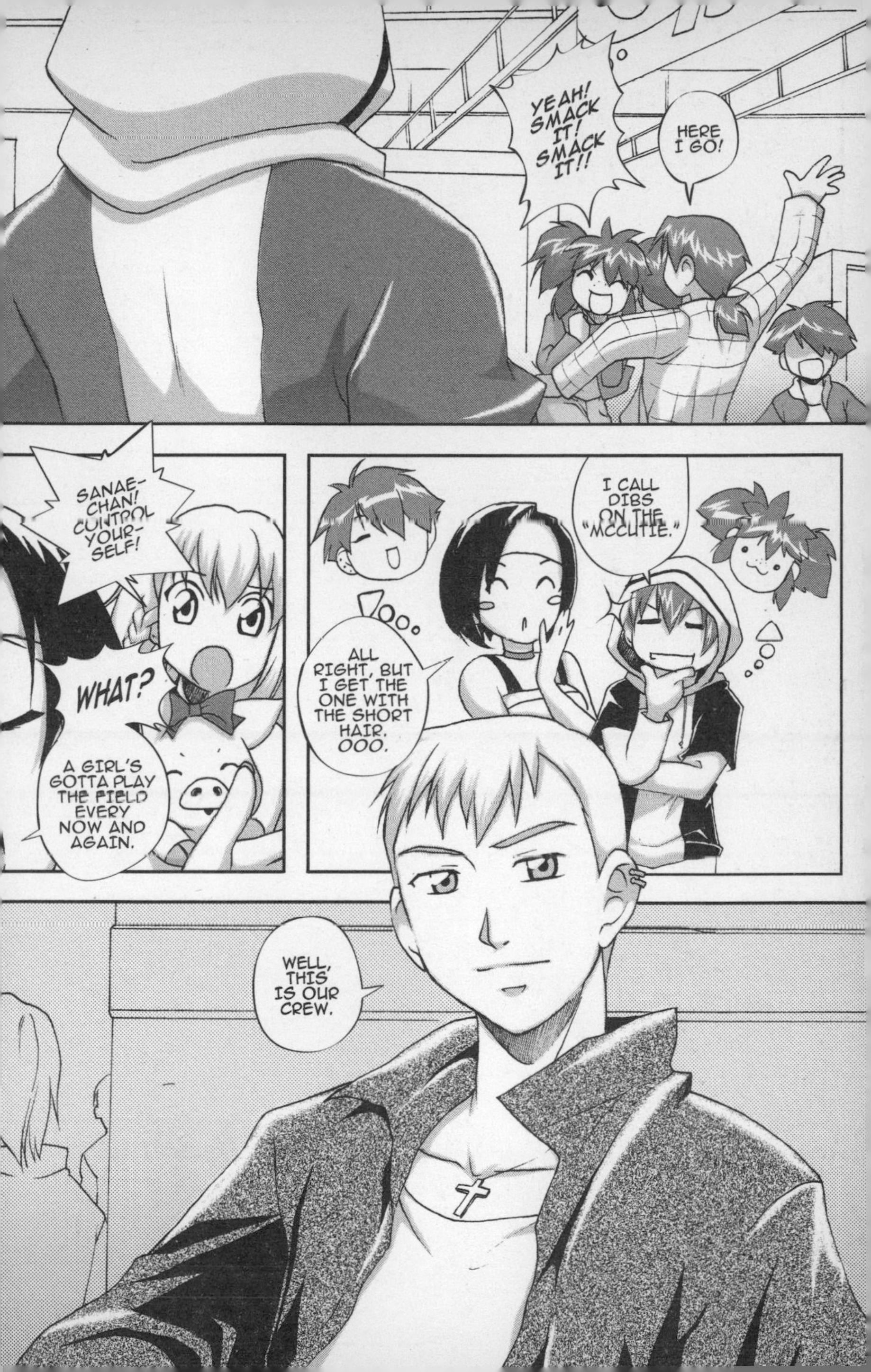
HERE I GO!
YEAH! SMACK IT! SMACK IT!!
I CALL DIBS ON THE "MCCUTIE."
ALL RIGHT, BUT I GET THE ONE WITH THE SHORT HAIR. OOO.
SANAE-CHAN! CONTROL YOURSELF!
WHAT?
A GIRL'S GOTTA PLAY THE FIELD EVERY NOW AND AGAIN.
WELL, THIS IS OUR CREW.

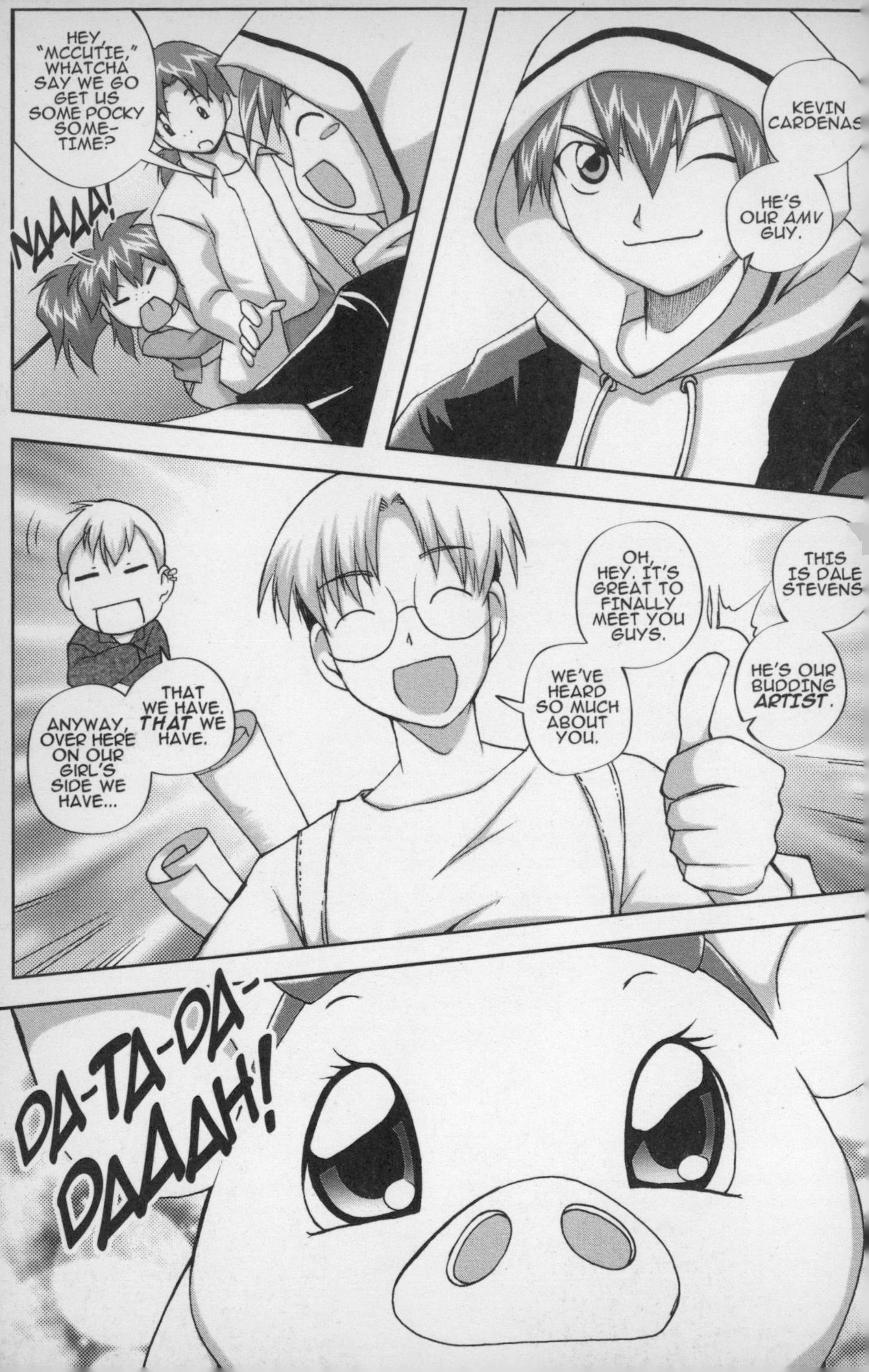
KEVIN CARDENAS
HE'S OUR AMV GUY.
HEY, "MCCUTIE," WHATCHA SAY WE GO GET US SOME POCKY SOME-TIME?
NAAAA!
THIS IS DALE STEVENS
HE'S OUR BUDDING ARTIST.
OH, HEY. IT'S GREAT TO FINALLY MEET YOU GUYS.
WE'VE HEARD SO MUCH ABOUT YOU.
THAT WE HAVE. THAT WE HAVE.
ANYWAY, OVER HERE ON OUR GIRL'S SIDE WE HAVE...
DA-TA-DA-DAAAH!

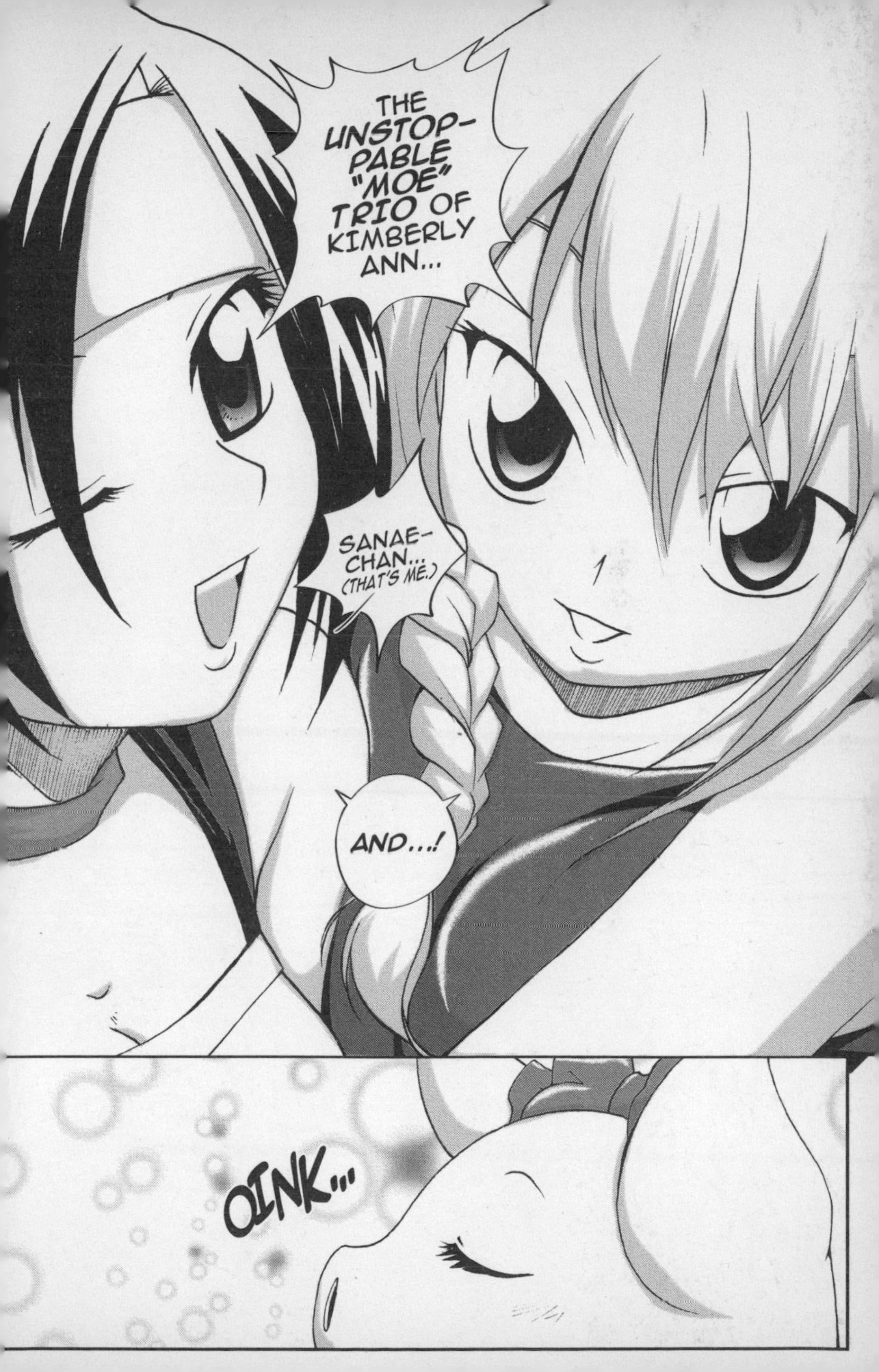
THE UNSTOPPABLE "MOE" TRIO OF KIMBERLY ANN...
SANAE-CHAN... (THAT'S ME.)
AND...!
OINK...

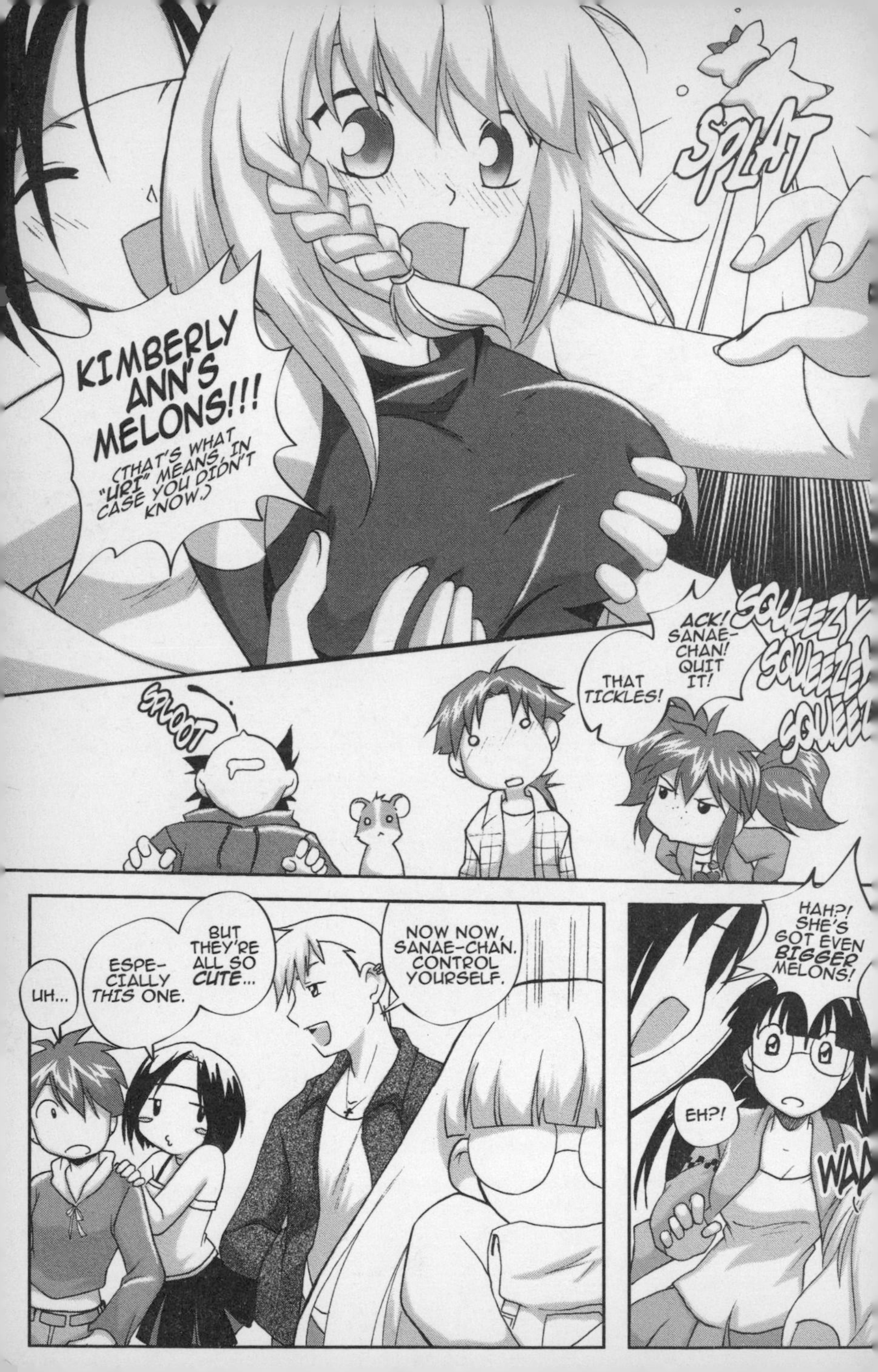
SPLAT
KIMBERLY ANN'S MELONS!!!
(THAT'S WHAT "URI" MEANS, IN CASE YOU DIDN'T KNOW.)
SQUEEZY
ACK! SANAE-CHAN! QUIT IT!
THAT TICKLES!
SPLOOT
HAH?! SHE'S GOT EVEN BIGGER MELONS!
EH?!
NOW NOW, SANAE-CHAN. CONTROL YOURSELF.
BUT THEY'RE ALL SO CUTE...
ESPE-CIALLY THIS ONE.
UH...

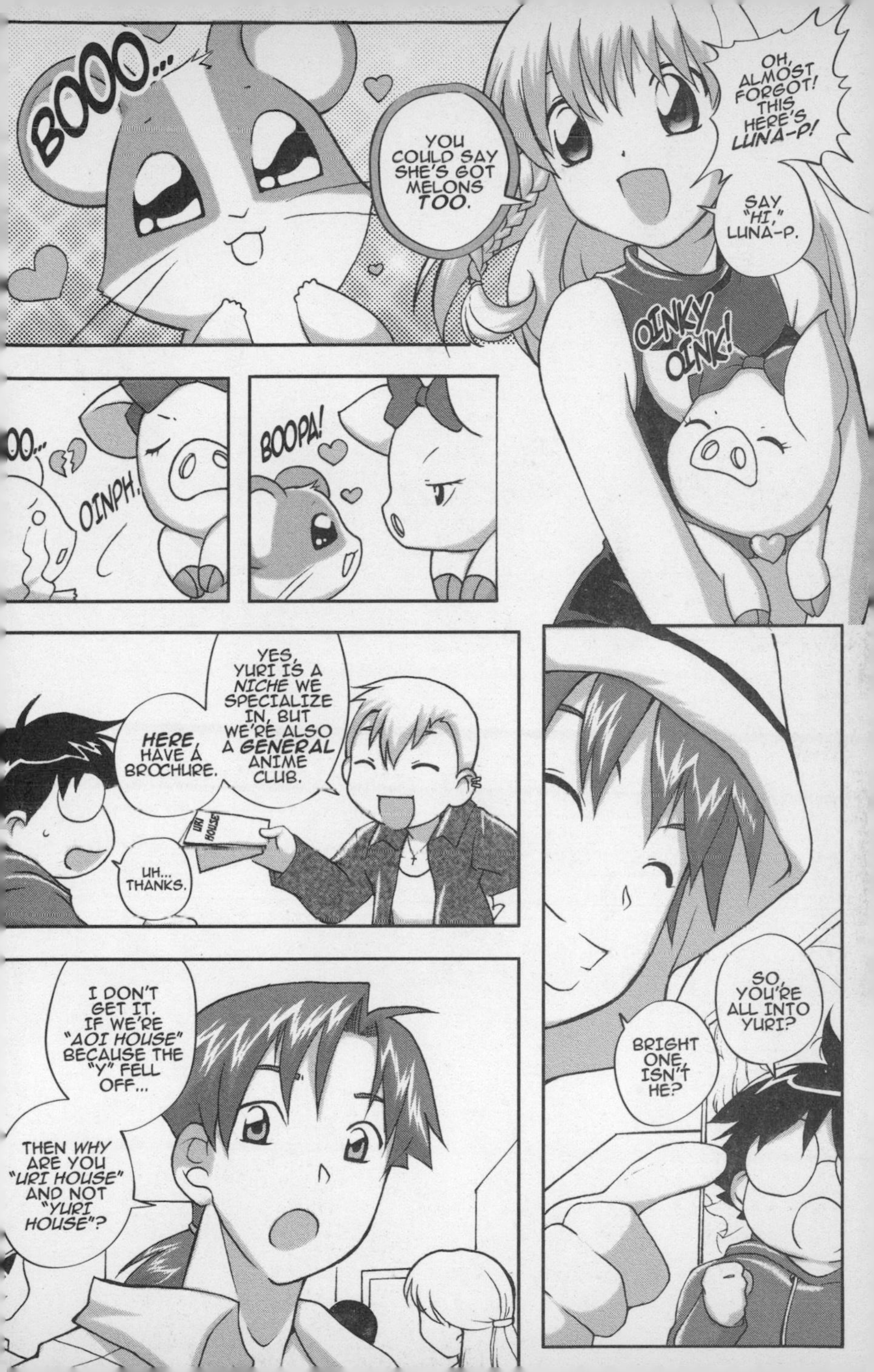
OH, ALMOST FORGOT! THIS HERE'S LUNA-P!
SAY "HI," LUNA-P.
OINKY OINK!
YOU COULD SAY SHE'S GOT MELONS TOO.
BOOO...
BOOPA!
OO...
OINPH.
SO, YOU'RE ALL INTO YURI?
BRIGHT ONE, ISN'T HE?
YES, YURI IS A NICHE WE SPECIALIZE IN, BUT WE'RE ALSO A GENERAL ANIME CLUB.
HERE, HAVE A BROCHURE.
URI HOUSE
UH... THANKS.
I DON'T GET IT. IF WE'RE "AOI HOUSE" BECAUSE THE "Y" FELL OFF...
THEN WHY ARE YOU "URI HOUSE" AND NOT "YURI HOUSE"?

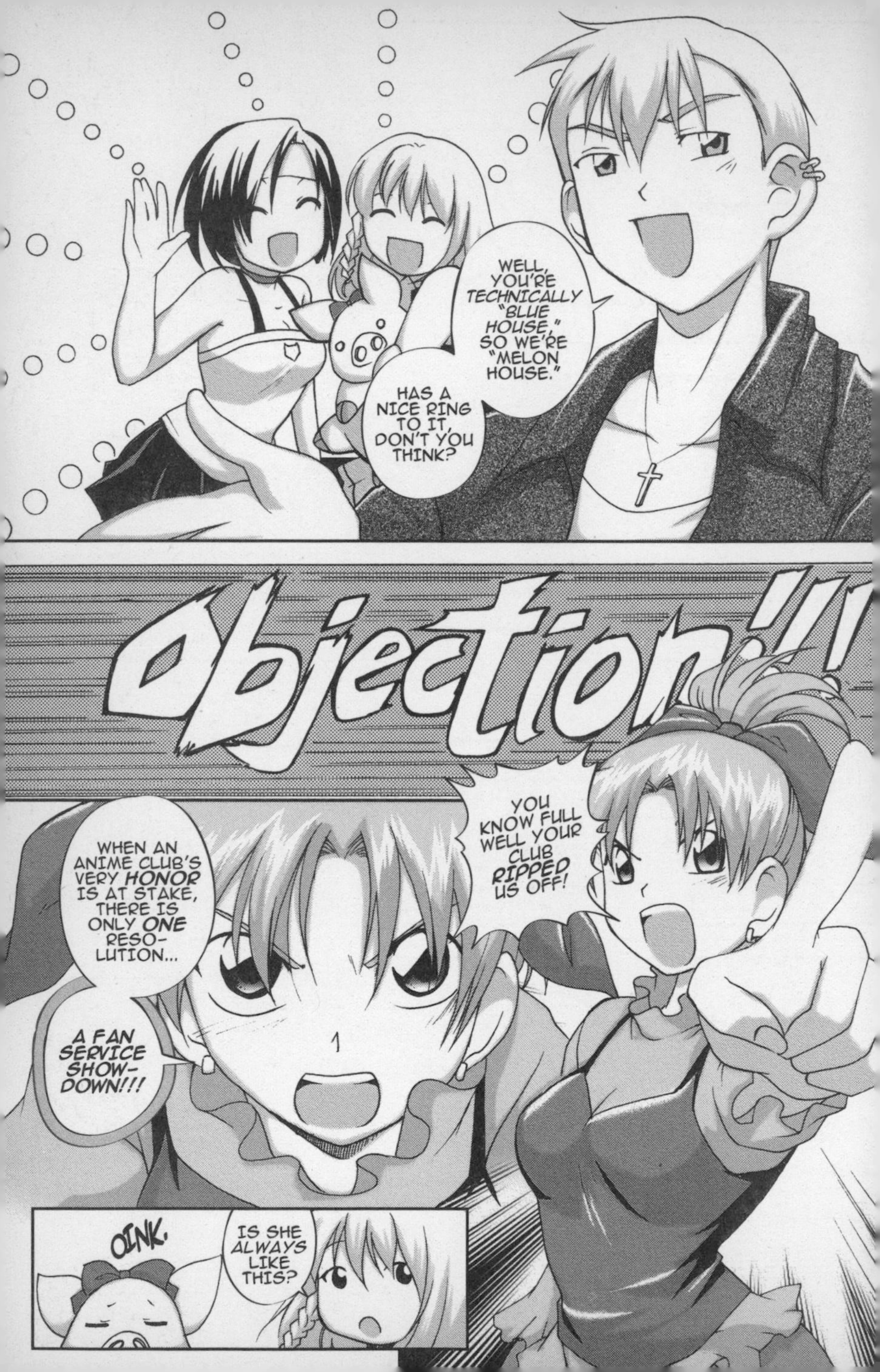
WELL, YOU'RE TECHNICALLY "BLUE HOUSE," SO WE'RE "MELON HOUSE."
HAS A NICE RING TO IT, DON'T YOU THINK?
Objection!!
YOU KNOW FULL WELL YOUR CLUB RIPPED US OFF!
WHEN AN ANIME CLUB'S VERY HONOR IS AT STAKE, THERE IS ONLY ONE RESO-LUTION...
A FAN SERVICE SHOW-DOWN!!!
IS SHE ALWAYS LIKE THIS?
OINK.

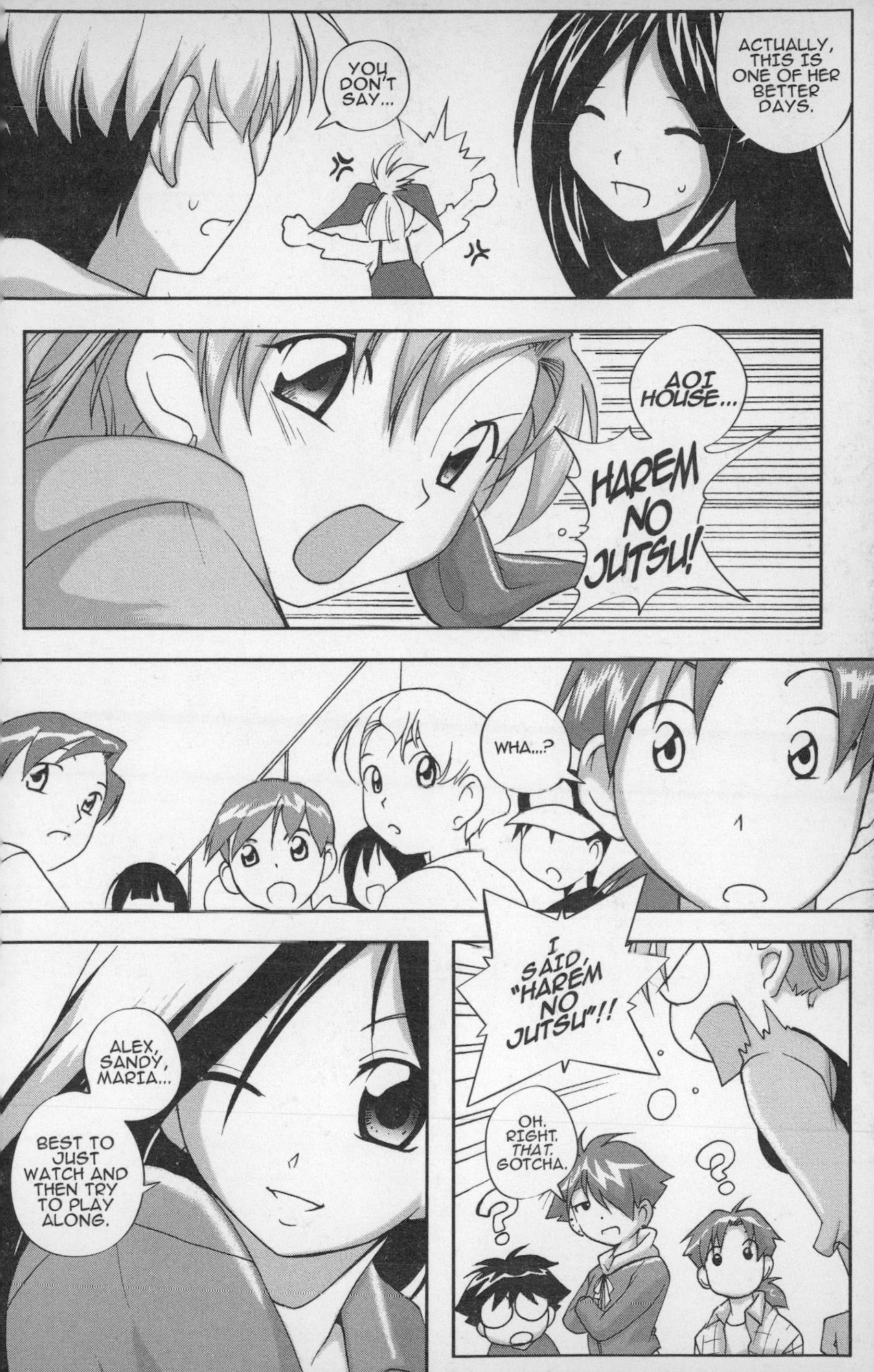
ACTUALLY, THIS IS ONE OF HER BETTER DAYS.
YOU DON'T SAY...
AOI HOUSE...
HAREM NO JUTSU!
WHA...?
I SAID, "HAREM NO JUTSU"!!
OH. RIGHT. THAT. GOTCHA.
ALEX, SANDY, MARIA...
BEST TO JUST WATCH AND THEN TRY TO PLAY ALONG.

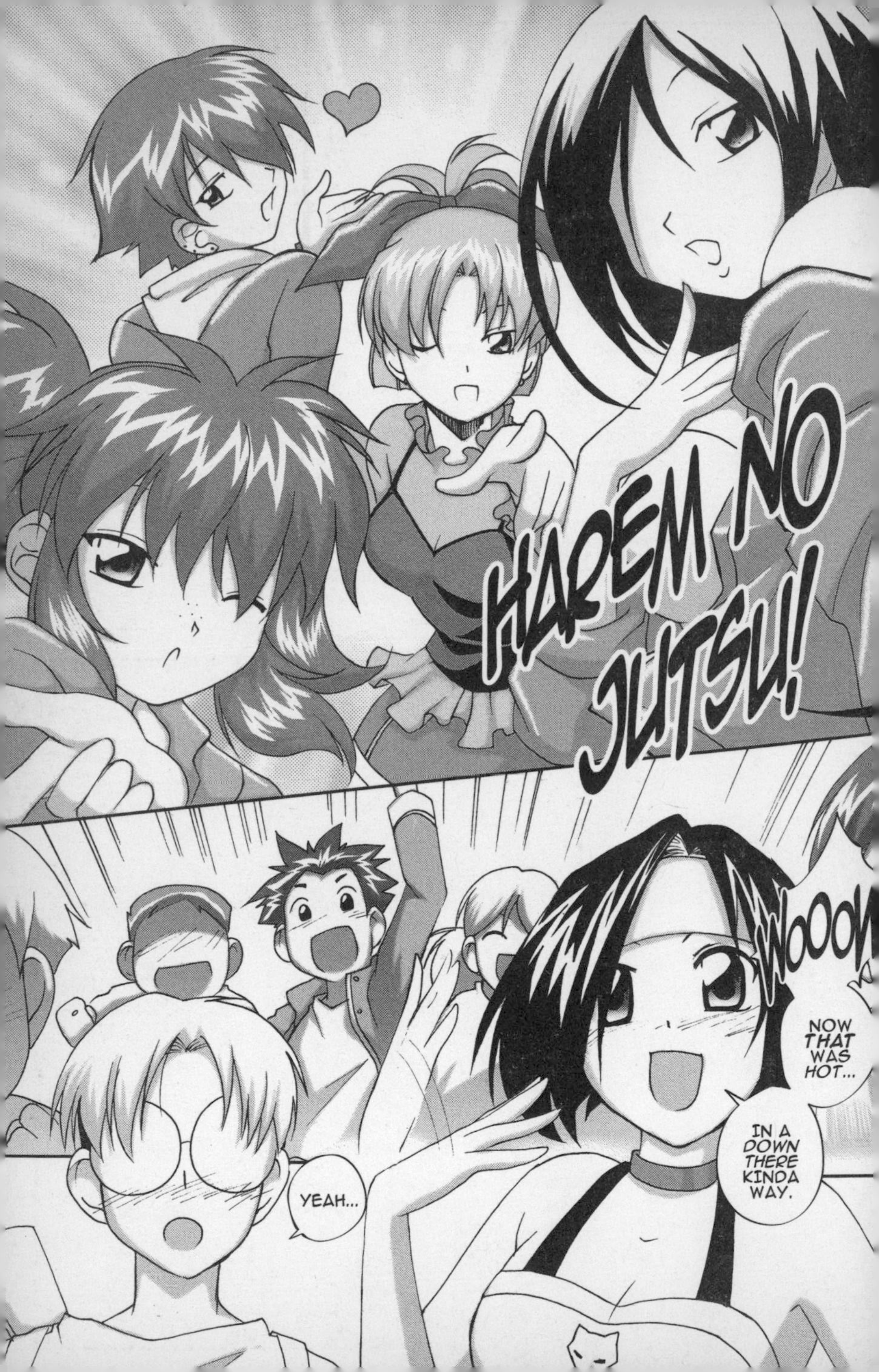
HAREM NO JUTSU!
WOOOW
NOW THAT WAS HOT...
IN A DOWN THERE KINDA WAY.
YEAH...

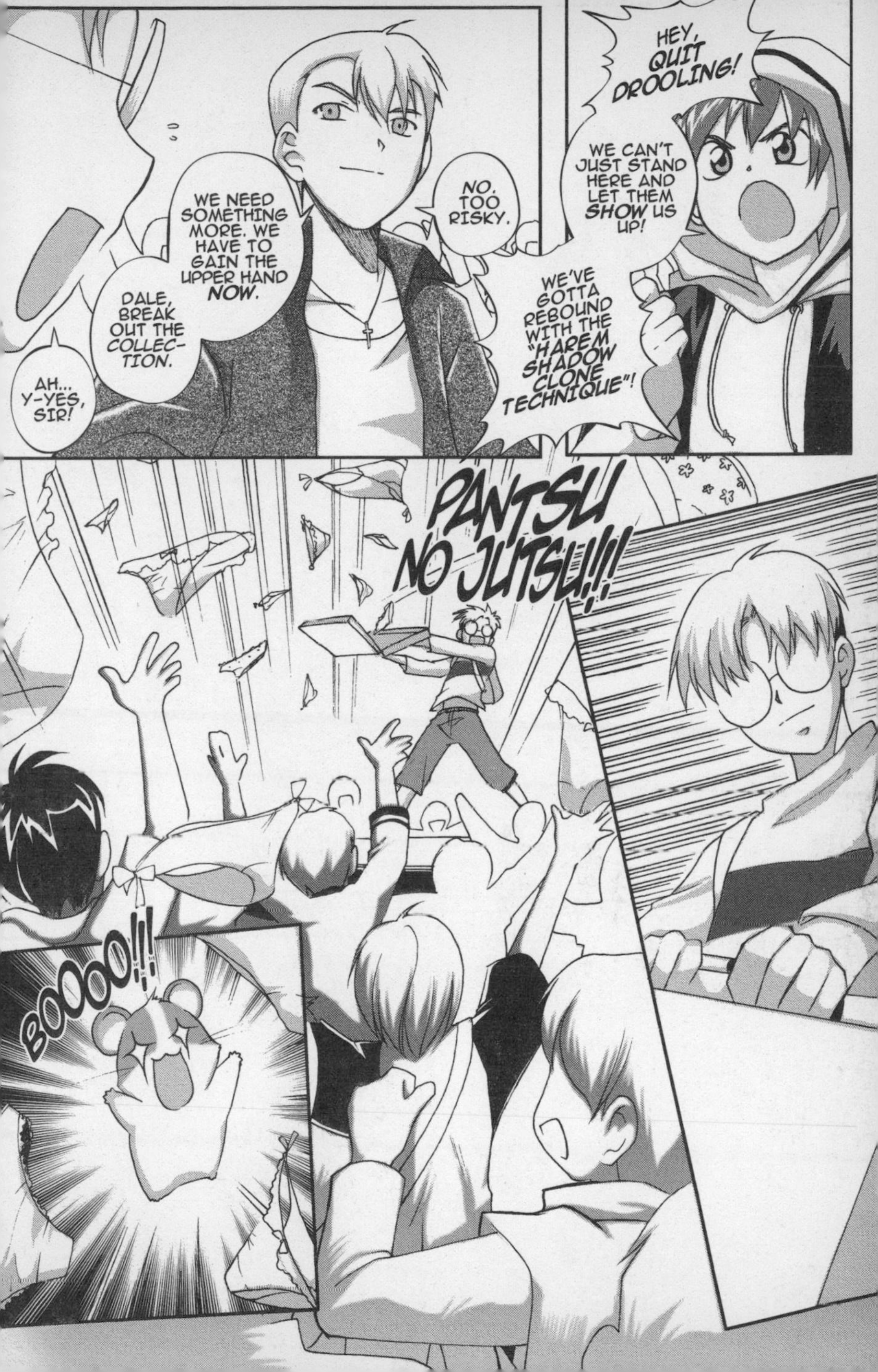
HEY, QUIT DROOLING!
WE CAN'T JUST STAND HERE AND LET THEM SHOW US UP!
WE'VE GOTTA REBOUND WITH THE "HAREM SHADOW CLONE TECHNIQUE"!
NO. TOO RISKY.
WE NEED SOMETHING MORE. WE HAVE TO GAIN THE UPPER HAND NOW.
DALE, BREAK OUT THE COLLEC-TION.
AH... Y-YES, SIR!
PANTSU NO JUTSU!!!
BOOOO!!!

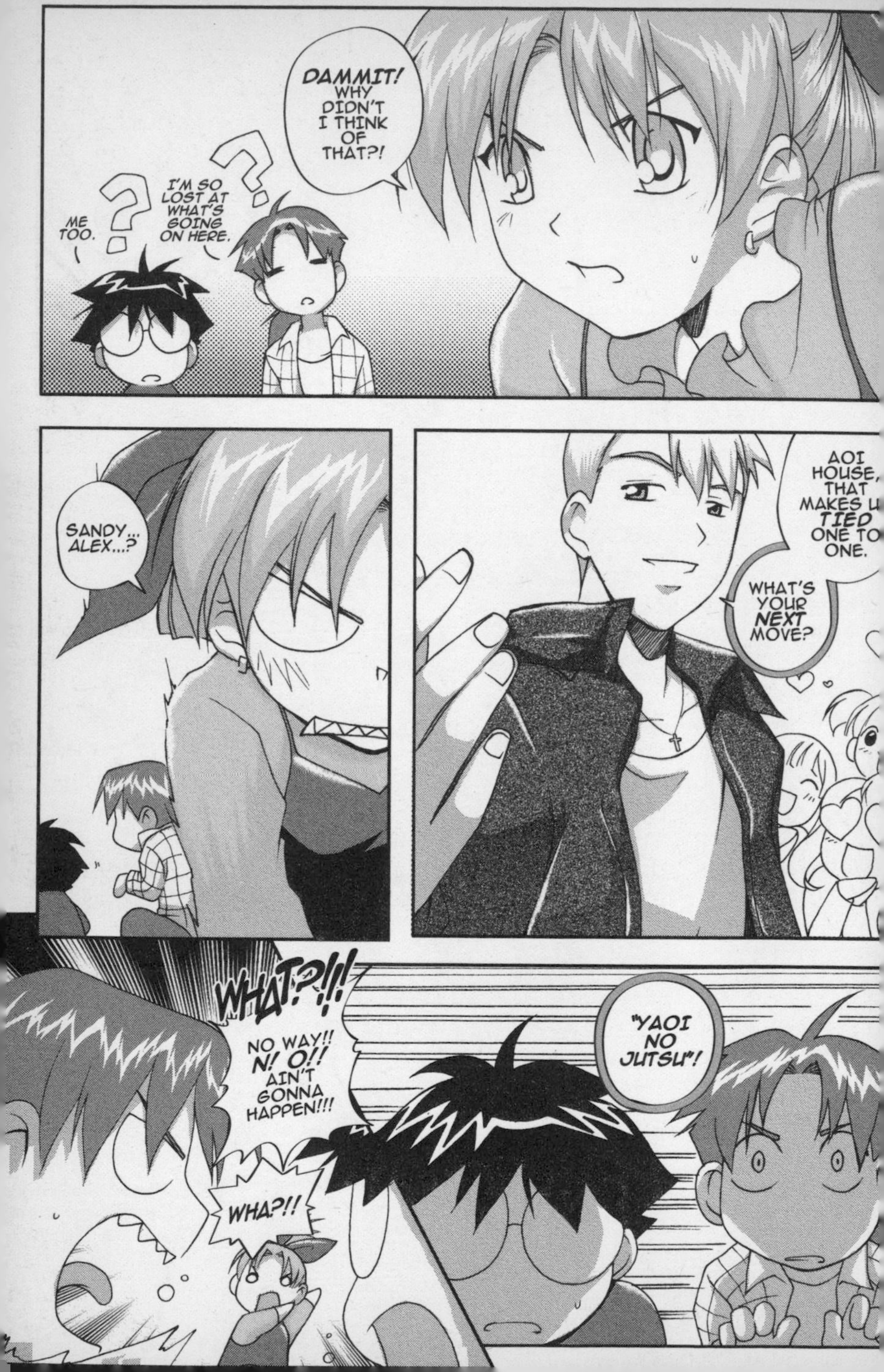
DAMMIT! WHY DIDN'T I THINK OF THAT?!
I'M SO LOST AT WHAT'S GOING ON HERE.
ME TOO.
AOI HOUSE, THAT MAKES U TIED ONE TO ONE.
WHAT'S YOUR NEXT MOVE?
SANDY... ALEX...?
"YAOI NO JUTSU"!
WHAT?!!!
NO WAY!! N! O!! AIN'T GONNA HAPPEN!!!
WHA?!!

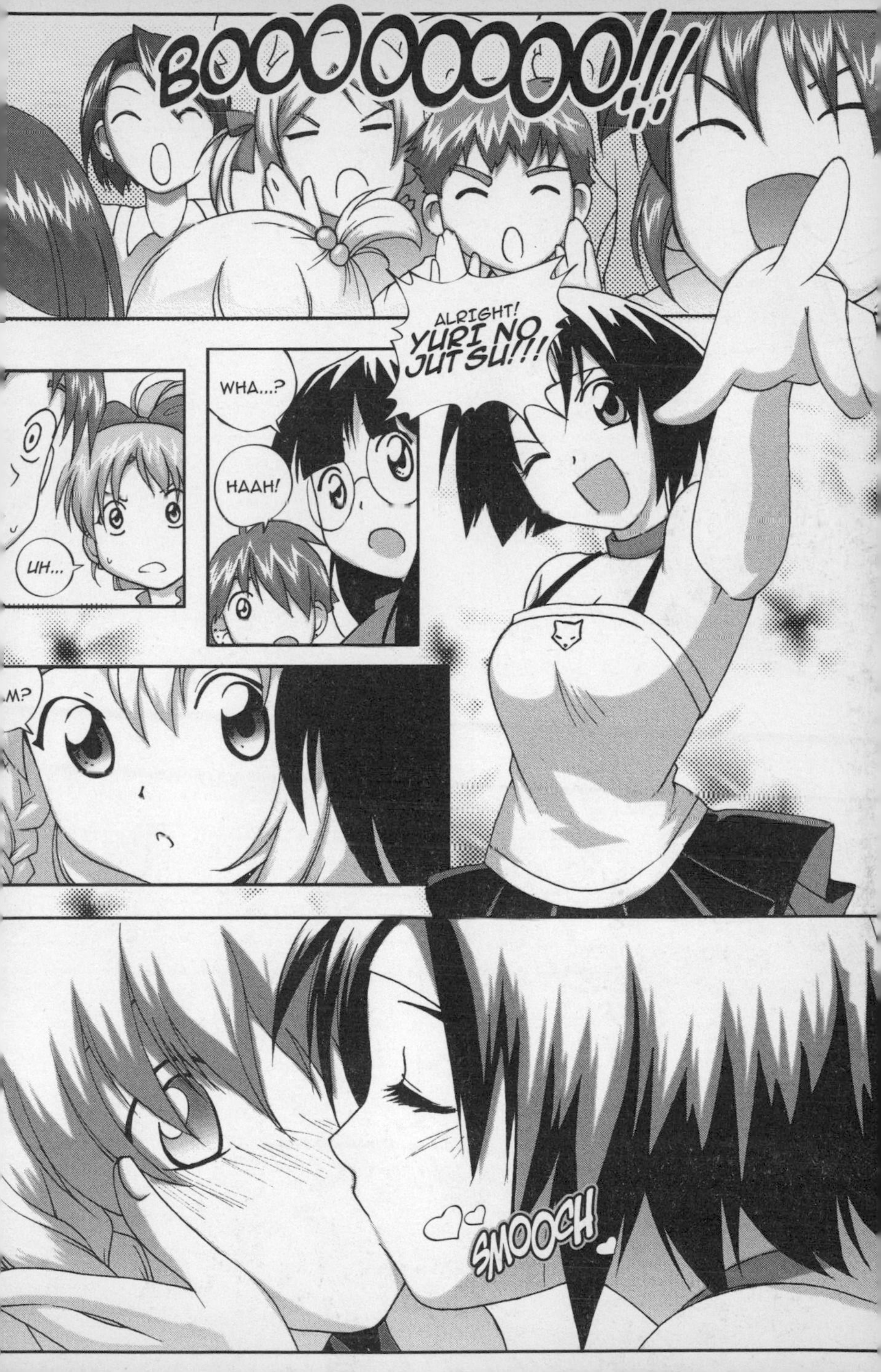
BOOOOOOOOO!!!
ALRIGHT! YURI NO JUTSU!!!
WHA...?
HAAH!
UH...
M?
SMOOCH

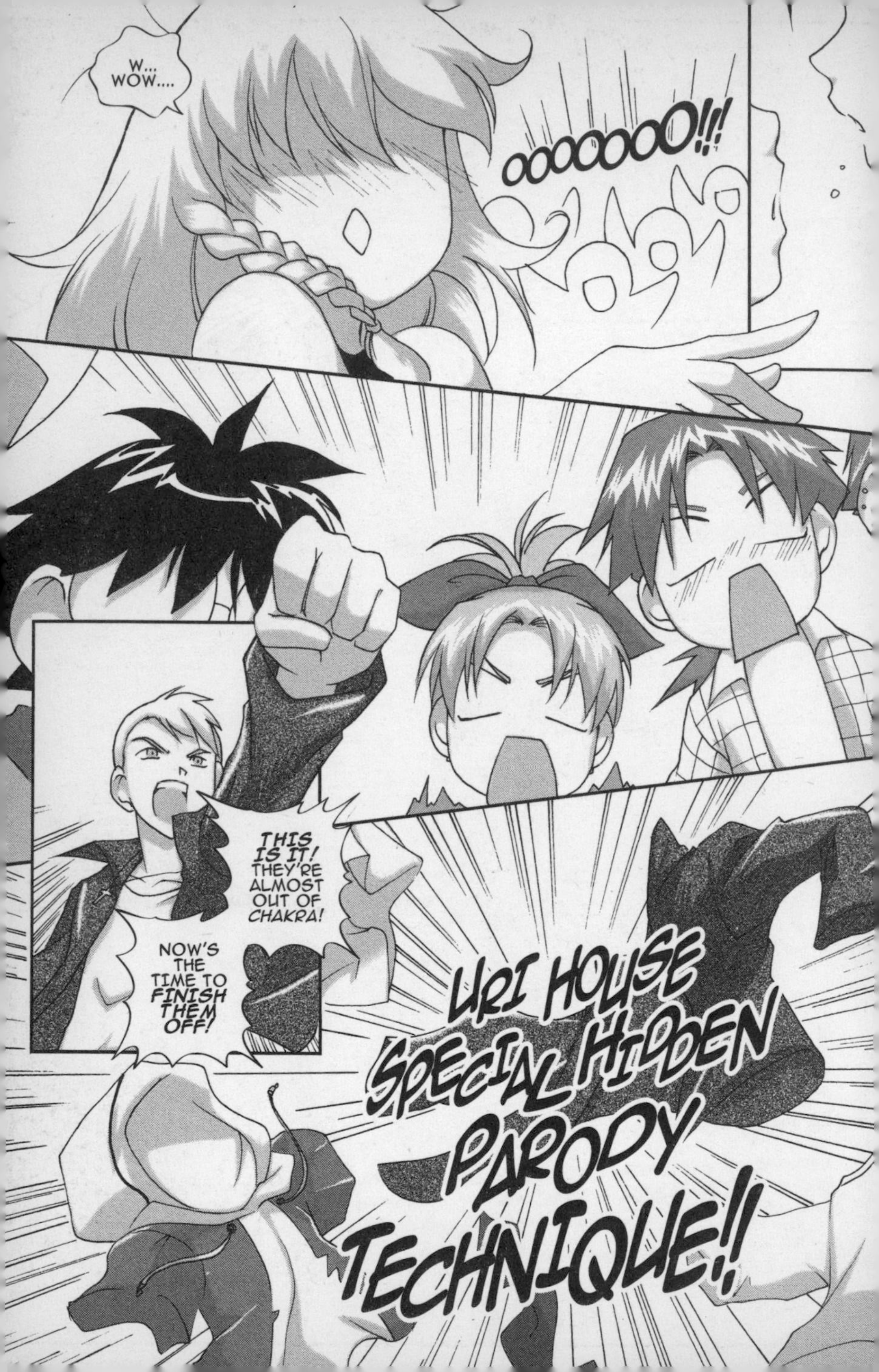
OOOOOOOO!!!
W... WOW....
THIS IS IT! THEY'RE ALMOST OUT OF CHAKRA!
NOW'S THE TIME TO FINISH THEM OFF!
URI HOUSE SPECIAL HIDDEN PARODY TECHNIQUE!

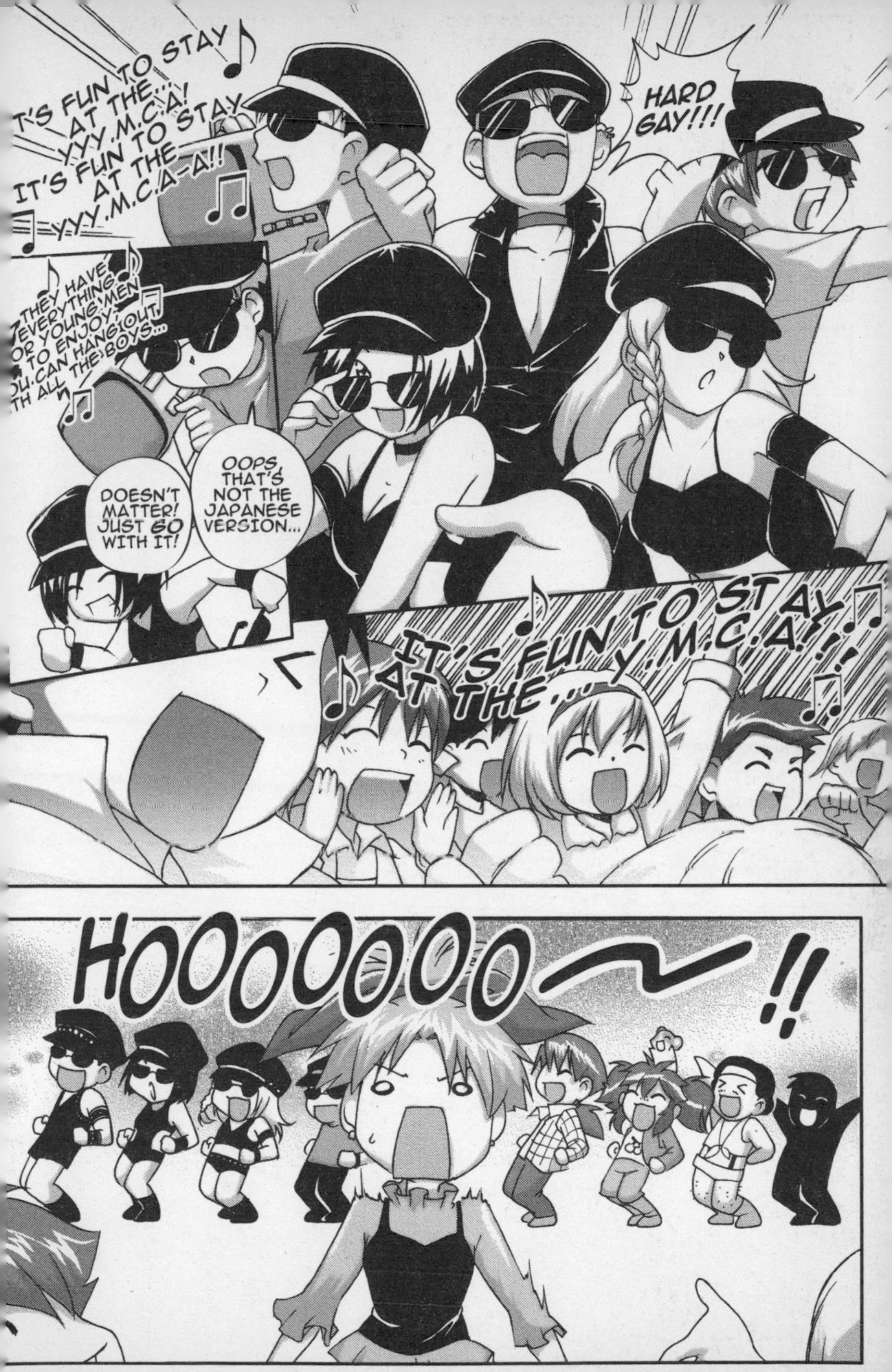
HARD GAY!!!
T'S FUN TO STAY AT THE... YYY.M.C.A! IT'S FUN TO STAY AT THE YYY.M.C.A-A!!
THEY HAVE EVERYTHING OR YOUNG MEN TO ENJOY, OU CAN HANG OUT TH ALL THE BOYS...
OOPS, THAT'S NOT THE JAPANESE VERSION...
DOESN'T MATTER! JUST GO WITH IT!
IT'S FUN TO STAY AT THE... Y.M.C.A!!!
HOOOOOOO~!!

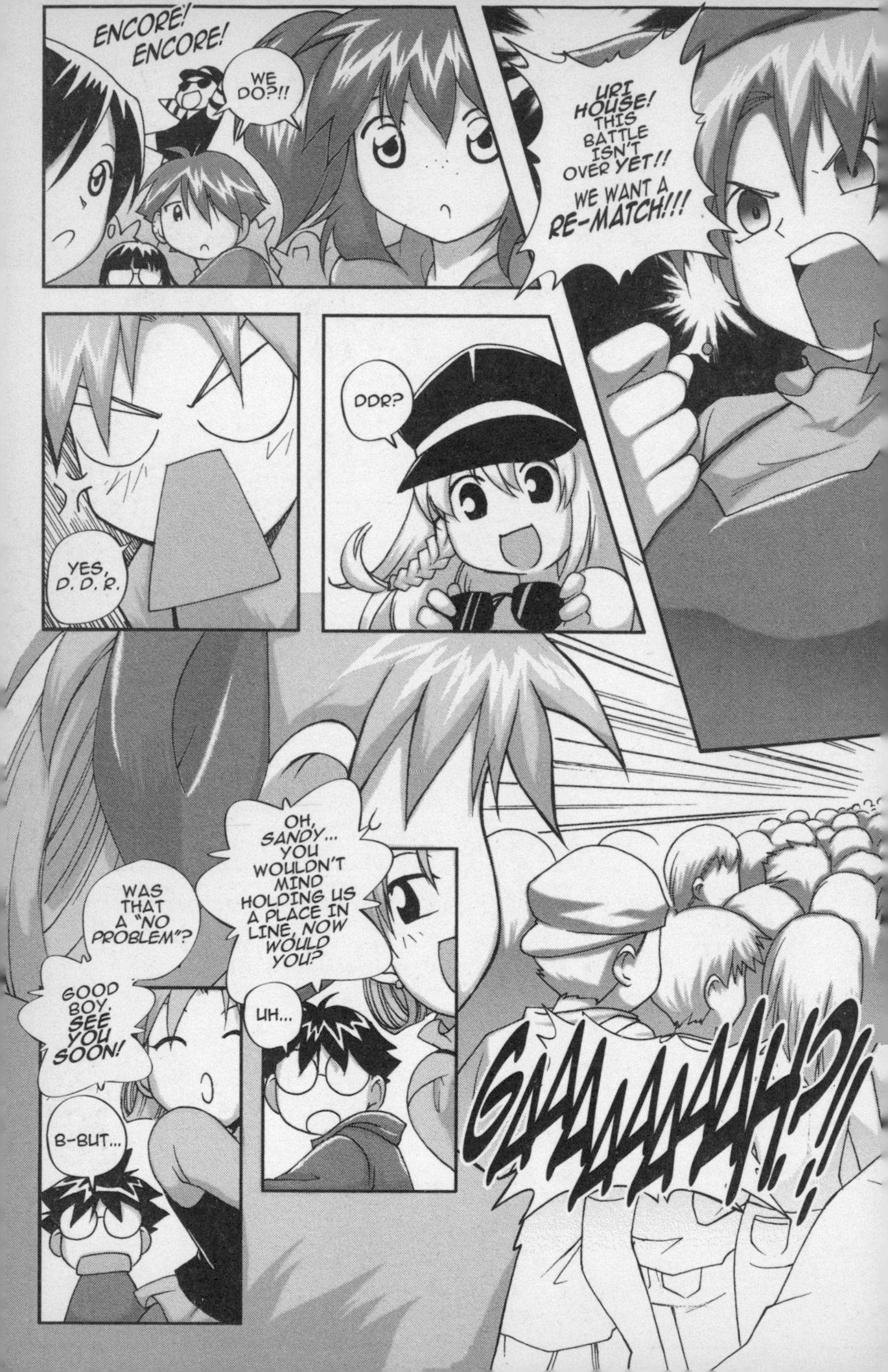
URI HOUSE! THIS BATTLE ISN'T OVER YET!! WE WANT A RE-MATCH!!!
ENCORE! ENCORE!
WE DO?!!
DDR?
YES, D. D. R.
OH, SANDY... YOU WOULDN'T MIND HOLDING US A PLACE IN LINE, NOW WOULD YOU?
GYAAAAAH?!!
WAS THAT A "NO PROBLEM"?
UH...
GOOD BOY. SEE YOU SOON!
B-BUT...

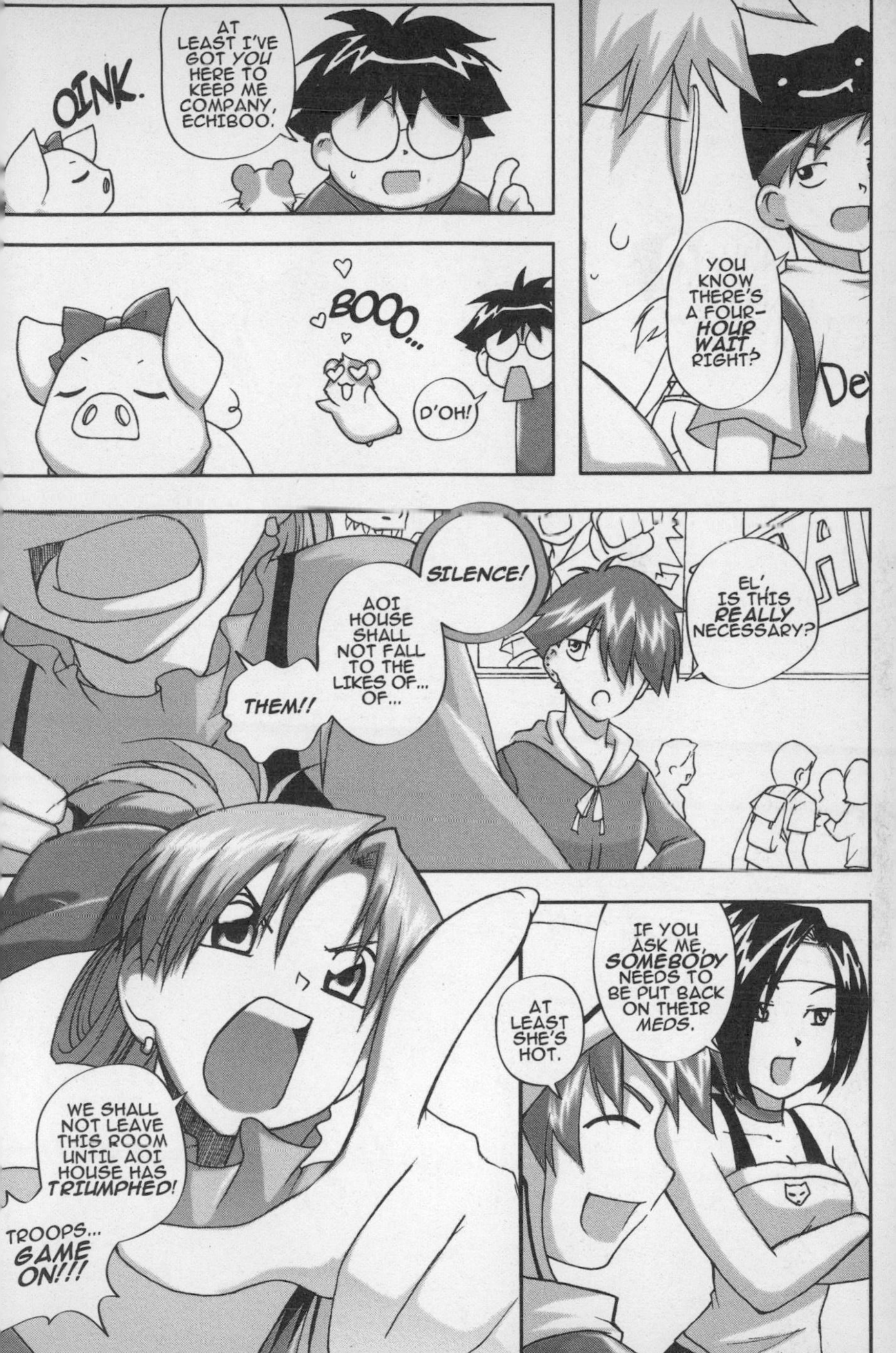
YOU KNOW THERE'S A FOUR-HOUR WAIT, RIGHT?
OINK.
AT LEAST I'VE GOT YOU HERE TO KEEP ME COMPANY, ECHIBOO.
BOOO...
D'OH!
EL', IS THIS REALLY NECESSARY?
SILENCE!
AOI HOUSE SHALL NOT FALL TO THE LIKES OF... OF...
THEM!!
IF YOU ASK ME, SOMEBODY NEEDS TO BE PUT BACK ON THEIR MEDS.
AT LEAST SHE'S HOT.
WE SHALL NOT LEAVE THIS ROOM UNTIL AOI HOUSE HAS TRIUMPHED!
TROOPS... GAME ON!!!

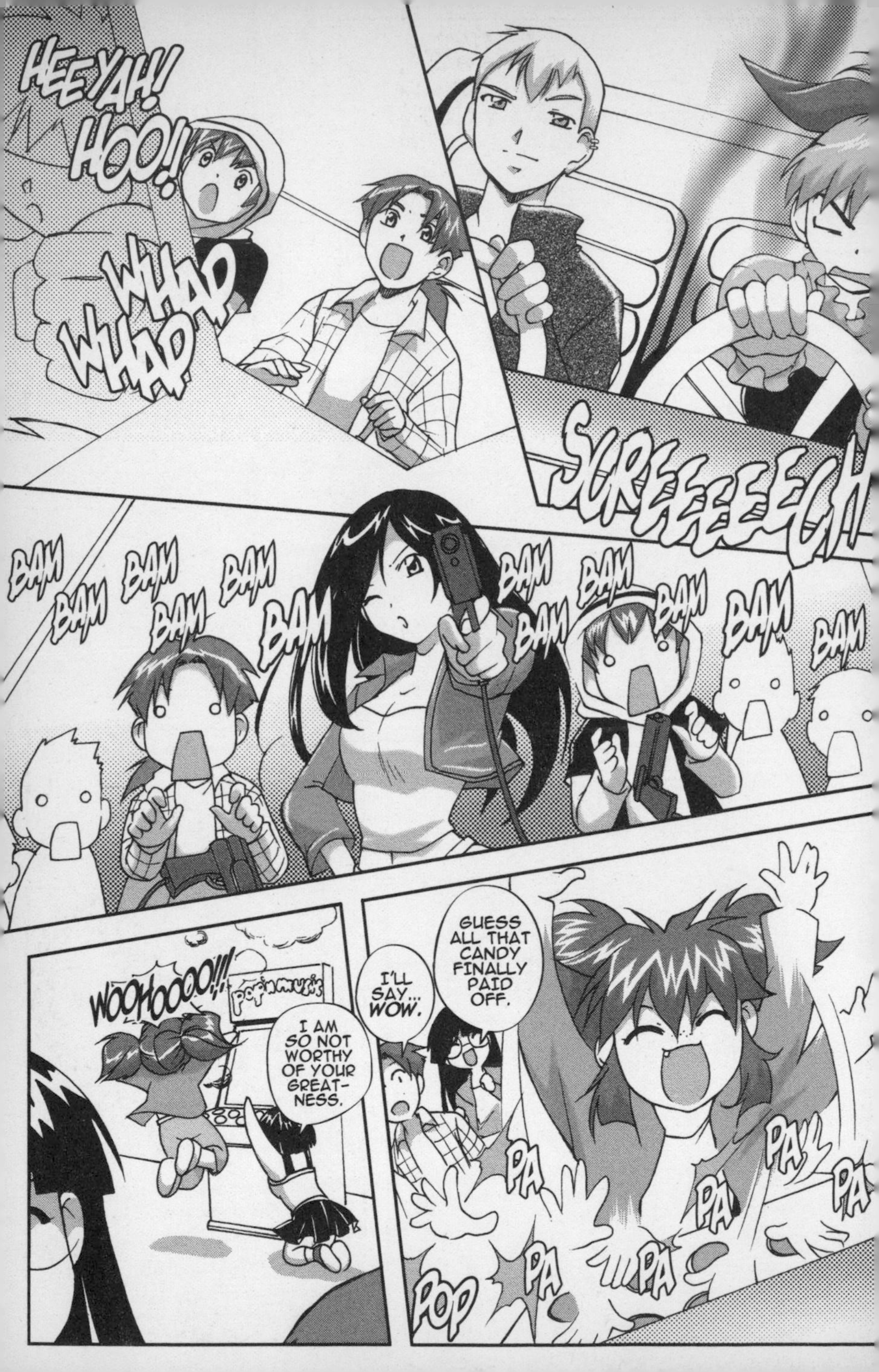
SCREEEEEECH
HEE YAH!
HOO!!
WHAP
WHAP
BAM
BAM
BAM
BAM
BAM
BAM
BAM
BAM
BAM
BAM
BAM
BAM
GUESS ALL THAT CANDY FINALLY PAID OFF.
I'LL SAY... WOW.
I AM SO NOT WORTHY OF YOUR GREATNESS.
PA
PA
PA
PA
PA
PA
POP
WOOHOOOO!!!
pop'n music

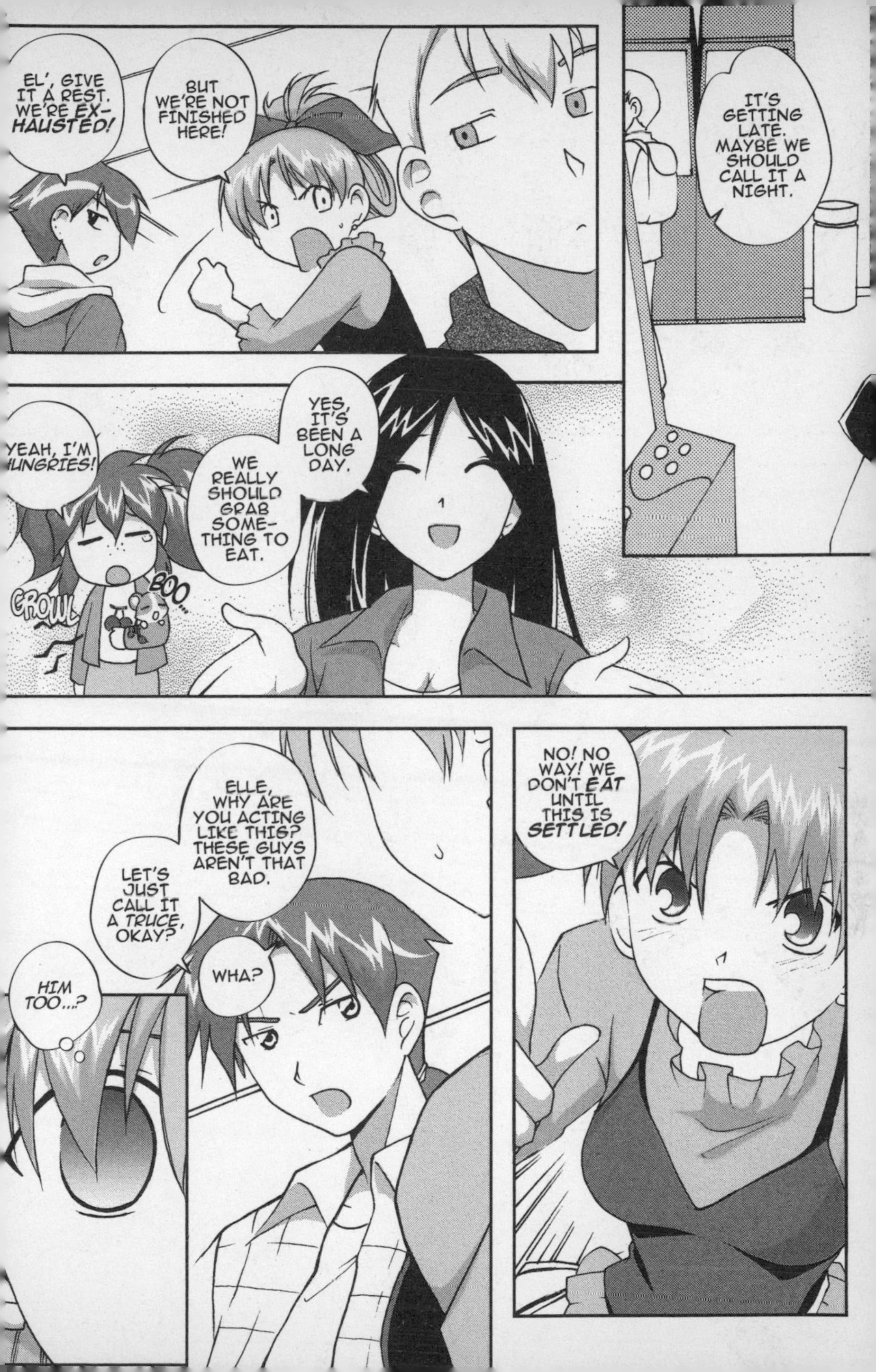
IT'S GETTING LATE. MAYBE WE SHOULD CALL IT A NIGHT.
BUT WE'RE NOT FINISHED HERE!
EL', GIVE IT A REST. WE'RE *EX-HAUSTED!*
YES, IT'S BEEN A LONG DAY.
WE REALLY SHOULD GRAB SOME-THING TO EAT.
YEAH, I'M HUNGRIES!
BOO...
GROWL
NO! NO WAY! WE DON'T *EAT* UNTIL THIS IS *SETTLED!*
ELLE, WHY ARE YOU ACTING LIKE THIS? THESE GUYS AREN'T THAT BAD.
LET'S JUST CALL IT A *TRUCE*, OKAY?
WHA?
HIM TOO...?

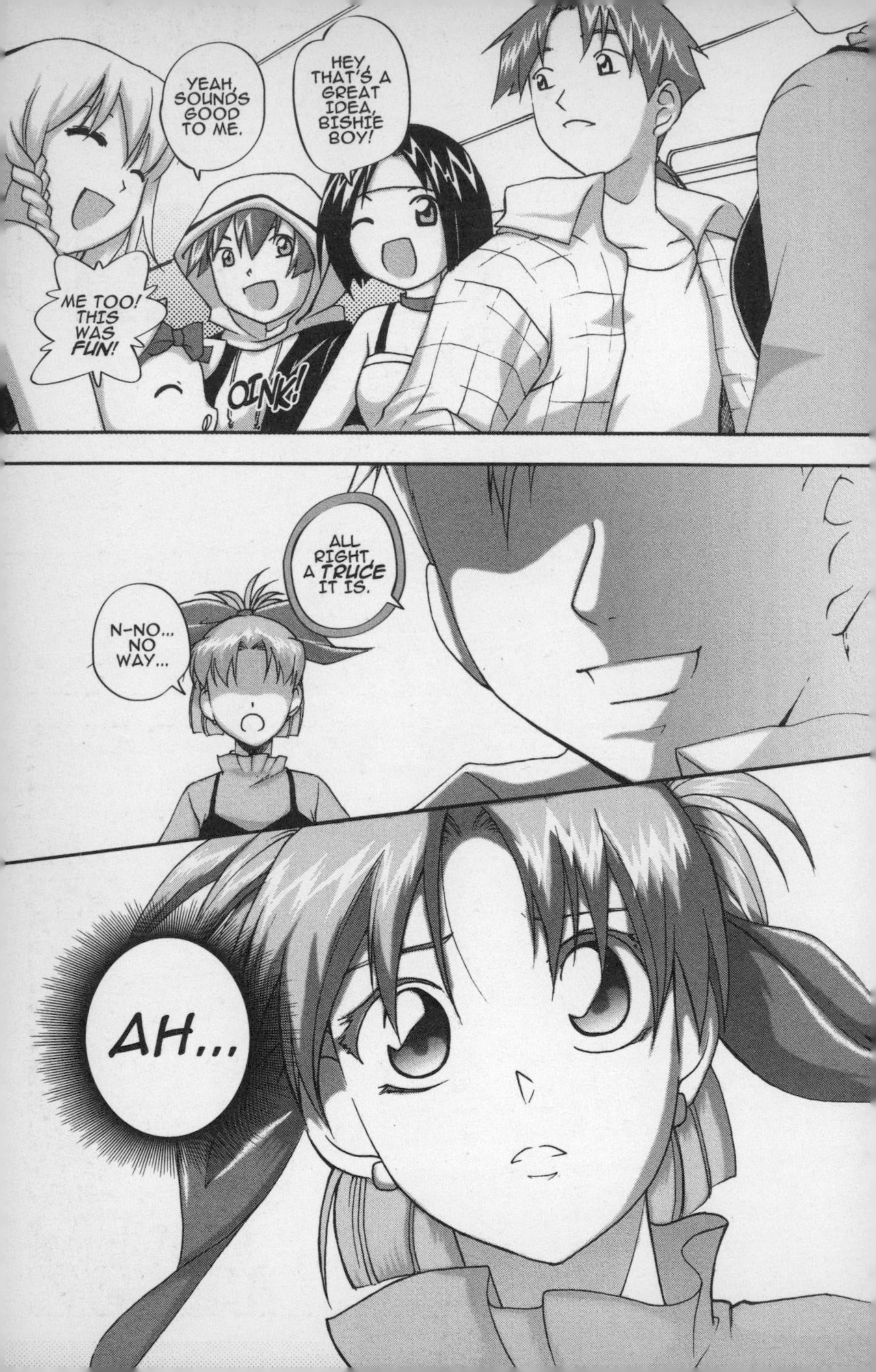
HEY, THAT'S A GREAT IDEA, BISHIE BOY!
YEAH, SOUNDS GOOD TO ME.
ME TOO! THIS WAS FUN!
OINK!
ALL RIGHT, A TRUCE IT IS.
N-NO... NO WAY...
AH...

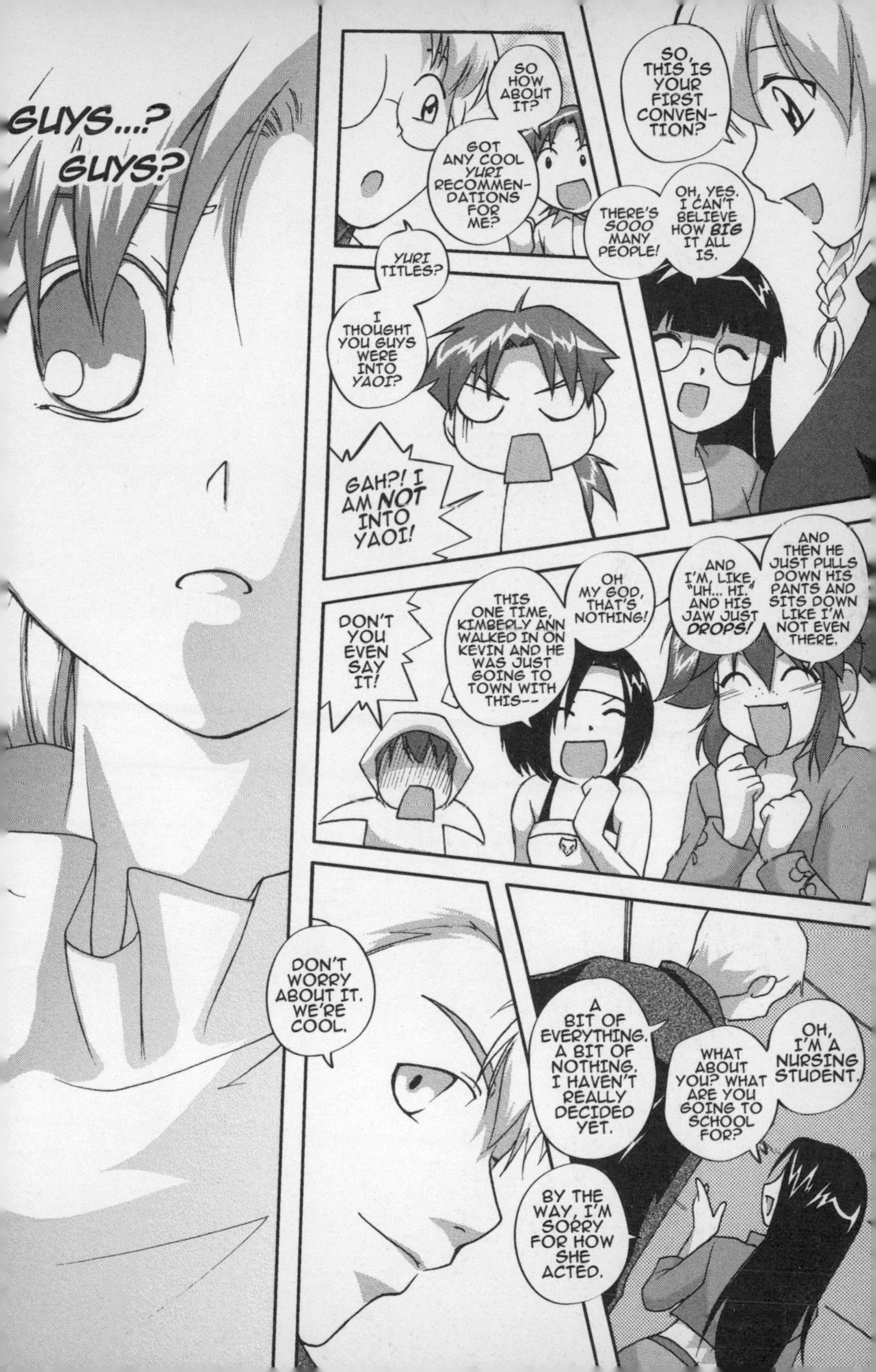
SO, THIS IS YOUR FIRST CONVENTION?
OH, YES. I CAN'T BELIEVE HOW BIG IT ALL IS.
THERE'S SOOO MANY PEOPLE!
SO HOW ABOUT IT?
GOT ANY COOL YURI RECOMMENDATIONS FOR ME?
YURI TITLES?
I THOUGHT YOU GUYS WERE INTO YAOI?
GAH?! I AM NOT INTO YAOI!
AND THEN HE JUST PULLS DOWN HIS PANTS AND SITS DOWN LIKE I'M NOT EVEN THERE.
AND I'M, LIKE, "UH... HI." AND HIS JAW JUST DROPS!
OH MY GOD, THAT'S NOTHING!
THIS ONE TIME, KIMBERLY ANN WALKED IN ON KEVIN AND HE WAS JUST GOING TO TOWN WITH THIS--
DON'T YOU EVEN SAY IT!
OH, I'M A NURSING STUDENT.
WHAT ABOUT YOU? WHAT ARE YOU GOING TO SCHOOL FOR?
A BIT OF EVERYTHING. A BIT OF NOTHING. I HAVEN'T REALLY DECIDED YET.
BY THE WAY, I'M SORRY FOR HOW SHE ACTED.
DON'T WORRY ABOUT IT. WE'RE COOL.
GUYS...? GUYS?

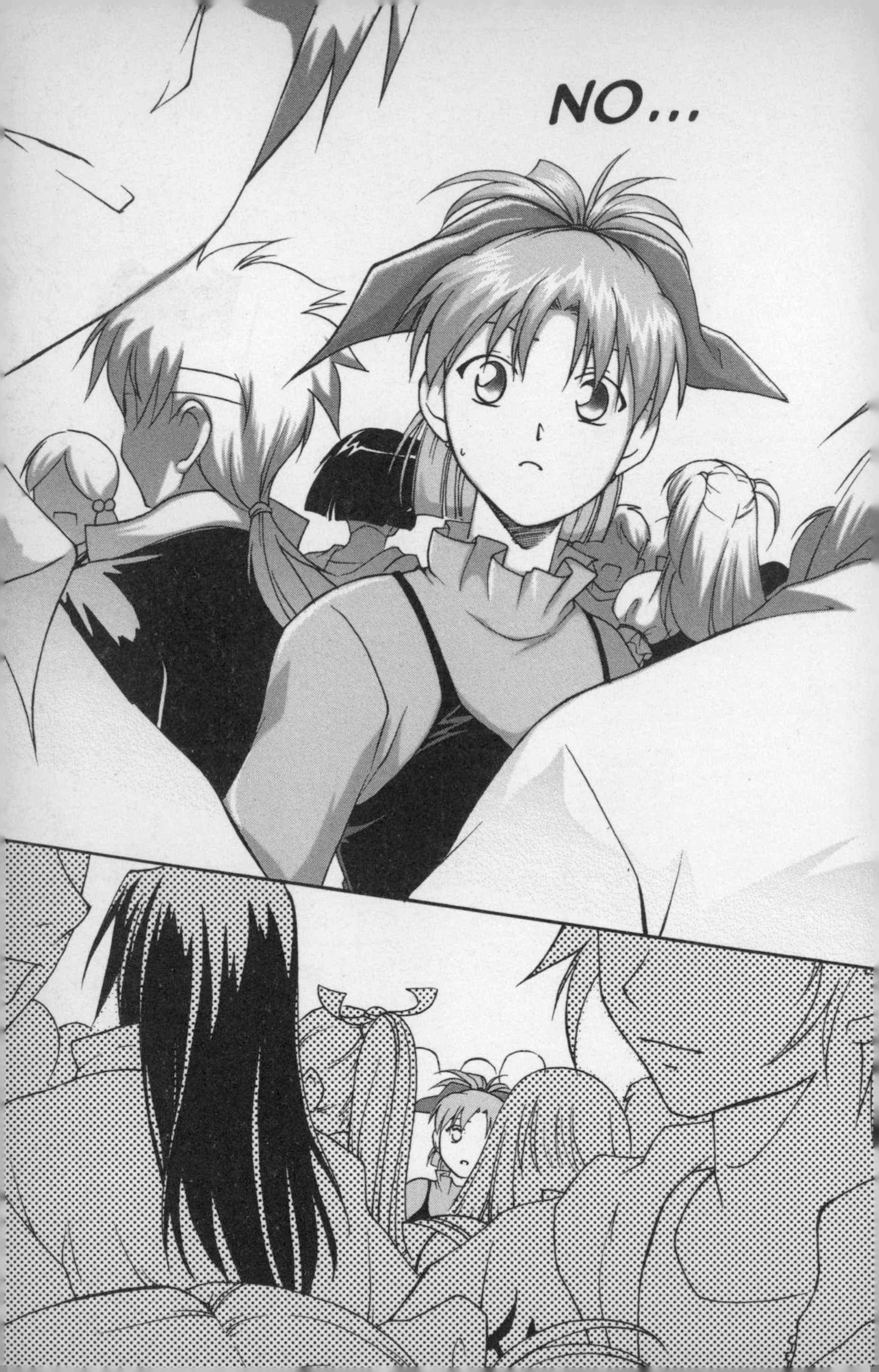
NO...

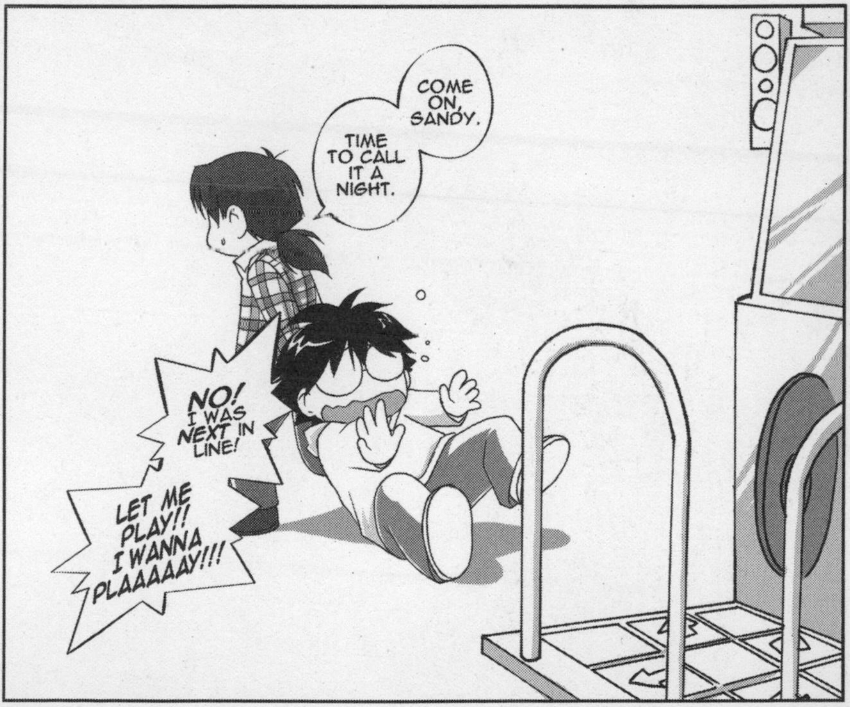
COME ON, SANDY.
TIME TO CALL IT A NIGHT.
NO! I WAS NEXT IN LINE!
LET ME PLAY!! I WANNA PLAAAAAY!!!

EPISODE 4:

D FOR DRAMA

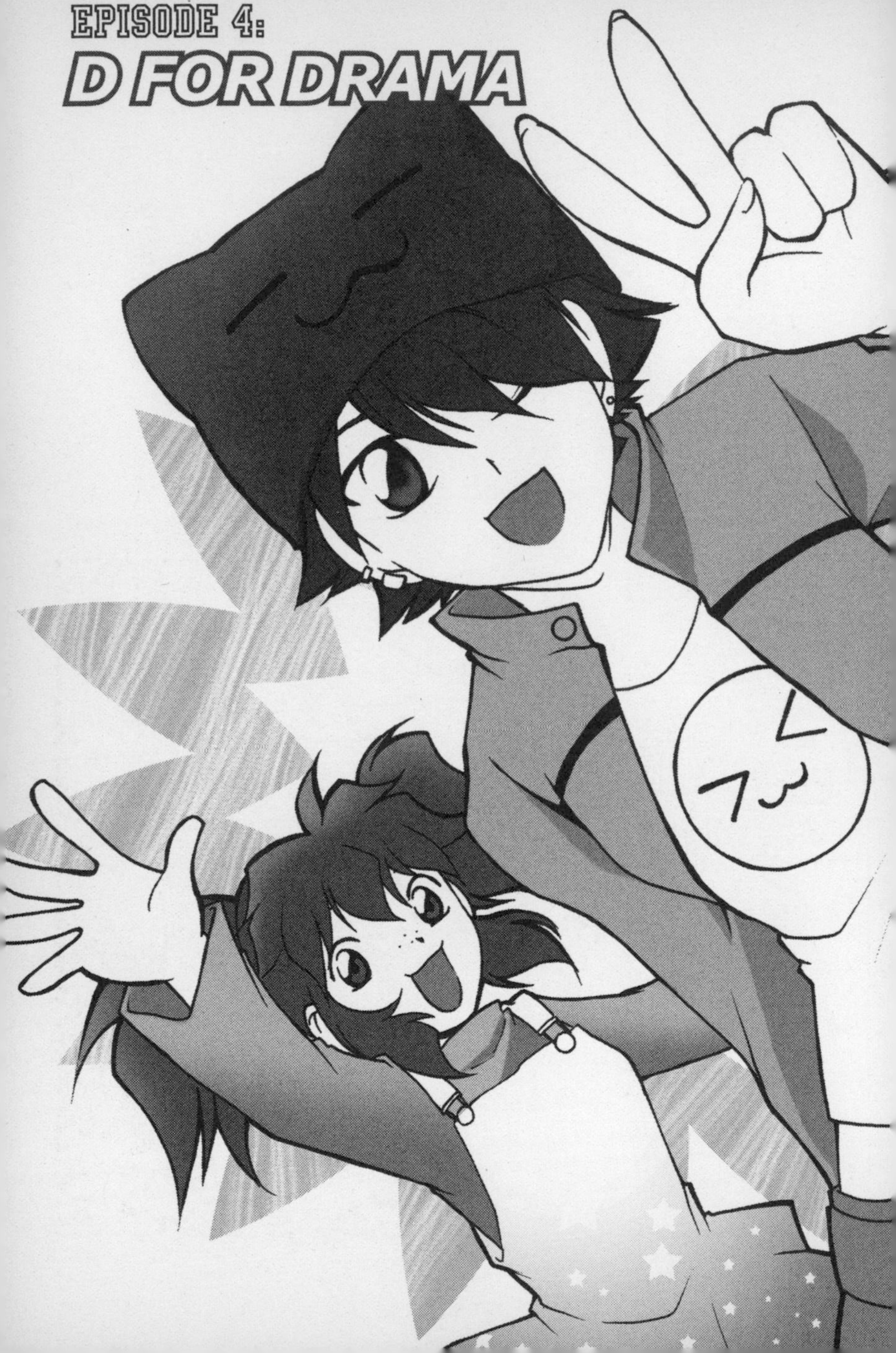

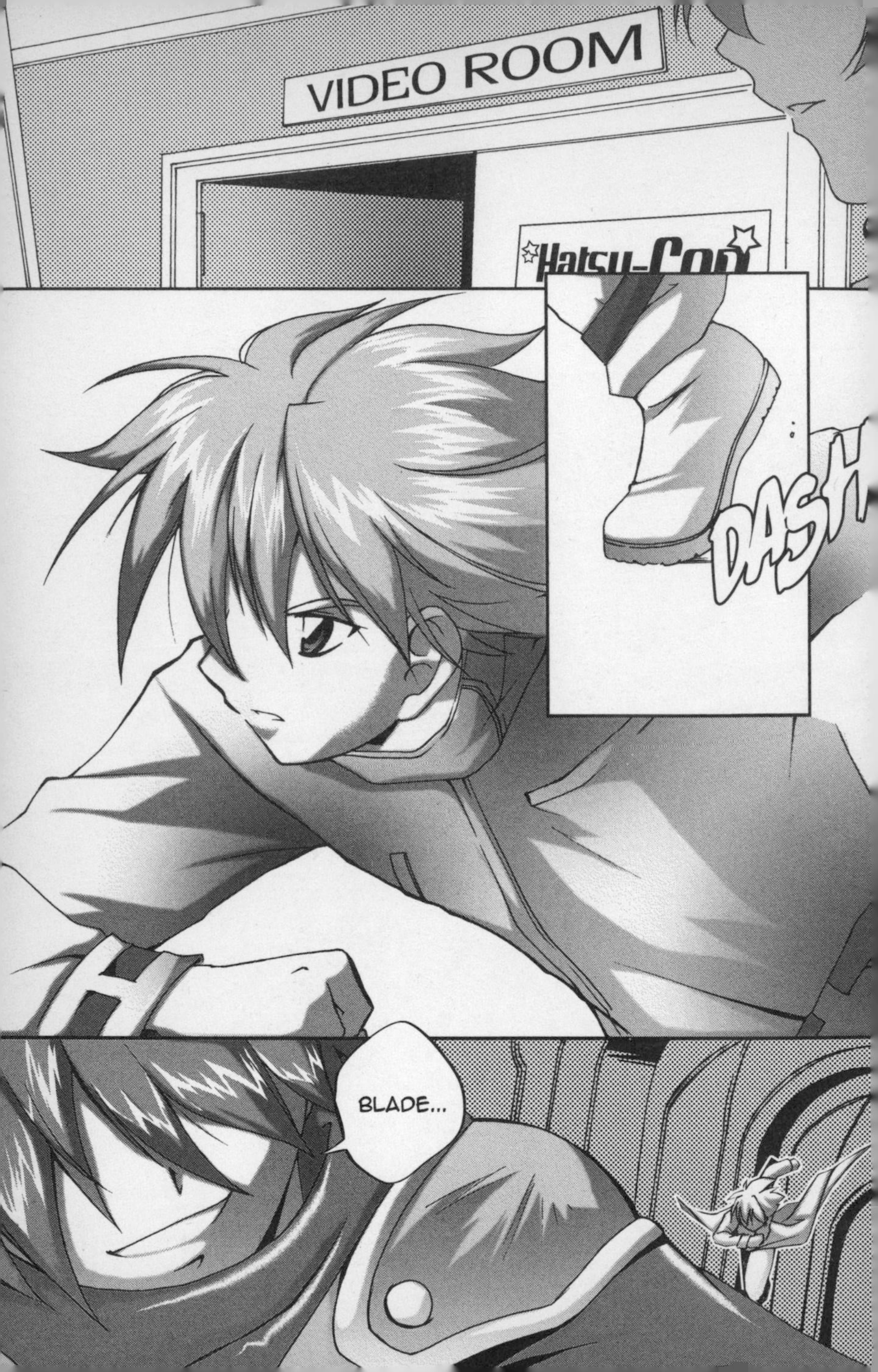
VIDEO ROOM
Hatsu-Cop
DASH
BLADE...

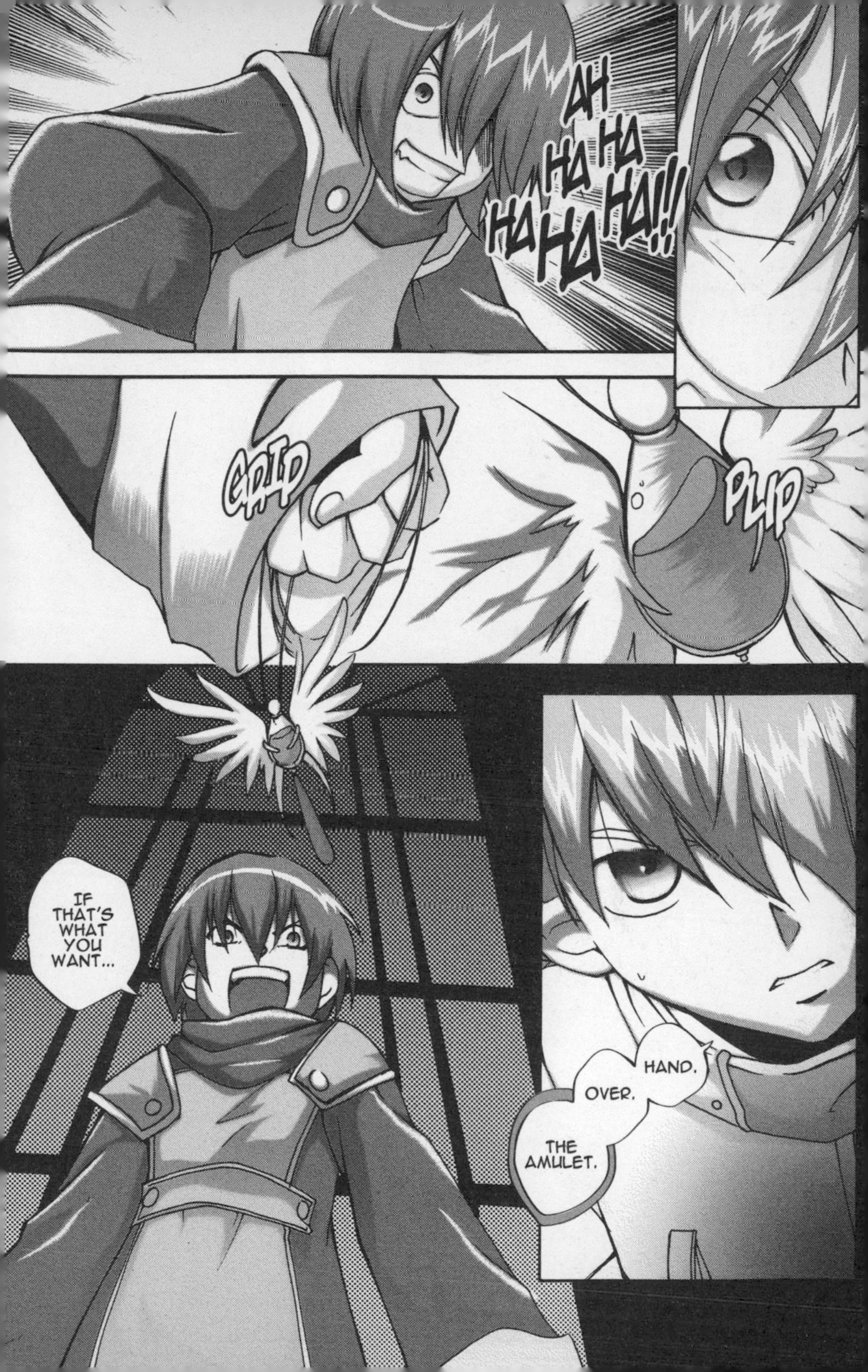
AH HA HA HA HA HA!!!
GRIP
PLIP
HAND. OVER. THE AMULET.
IF THAT'S WHAT YOU WANT...

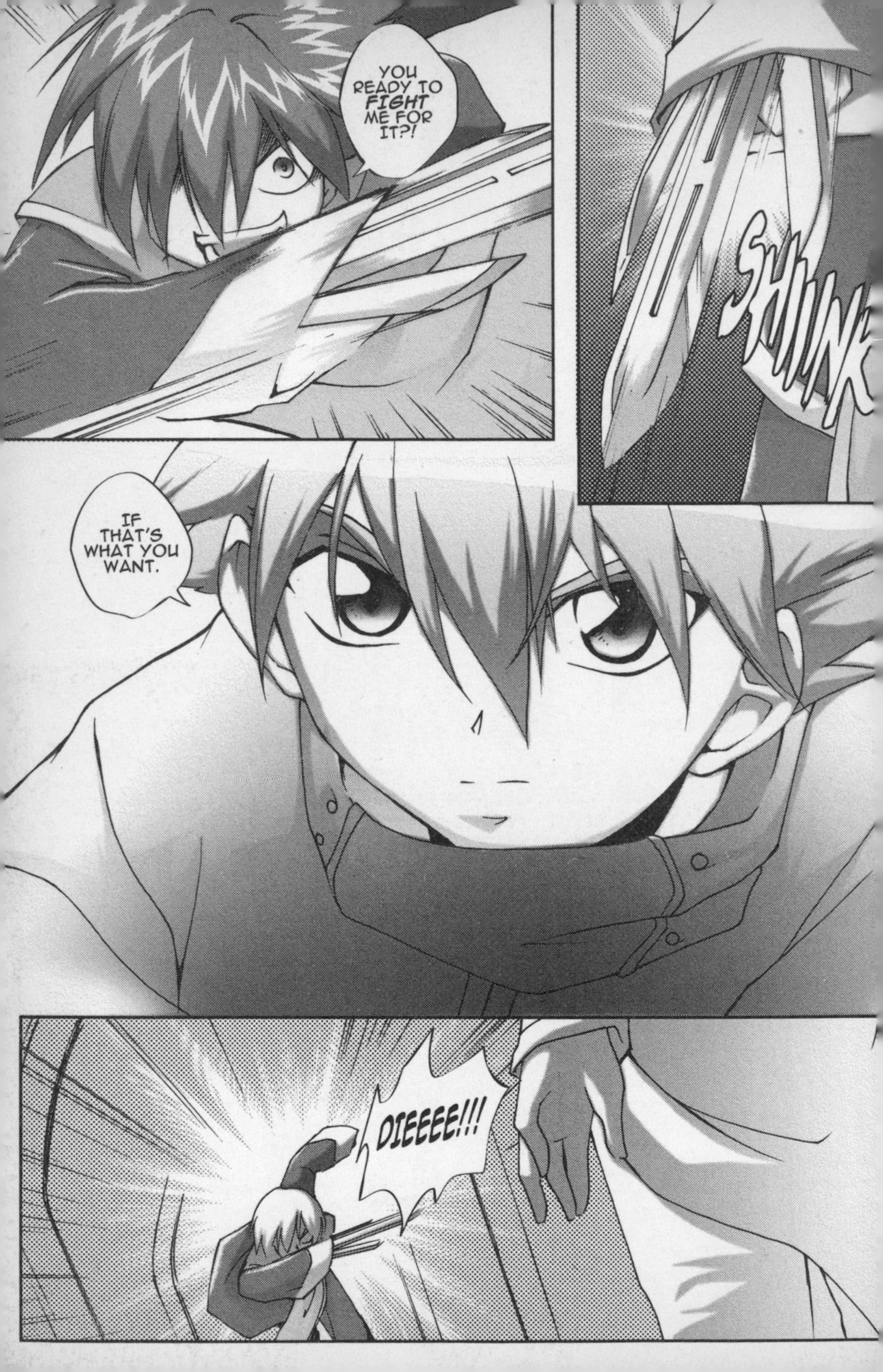
SHIINK
YOU READY TO FIGHT ME FOR IT?!
IF THAT'S WHAT YOU WANT.
DIEEEE!!!

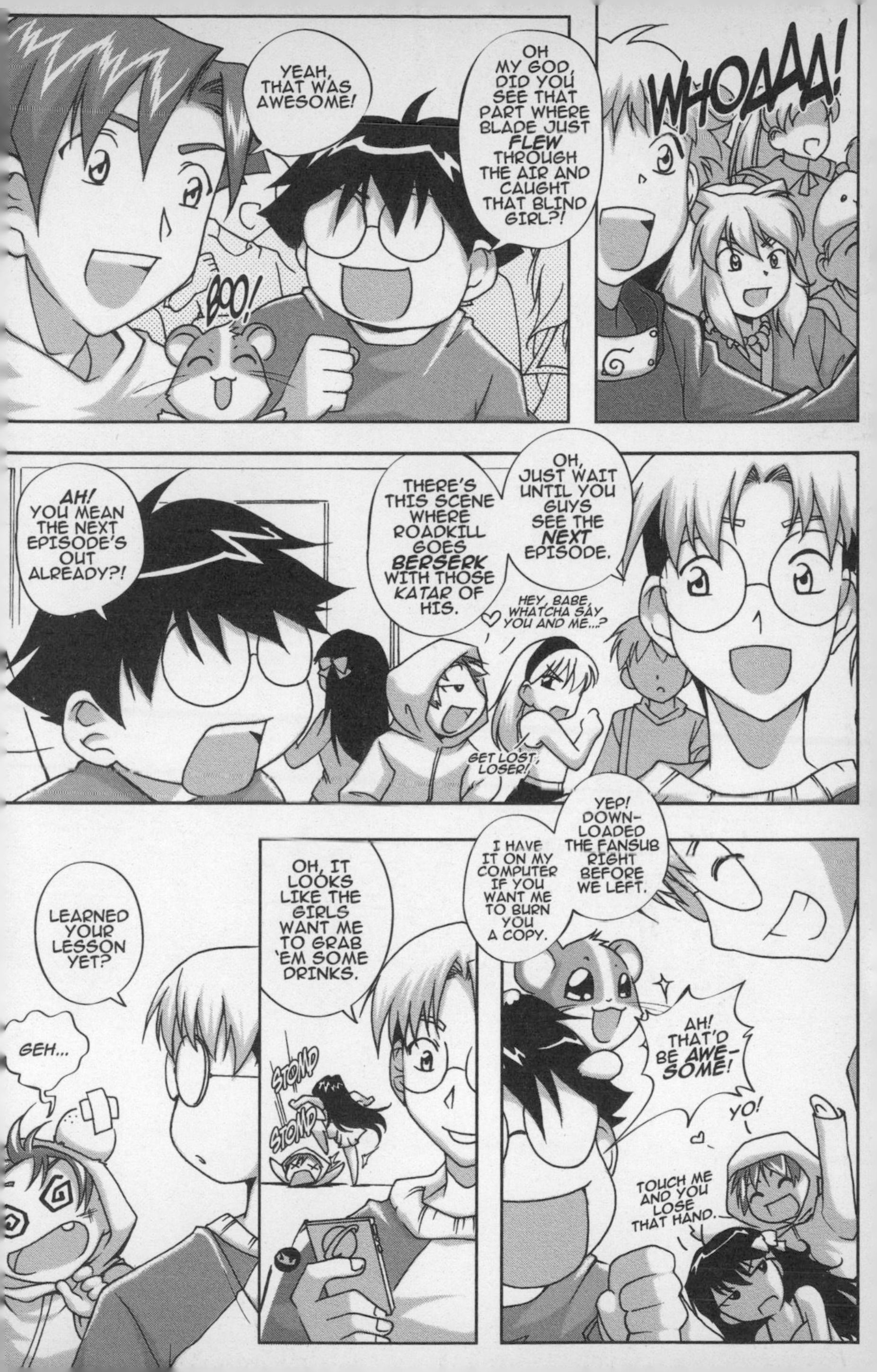
WHOAAA!
OH MY GOD, DID YOU SEE THAT PART WHERE BLADE JUST *FLEW* THROUGH THE AIR AND CAUGHT THAT BLIND GIRL?!
YEAH, THAT WAS AWESOME!
BOO!
OH, JUST WAIT UNTIL YOU GUYS SEE THE ***NEXT*** EPISODE.
THERE'S THIS SCENE WHERE ROADKILL GOES ***BERSERK*** WITH THOSE *KATAR* OF HIS.
AH! YOU MEAN THE NEXT EPISODE'S OUT ALREADY?!
HEY, BABE, WHATCHA SAY YOU AND ME...?
GET LOST, LOSER!
YEP! DOWN-LOADED THE FANSUB RIGHT BEFORE WE LEFT.
I HAVE IT ON MY COMPUTER IF YOU WANT ME TO BURN YOU A COPY.
AH! THAT'D BE ***AWE-SOME***!
YO!
TOUCH ME AND YOU LOSE THAT HAND.
OH, IT LOOKS LIKE THE GIRLS WANT ME TO GRAB 'EM SOME DRINKS.
STOMP
STOMP
LEARNED YOUR LESSON YET?
GEH...

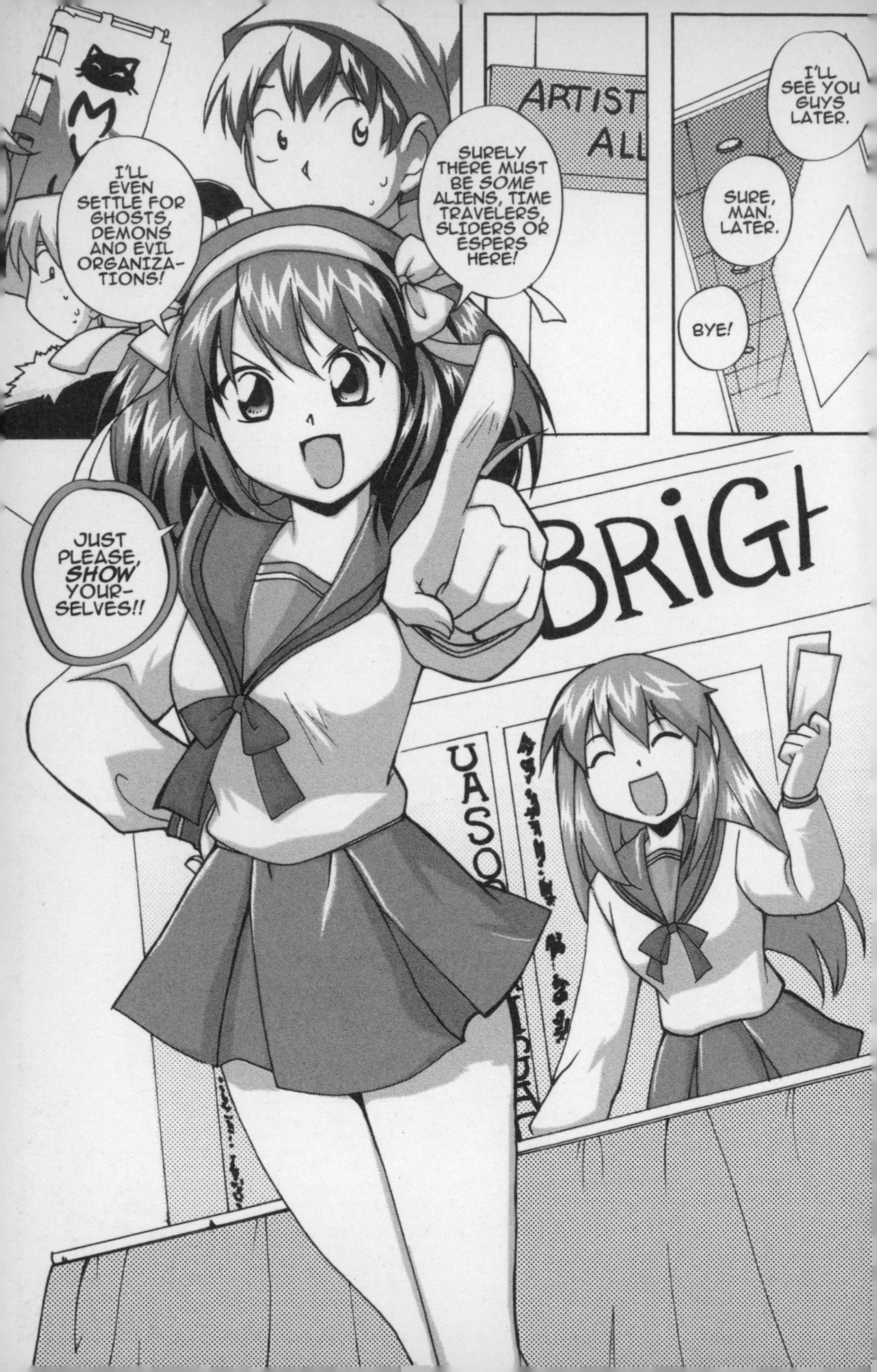
I'LL SEE YOU GUYS LATER.
SURE, MAN. LATER.
BYE!
ARTIST ALL
SURELY THERE MUST BE *SOME* ALIENS, TIME TRAVELERS, SLIDERS OR ESPERS HERE!
I'LL EVEN SETTLE FOR GHOSTS, DEMONS AND EVIL ORGANIZA-TIONS!
JUST PLEASE, ***SHOW*** YOUR-SELVES!!

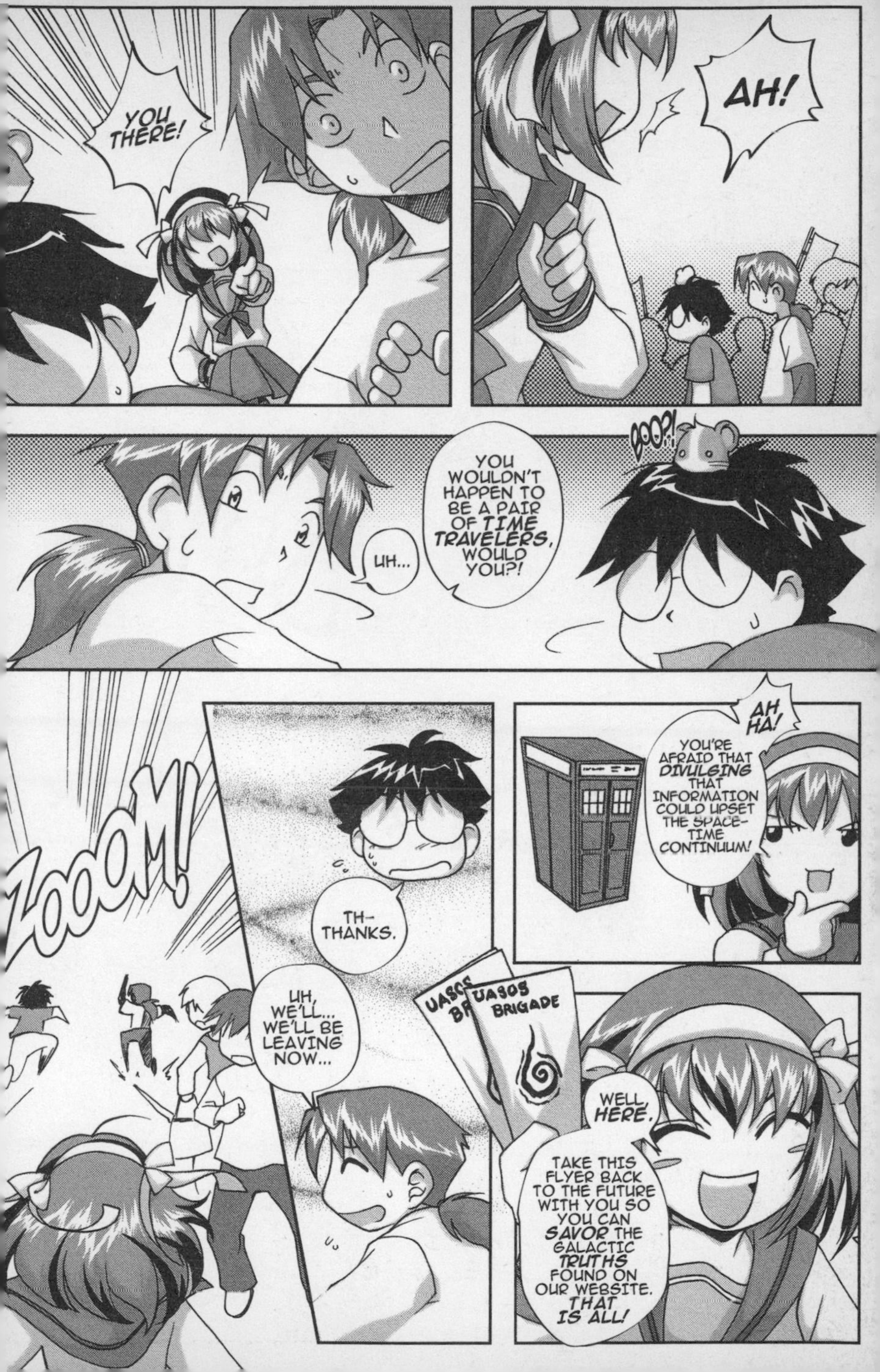

AH!
YOU THERE!
BOOP?!
YOU WOULDN'T HAPPEN TO BE A PAIR OF TIME TRAVELERS, WOULD YOU?!
UH...
AH, HA!
YOU'RE AFRAID THAT DIVULGING THAT INFORMATION COULD UPSET THE SPACE-TIME CONTINUUM!
UASOS BRIGADE
WELL, HERE.
TAKE THIS FLYER BACK TO THE FUTURE WITH YOU SO YOU CAN SAVOR THE GALACTIC TRUTHS FOUND ON OUR WEBSITE. THAT IS ALL!
TH-THANKS.
UH, WE'LL... WE'LL BE LEAVING NOW...
ZOOOM!

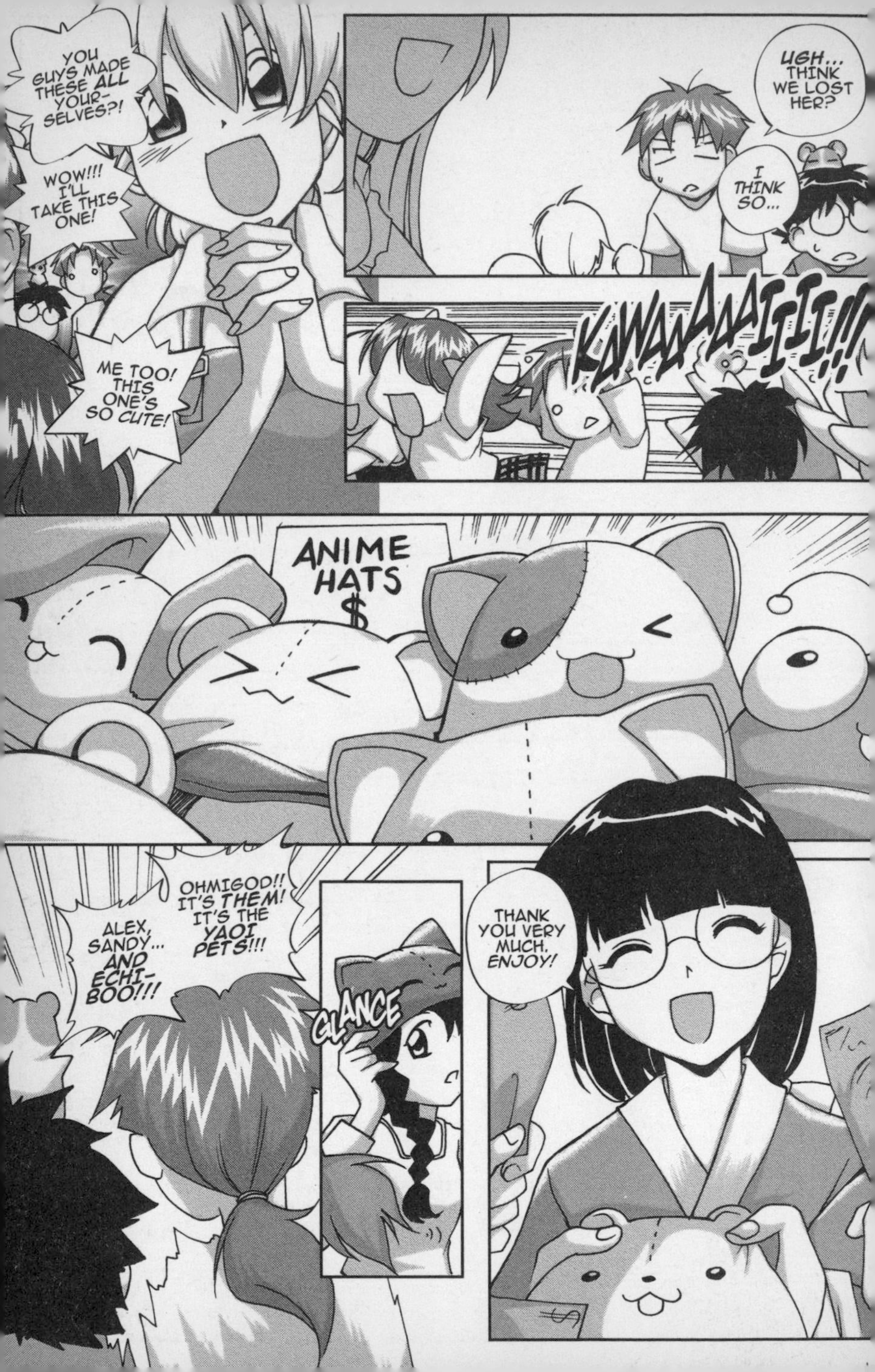
UGH... THINK WE LOST HER?
I THINK SO...
KAWAAAAIII!!!
YOU GUYS MADE THESE ALL YOUR-SELVES?!
WOW!!! I'LL TAKE THIS ONE!
ME TOO! THIS ONE'S SO CUTE!
ANIME HATS $
THANK YOU VERY MUCH. ENJOY!
GLANCE
OHMIGOD!! IT'S THEM! IT'S THE YAOI PETS!!!
ALEX, SANDY... AND ECHI-BOO!!!

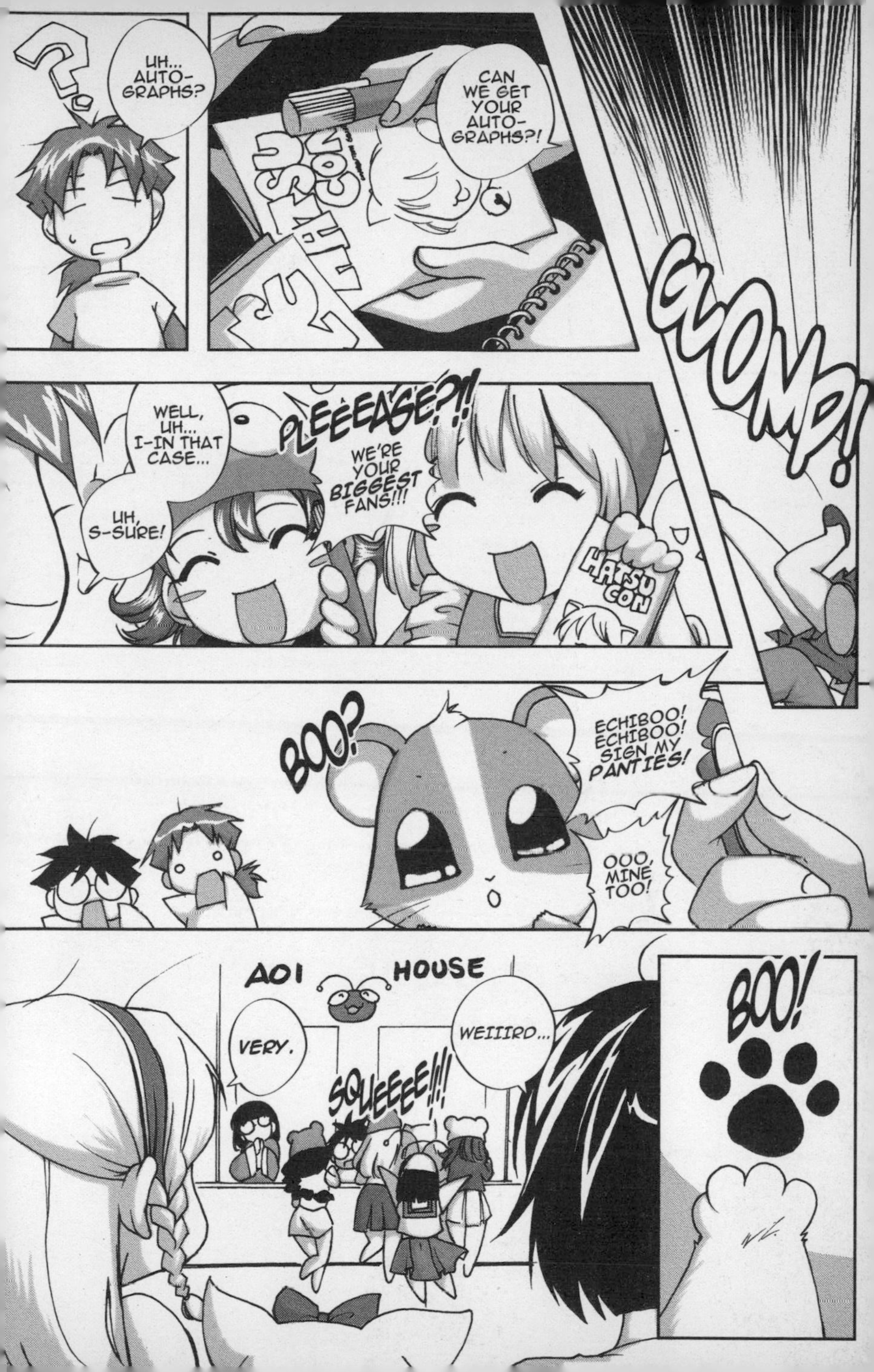
GLOMP!
CAN WE GET YOUR AUTO-GRAPHS?!
UH... AUTO-GRAPHS?
PLEEEASE?!!
WE'RE YOUR BIGGEST FANS!!!
HATSU CON
WELL, UH... I-IN THAT CASE...
UH, S-SURE!
ECHIBOO! ECHIBOO! SIGN MY PANTIES!
OOO, MINE TOO!
BOO?
BOO!
AOI HOUSE
WEIIIRD...
VERY.
SQUEEEE!!!!

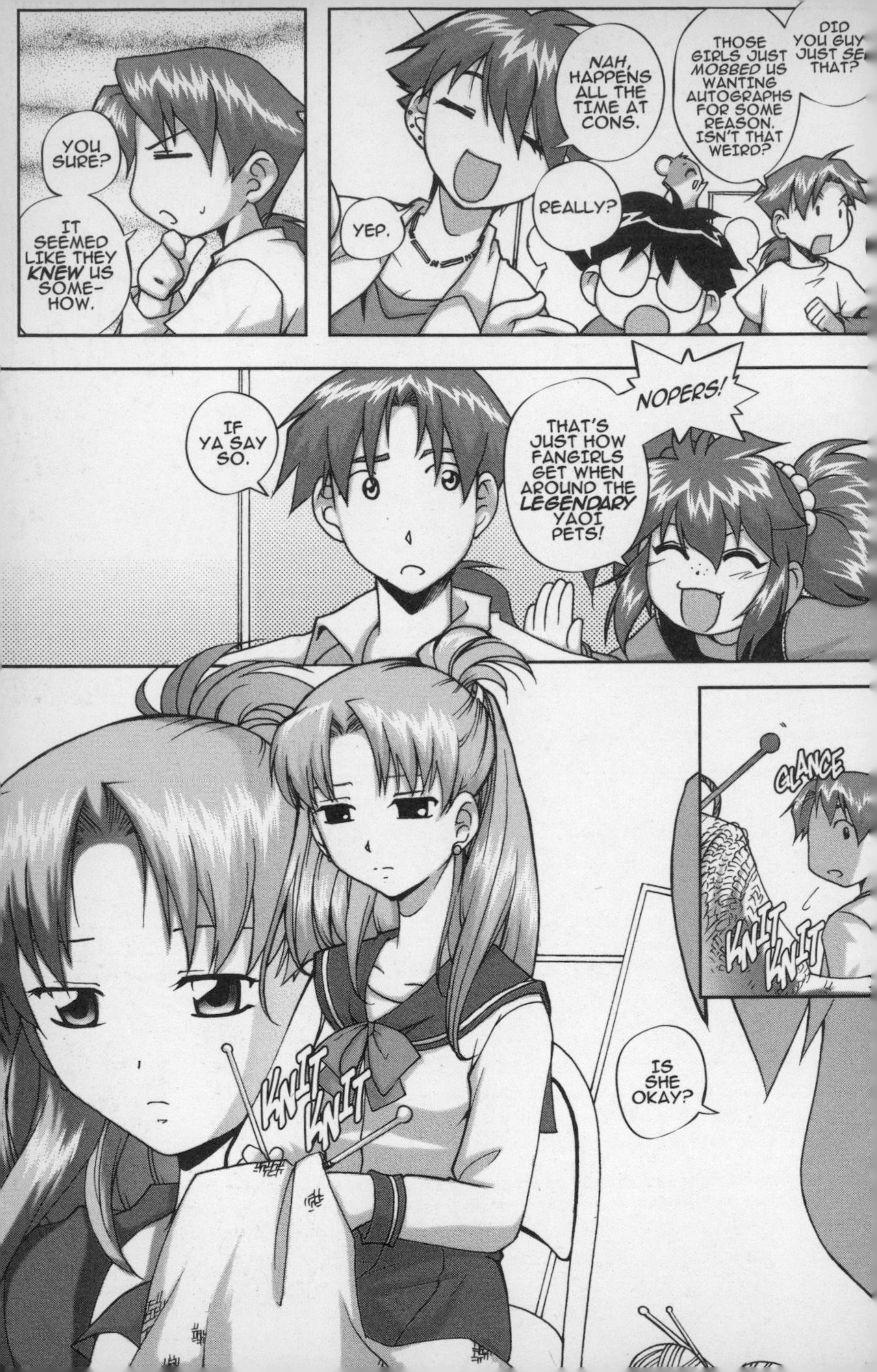

DID YOU GUY JUST SE THAT?
THOSE GIRLS JUST MOBBED US WANTING AUTOGRAPHS FOR SOME REASON. ISN'T THAT WEIRD?
NAH, HAPPENS ALL THE TIME AT CONS.
REALLY?
YEP.
YOU SURE?
IT SEEMED LIKE THEY KNEW US SOME-HOW.
NOPERS!
THAT'S JUST HOW FANGIRLS GET WHEN AROUND THE LEGENDARY YAOI PETS!
IF YA SAY SO.
GLANCE
KNIT KNIT
IS SHE OKAY?
KNIT KNIT

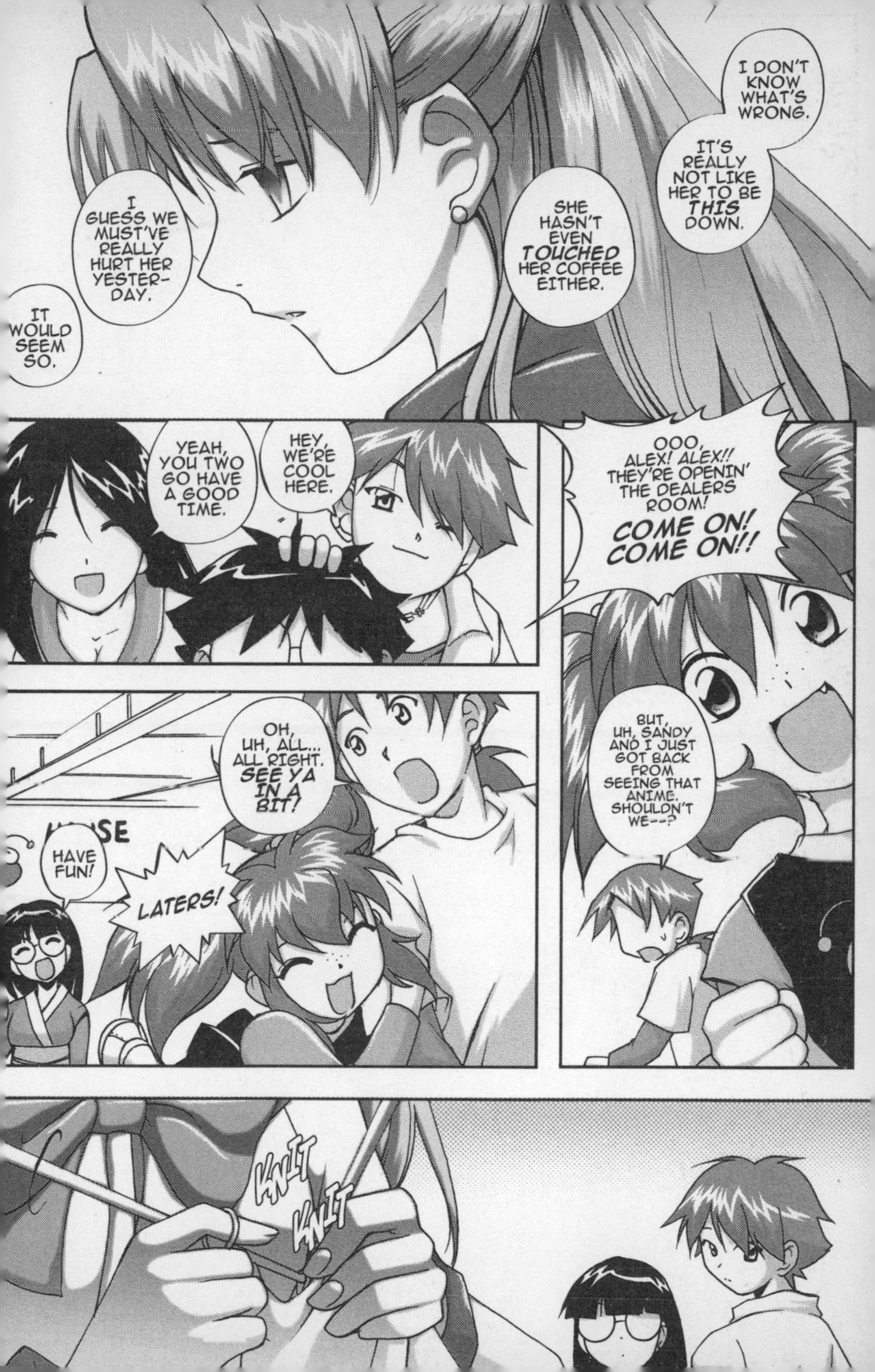
I DON'T KNOW WHAT'S WRONG.
IT'S REALLY NOT LIKE HER TO BE THIS DOWN.
SHE HASN'T EVEN TOUCHED HER COFFEE EITHER.
I GUESS WE MUST'VE REALLY HURT HER YESTER-DAY.
IT WOULD SEEM SO.
OOO, ALEX! ALEX!! THEY'RE OPENIN' THE DEALERS ROOM!
COME ON! COME ON!!
BUT, UH, SANDY AND I JUST GOT BACK FROM SEEING THAT ANIME. SHOULDN'T WE--?
HEY, WE'RE COOL HERE.
YEAH, YOU TWO GO HAVE A GOOD TIME.
OH, UH, ALL... ALL RIGHT. SEE YA IN A BIT!
LATERS!
HAVE FUN!
KNIT
KNIT

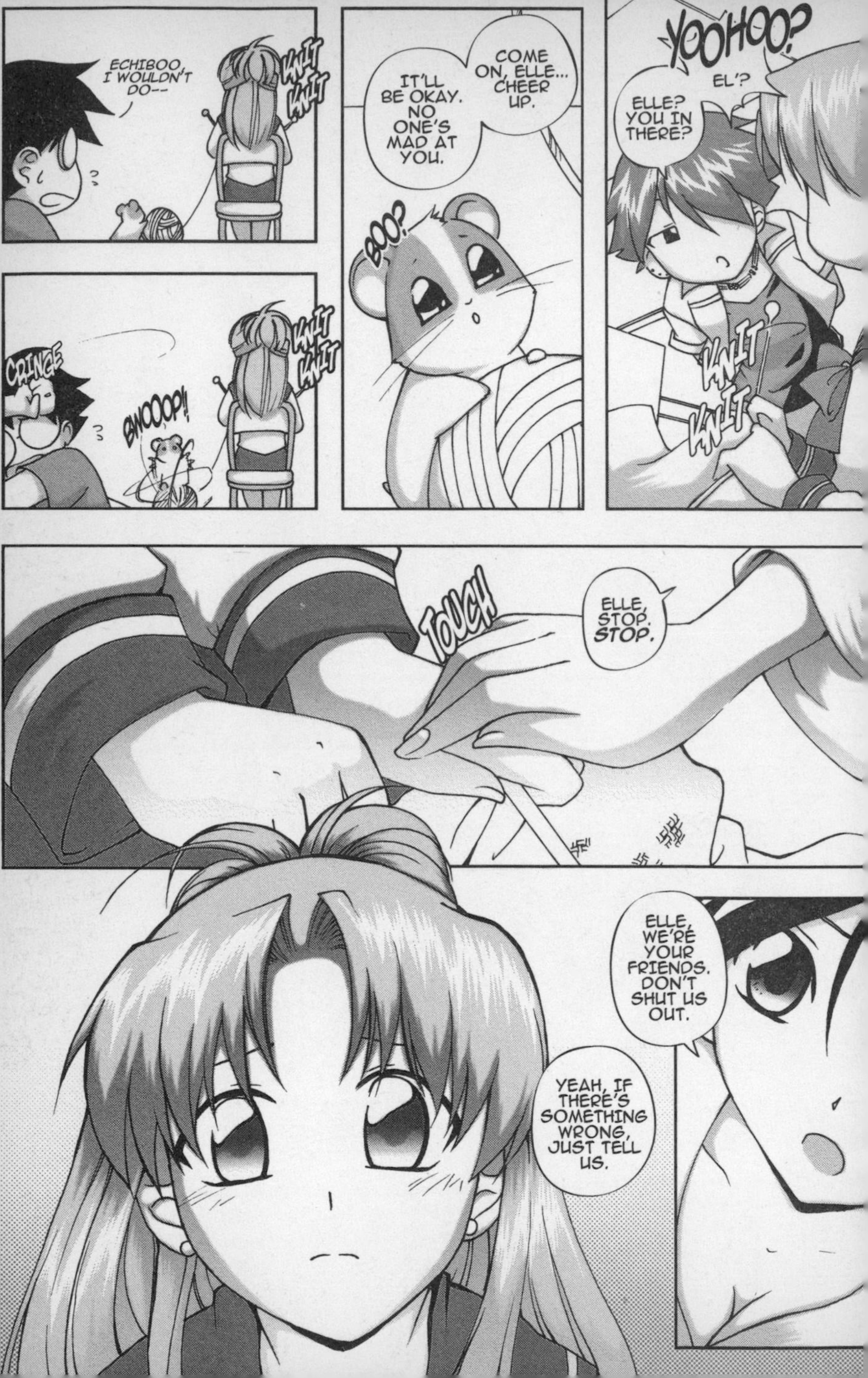
YOOHOO?
EL'?
ELLE? YOU IN THERE?
KNIT KNIT
COME ON, ELLE... CHEER UP.
IT'LL BE OKAY. NO ONE'S MAD AT YOU.
BOO?
KNIT KNIT
ECHIBOO, I WOULDN'T DO--
KNIT KNIT
CRINGE
BWOOOP!!
ELLE, STOP. STOP.
TOUCH
ELLE, WE'RE YOUR FRIENDS. DON'T SHUT US OUT.
YEAH, IF THERE'S SOMETHING WRONG, JUST TELL US.

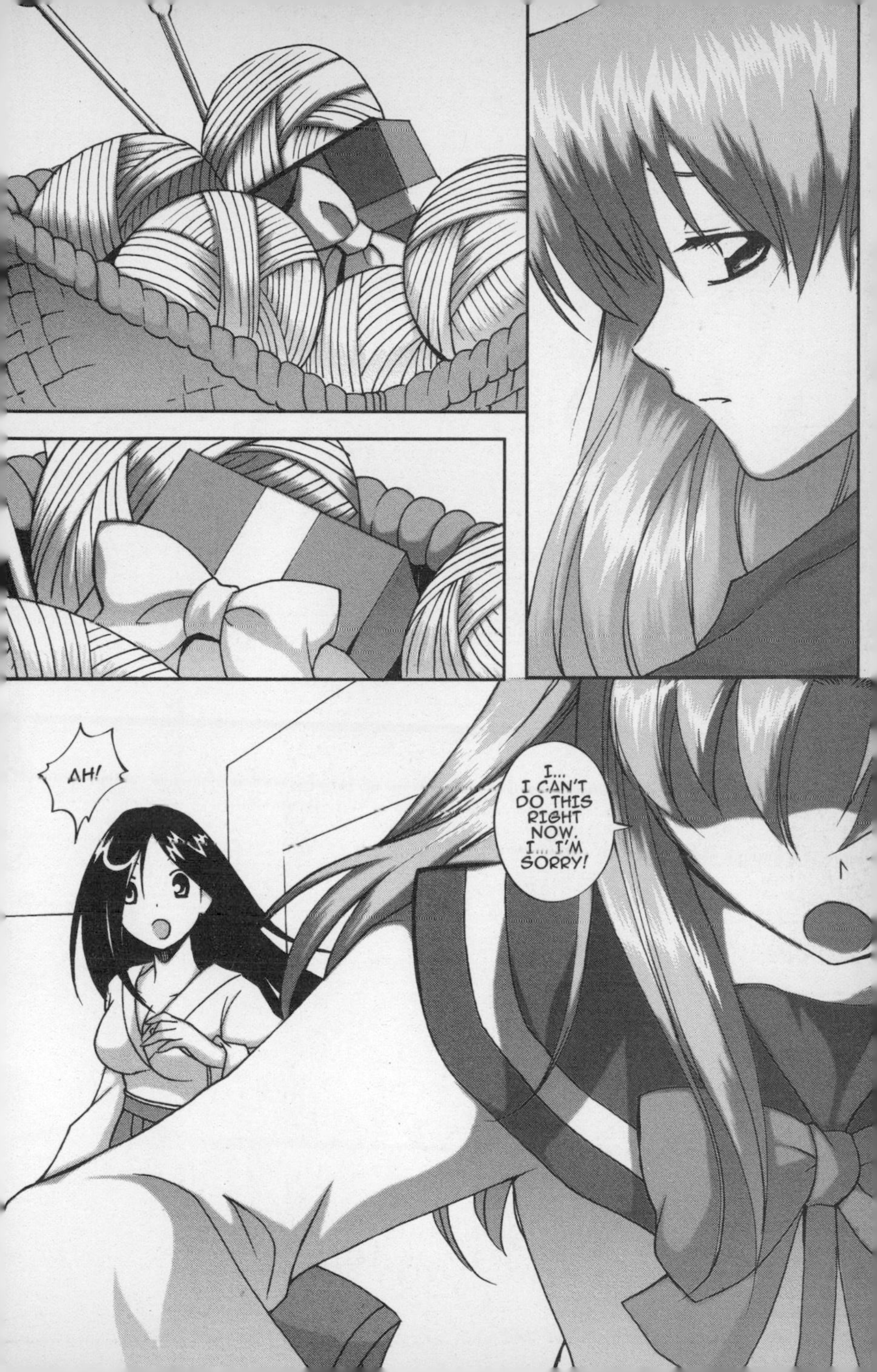
I... I CAN'T DO THIS RIGHT NOW. I... I'M SORRY!
AH!

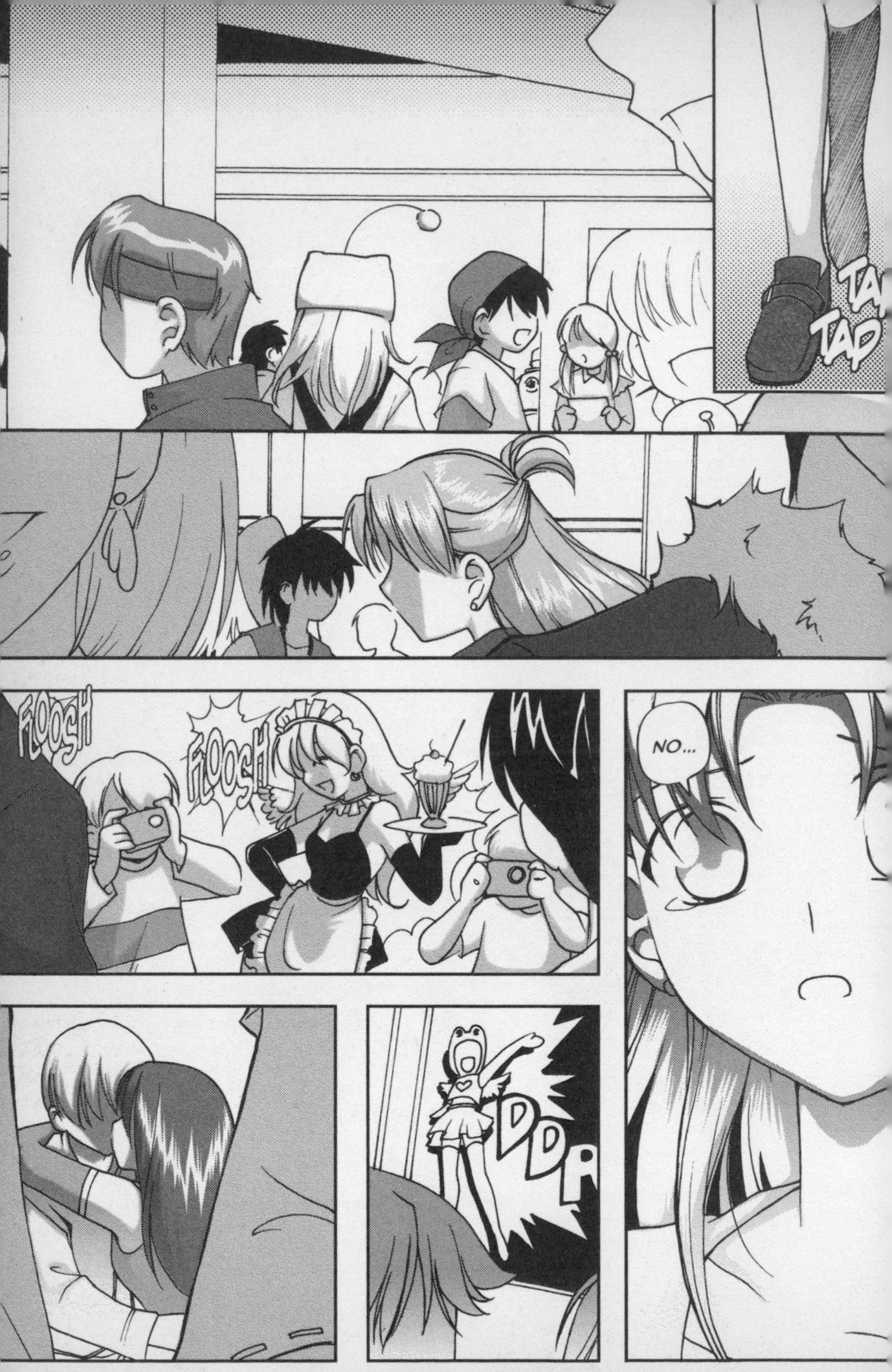
TAP
NO...
FLOOSH
FLOOSH

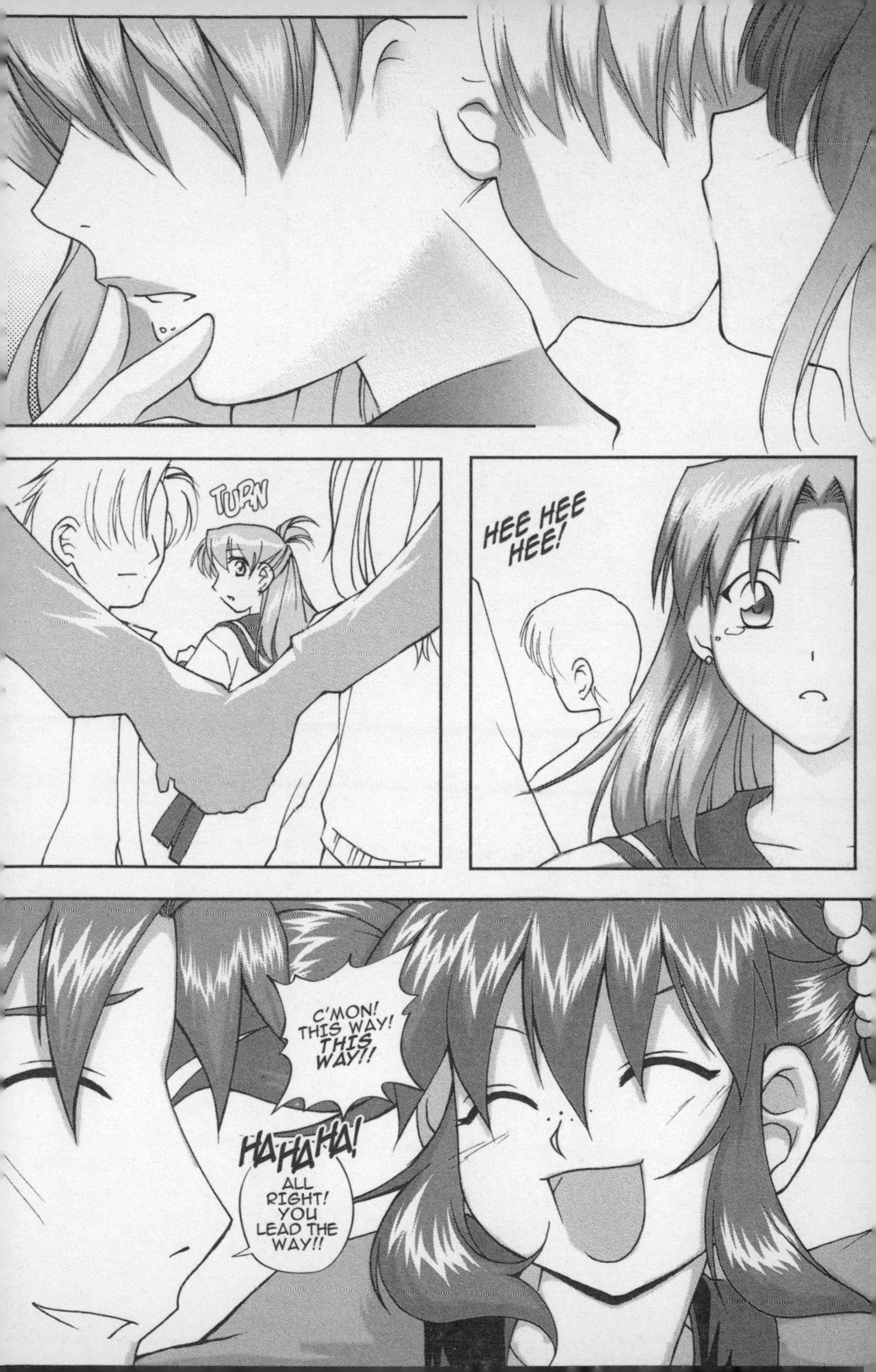
HEE HEE HEE!
TURN
C'MON! THIS WAY! THIS WAY!!
HA HA HA!
ALL RIGHT! YOU LEAD THE WAY!!

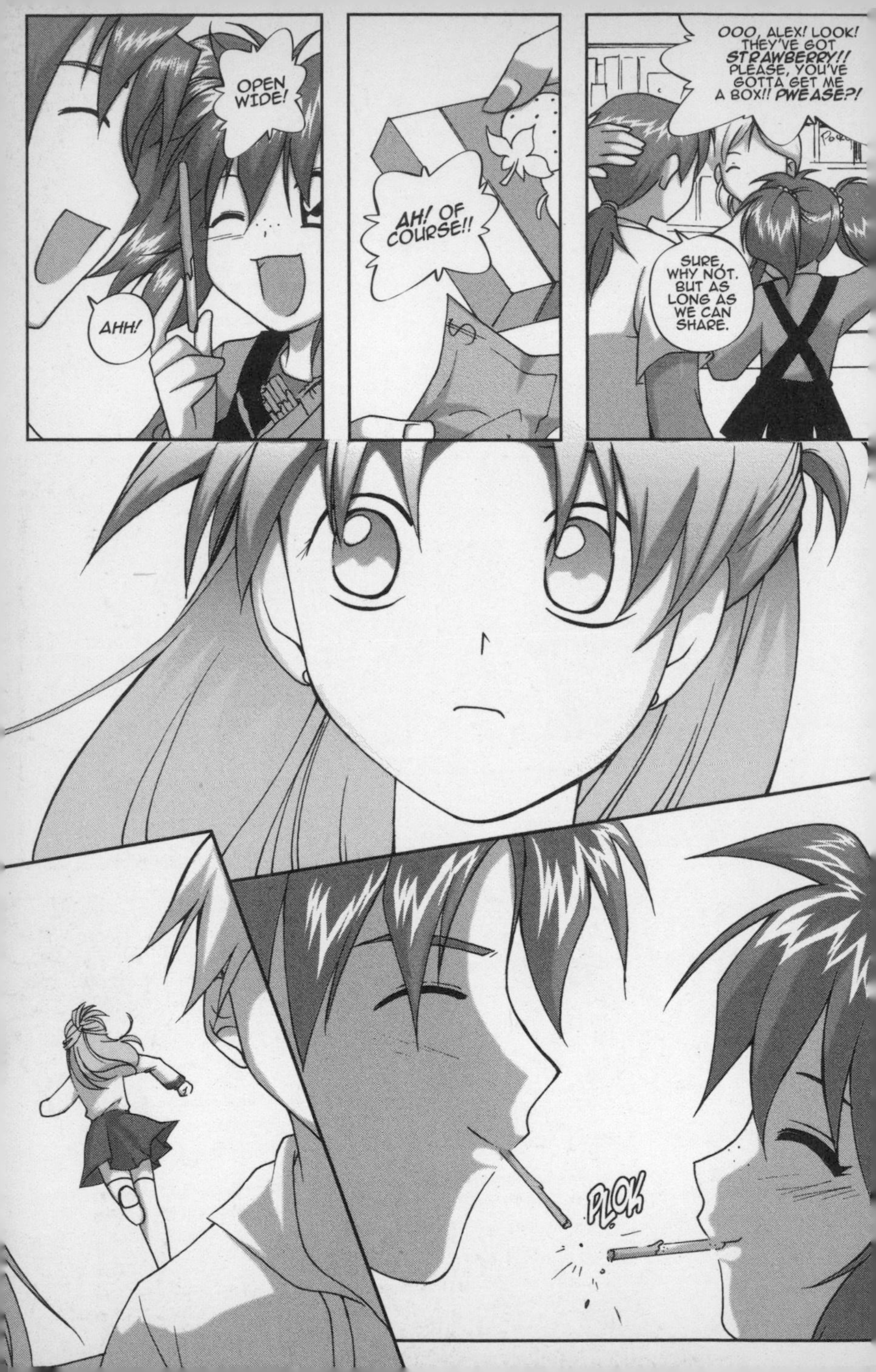
OOO, ALEX! LOOK! THEY'VE GOT STRAWBERRY!! PLEASE, YOU'VE GOTTA GET ME A BOX!! PWEASE?!
SURE, WHY NOT. BUT AS LONG AS WE CAN SHARE.
AH! OF COURSE!!
OPEN WIDE!
AHH!
PLOK

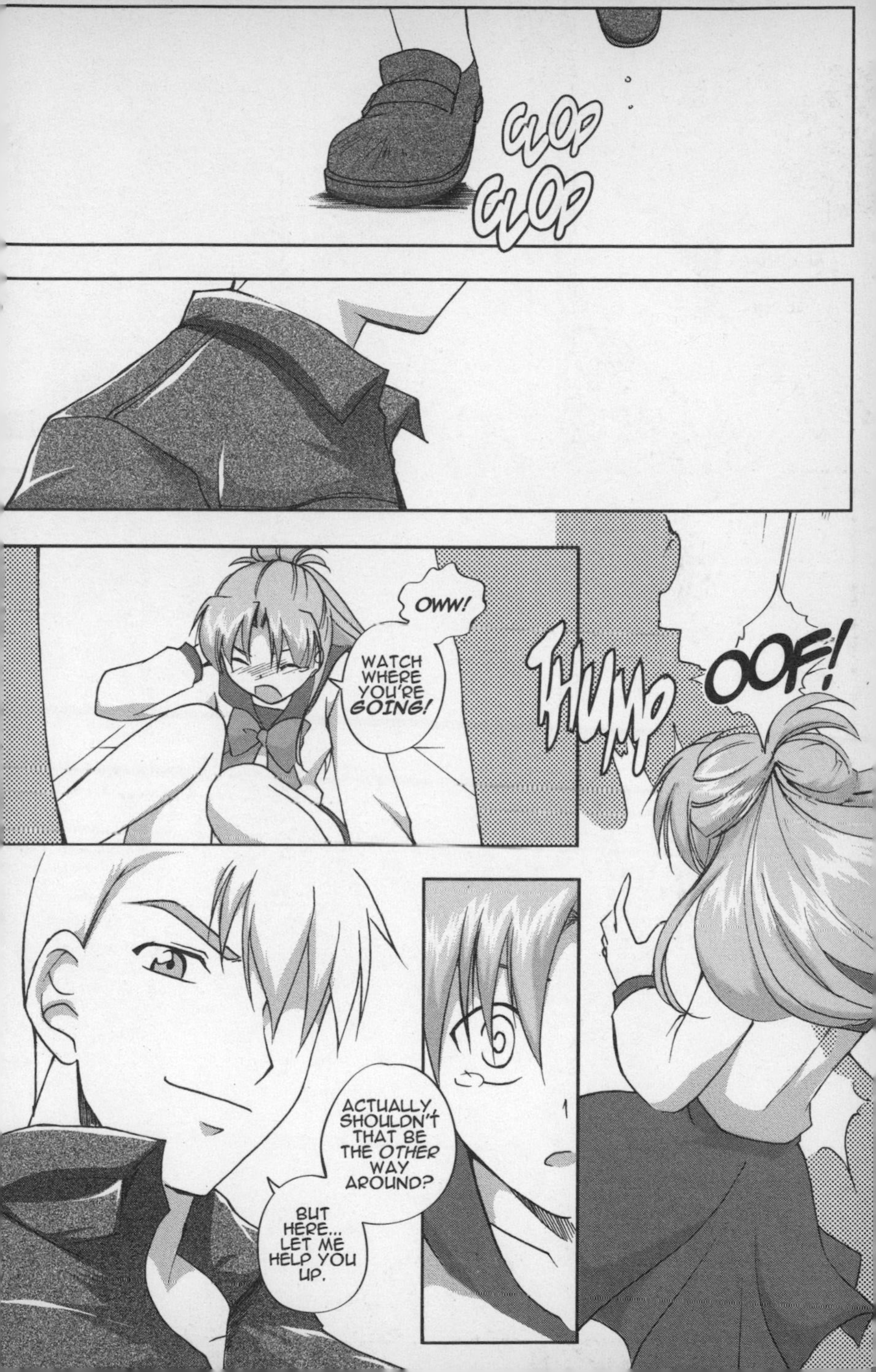
CLOP CLOP
THUMP
OOF!
OWW!
WATCH WHERE YOU'RE GOING!
ACTUALLY, SHOULDN'T THAT BE THE OTHER WAY AROUND?
BUT HERE... LET ME HELP YOU UP.

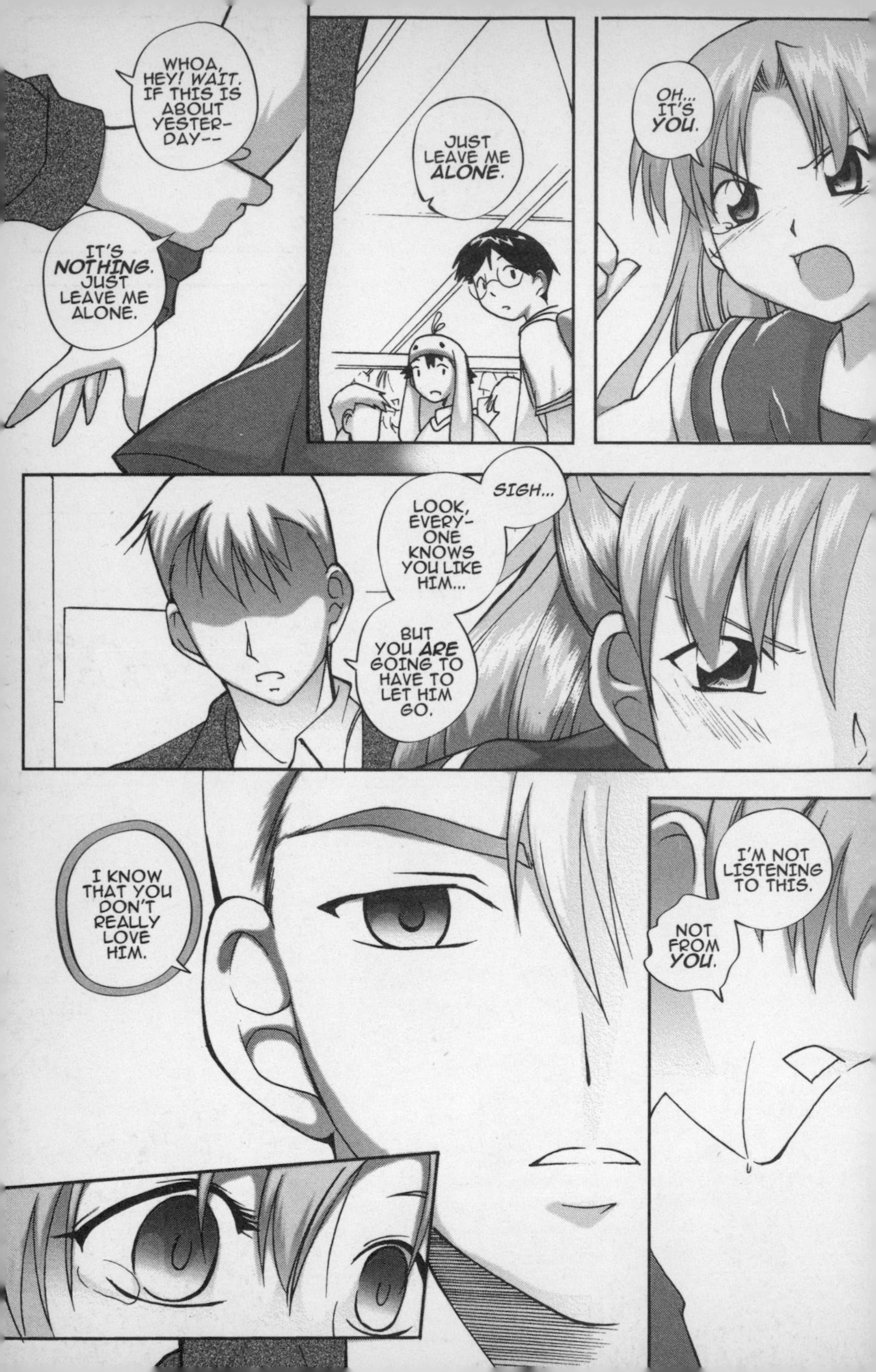
OH... IT'S ***YOU***.
JUST LEAVE ME ***ALONE***.
WHOA, HEY! *WAIT*. IF THIS IS ABOUT YESTER-DAY--
IT'S ***NOTHING***. JUST LEAVE ME ALONE.
SIGH...
LOOK, EVERY-ONE KNOWS YOU LIKE HIM...
BUT YOU ***ARE*** GOING TO HAVE TO LET HIM GO.
I'M NOT LISTENING TO THIS.
NOT FROM ***YOU***.
I KNOW THAT YOU DON'T REALLY LOVE HIM.

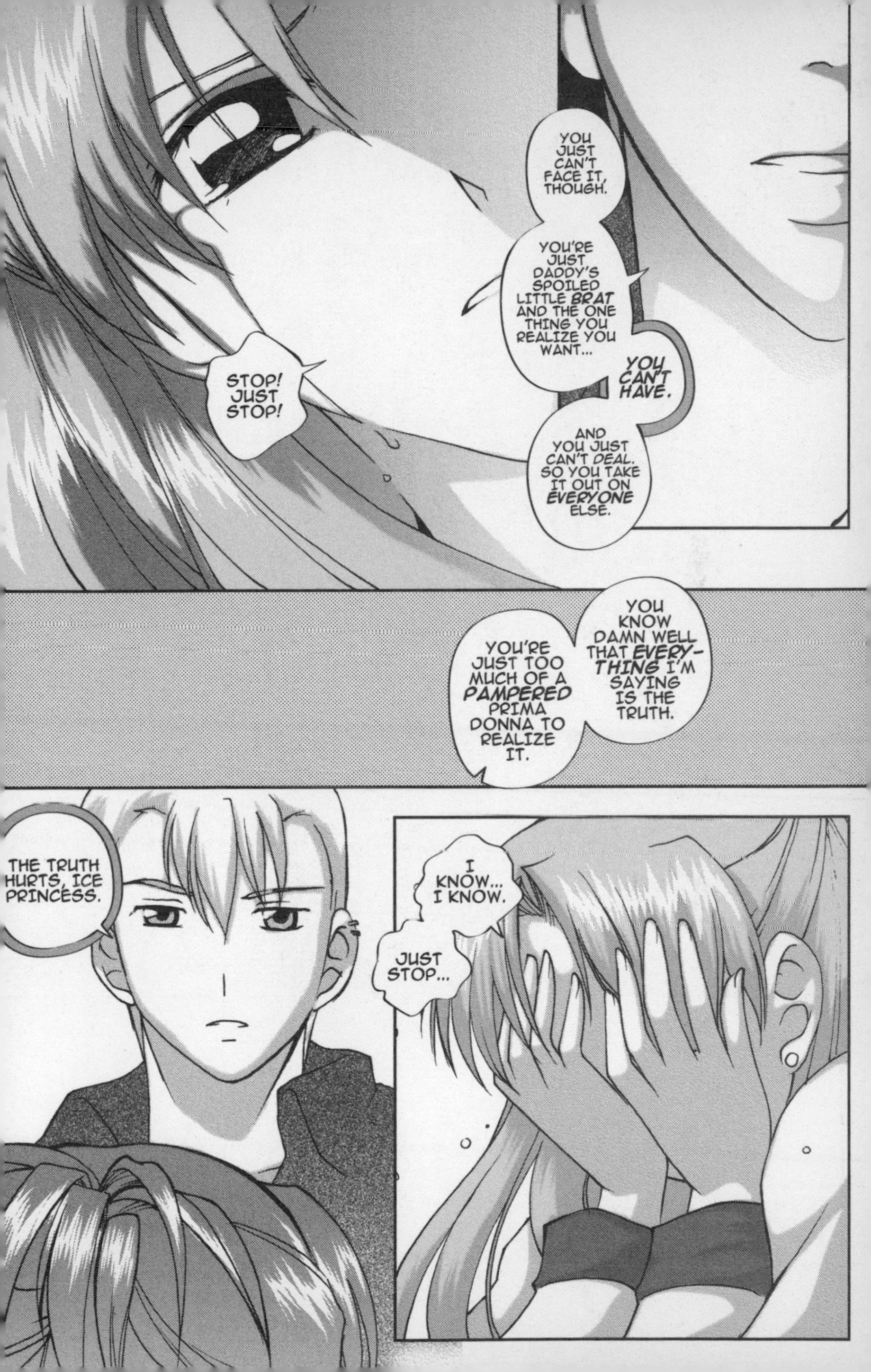
YOU JUST CAN'T FACE IT, THOUGH.
YOU'RE JUST DADDY'S SPOILED LITTLE BRAT AND THE ONE THING YOU REALIZE YOU WANT...
YOU CAN'T HAVE.
AND YOU JUST CAN'T DEAL. SO YOU TAKE IT OUT ON EVERYONE ELSE.
STOP! JUST STOP!
YOU KNOW DAMN WELL THAT EVERY-THING I'M SAYING IS THE TRUTH.
YOU'RE JUST TOO MUCH OF A PAMPERED PRIMA DONNA TO REALIZE IT.
I KNOW... I KNOW.
JUST STOP...
THE TRUTH HURTS, ICE PRINCESS.

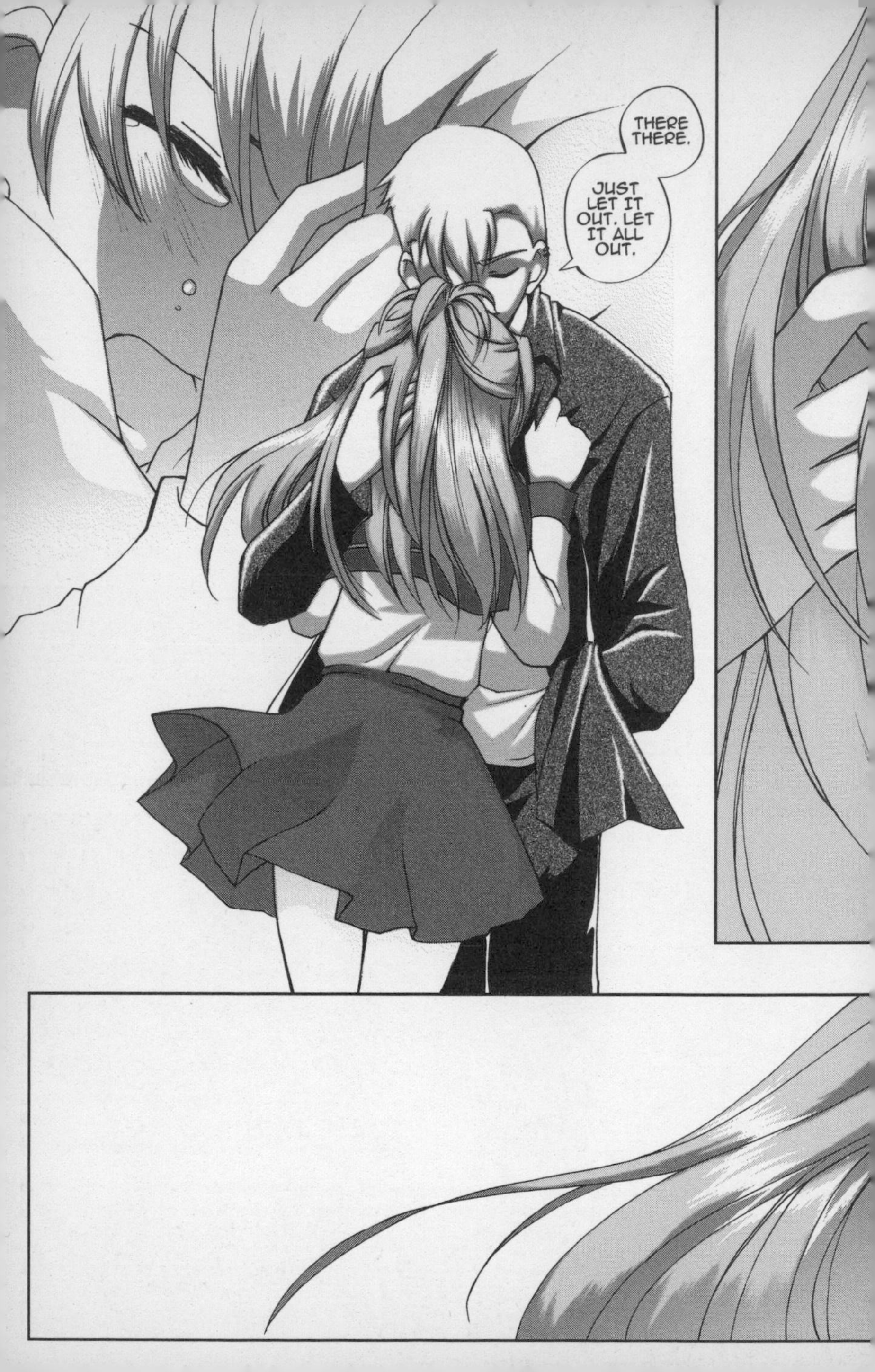
THERE THERE.
JUST LET IT OUT. LET IT ALL OUT.

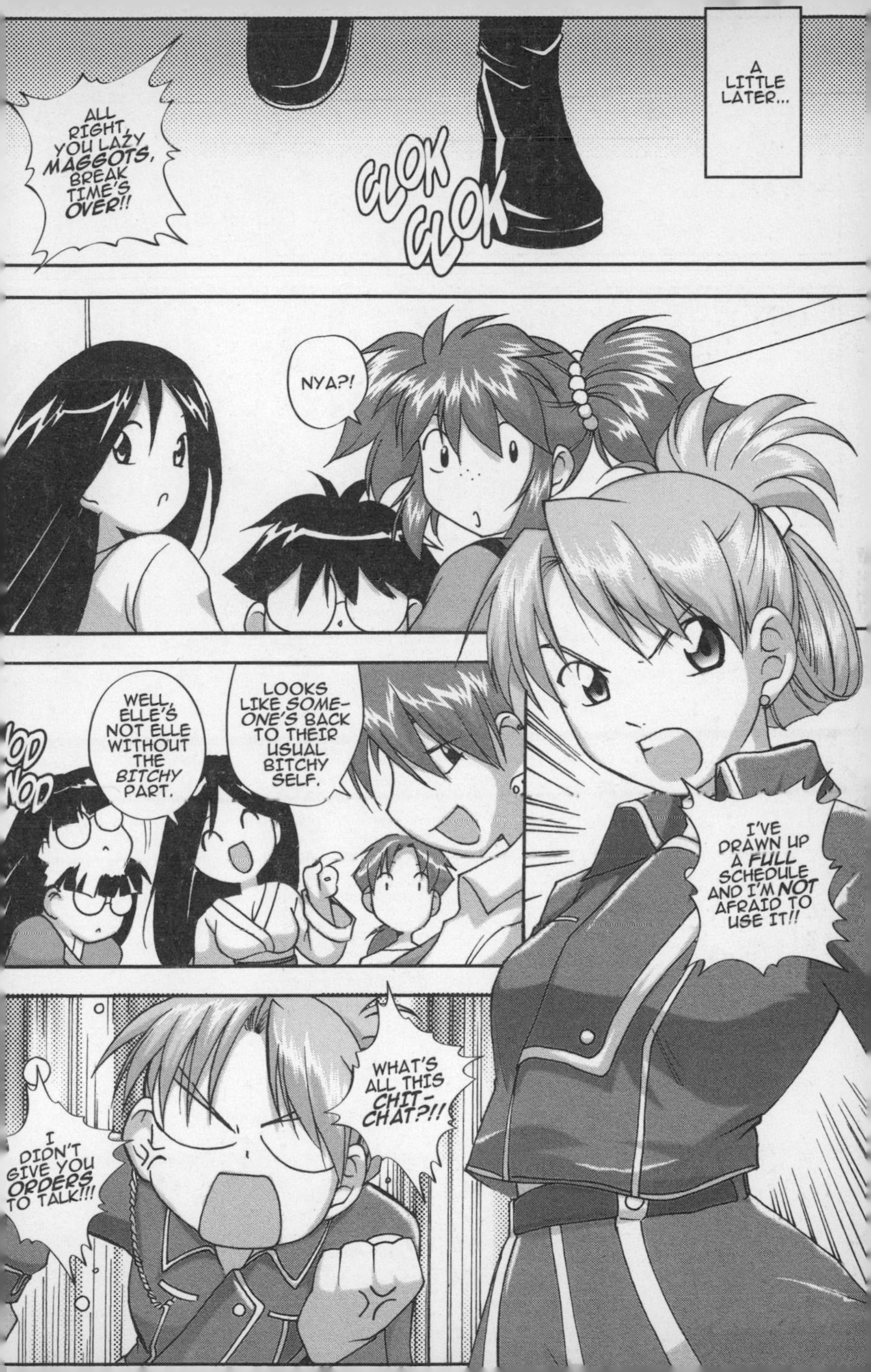
A LITTLE LATER...
CLOK CLOK
ALL RIGHT, YOU LAZY MAGGOTS, BREAK TIME'S OVER!!
NYA?!
I'VE DRAWN UP A FULL SCHEDULE AND I'M NOT AFRAID TO USE IT!!
LOOKS LIKE SOME-ONE'S BACK TO THEIR USUAL BITCHY SELF.
WELL, ELLE'S NOT ELLE WITHOUT THE BITCHY PART.
WHAT'S ALL THIS CHIT-CHAT?!!
I DIDN'T GIVE YOU ORDERS TO TALK!!!

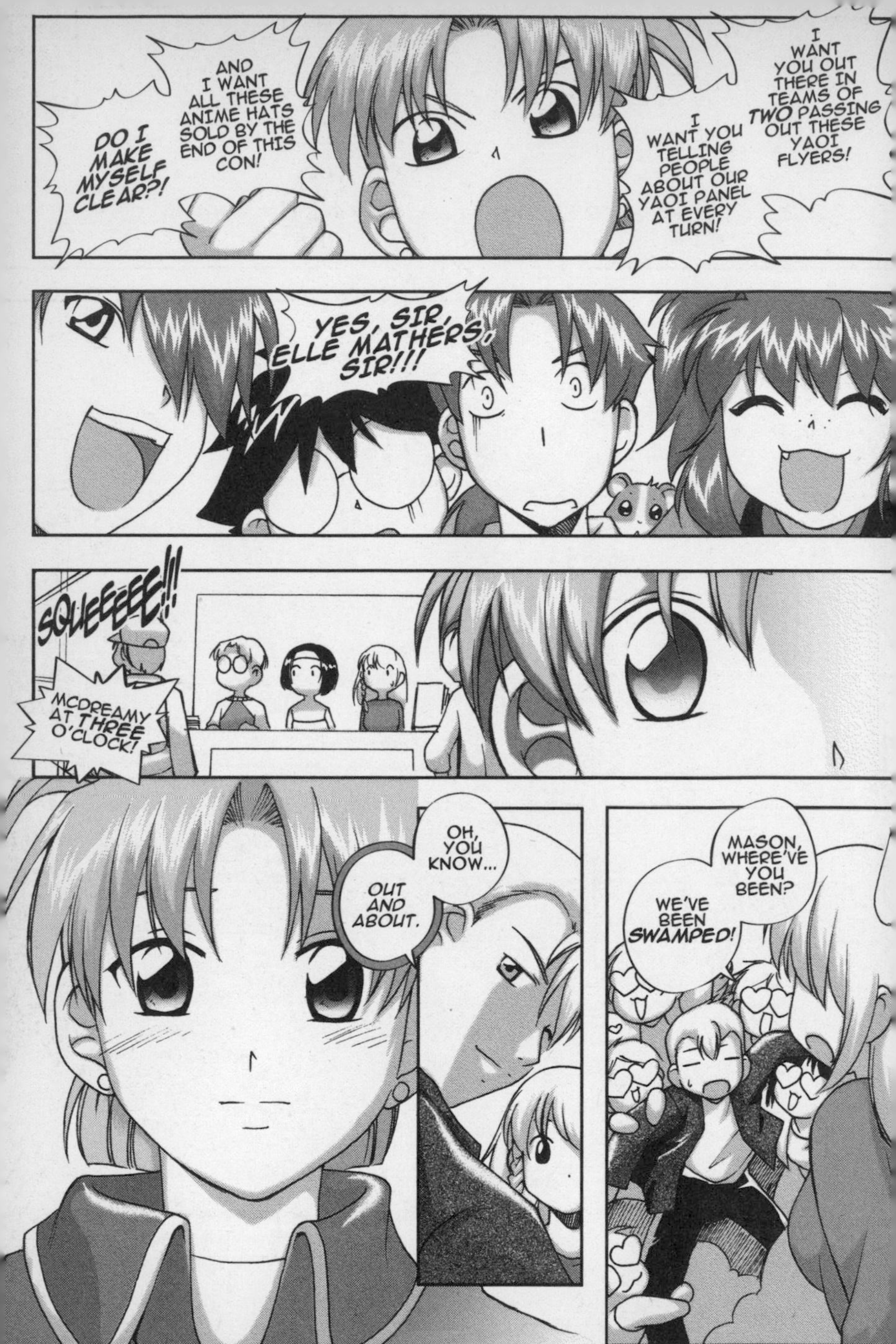
I WANT YOU OUT THERE IN TEAMS OF TWO PASSING OUT THESE YAOI FLYERS!
I WANT YOU TELLING PEOPLE ABOUT OUR YAOI PANEL AT EVERY TURN!
AND I WANT ALL THESE ANIME HATS SOLD BY THE END OF THIS CON!
DO I MAKE MYSELF CLEAR?!
YES, SIR, ELLE MATHERS, SIR!!!
SQUEEEEEE!!!
MCDREAMY AT THREE O'CLOCK!
MASON, WHERE'VE YOU BEEN?
WE'VE BEEN SWAMPED!
OH, YOU KNOW...
OUT AND ABOUT.

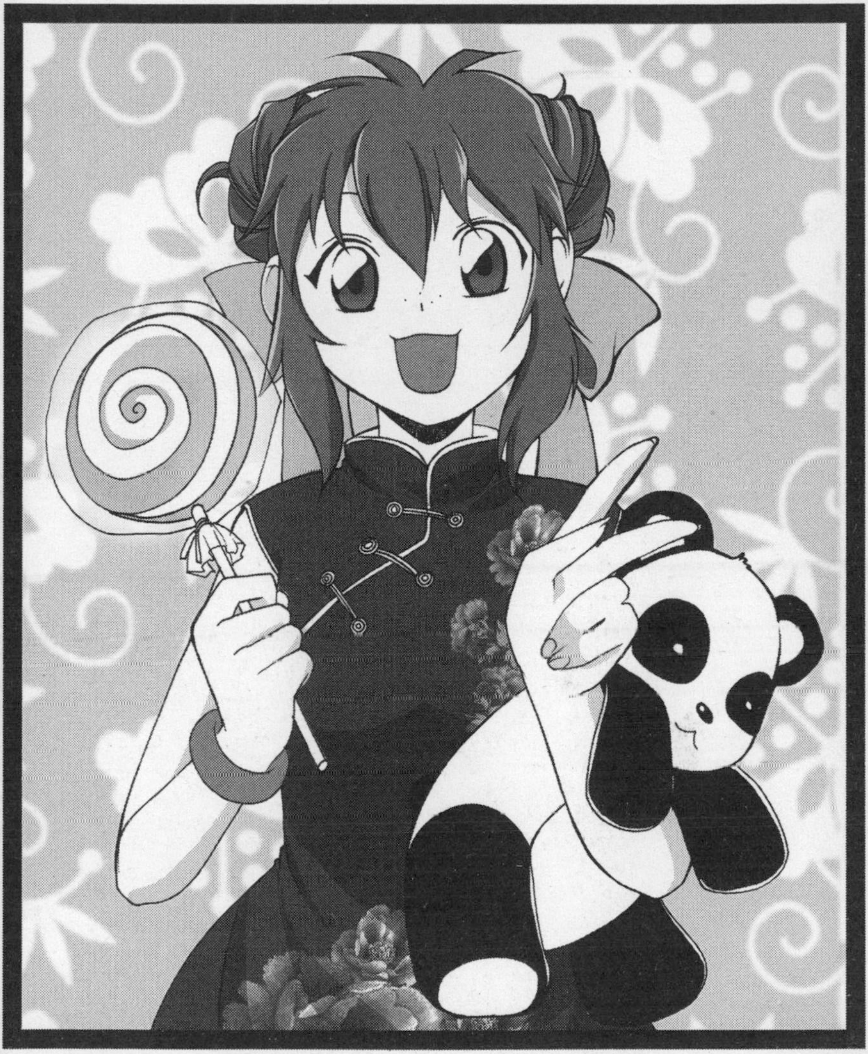

EPISODE 5:
MR. WONDERFUL

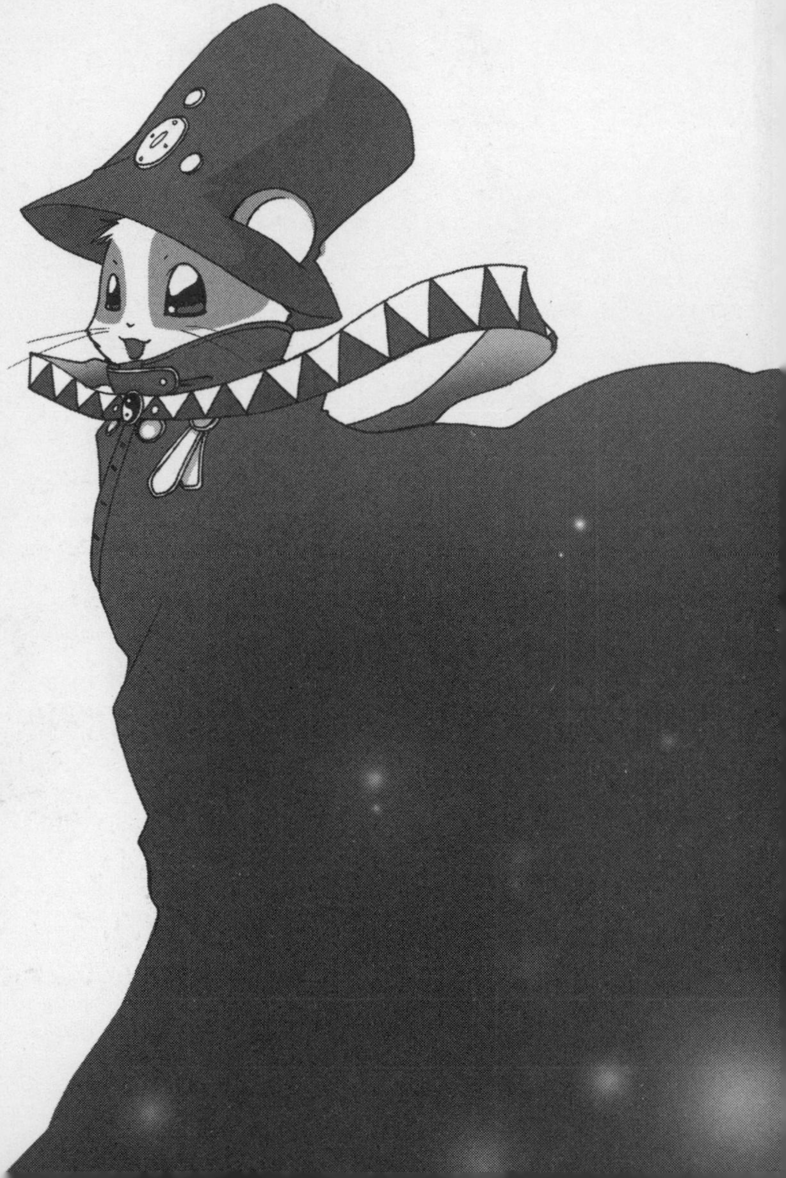

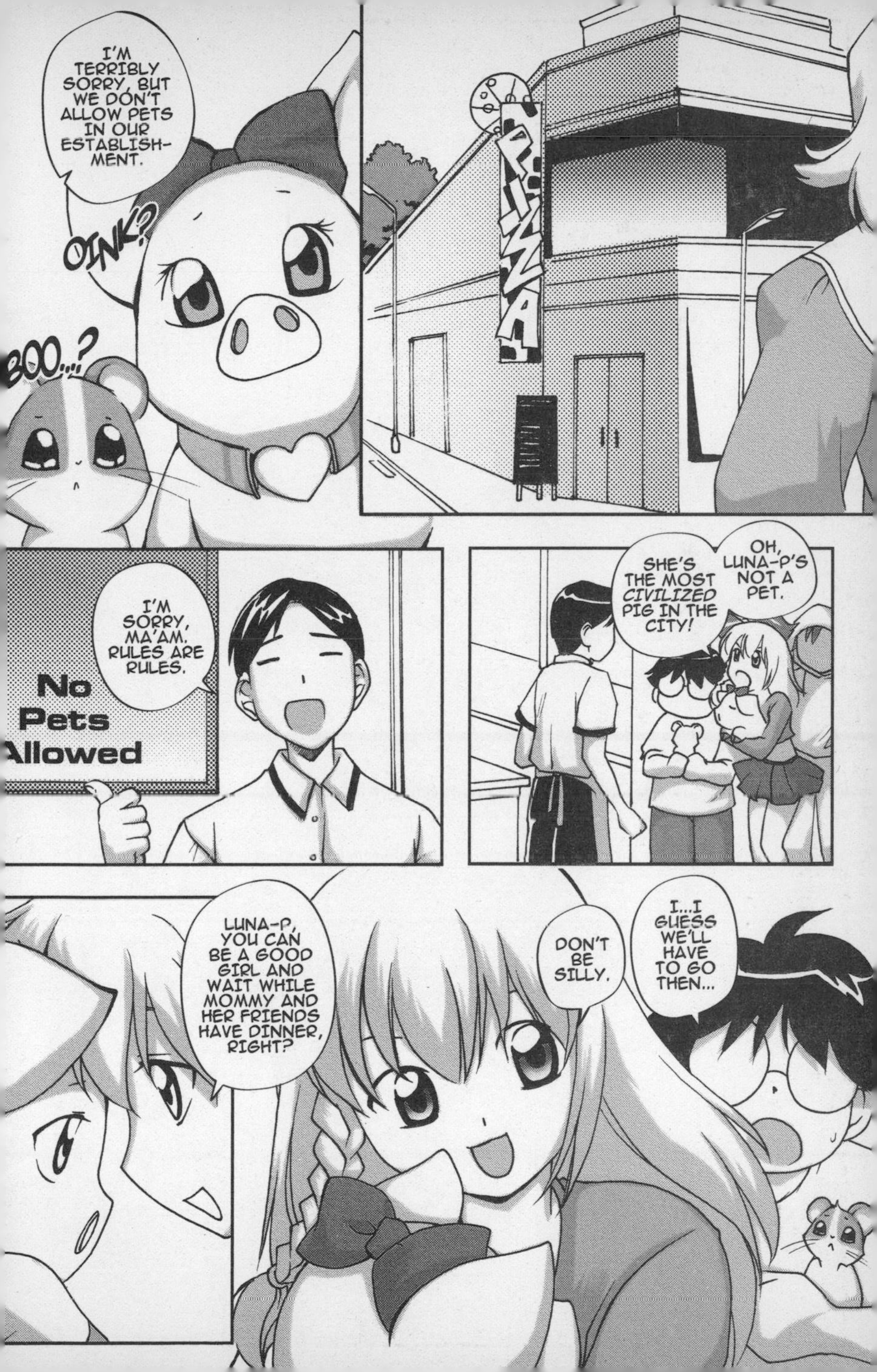

I'M TERRIBLY SORRY, BUT WE DON'T ALLOW PETS IN OUR ESTABLISH-MENT.
OINK?
BOO...?
OH, LUNA-P'S NOT A PET.
SHE'S THE MOST *CIVILIZED* PIG IN THE CITY!
I'M SORRY, MA'AM. RULES ARE RULES.
No Pets Allowed
I...I GUESS WE'LL HAVE TO GO THEN...
DON'T BE SILLY.
LUNA-P, YOU CAN BE A GOOD GIRL AND WAIT WHILE MOMMY AND HER FRIENDS HAVE DINNER, RIGHT?

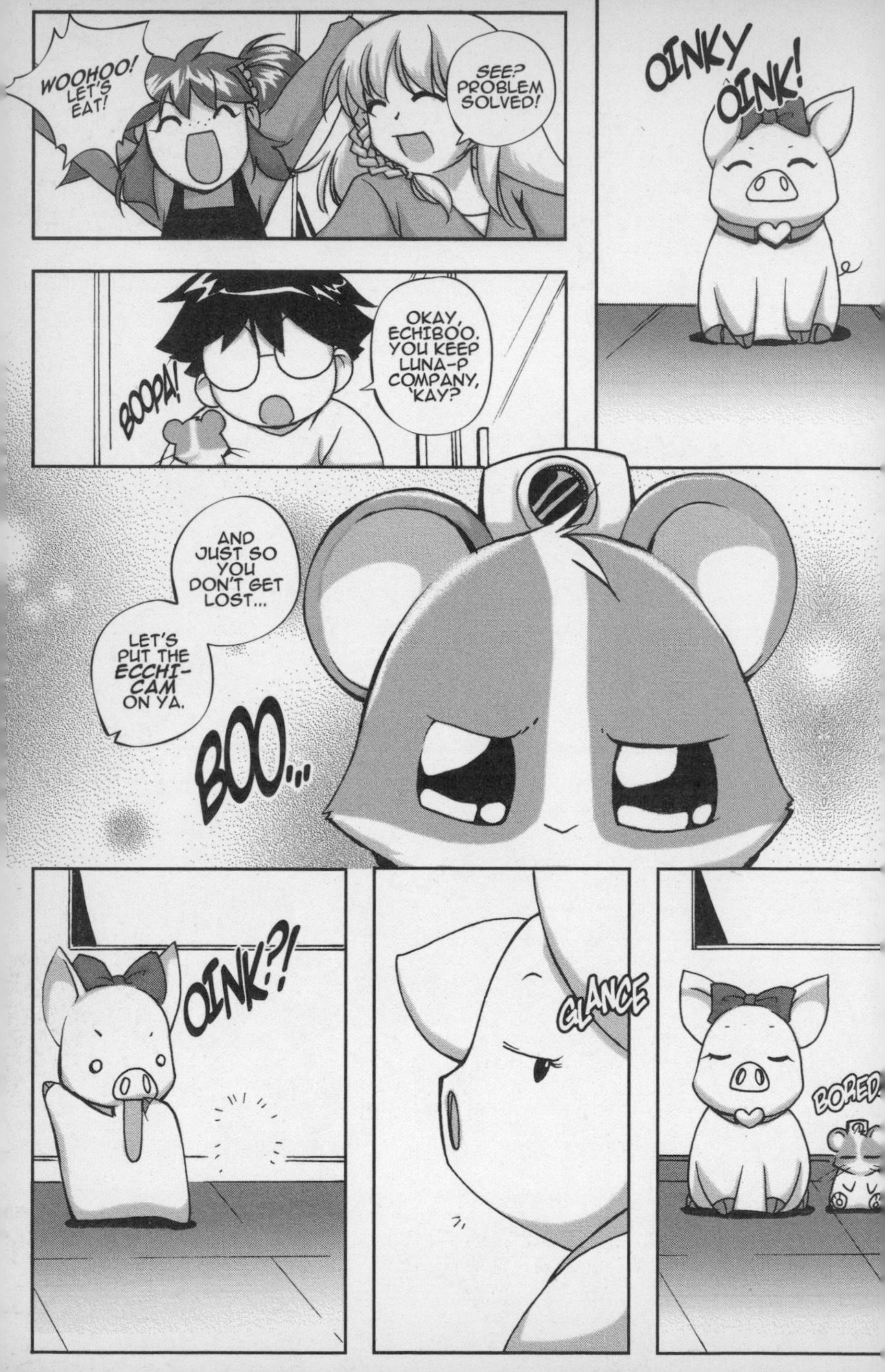

OINKY OINK!
SEE? PROBLEM SOLVED!
WOOHOO! LET'S EAT!
OKAY, ECHIBOO. YOU KEEP LUNA-P COMPANY, 'KAY?
BOOPA!
AND JUST SO YOU DON'T GET LOST...
LET'S PUT THE ECCHI-CAM ON YA.
BOO...
BORED.
GLANCE
OINK?!

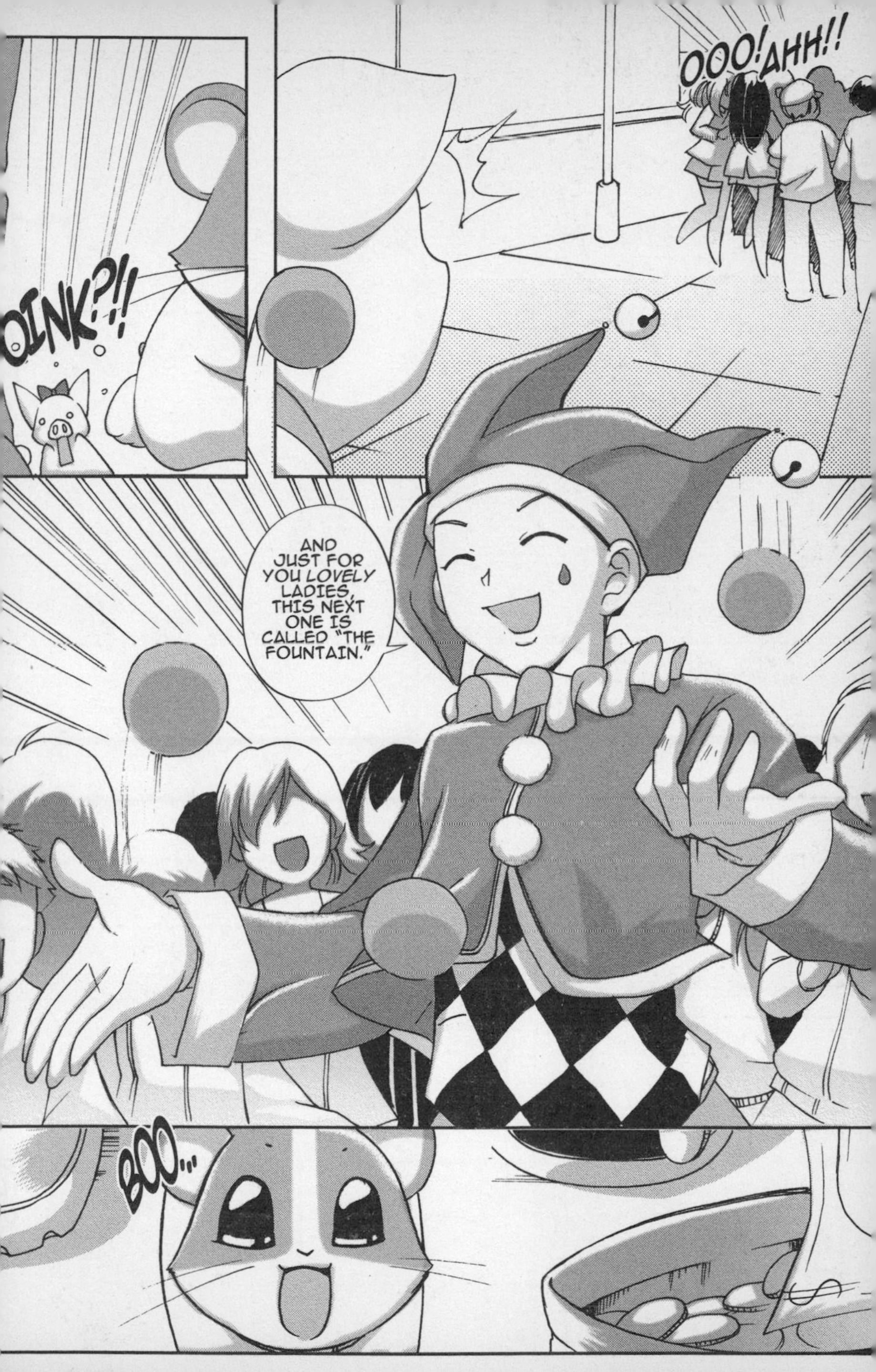
OOO! AHH!!
OINK?!!
AND JUST FOR YOU *LOVELY* LADIES, THIS NEXT ONE IS CALLED "THE FOUNTAIN."
BOO...

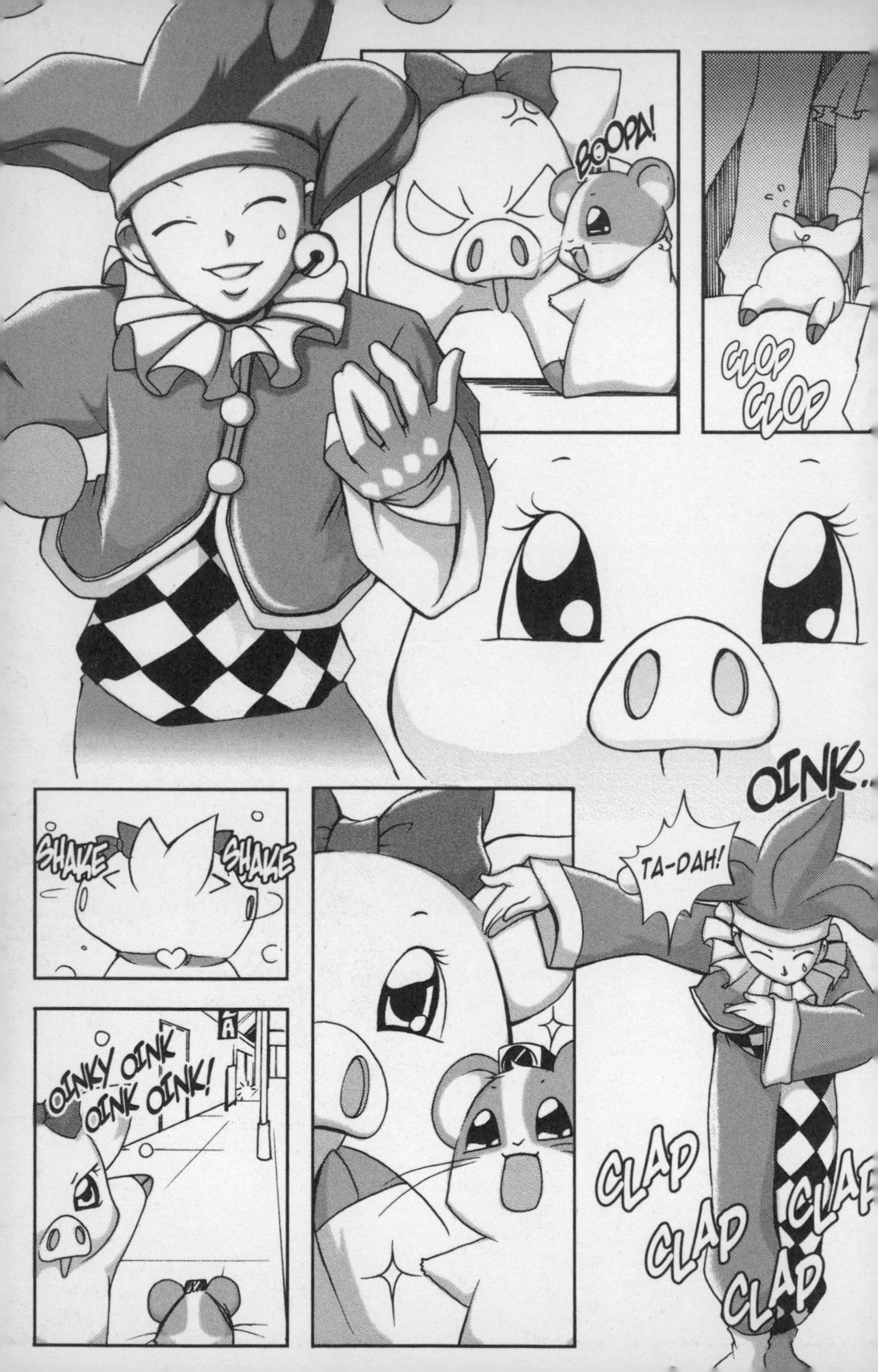
CLOP CLOP
BOOPA!
OINK...
TA-DAH!
CLAP
CLAP
CLAP
CLAP
CLAP
SHAKE SHAKE
OINKY OINK OINK OINK!

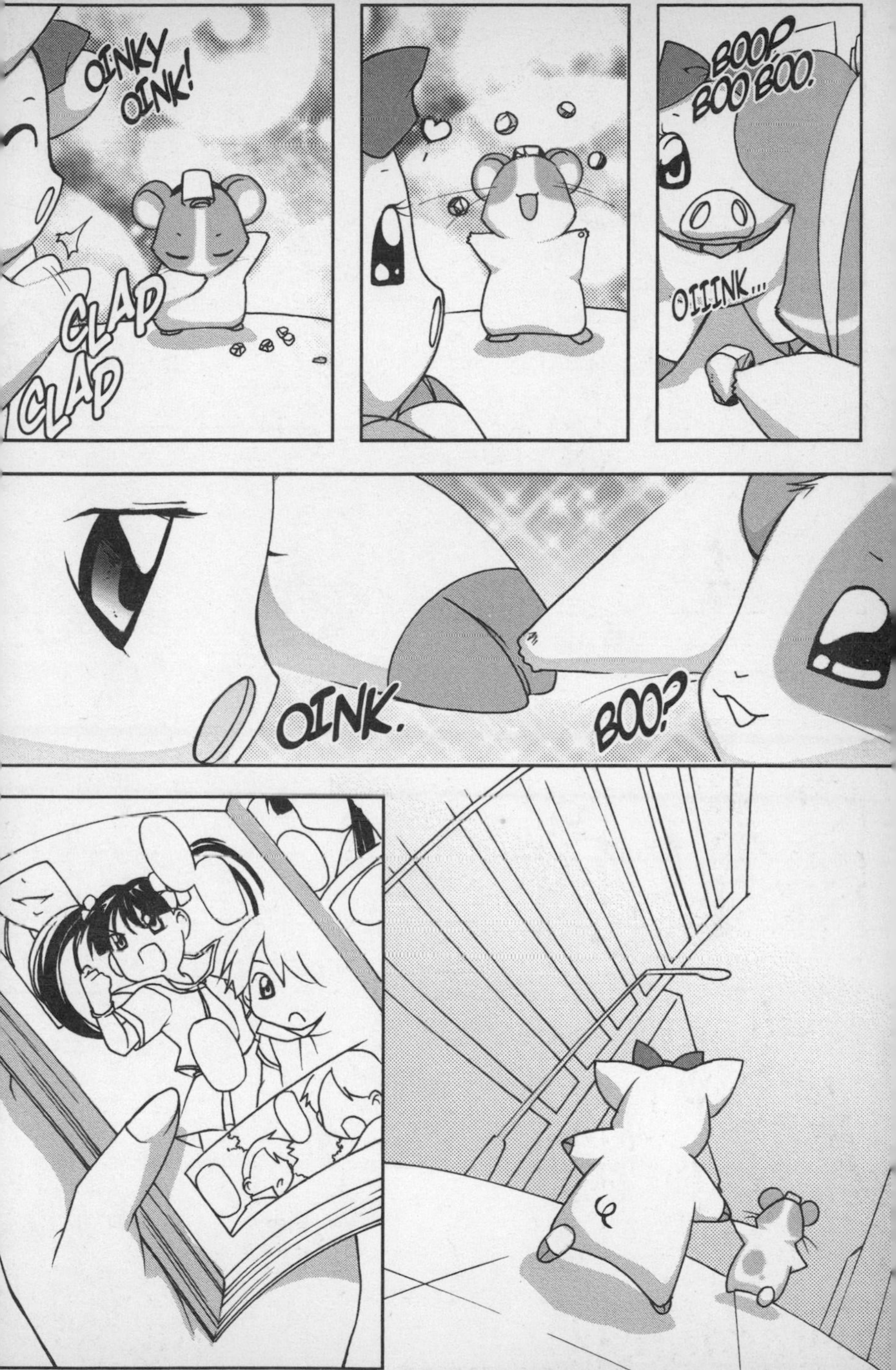
BOOP, BOO BOO.
OIIINK...
OINKY OINK!
CLAP
CLAP
BOO?
OINK.

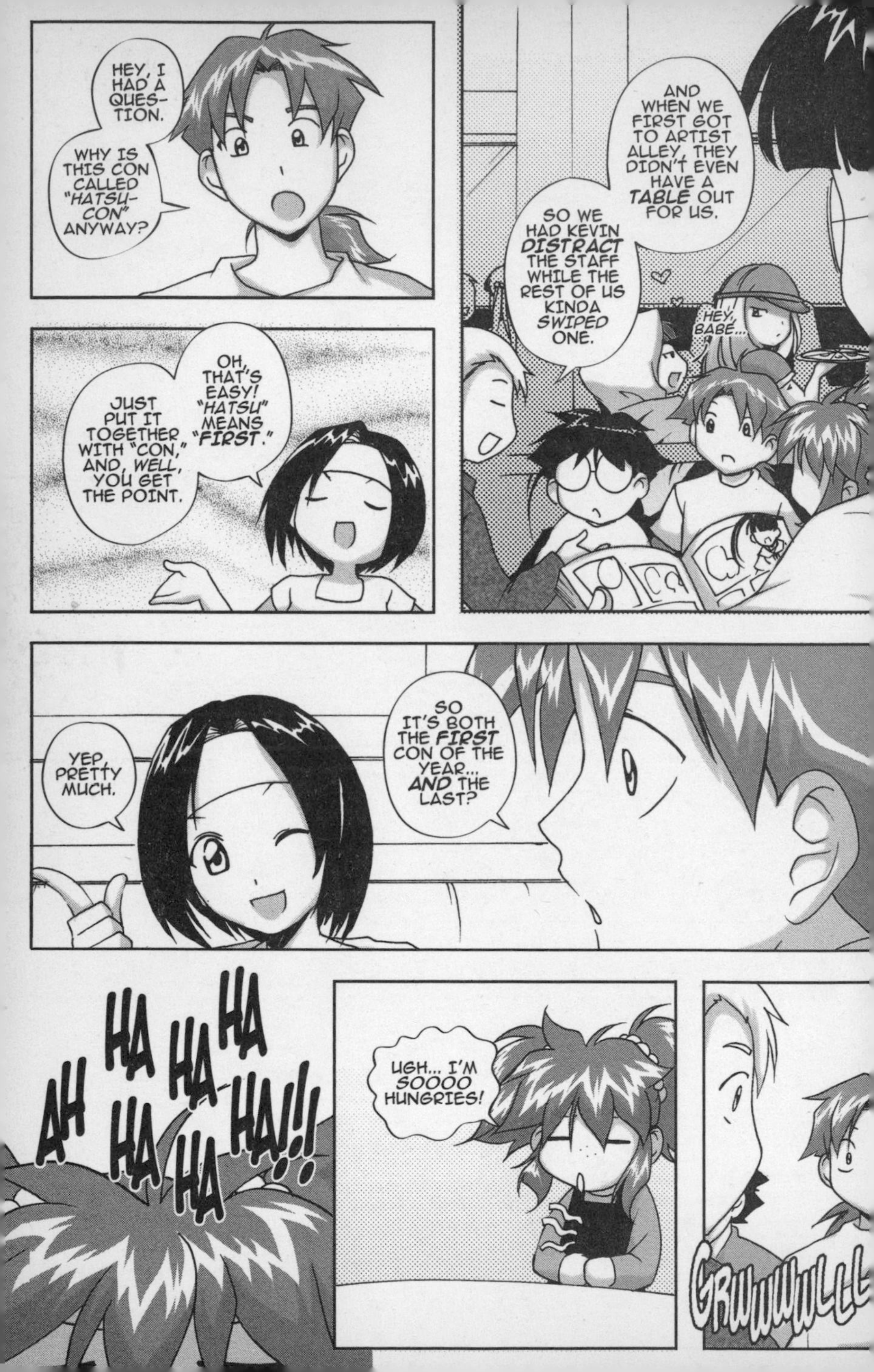
AND WHEN WE FIRST GOT TO ARTIST ALLEY, THEY DIDN'T EVEN HAVE A TABLE OUT FOR US.
SO WE HAD KEVIN DISTRACT THE STAFF WHILE THE REST OF US KINDA SWIPED ONE.
HEY, BABE...
HEY, I HAD A QUESTION.
WHY IS THIS CON CALLED "HATSU-CON" ANYWAY?
OH, THAT'S EASY! "HATSU" MEANS "FIRST."
JUST PUT IT TOGETHER WITH "CON," AND, WELL, YOU GET THE POINT.
SO IT'S BOTH THE FIRST CON OF THE YEAR... AND THE LAST?
YEP, PRETTY MUCH.
GRWWWLLL
UGH... I'M SOOOO HUNGRIES!
AH HA HA HA HA HA-HA HA HA HA!!!

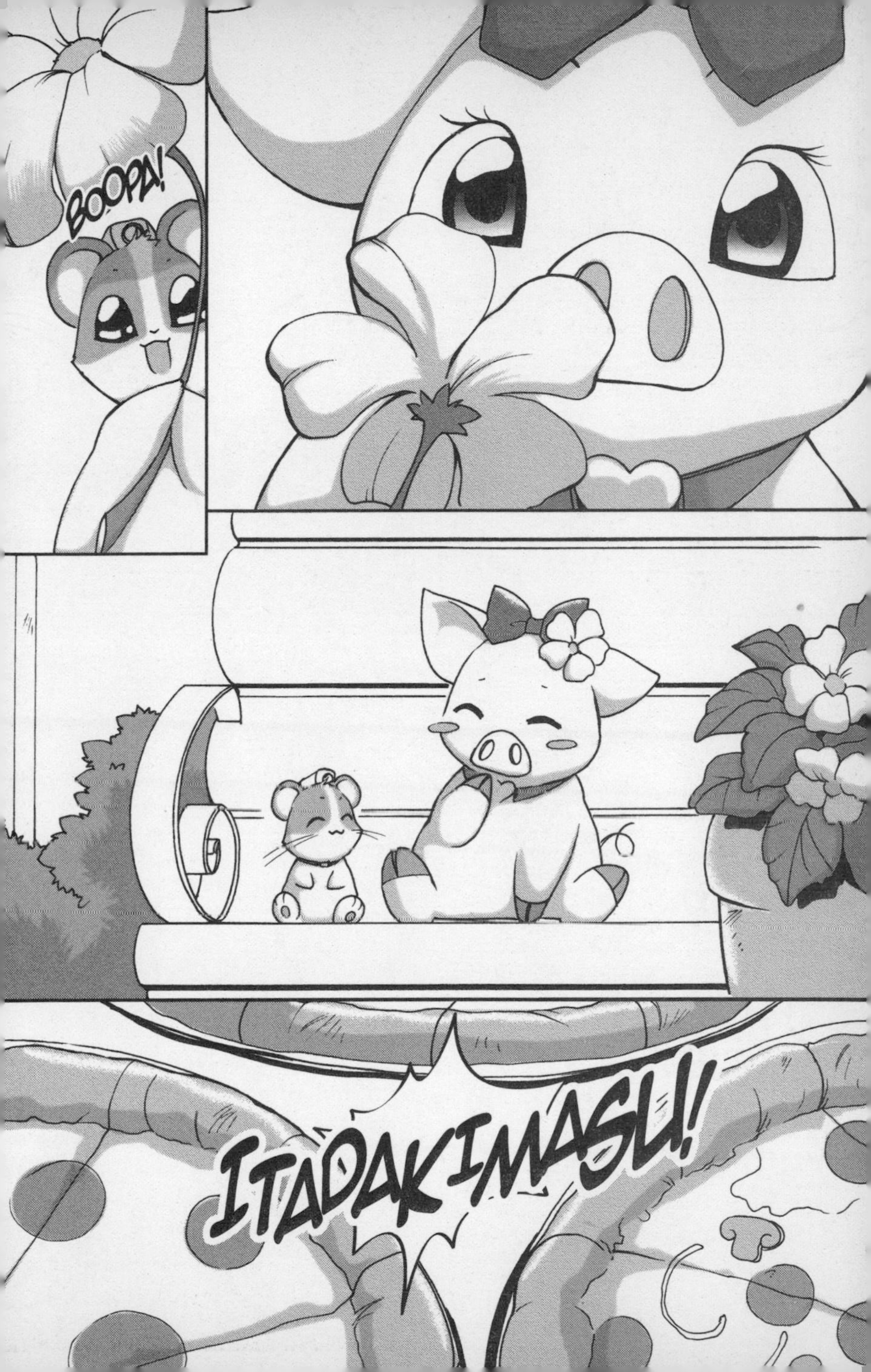
BOOPA!
ITADAKIMASU!

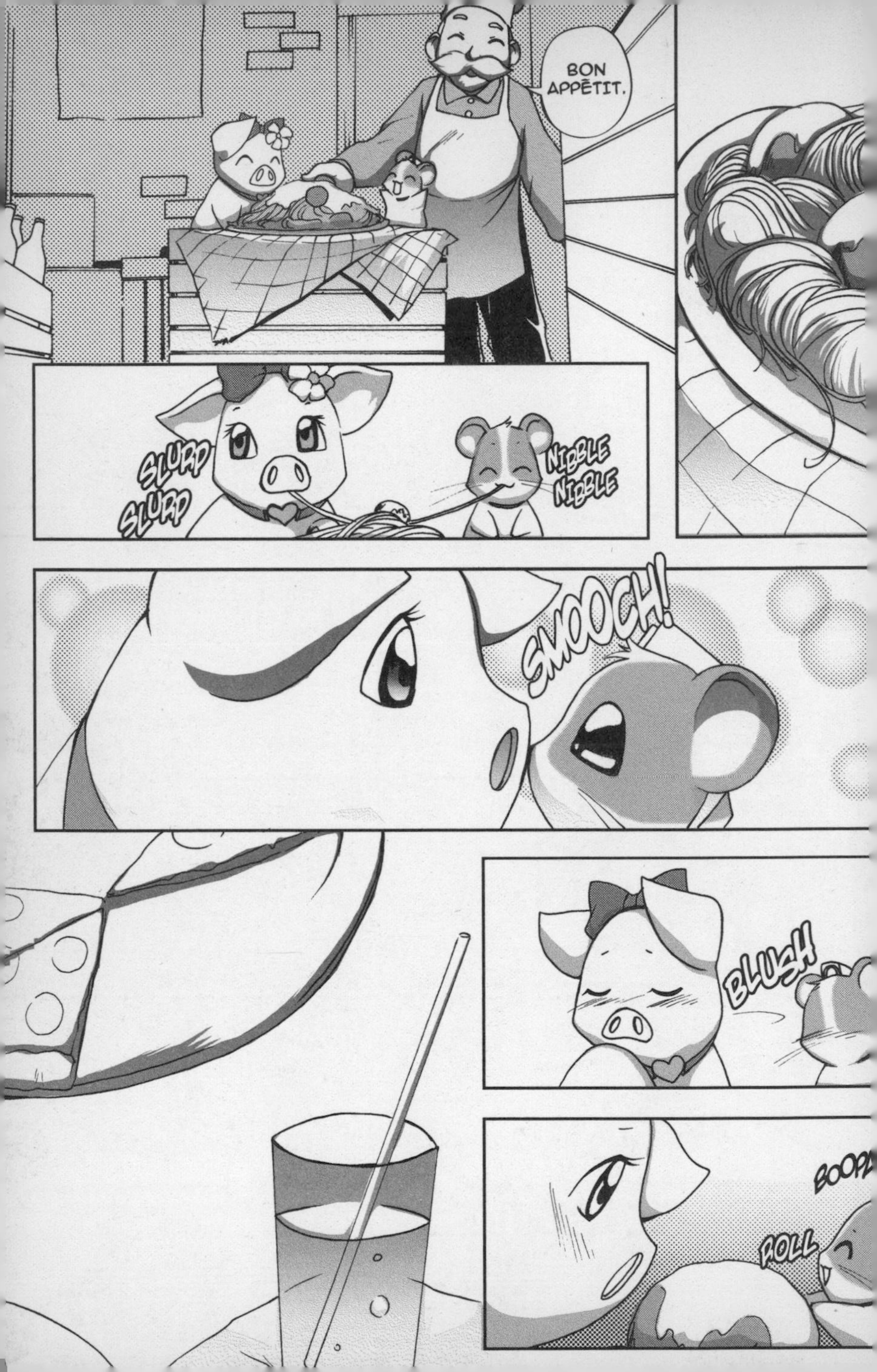
BON APPÊTIT.
SLURP SLURP
NIBBLE NIBBLE
SMOOCH!
BLUSH
ROLL

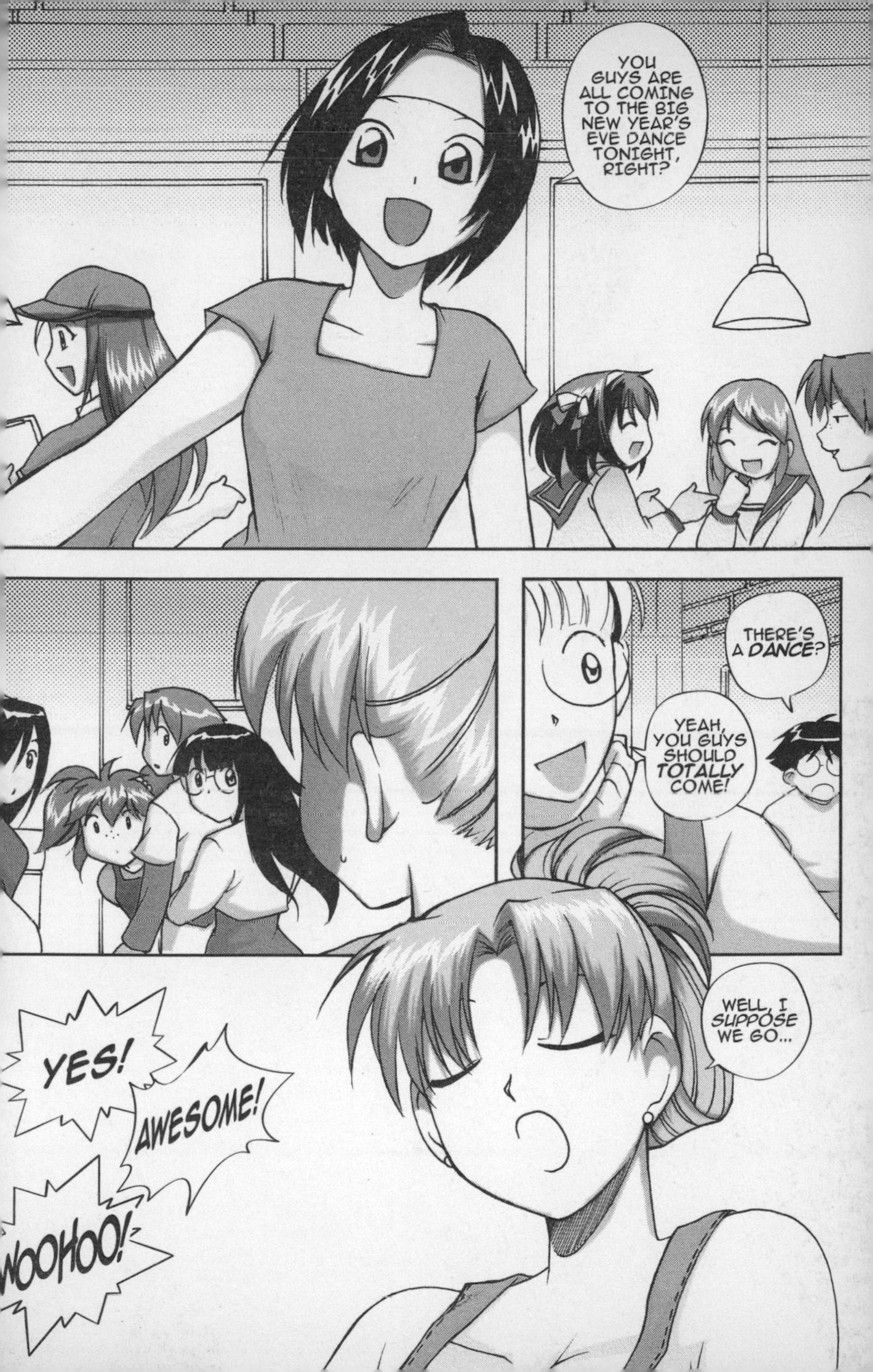
YOU GUYS ARE ALL COMING TO THE BIG NEW YEAR'S EVE DANCE TONIGHT, RIGHT?
THERE'S A *DANCE*?
YEAH, YOU GUYS SHOULD *TOTALLY* COME!
WELL, I *SUPPOSE* WE GO...
YES!
AWESOME!
WOOHOO!

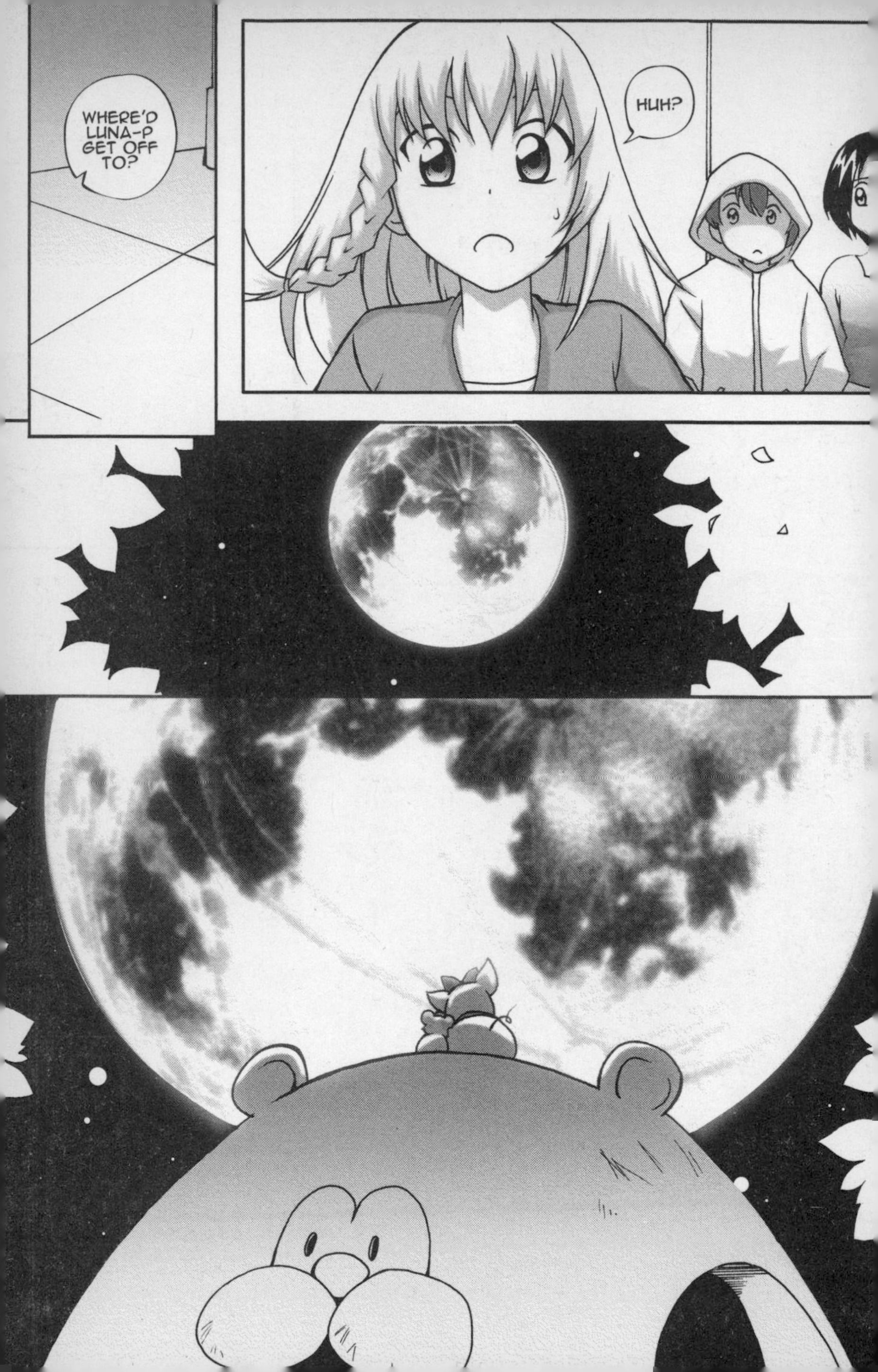
HUH?
WHERE'D LUNA-P GET OFF TO?

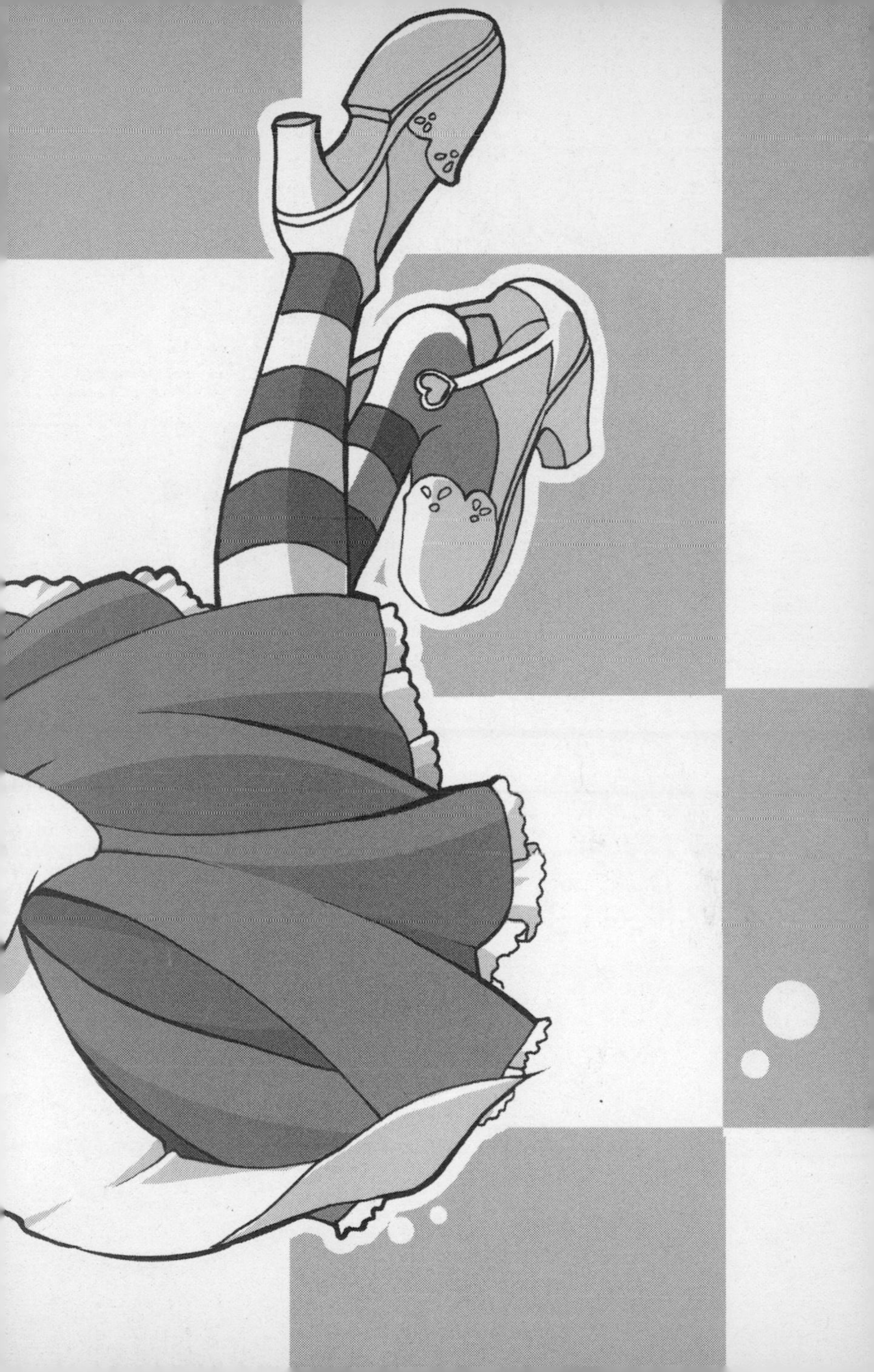

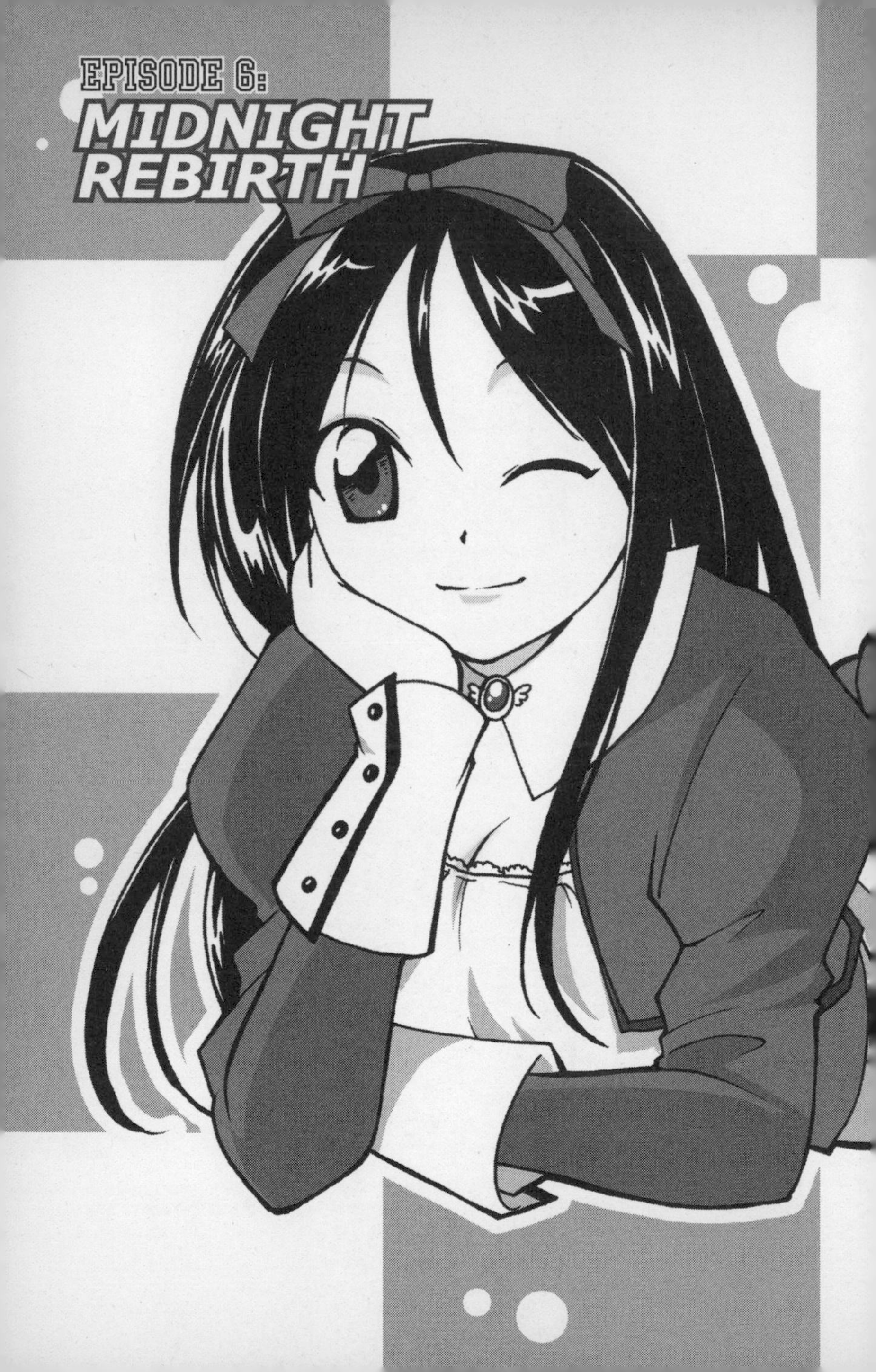
EPISODE 6:
MIDNIGHT REBIRTH

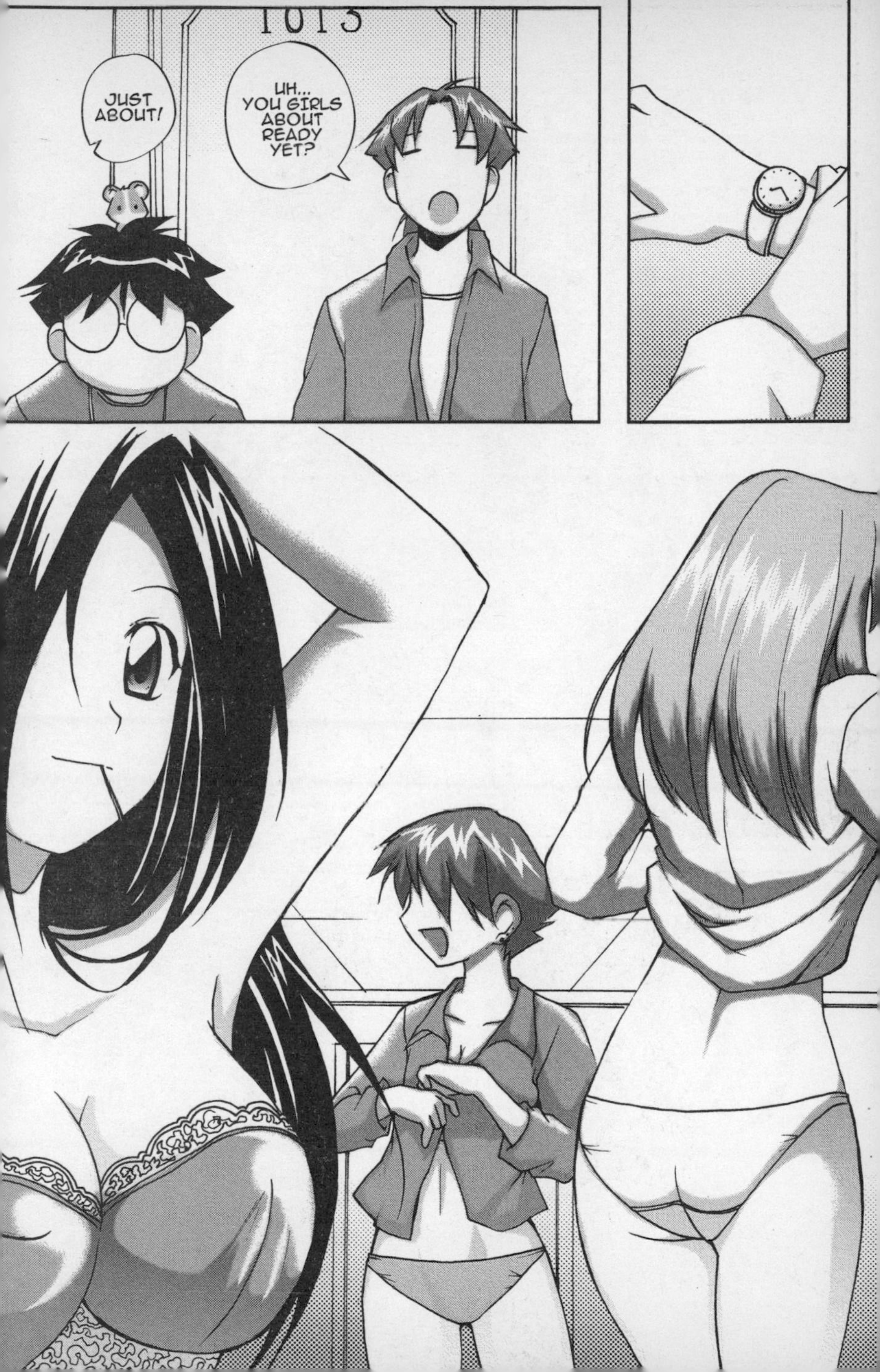
1013
UH... YOU GIRLS ABOUT READY YET?
JUST ABOUT!

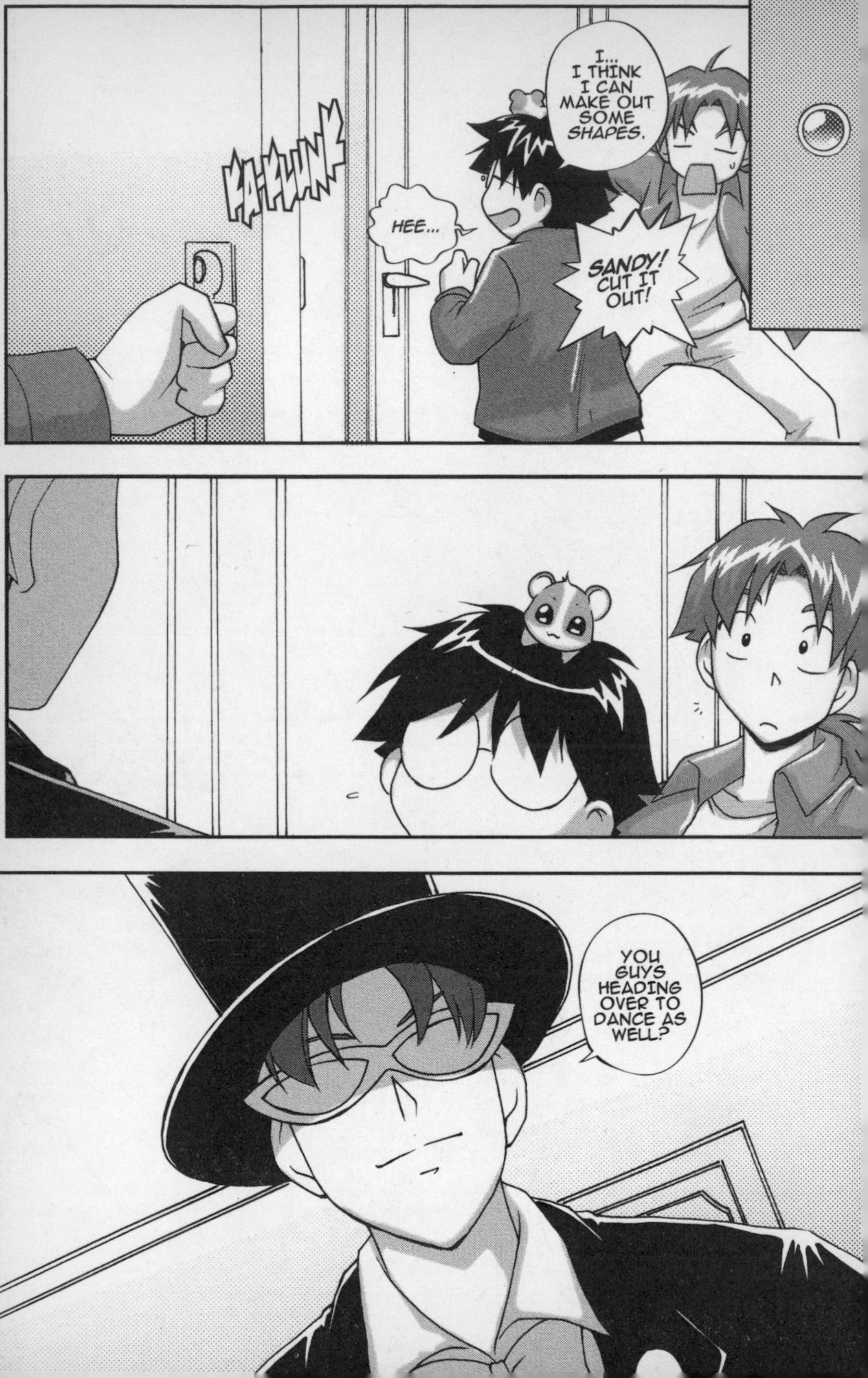
I... I THINK I CAN MAKE OUT SOME SHAPES.
SANDY! CUT IT OUT!
HEE...
KA-KLUNK
YOU GUYS HEADING OVER TO DANCE AS WELL?

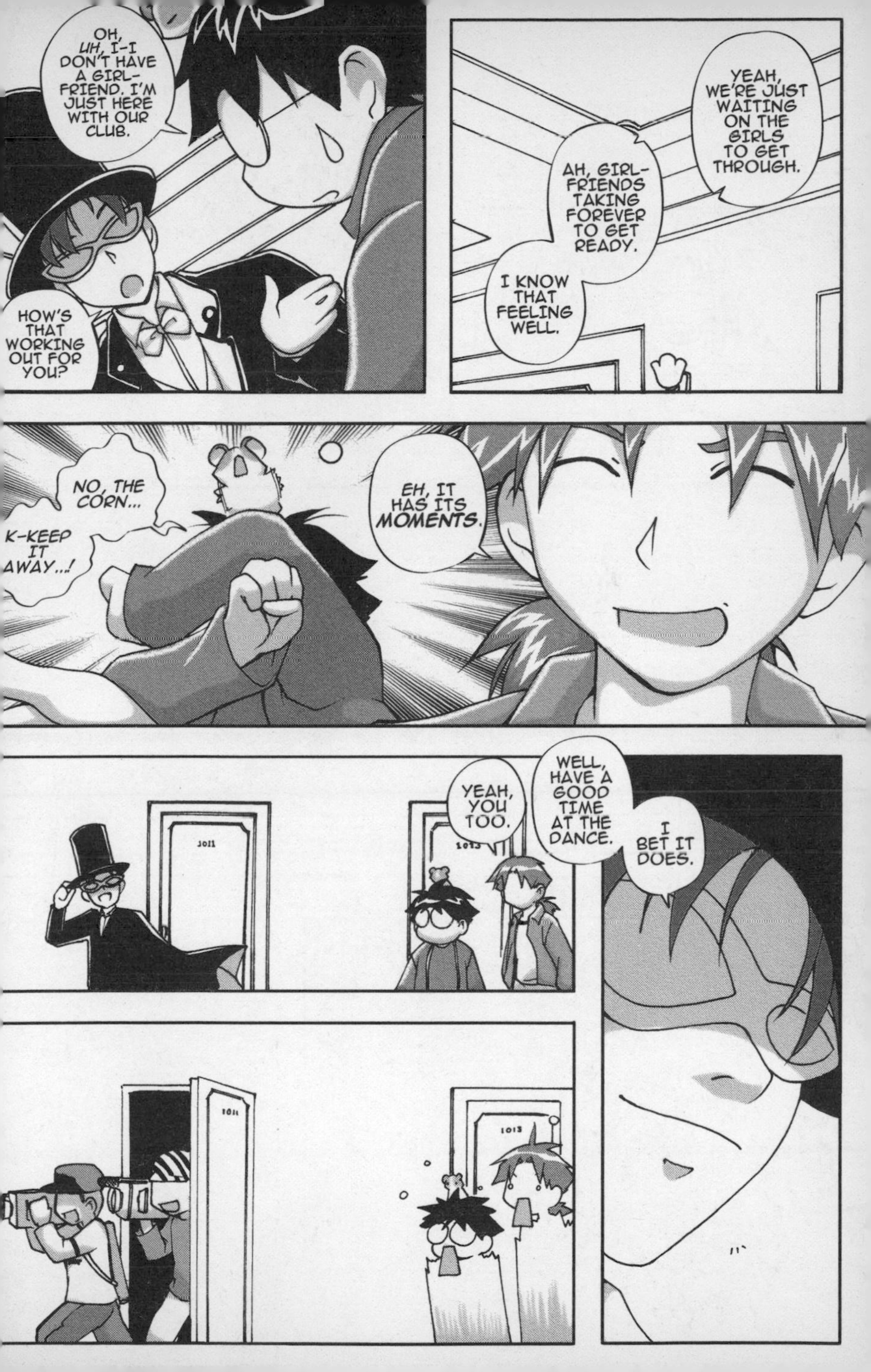
YEAH, WE'RE JUST WAITING ON THE GIRLS TO GET THROUGH.
AH, GIRL-FRIENDS TAKING FOREVER TO GET READY.
I KNOW THAT FEELING WELL.
OH, UH, I-I DON'T HAVE A GIRL-FRIEND. I'M JUST HERE WITH OUR CLUB.
HOW'S THAT WORKING OUT FOR YOU?
EH, IT HAS ITS MOMENTS.
NO, THE CORN...
K-KEEP IT AWAY...!
I BET IT DOES.
WELL, HAVE A GOOD TIME AT THE DANCE.
YEAH, YOU TOO.

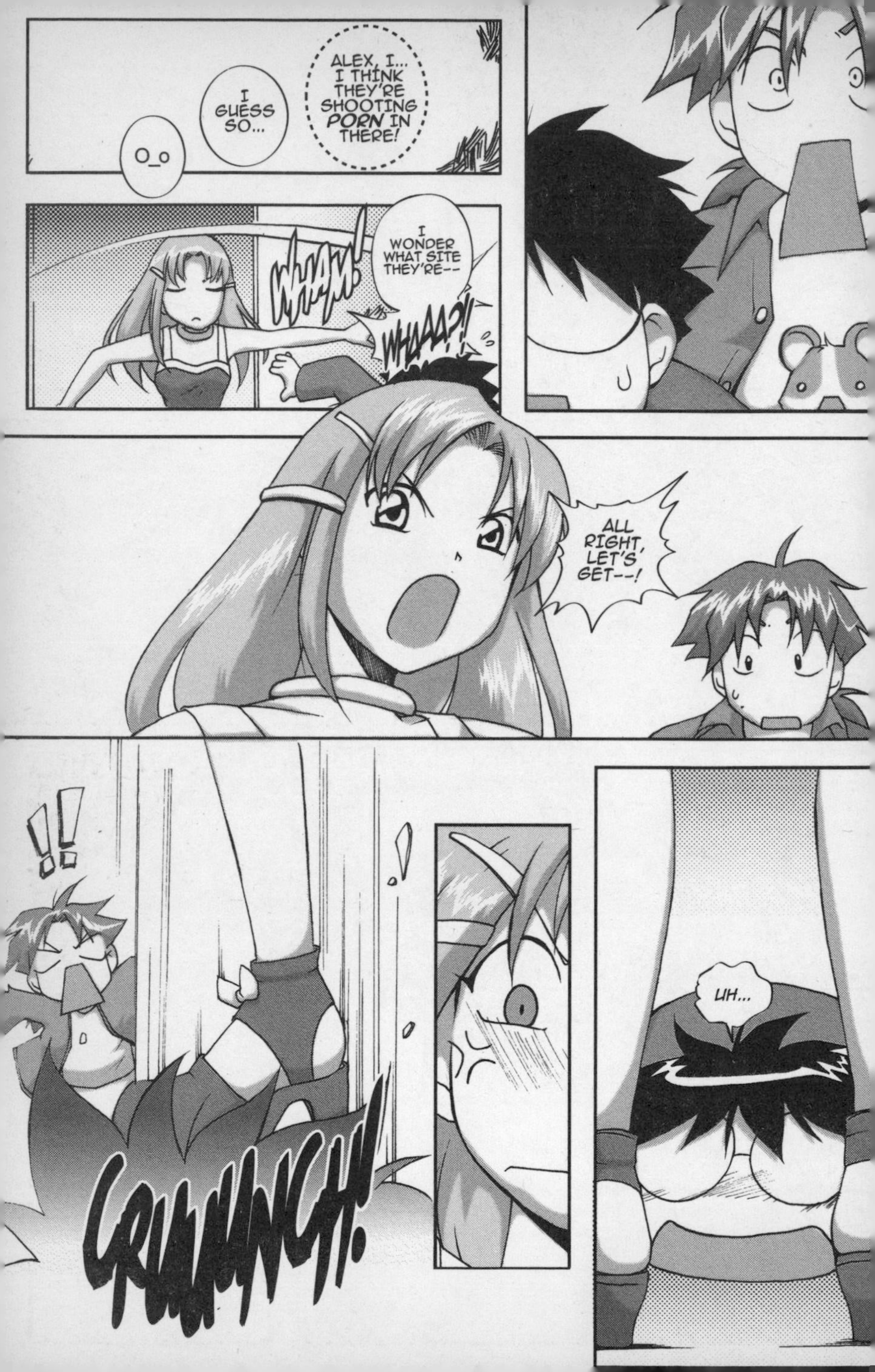
ALEX, I... I THINK THEY'RE SHOOTING PORN IN THERE!
I GUESS SO...
O_o
I WONDER WHAT SITE THEY'RE--
WHAM!
WHAAA?!
ALL RIGHT, LET'S GET--!
UH...
!
!!
CRUNNCH!

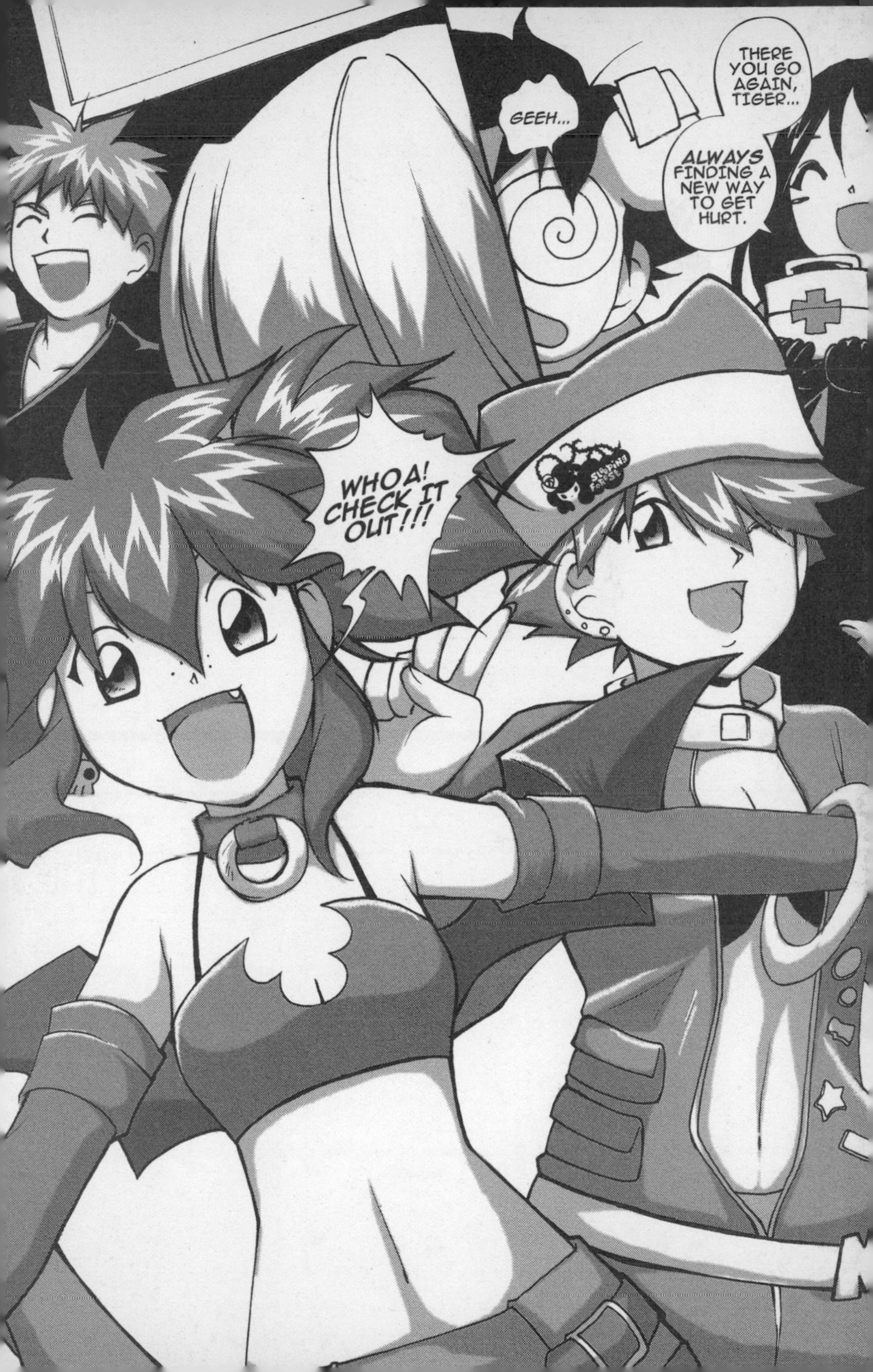
THERE YOU GO AGAIN, TIGER...
ALWAYS FINDING A NEW WAY TO GET HURT.
GEEH...
WHOA! CHECK IT OUT!!!

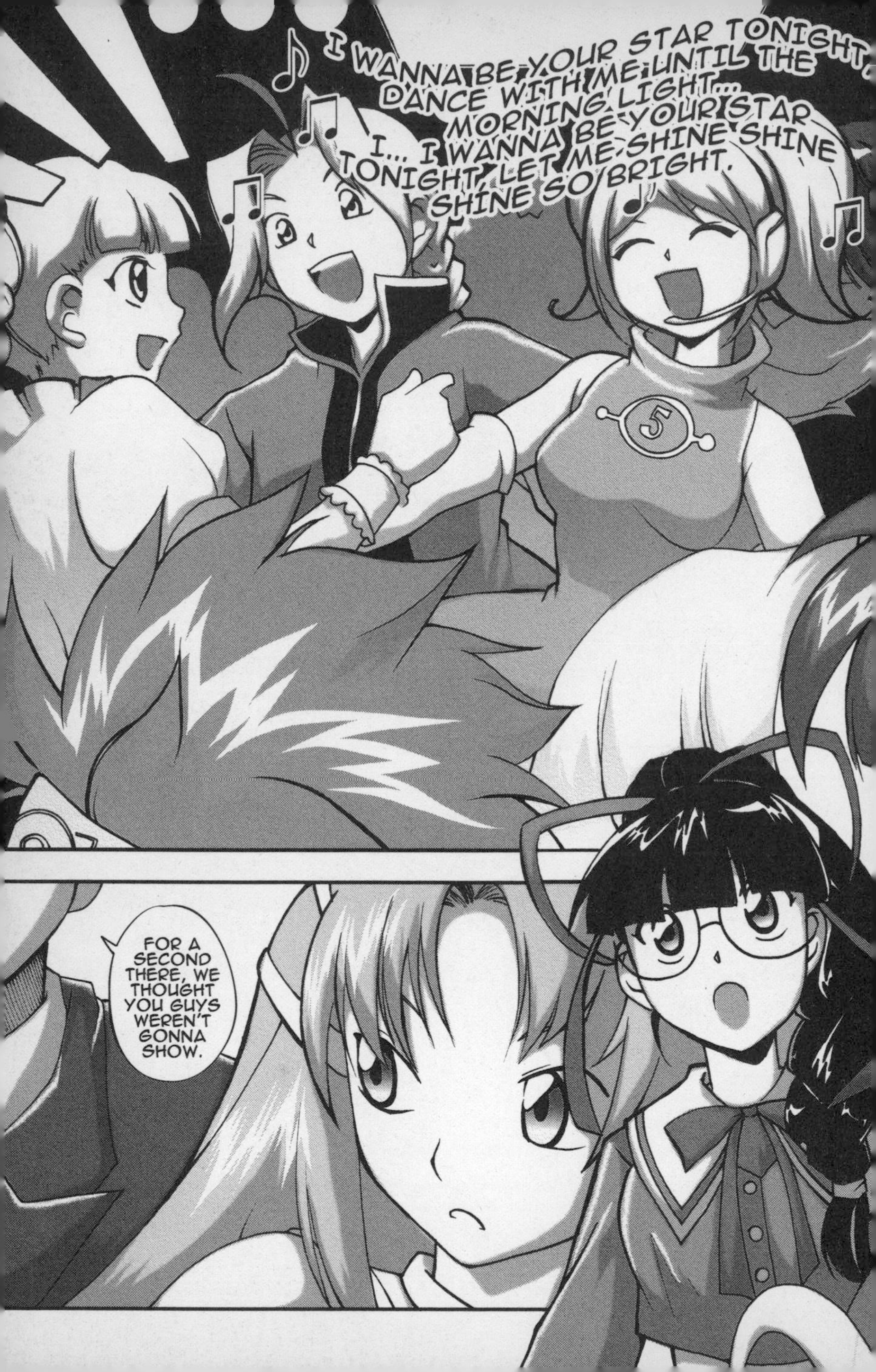
I WANNA BE YOUR STAR TONIGHT, DANCE WITH ME UNTIL THE MORNING LIGHT... I... I WANNA BE YOUR STAR TONIGHT, LET ME SHINE SHINE SHINE SO BRIGHT.
FOR A SECOND THERE, WE THOUGHT YOU GUYS WEREN'T GONNA SHOW.

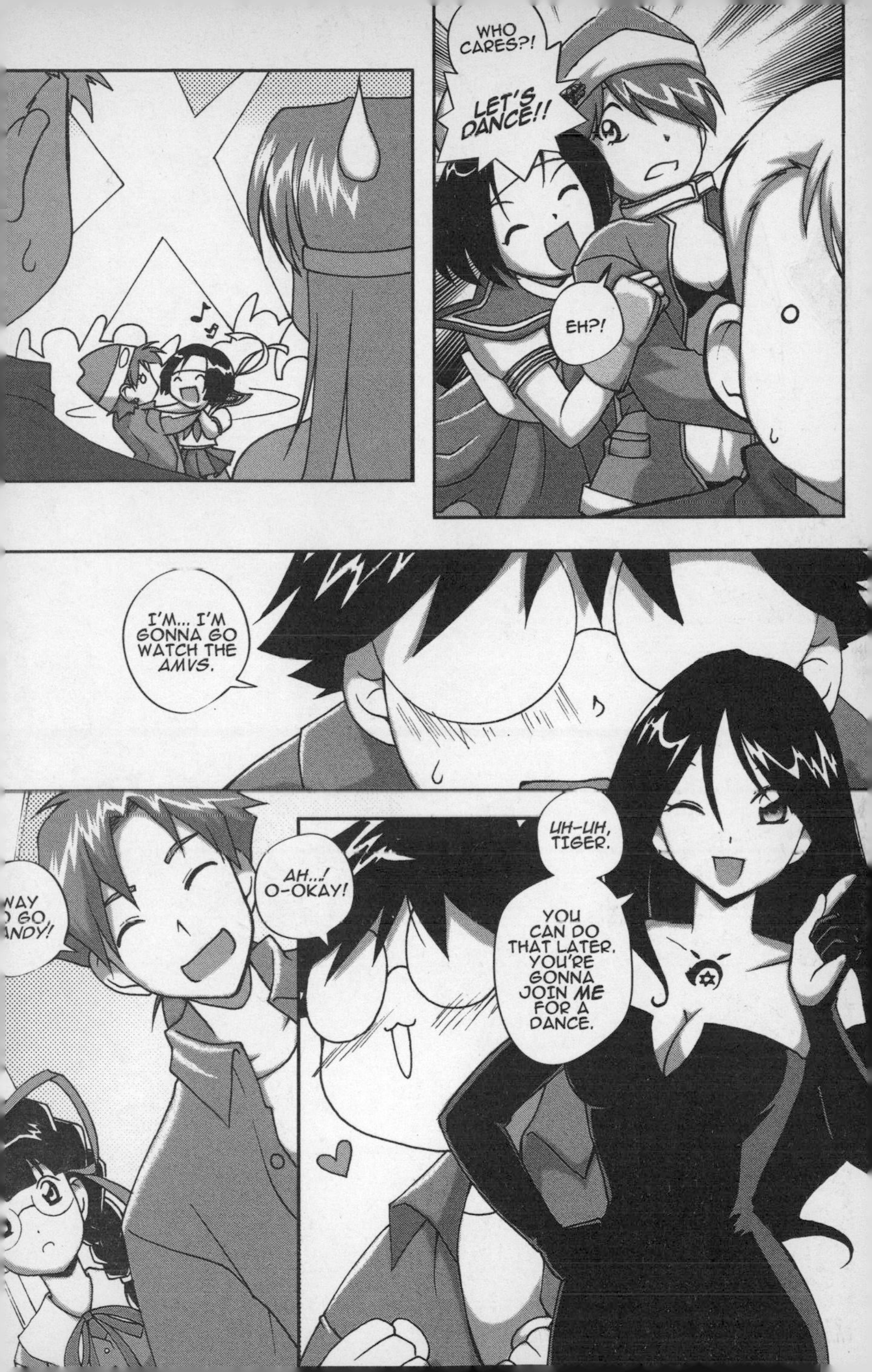
WHO CARES?!
LET'S DANCE!!
EH?!
I'M... I'M GONNA GO WATCH THE AMVS.
UH-UH, TIGER.
YOU CAN DO THAT LATER. YOU'RE GONNA JOIN *ME* FOR A DANCE.
AH...! O-OKAY!
WAY
O GO
ANDY!

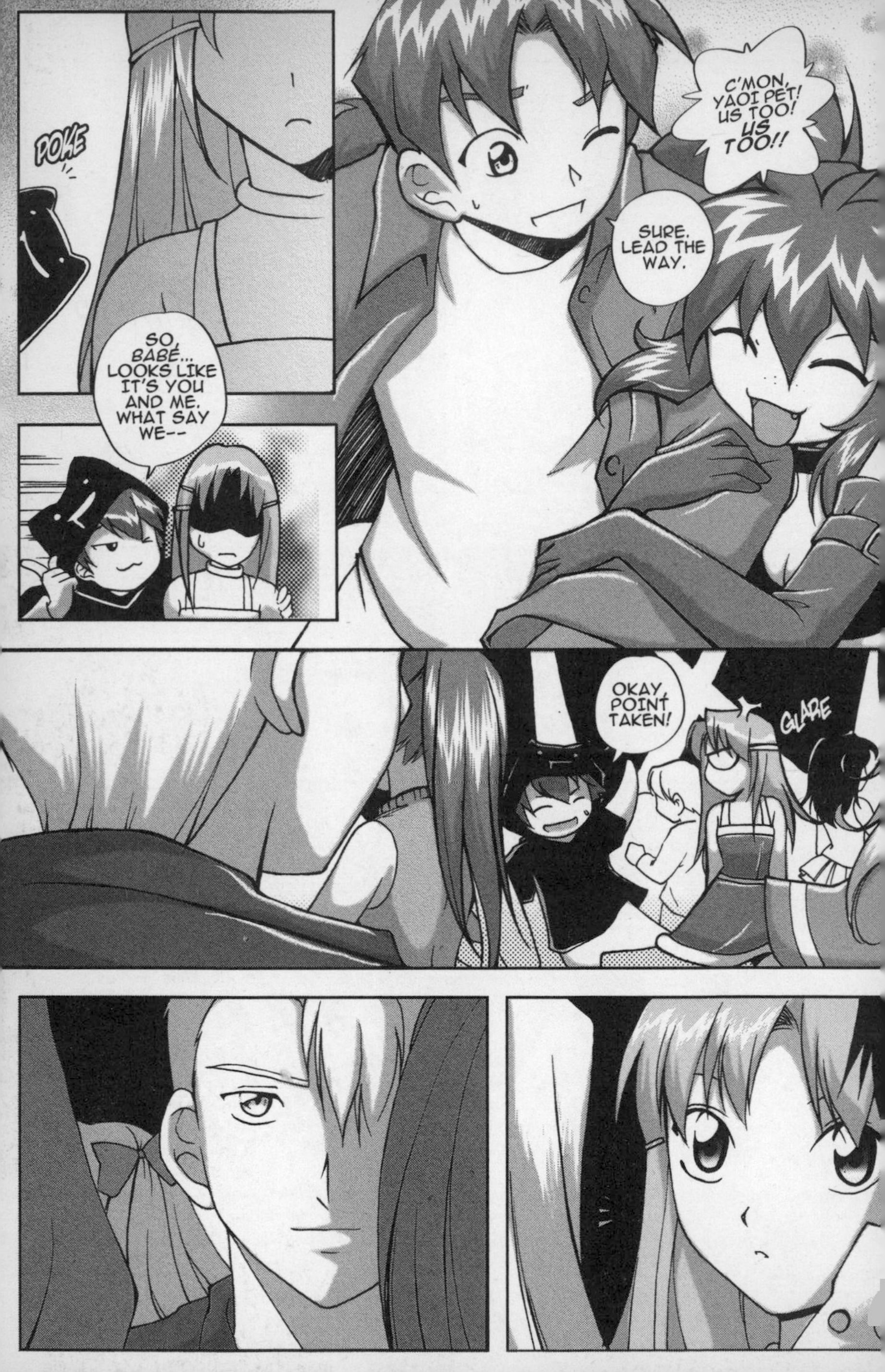
C'MON, YAOI PET! US TOO! US TOO!!
SURE. LEAD THE WAY.
POKE
SO, BABE... LOOKS LIKE IT'S YOU AND ME. WHAT SAY WE--
GLARE
OKAY, POINT TAKEN!

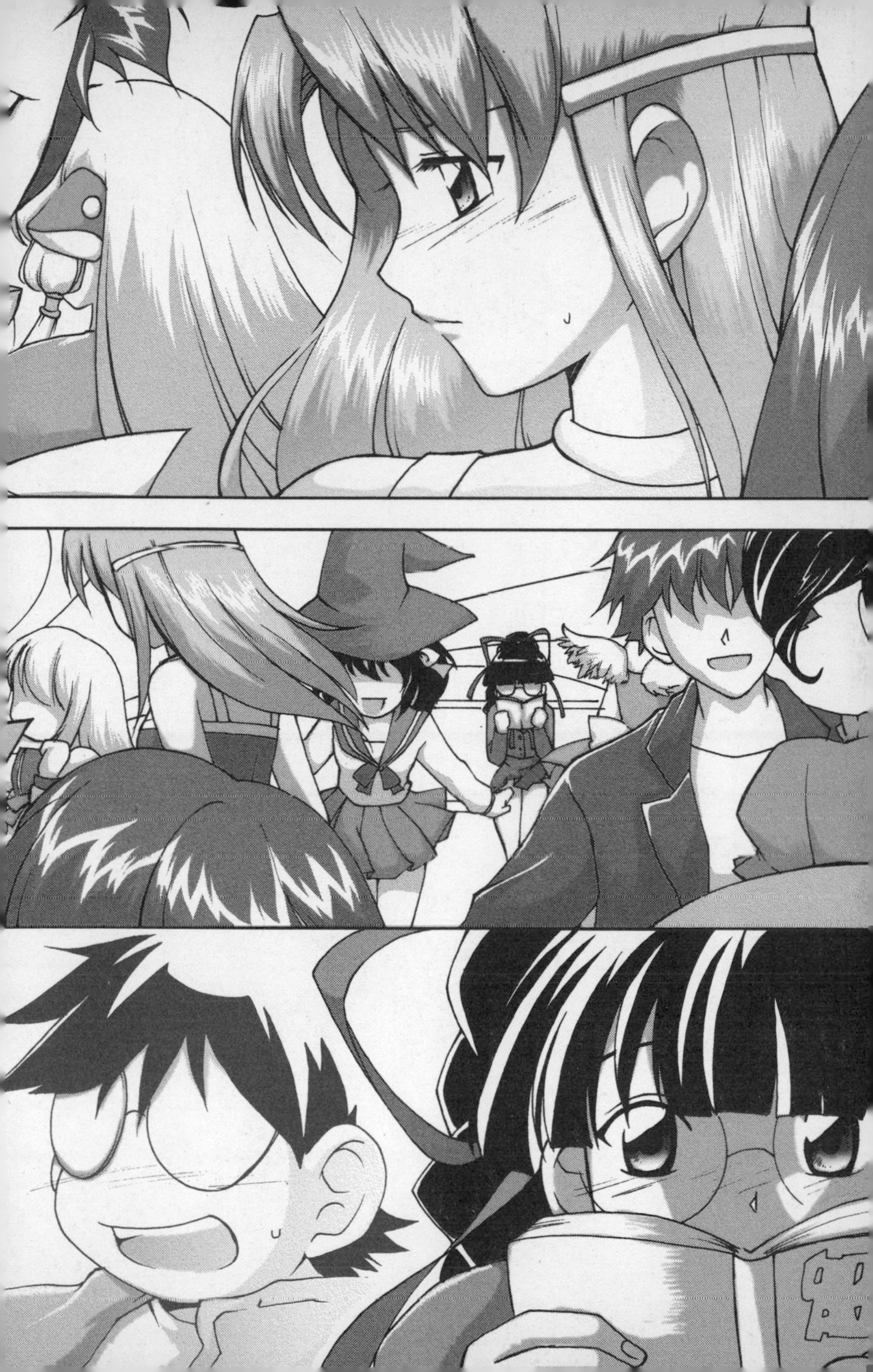

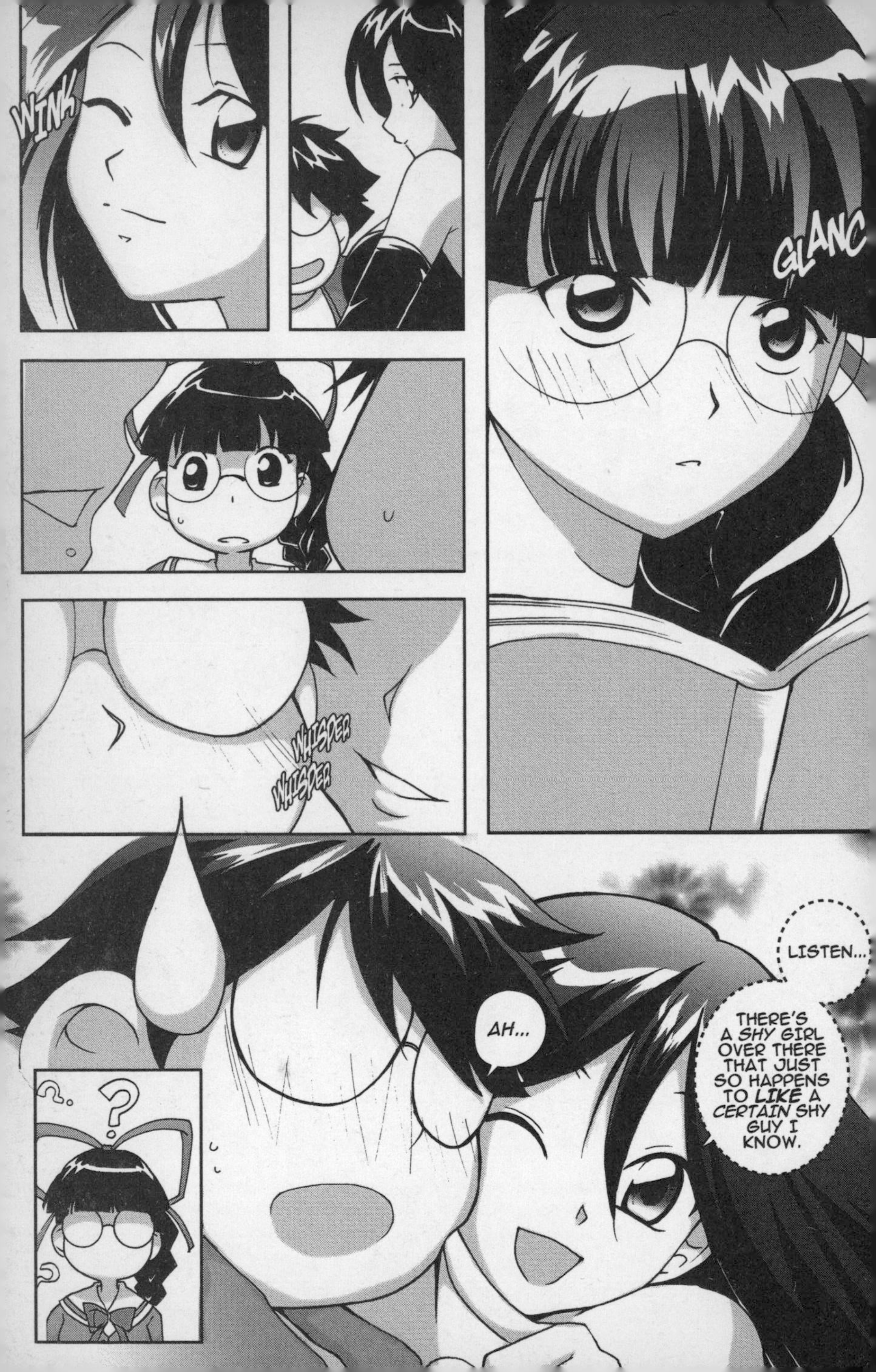
GLANC
WINK
WHISPER
WHISPER
LISTEN...
THERE'S A SHY GIRL OVER THERE THAT JUST SO HAPPENS TO LIKE A CERTAIN SHY GUY I KNOW.
AH...

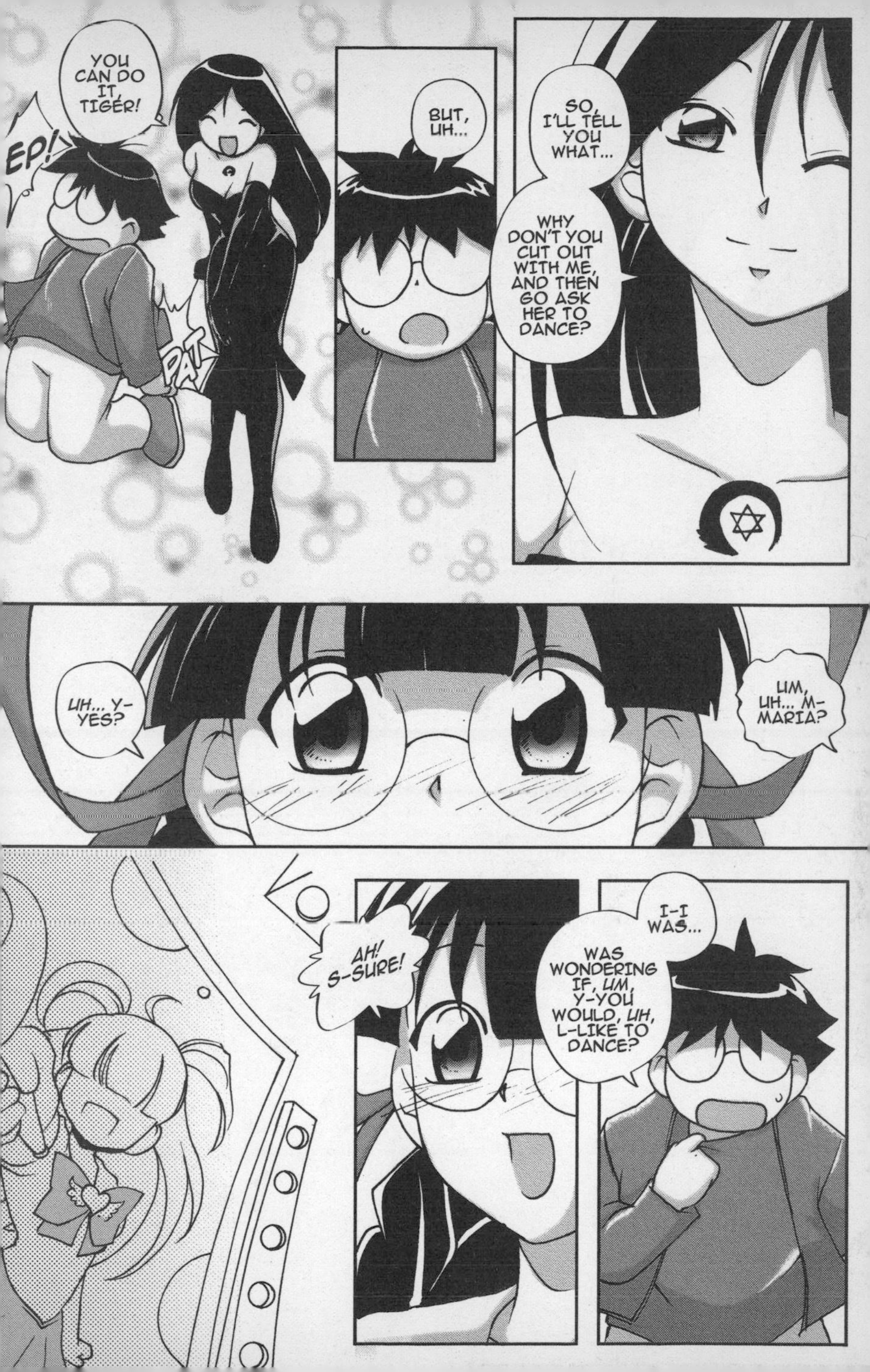
SO, I'LL TELL YOU WHAT...
WHY DON'T YOU CUT OUT WITH ME, AND THEN GO ASK HER TO DANCE?
BUT, UH...
YOU CAN DO IT, TIGER!
EP!
PAT
UM, UH... M-MARIA?
UH... Y-YES?
I-I WAS...
WAS WONDERING IF, UM, Y-YOU WOULD, UH, L-LIKE TO DANCE?
AH! S-SURE!

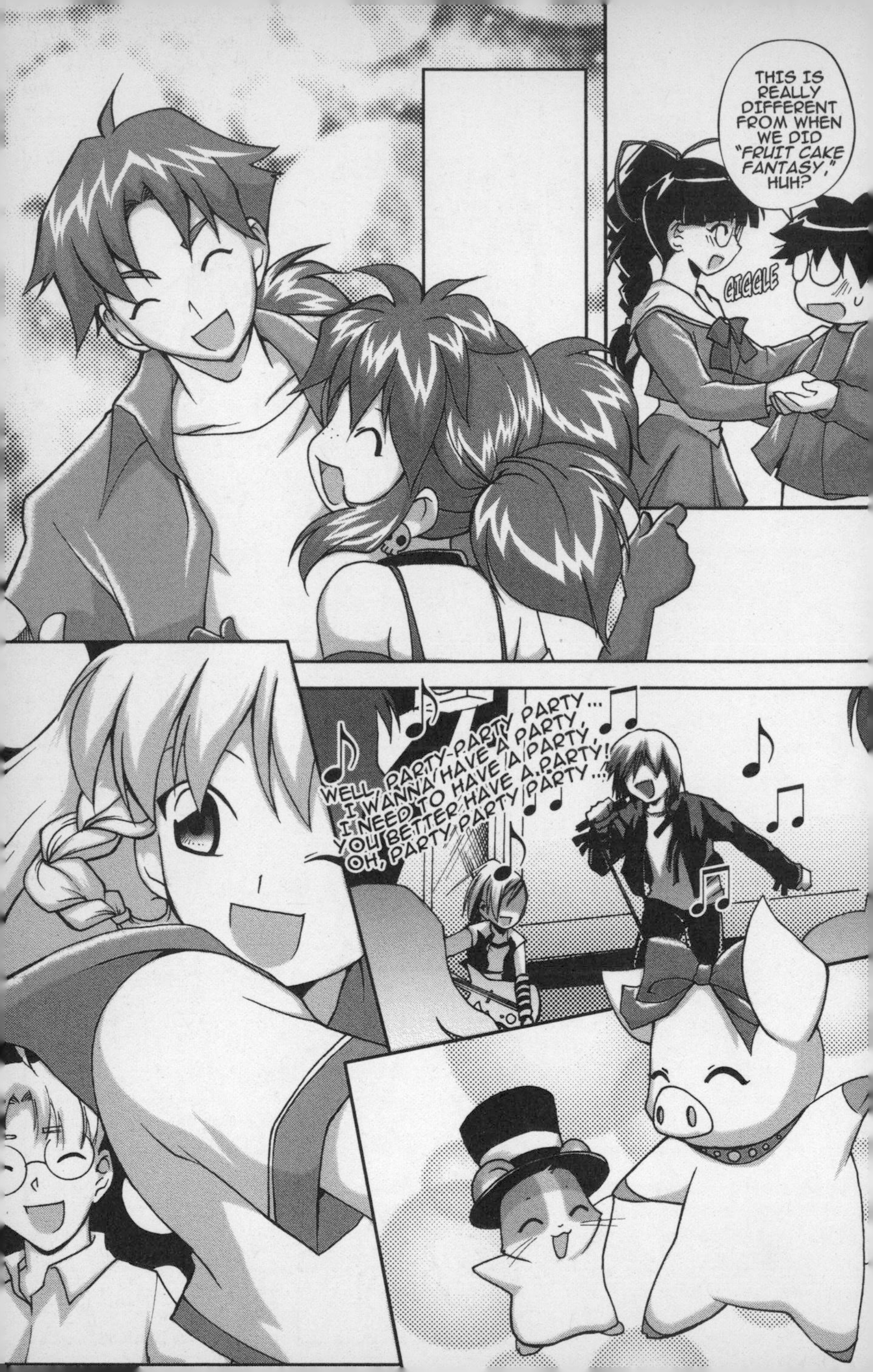
THIS IS REALLY DIFFERENT FROM WHEN WE DID "FRUIT CAKE FANTASY," HUH?
GIGGLE
WELL, PARTY-PARTY PARTY...
I WANNA HAVE A PARTY,
I NEED TO HAVE A PARTY,
YOU BETTER HAVE A PARTY!
OH, PARTY PARTY PARTY...!

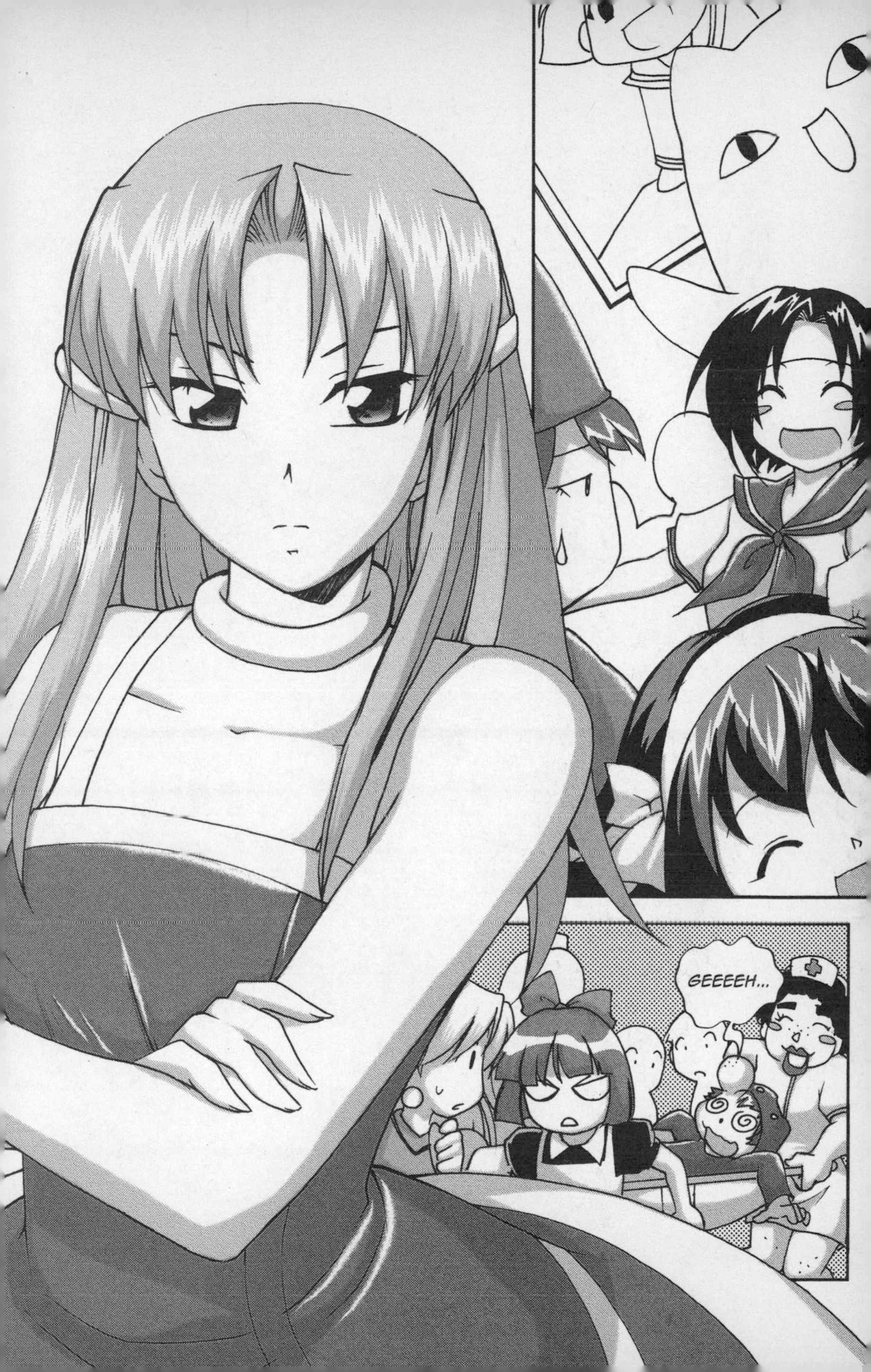
GEEEEH...

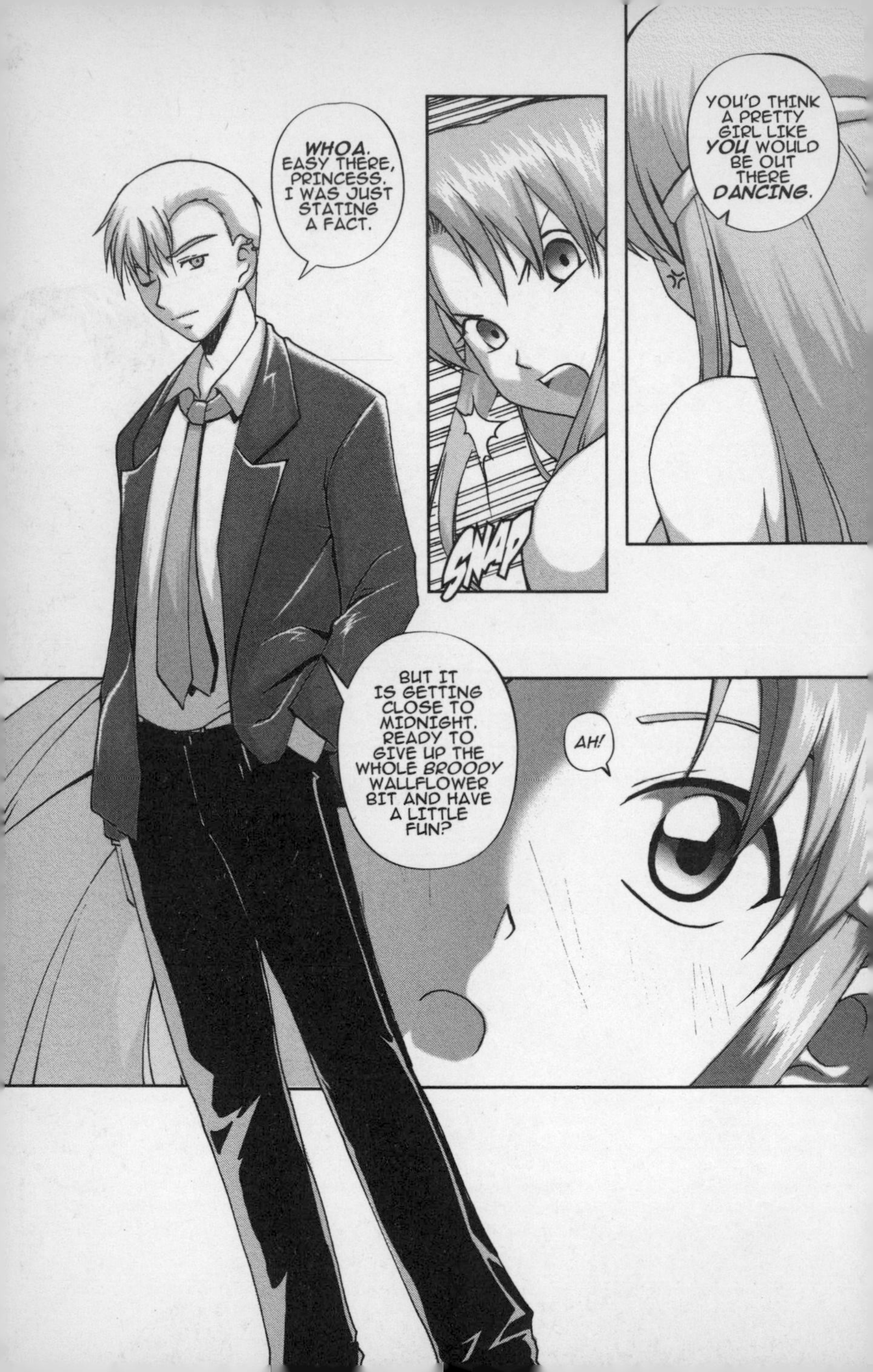
YOU'D THINK A PRETTY GIRL LIKE *YOU* WOULD BE OUT THERE *DANCING*.
SNAP
WHOA. EASY THERE, PRINCESS. I WAS JUST STATING A FACT.
AH!
BUT IT IS GETTING CLOSE TO MIDNIGHT. READY TO GIVE UP THE WHOLE *BROODY* WALLFLOWER BIT AND HAVE A LITTLE FUN?

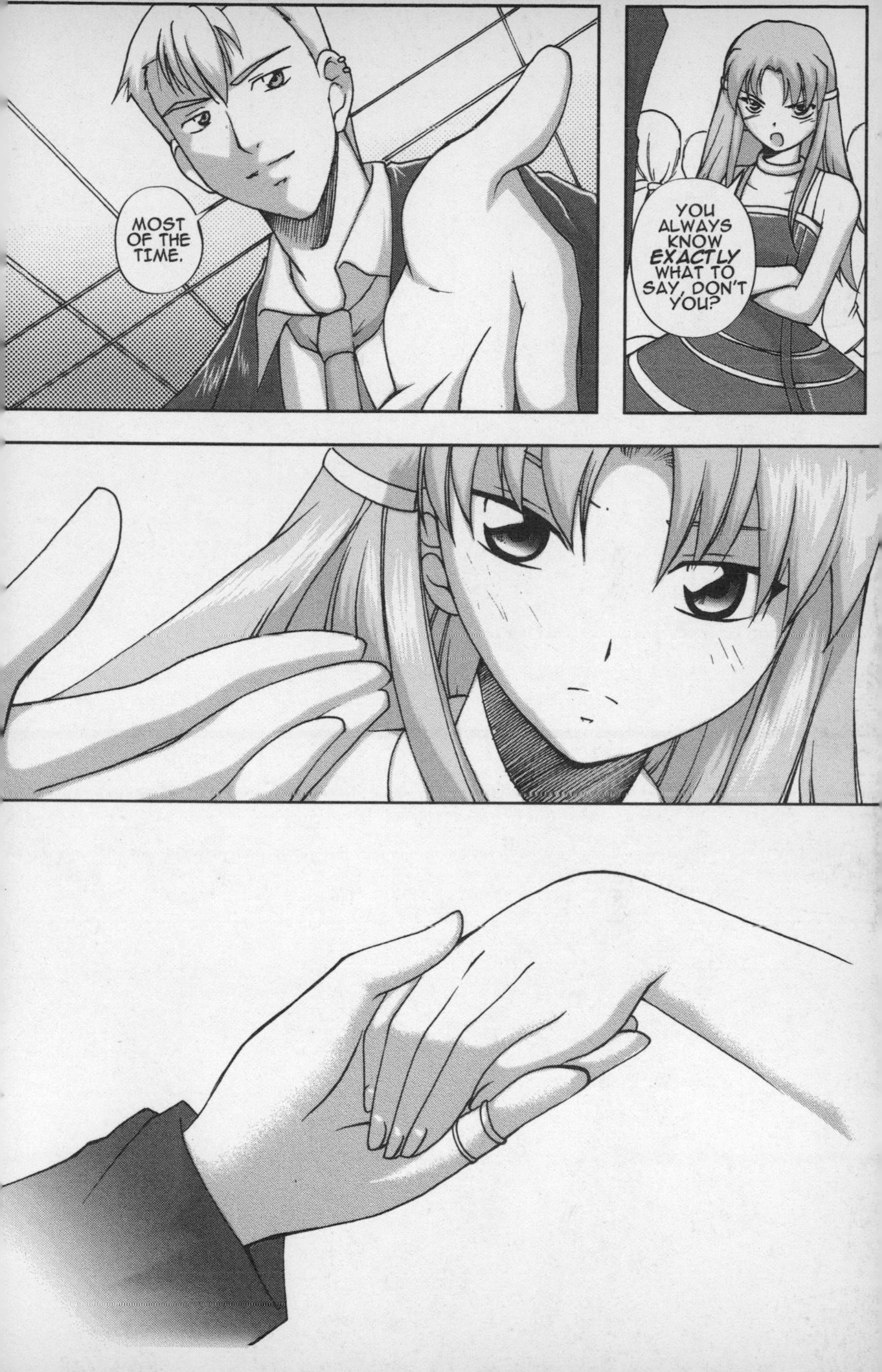
YOU ALWAYS KNOW EXACTLY WHAT TO SAY, DON'T YOU?
MOST OF THE TIME.

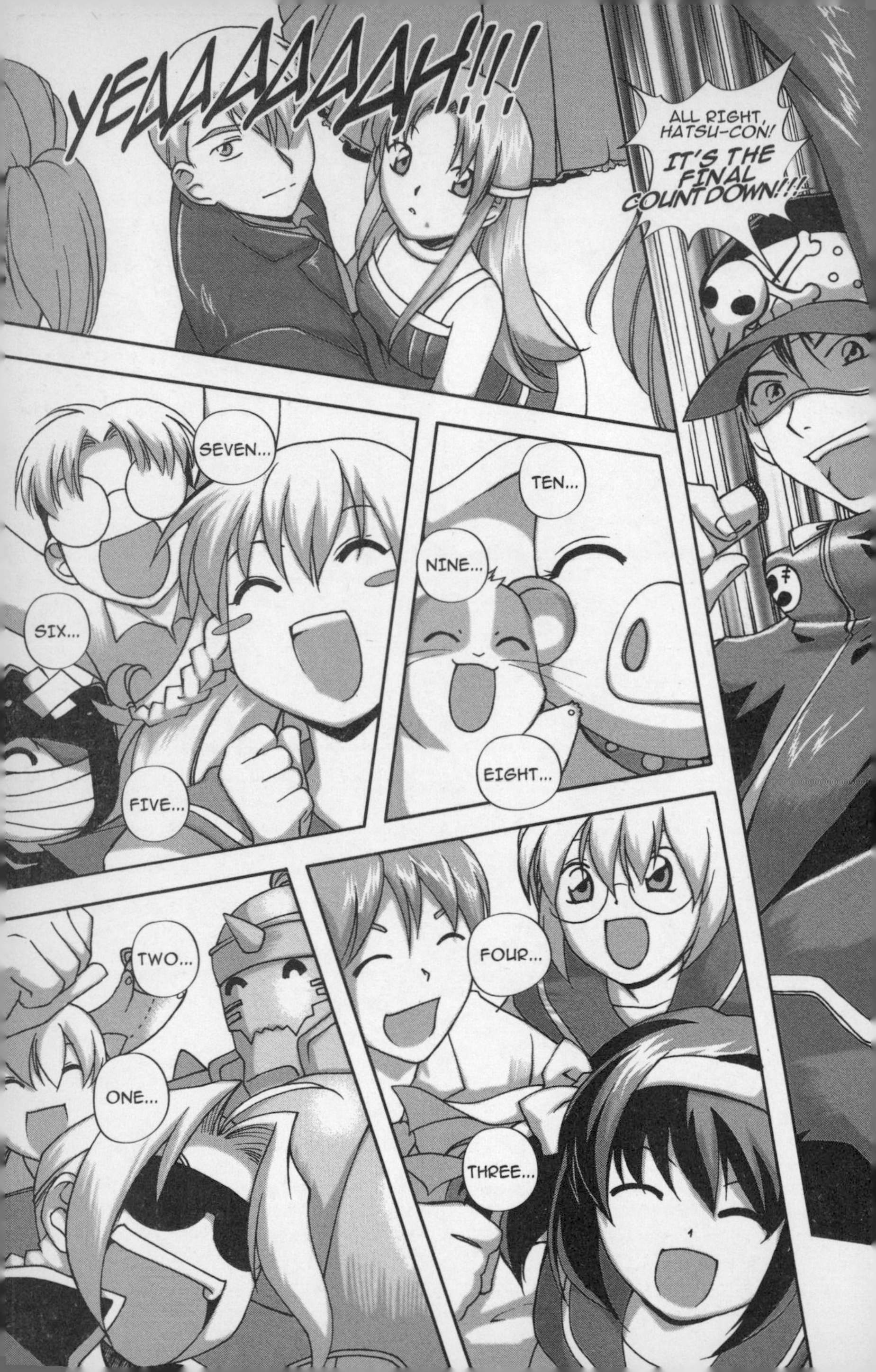
ALL RIGHT, HATSU-CON!
IT'S THE FINAL COUNTDOWN!!!
TEN...
NINE...
EIGHT...
SEVEN...
SIX...
FIVE...
FOUR...
THREE...
TWO...
ONE...
YEAAAAAAH!!!

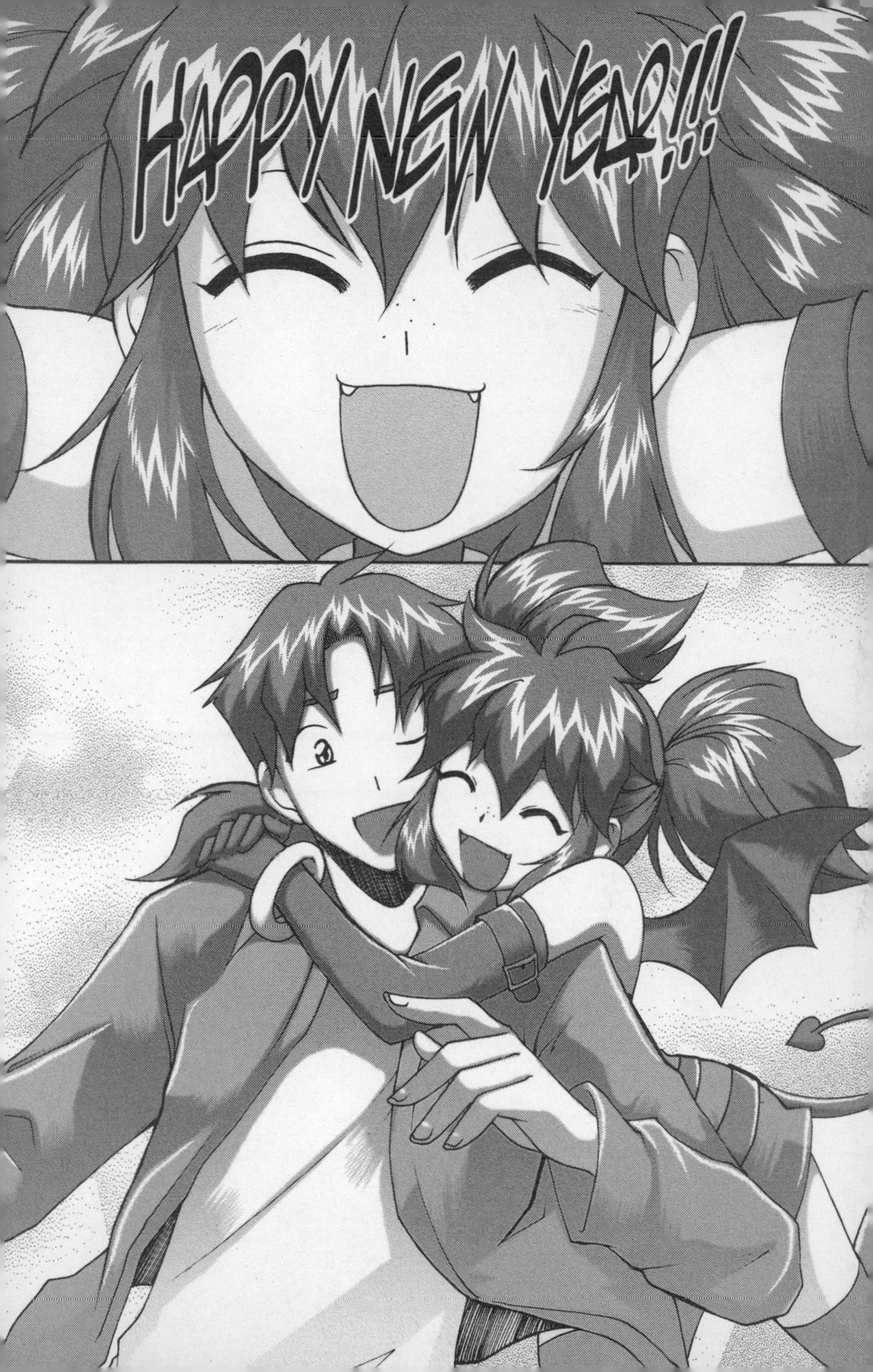
HAPPY NEW YEAR!!!

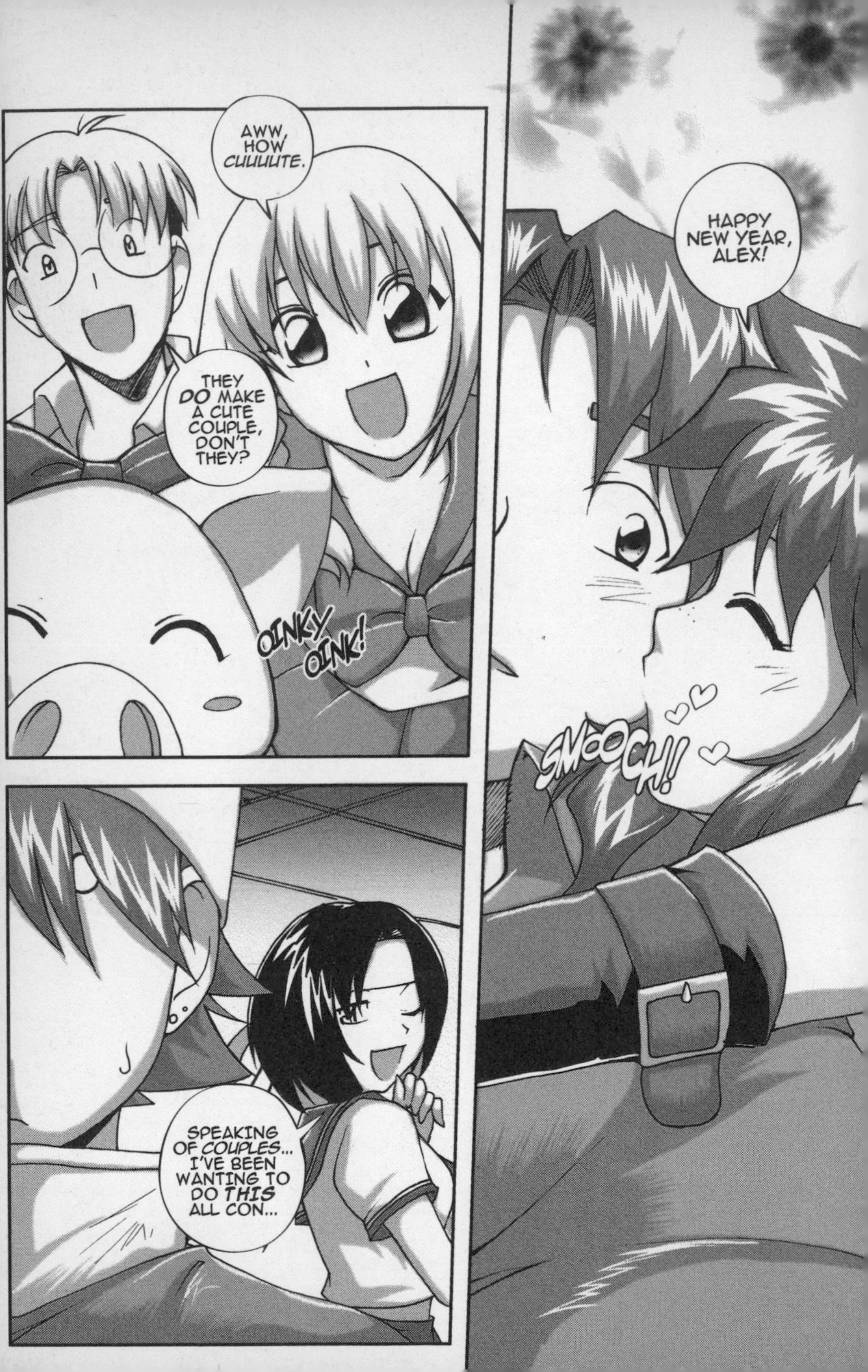
HAPPY NEW YEAR, ALEX!
SMOOCH!
AWW, HOW CUUUUTE.
THEY *DO* MAKE A CUTE COUPLE, DON'T THEY?
OINKY OINK!
SPEAKING OF *COUPLES*... I'VE BEEN WANTING TO DO ***THIS*** ALL CON...

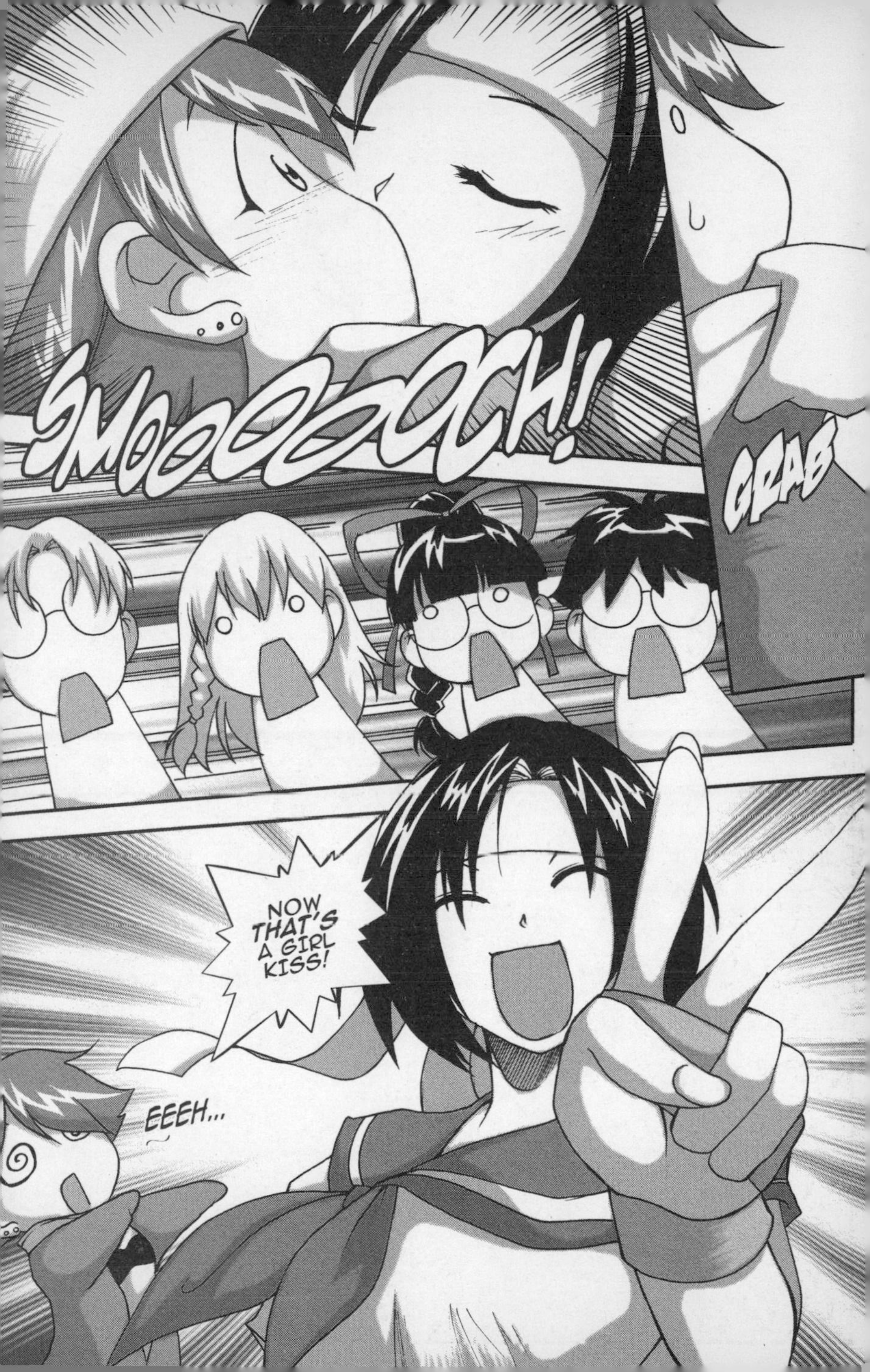
GRAB
SMOOOOOCH!
NOW THAT'S A GIRL KISS!
EEEH...

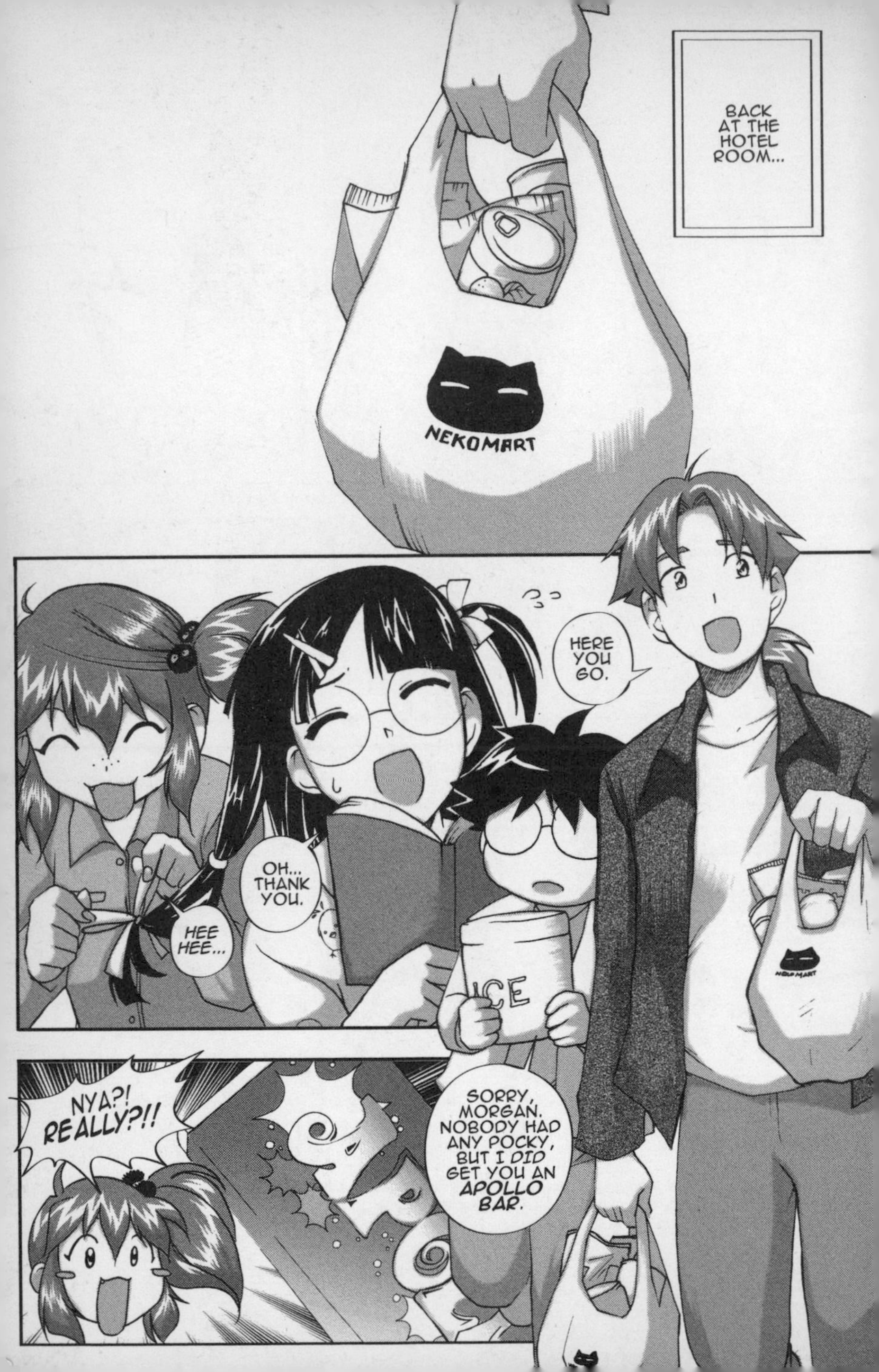
BACK AT THE HOTEL ROOM...
NEKOMART
HERE YOU GO.
OH... THANK YOU.
HEE HEE...
ICE
SORRY, MORGAN. NOBODY HAD ANY POCKY, BUT I *DID* GET YOU AN **APOLLO BAR**.
NYA?! **REALLY?!!**

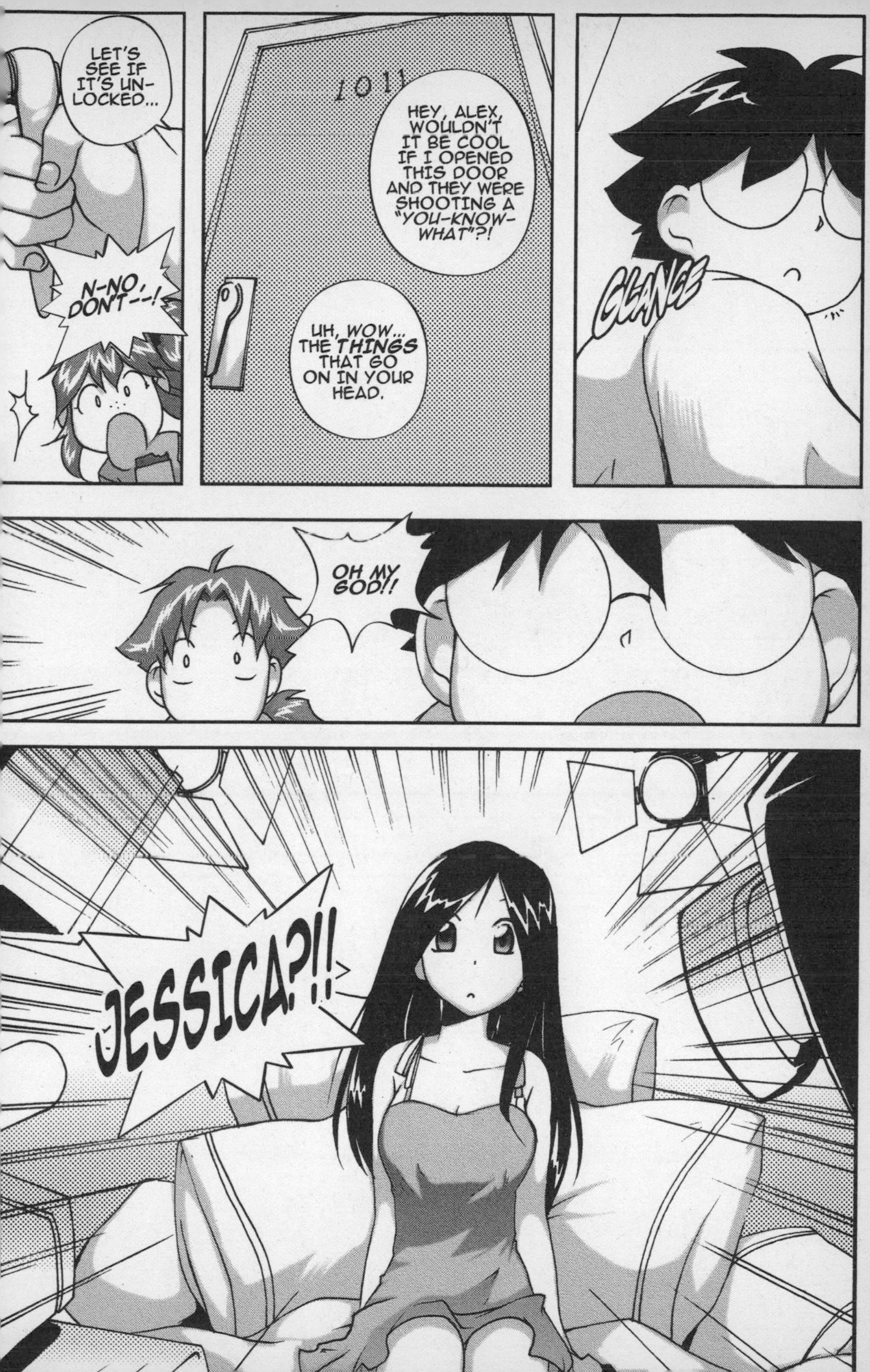
GLANCE
1011
HEY, ALEX, WOULDN'T IT BE COOL IF I OPENED THIS DOOR AND THEY WERE SHOOTING A "YOU-KNOW-WHAT"?!
UH, WOW... THE THINGS THAT GO ON IN YOUR HEAD.
LET'S SEE IF IT'S UN-LOCKED...
N-NO, DON'T--!
OH MY GOD!!
JESSICA?!!

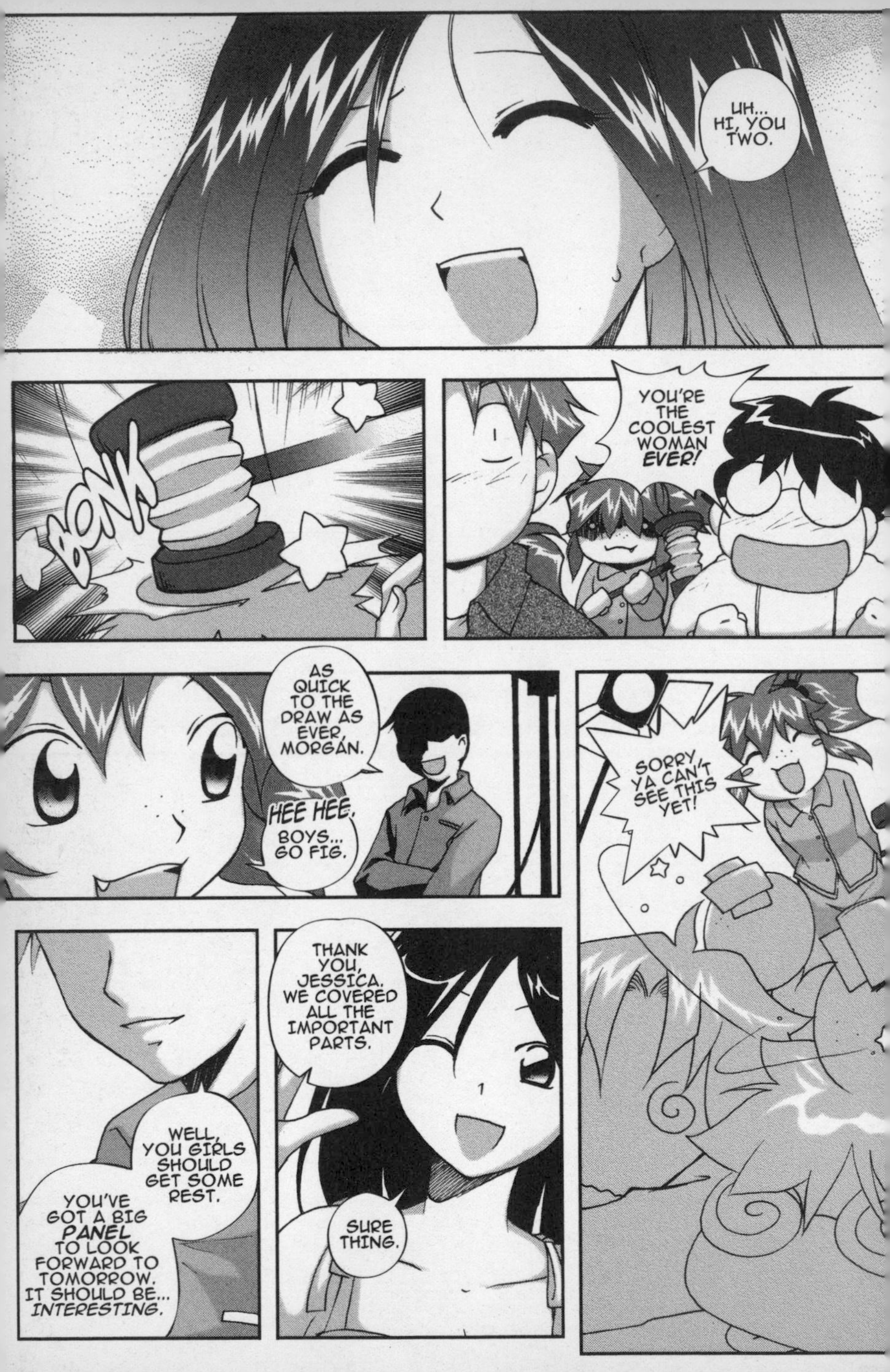
UH... HI, YOU TWO.
YOU'RE THE COOLEST WOMAN *EVER!*
BONK
SORRY, YA CAN'T SEE THIS YET!
AS QUICK TO THE DRAW AS EVER, MORGAN.
HEE HEE.
BOYS... GO FIG.
THANK YOU, JESSICA. WE COVERED ALL THE IMPORTANT PARTS.
SURE THING.
WELL, YOU GIRLS SHOULD GET SOME REST.
YOU'VE GOT A BIG *PANEL* TO LOOK FORWARD TO TOMORROW. IT SHOULD BE... *INTERESTING.*

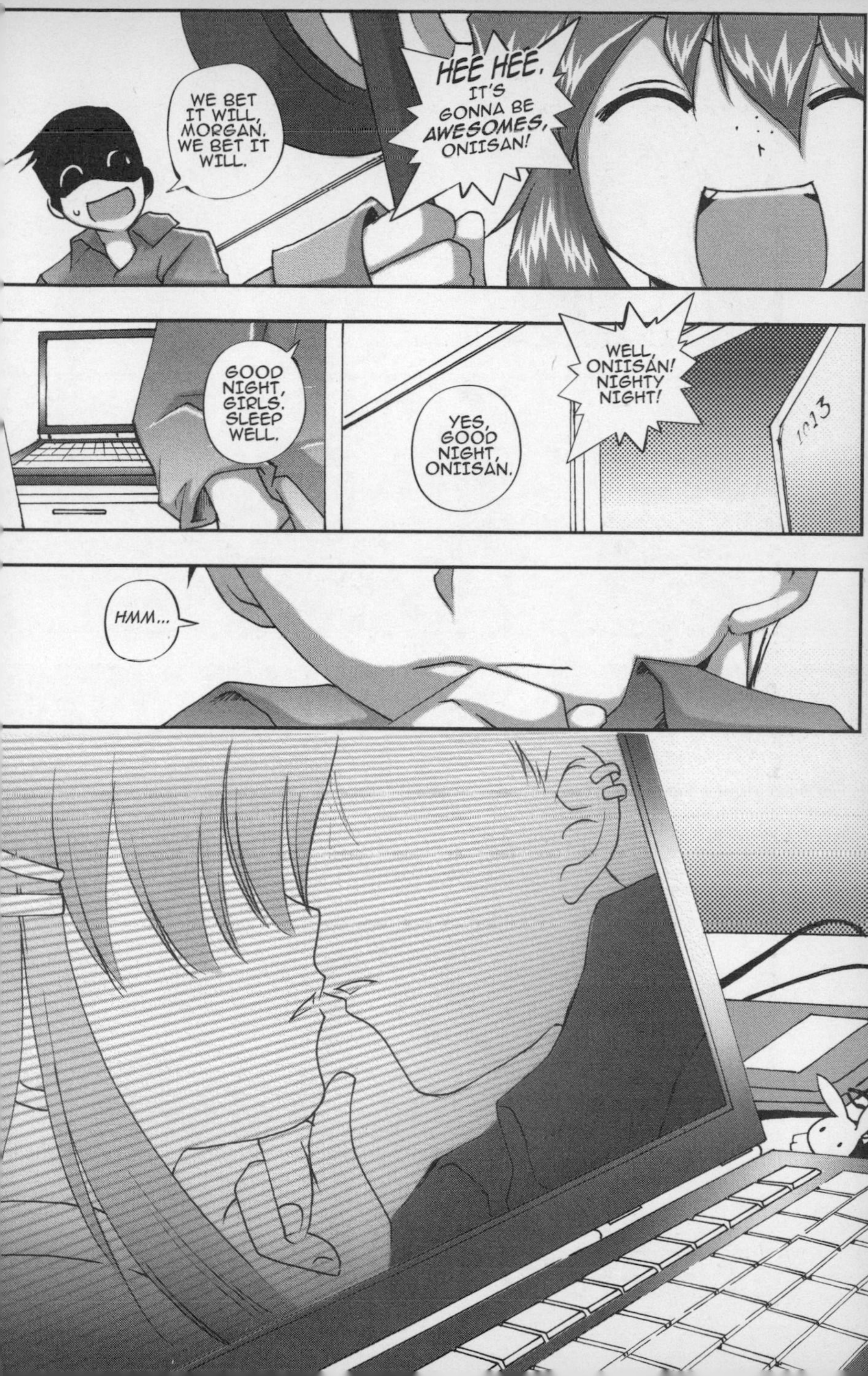
HEE HEE, IT'S GONNA BE AWESOMES, ONIISAN!
WE BET IT WILL, MORGAN. WE BET IT WILL.
WELL, ONIISAN! NIGHTY NIGHT!
1013
YES, GOOD NIGHT, ONIISAN.
GOOD NIGHT, GIRLS. SLEEP WELL.
HMM...

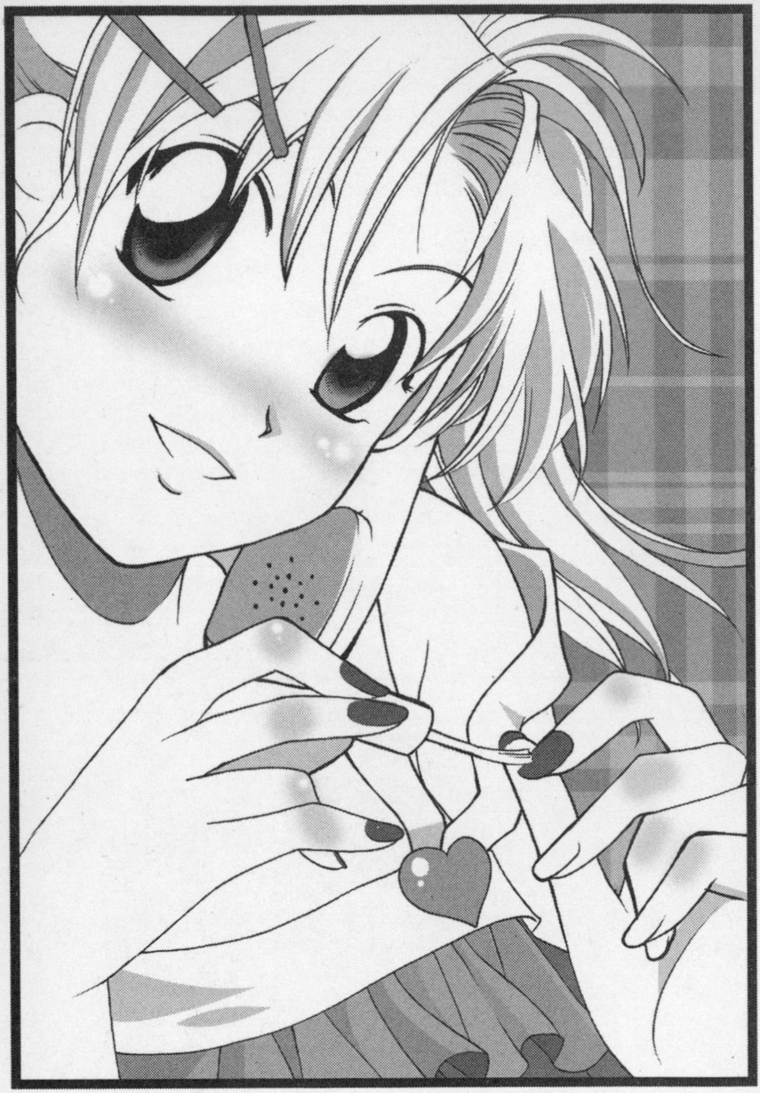

EPISODE 7:

YAOI 801

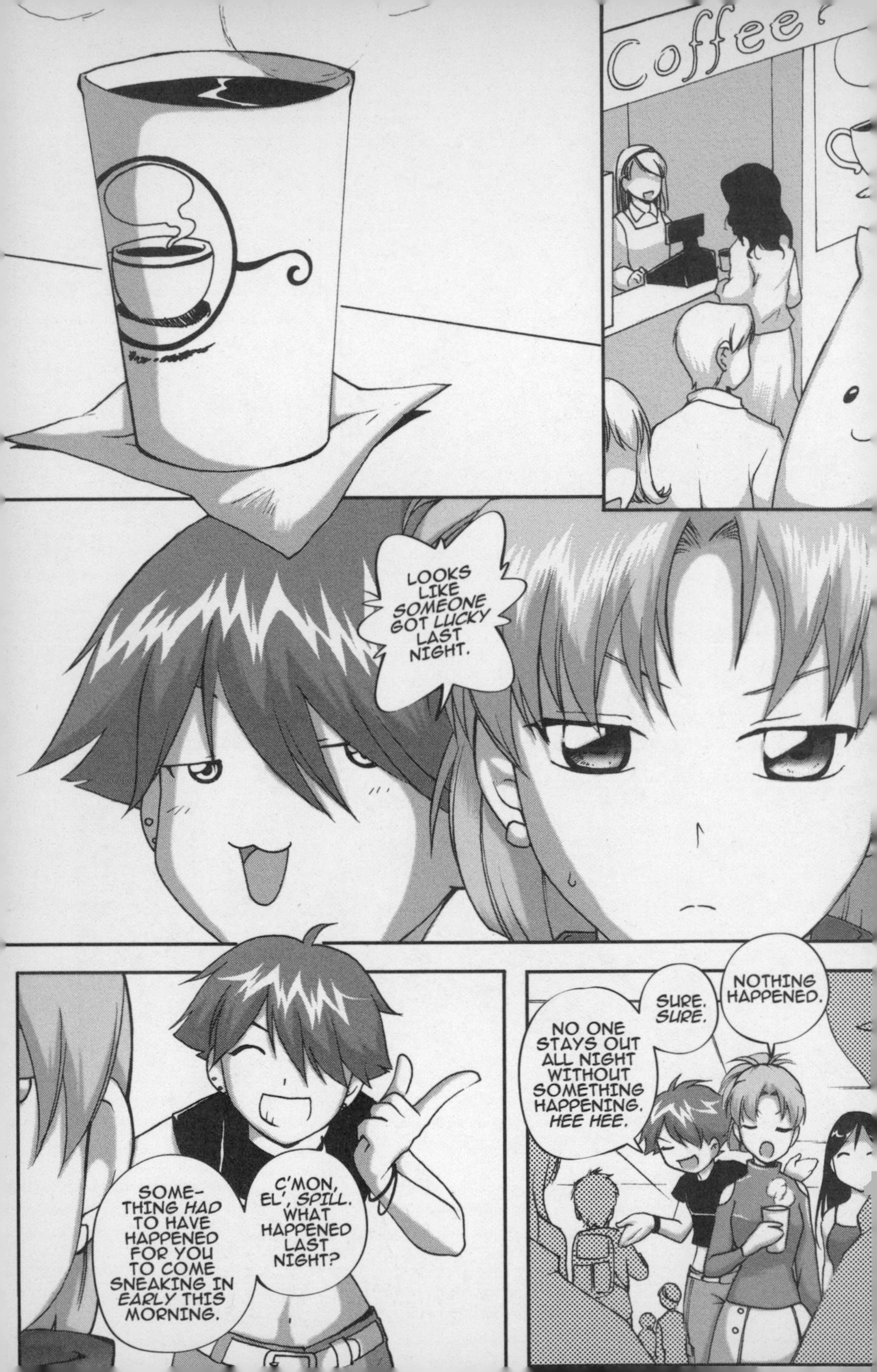
Coffee
LOOKS LIKE SOMEONE GOT *LUCKY* LAST NIGHT.
NOTHING HAPPENED.
SURE. SURE.
NO ONE STAYS OUT ALL NIGHT WITHOUT SOMETHING HAPPENING. *HEE HEE.*
C'MON, EL', *SPILL*. WHAT HAPPENED LAST NIGHT?
SOME-THING *HAD* TO HAVE HAPPENED FOR YOU TO COME SNEAKING IN *EARLY* THIS MORNING.

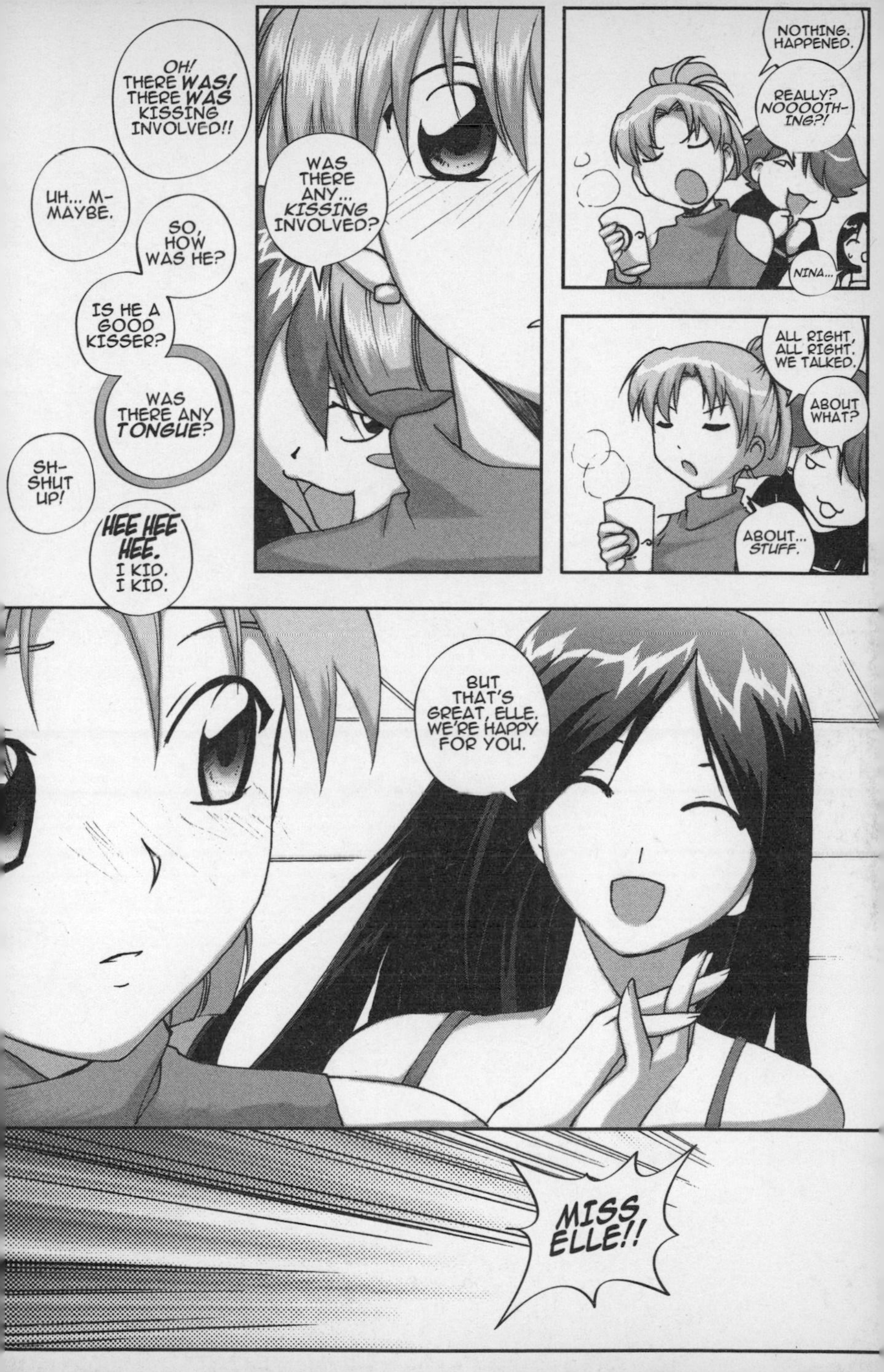
NOTHING. HAPPENED.
REALLY? NOOOOTHING?!
NINA...
ALL RIGHT, ALL RIGHT. WE TALKED.
ABOUT WHAT?
ABOUT... STUFF.
WAS THERE ANY... KISSING INVOLVED?
UH... M-MAYBE.
OH! THERE WAS! THERE WAS KISSING INVOLVED!!
SO, HOW WAS HE?
IS HE A GOOD KISSER?
WAS THERE ANY TONGUE?
SH-SHUT UP!
HEE HEE HEE. I KID. I KID.
BUT THAT'S GREAT, ELLE. WE'RE HAPPY FOR YOU.
MISS ELLE!!

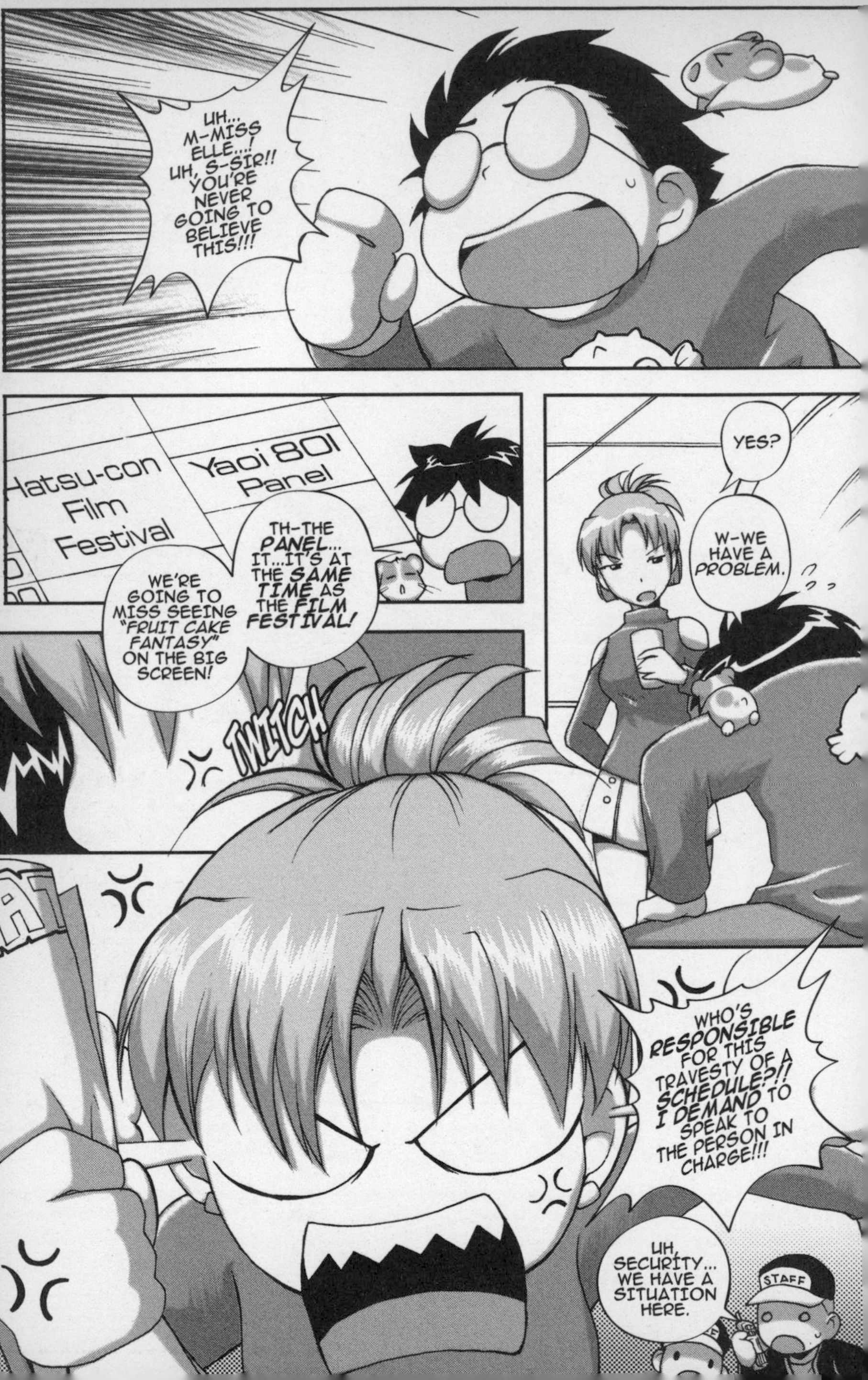
UH... M-MISS ELLE...! UH, S-SIR!! YOU'RE NEVER GOING TO BELIEVE THIS!!!
YES?
W-WE HAVE A PROBLEM.
Hatsu-con Film Festival
Yaoi 801 Panel
TH-THE PANEL... IT...IT'S AT THE SAME TIME AS THE FILM FESTIVAL!
WE'RE GOING TO MISS SEEING "FRUIT CAKE FANTASY" ON THE BIG SCREEN!
TWITCH
WHO'S RESPONSIBLE FOR THIS TRAVESTY OF A SCHEDULE?!! I DEMAND TO SPEAK TO THE PERSON IN CHARGE!!!
UH, SECURITY... WE HAVE A SITUATION HERE.
STAFF

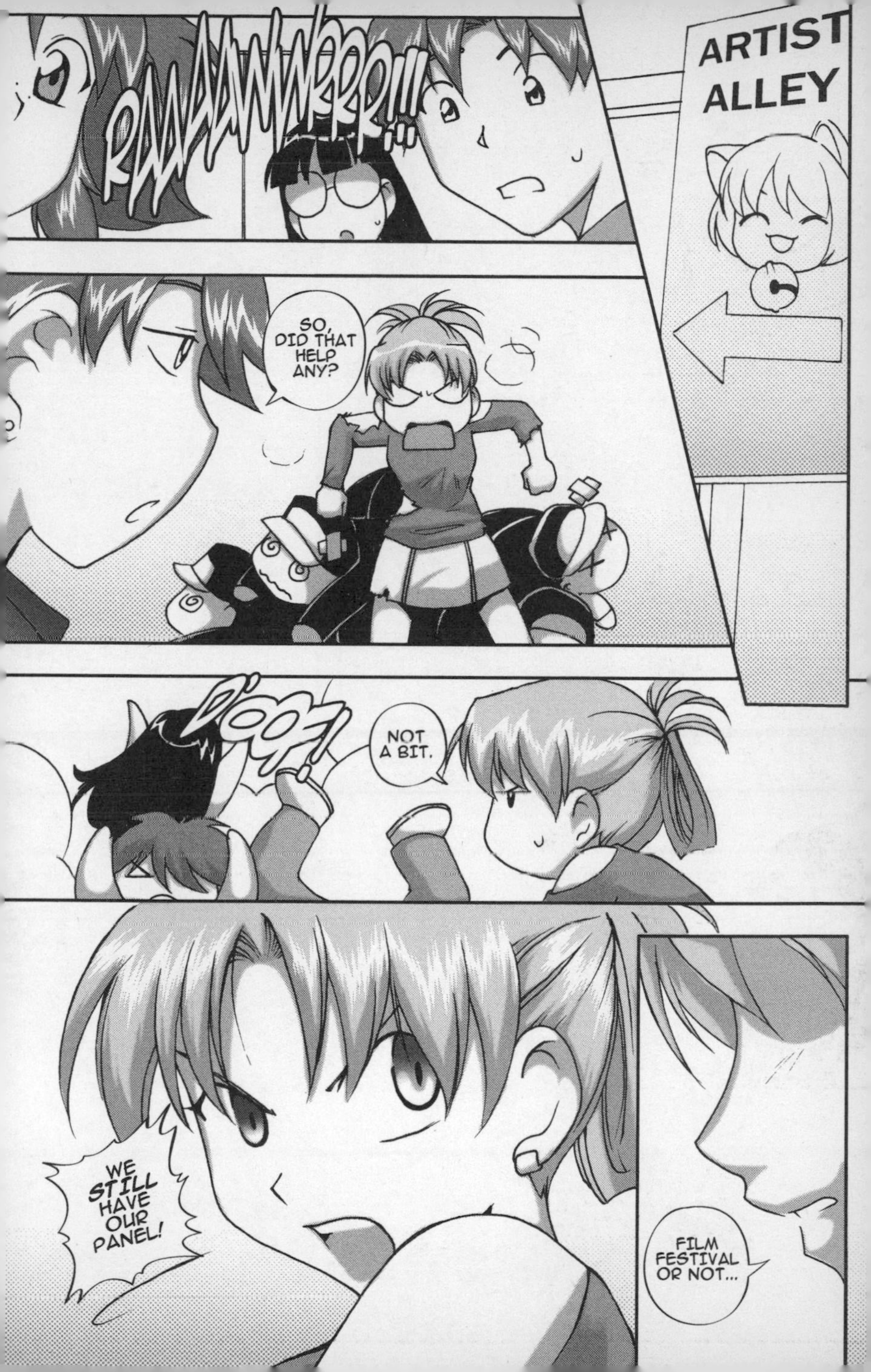
ARTIST ALLEY
RAAAAWKRR!!!
SO, DID THAT HELP ANY?
NOT A BIT.
D'OOF!
FILM FESTIVAL OR NOT...
WE STILL HAVE OUR PANEL!

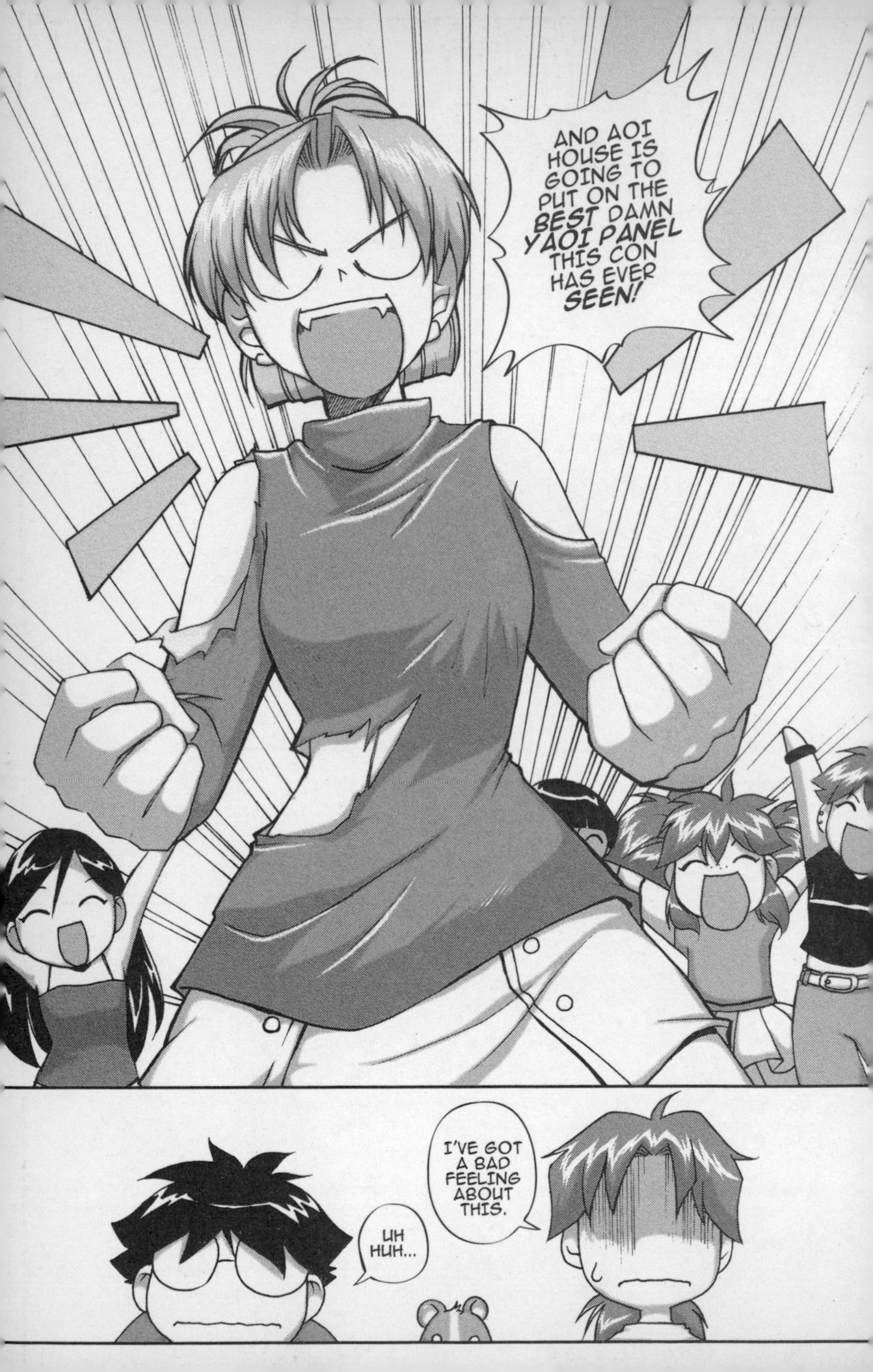
AND AOI HOUSE IS GOING TO PUT ON THE BEST DAMN YAOI PANEL THIS CON HAS EVER SEEN!
I'VE GOT A BAD FEELING ABOUT THIS.
UH HUH...

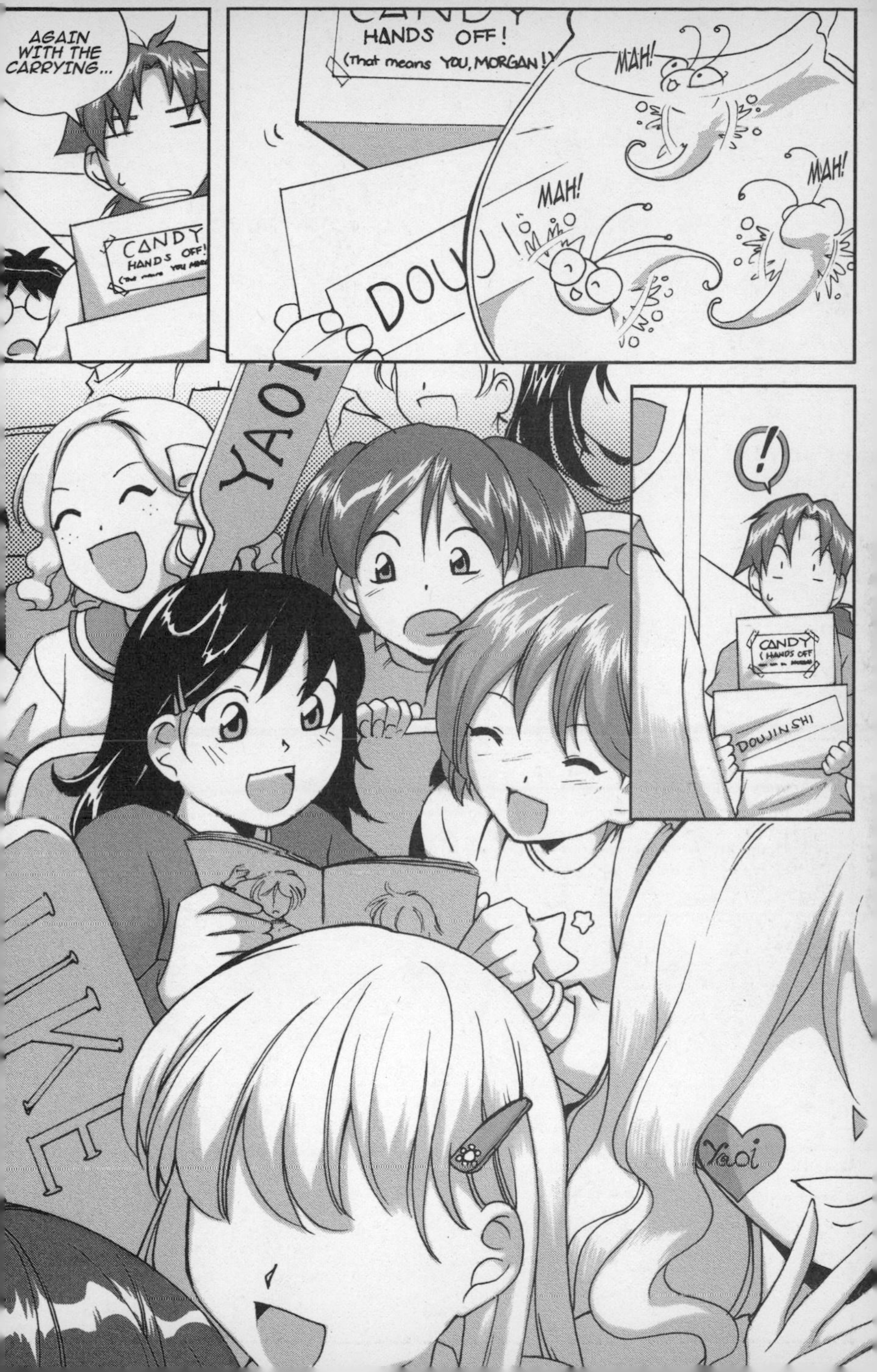
HANDS OFF!
(That means YOU, MORGAN!)
MAH!
MAH!
MAH!
DOUJ
AGAIN WITH THE CARRYING...
CANDY
HANDS OFF!
!
CANDY
HANDS OFF
DOUJINSHI
YAOI
Yaoi

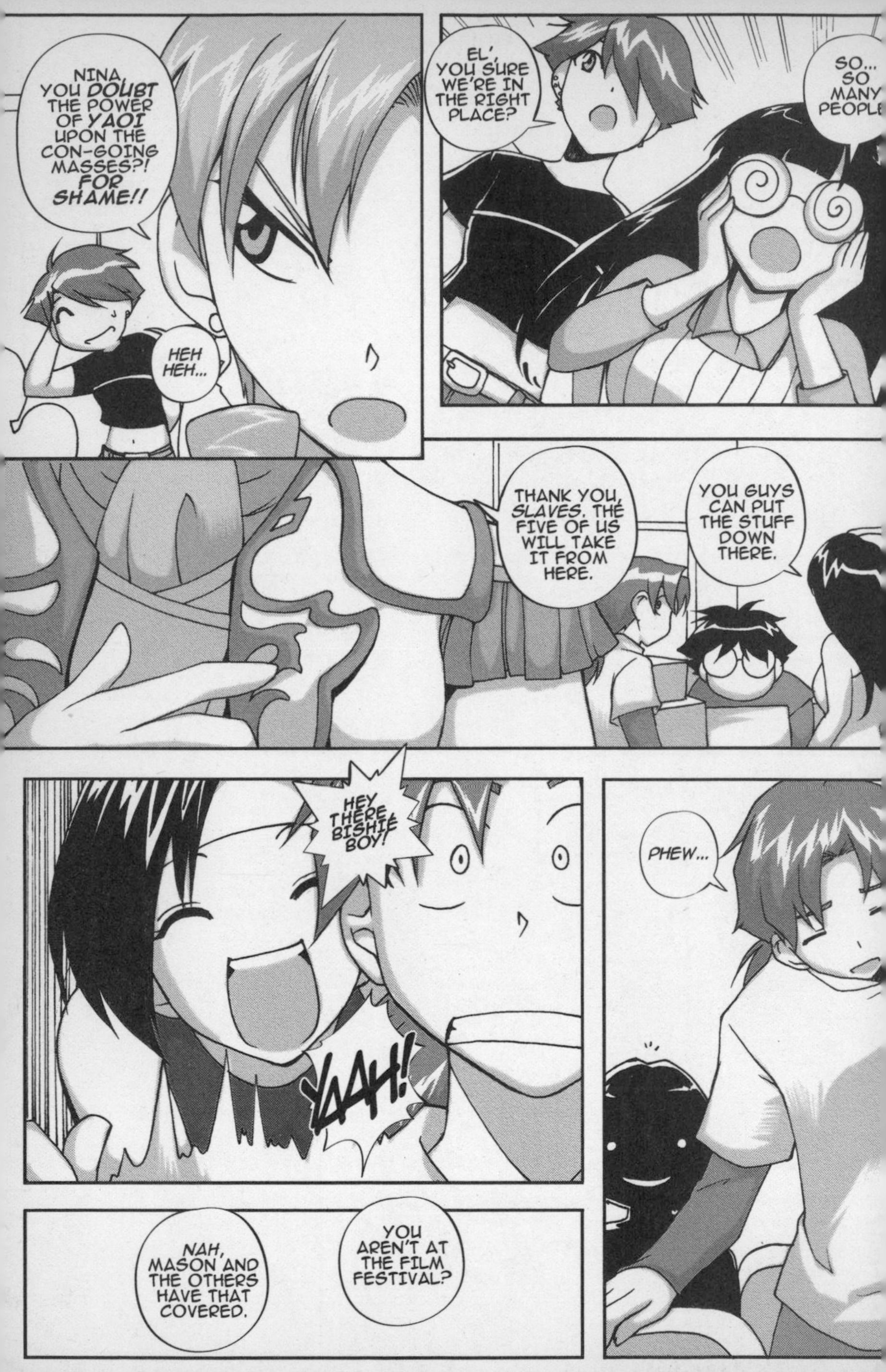
SO... SO MANY PEOPLE
EL', YOU SURE WE'RE IN THE RIGHT PLACE?
NINA, YOU DOUBT THE POWER OF YAOI UPON THE CON-GOING MASSES?! FOR SHAME!!
HEH HEH...
YOU GUYS CAN PUT THE STUFF DOWN THERE.
THANK YOU, SLAVES. THE FIVE OF US WILL TAKE IT FROM HERE.
PHEW...
HEY THERE BISHIE BOY!
YAAH!
YOU AREN'T AT THE FILM FESTIVAL?
NAH, MASON AND THE OTHERS HAVE THAT COVERED.

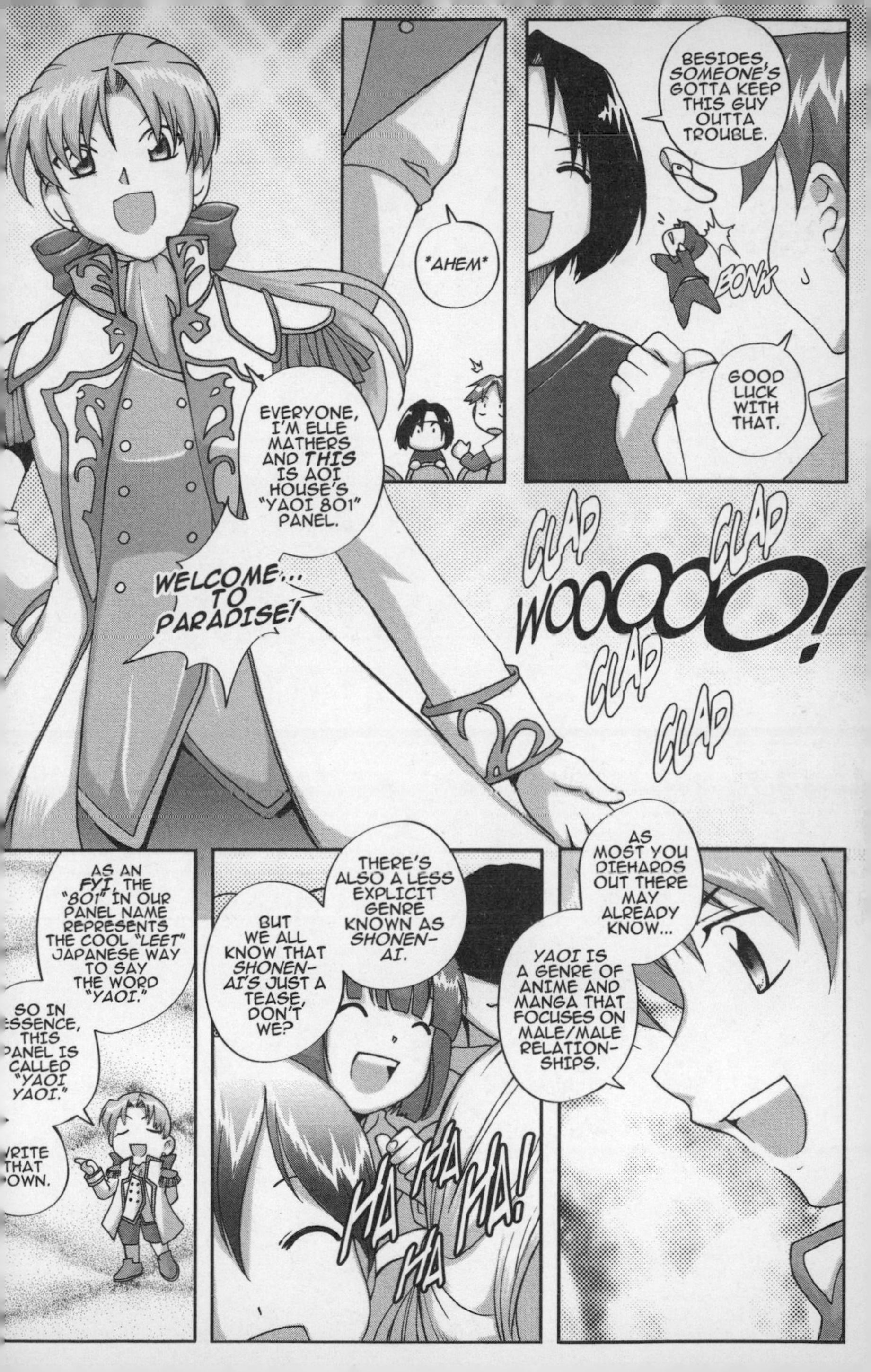
BESIDES, SOMEONE'S GOTTA KEEP THIS GUY OUTTA TROUBLE.
BONK
GOOD LUCK WITH THAT.
AHEM
EVERYONE, I'M ELLE MATHERS AND THIS IS AOI HOUSE'S "YAOI 801" PANEL.
WELCOME... TO PARADISE!
CLAP CLAP
WOOOOOO!
CLAP
CLAP
AS MOST YOU DIEHARDS OUT THERE MAY ALREADY KNOW...
YAOI IS A GENRE OF ANIME AND MANGA THAT FOCUSES ON MALE/MALE RELATION-SHIPS.
THERE'S ALSO A LESS EXPLICIT GENRE KNOWN AS SHONEN-AI.
BUT WE ALL KNOW THAT SHONEN-AI'S JUST A TEASE, DON'T WE?
HA HA HA HA HA!
AS AN FYI, THE "801" IN OUR PANEL NAME REPRESENTS THE COOL "LEET" JAPANESE WAY TO SAY THE WORD "YAOI."
SO IN SSENCE, THIS PANEL IS CALLED "YAOI YAOI."
RITE THAT OWN.

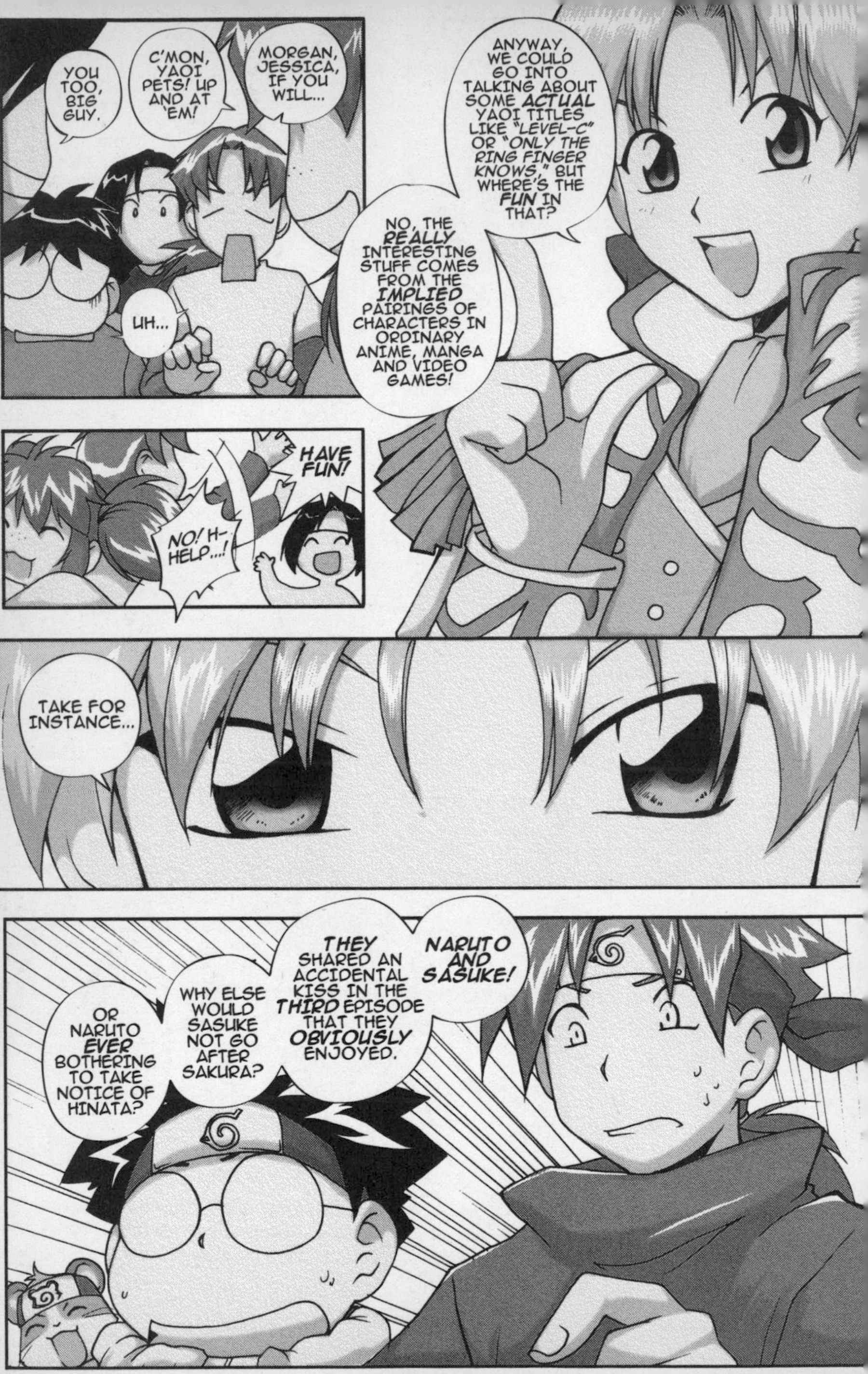

ANYWAY, WE COULD GO INTO TALKING ABOUT SOME ACTUAL YAOI TITLES LIKE "LEVEL-C" OR "ONLY THE RING FINGER KNOWS," BUT WHERE'S THE FUN IN THAT?
NO, THE REALLY INTERESTING STUFF COMES FROM THE IMPLIED PAIRINGS OF CHARACTERS IN ORDINARY ANIME, MANGA AND VIDEO GAMES!
MORGAN, JESSICA, IF YOU WILL...
C'MON, YAOI PETS! UP AND AT 'EM!
YOU TOO, BIG GUY.
UH...
HAVE FUN!
NO! H-HELP...!
TAKE FOR INSTANCE...
NARUTO AND SASUKE!
THEY SHARED AN ACCIDENTAL KISS IN THE THIRD EPISODE THAT THEY OBVIOUSLY ENJOYED.
WHY ELSE WOULD SASUKE NOT GO AFTER SAKURA?
OR NARUTO EVER BOTHERING TO TAKE NOTICE OF HINATA?

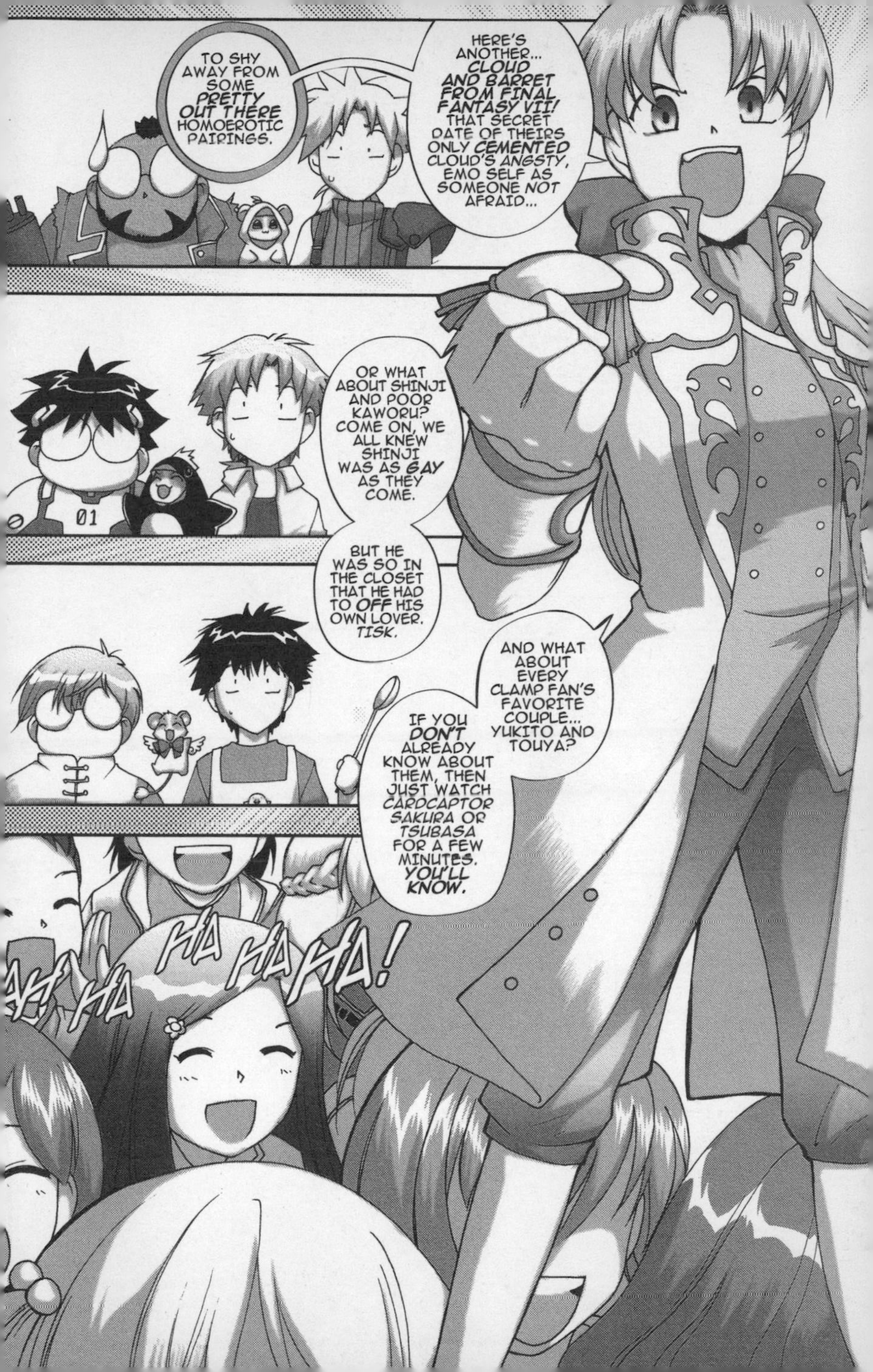
HERE'S ANOTHER... CLOUD AND BARRET FROM FINAL FANTASY VII! THAT SECRET DATE OF THEIRS ONLY CEMENTED CLOUD'S ANGSTY, EMO SELF AS SOMEONE NOT AFRAID...
TO SHY AWAY FROM SOME PRETTY OUT THERE HOMOEROTIC PAIRINGS.
01
OR WHAT ABOUT SHINJI AND POOR KAWORU? COME ON, WE ALL KNEW SHINJI WAS AS GAY AS THEY COME.
BUT HE WAS SO IN THE CLOSET THAT HE HAD TO OFF HIS OWN LOVER. TISK.
AND WHAT ABOUT EVERY CLAMP FAN'S FAVORITE COUPLE... YUKITO AND TOUYA?
IF YOU DON'T ALREADY KNOW ABOUT THEM, THEN JUST WATCH CARDCAPTOR SAKURA OR TSUBASA FOR A FEW MINUTES. YOU'LL KNOW.
HA HA HA HAHA!

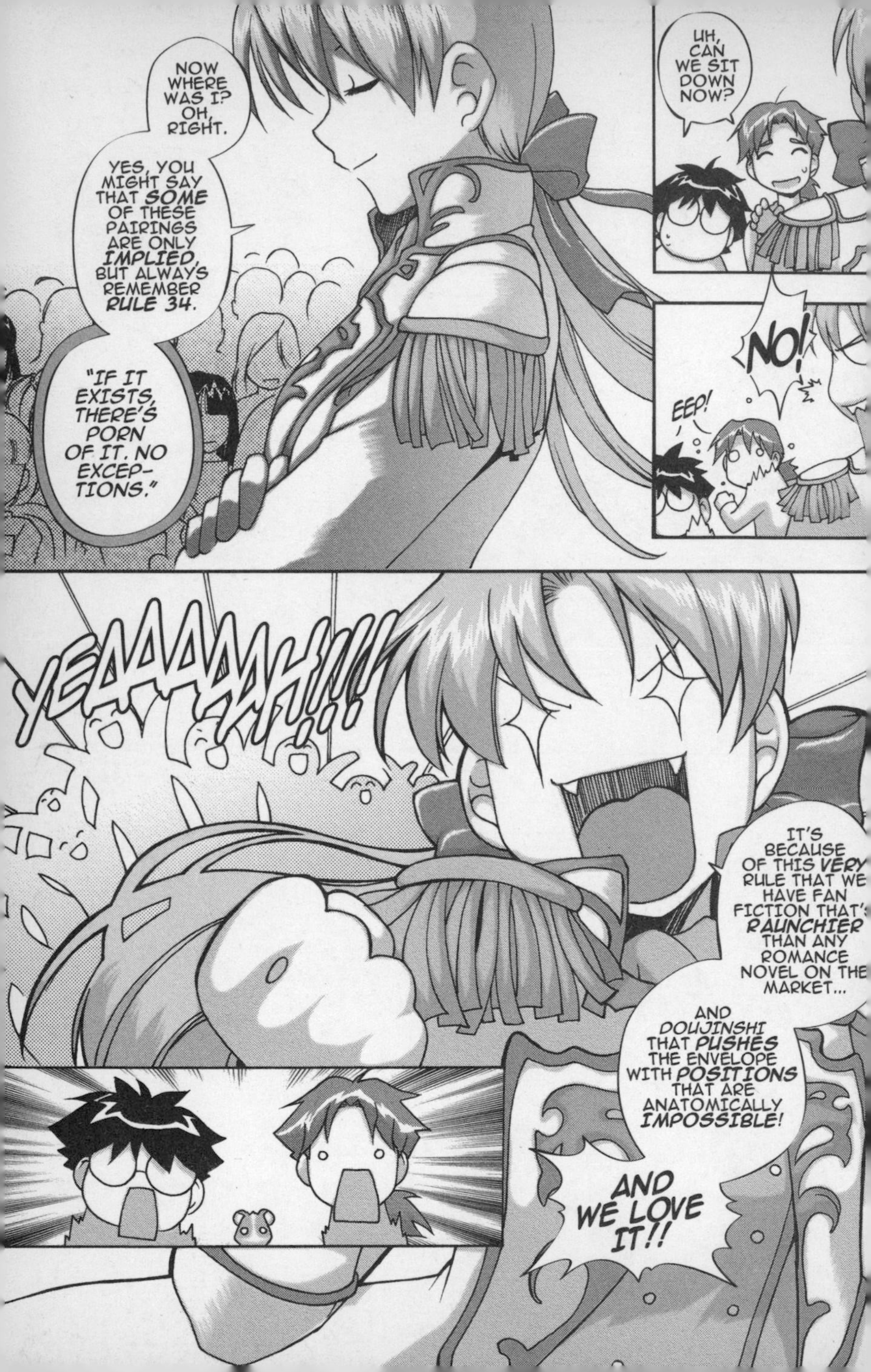
UH, CAN WE SIT DOWN NOW?
NO!
EEP!
NOW WHERE WAS I? OH, RIGHT.
YES, YOU MIGHT SAY THAT **SOME** OF THESE PAIRINGS ARE ONLY **IMPLIED**, BUT ALWAY'S REMEMBER **RULE 34**.
"IF IT EXISTS, THERE'S PORN OF IT. NO EXCEP-TIONS."
YEAAAAAAH!!!!
IT'S BECAUSE OF THIS **VERY** RULE THAT WE HAVE FAN FICTION THAT'S **RAUNCHIER** THAN ANY ROMANCE NOVEL ON THE MARKET...
AND **DOUJINSHI** THAT **PUSHES** THE ENVELOPE WITH **POSITIONS** THAT ARE ANATOMICALLY **IMPOSSIBLE**!
AND WE LOVE IT!!

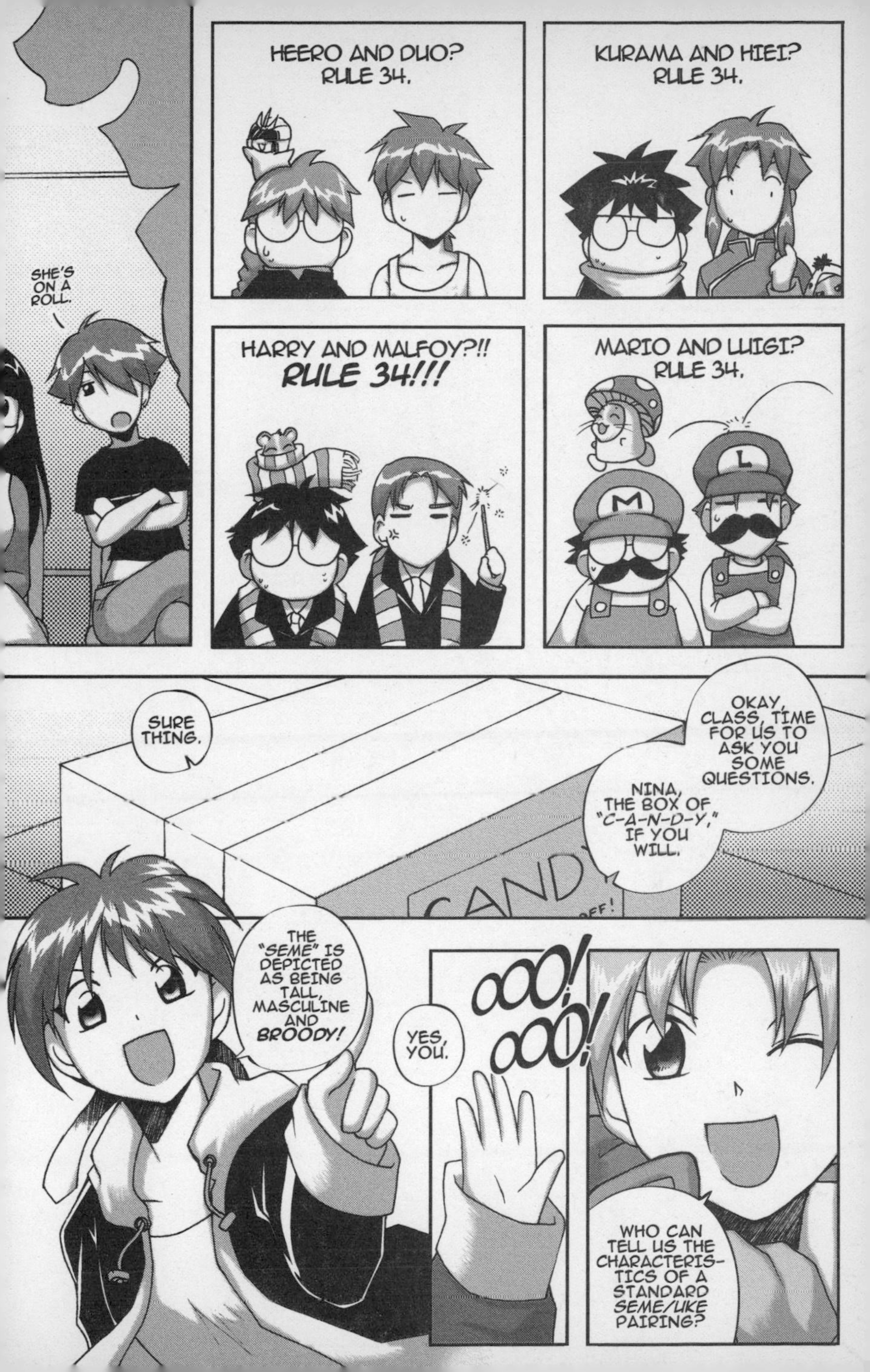
KURAMA AND HIEI? RULE 34.
HEERO AND DUO? RULE 34.
MARIO AND LUIGI? RULE 34.
HARRY AND MALFOY?!! RULE 34!!!
SHE'S ON A ROLL.
OKAY, CLASS, TIME FOR US TO ASK YOU SOME QUESTIONS.
NINA, THE BOX OF "C-A-N-D-Y," IF YOU WILL.
SURE THING.
CANDY
WHO CAN TELL US THE CHARACTERIS-TICS OF A STANDARD SEME/UKE PAIRING?
OOO! OOO!
YES, YOU.
THE "SEME" IS DEPICTED AS BEING TALL, MASCULINE AND BROODY!

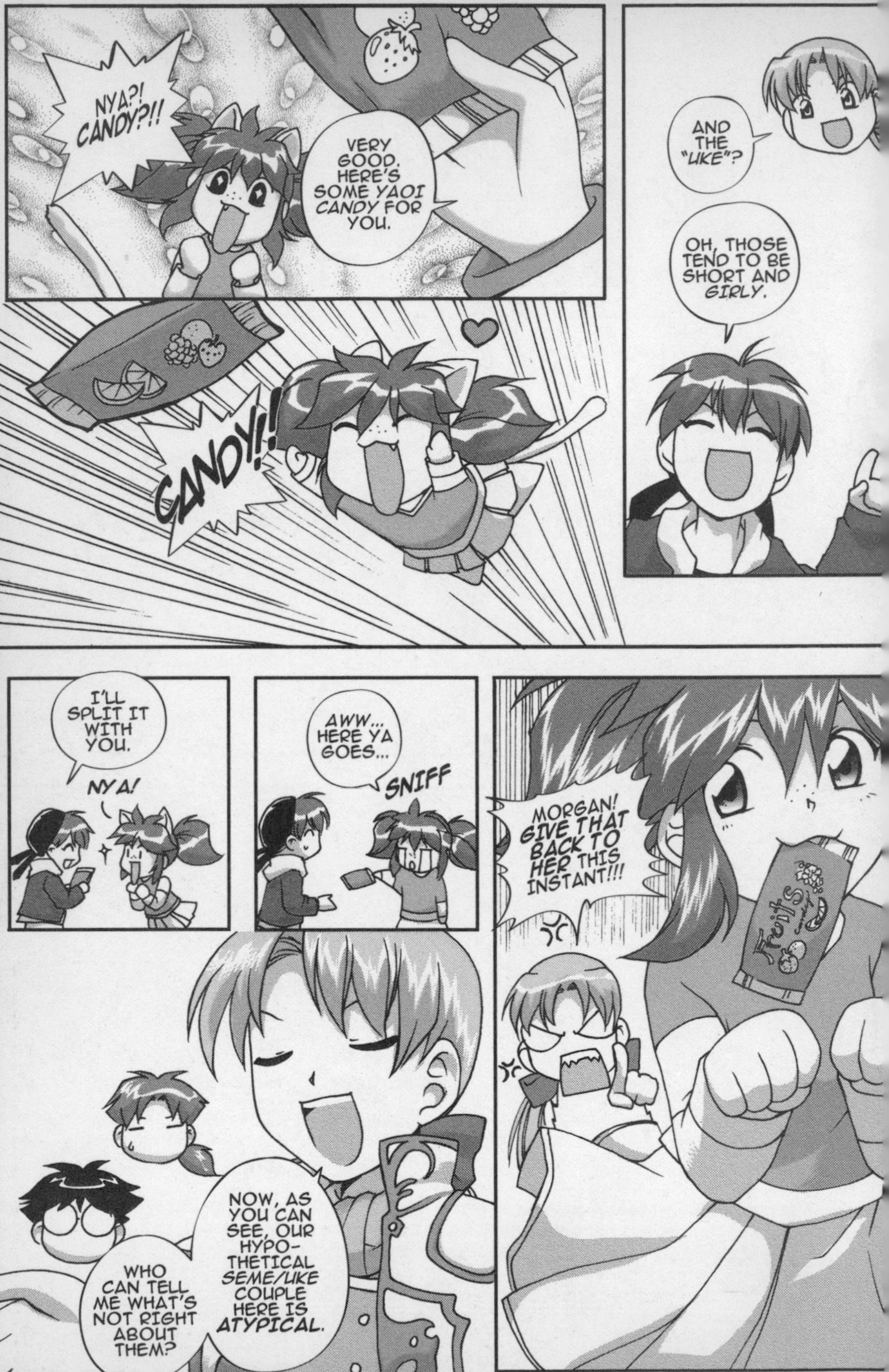
AND THE "UKE"?
OH, THOSE TEND TO BE SHORT AND GIRLY.
VERY GOOD. HERE'S SOME YAOI CANDY FOR YOU.
NYA?! CANDY?!!
CANDY!!
MORGAN! GIVE THAT BACK TO HER THIS INSTANT!!!
AWW... HERE YA GOES...
SNIFF
I'LL SPLIT IT WITH YOU.
NYA!
NOW, AS YOU CAN SEE, OUR HYPOTHETICAL SEME/UKE COUPLE HERE IS ATYPICAL.
WHO CAN TELL ME WHAT'S NOT RIGHT ABOUT THEM?

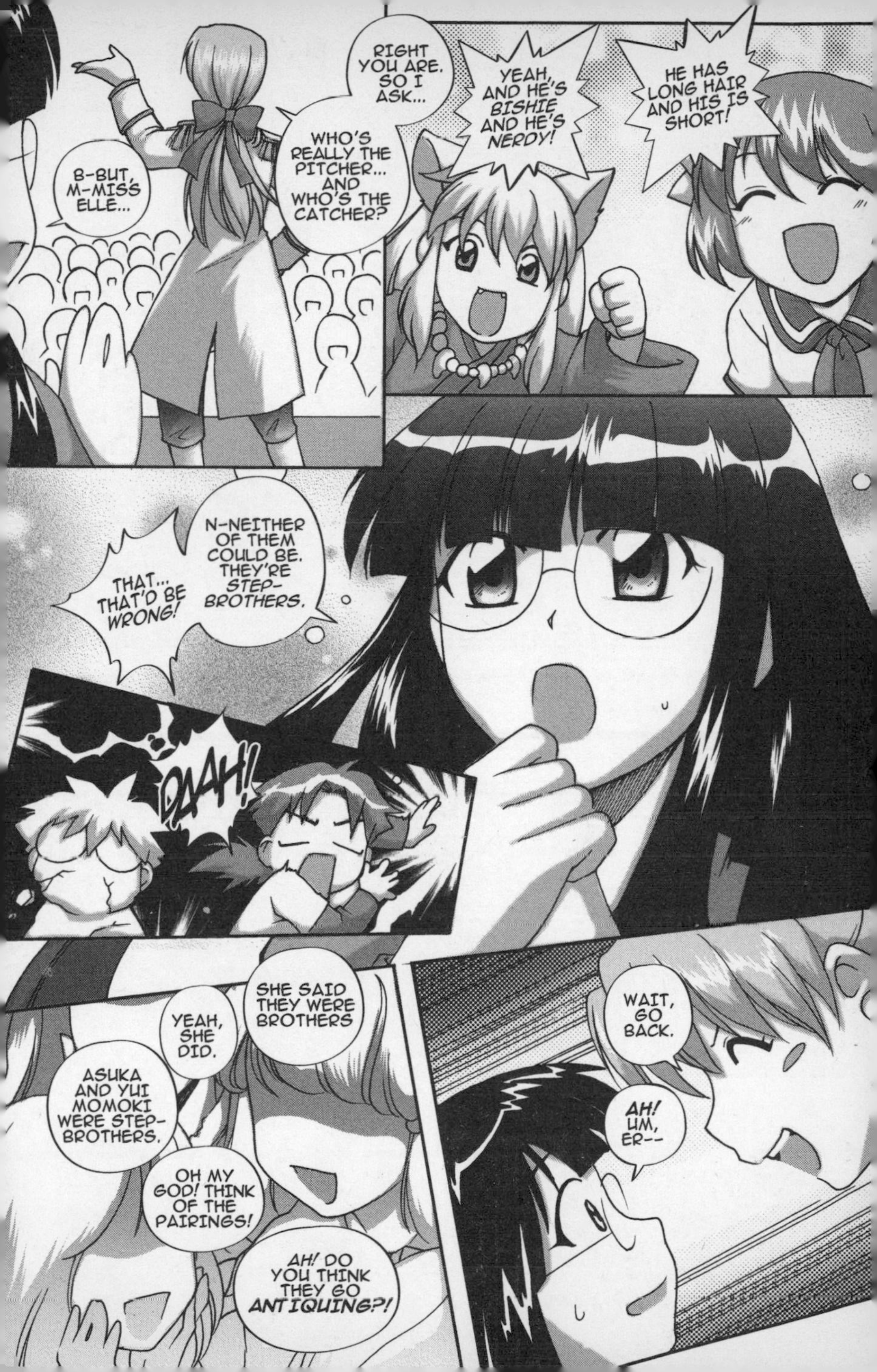
HE HAS LONG HAIR AND HIS IS SHORT!
YEAH, AND HE'S BISHIE AND HE'S NERDY!
RIGHT YOU ARE. SO I ASK...
WHO'S REALLY THE PITCHER... AND WHO'S THE CATCHER?
B-BUT, M-MISS ELLE...
N-NEITHER OF THEM COULD BE. THEY'RE STEP-BROTHERS.
THAT... THAT'D BE WRONG!
DAAH!
WAIT, GO BACK.
AH! UM, ER--
SHE SAID THEY WERE BROTHERS
YEAH, SHE DID.
ASUKA AND YUI MOMOKI WERE STEP-BROTHERS.
OH MY GOD! THINK OF THE PAIRINGS!
AH! DO YOU THINK THEY GO ANTIQUING?!

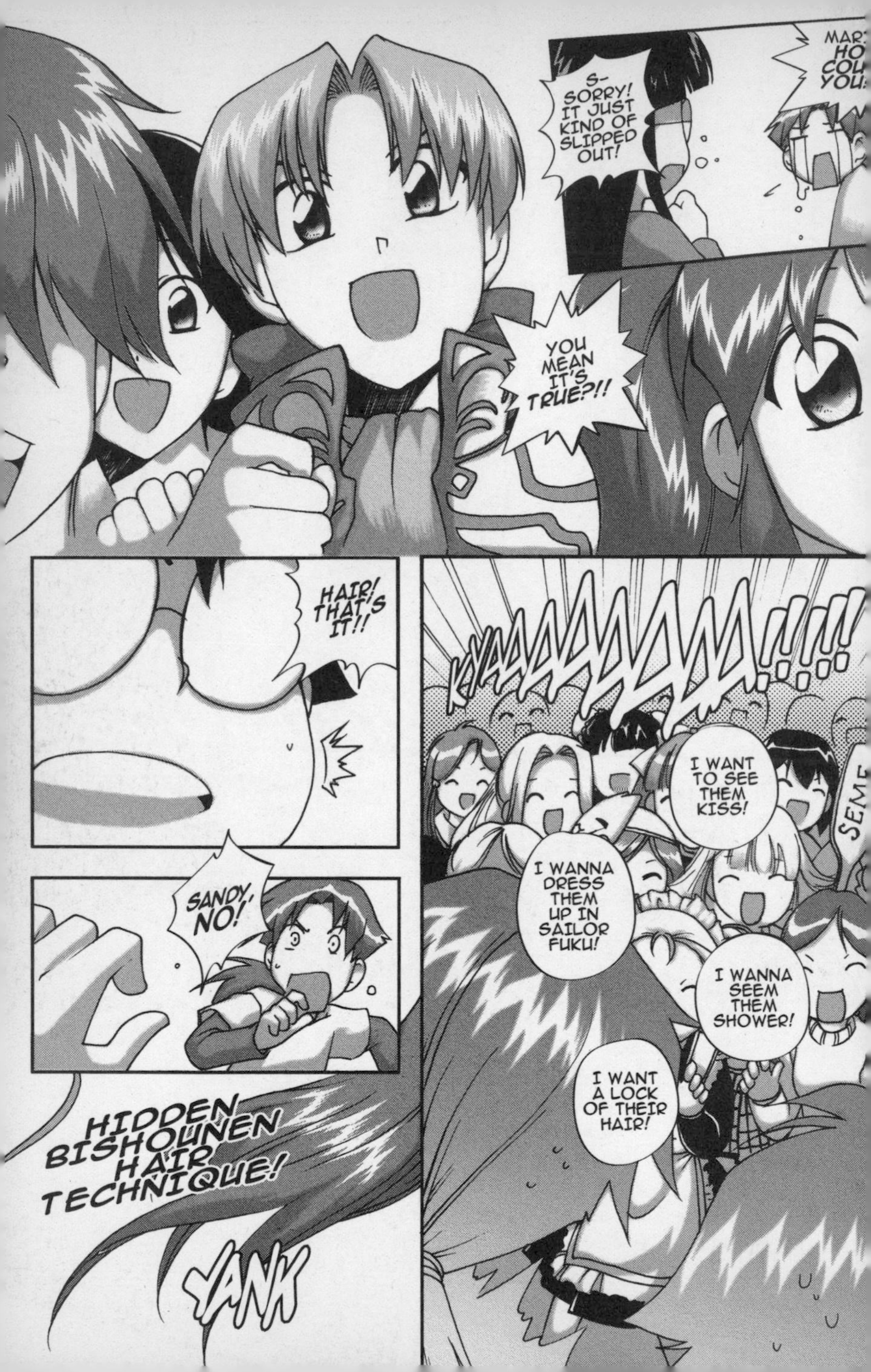

MAR? HO COU YOU?
S-SORRY! IT JUST KIND OF SLIPPED OUT!
YOU MEAN IT'S TRUE?!!
KYAAAAAAAAAA!!!!!
SEME
I WANT TO SEE THEM KISS!
I WANNA DRESS THEM UP IN SAILOR FUKU!
I WANNA SEEM THEM SHOWER!
I WANT A LOCK OF THEIR HAIR!
HAIR! THAT'S IT!!
SANDY, NO!
HIDDEN BISHOUNEN HAIR TECHNIQUE!
YANK

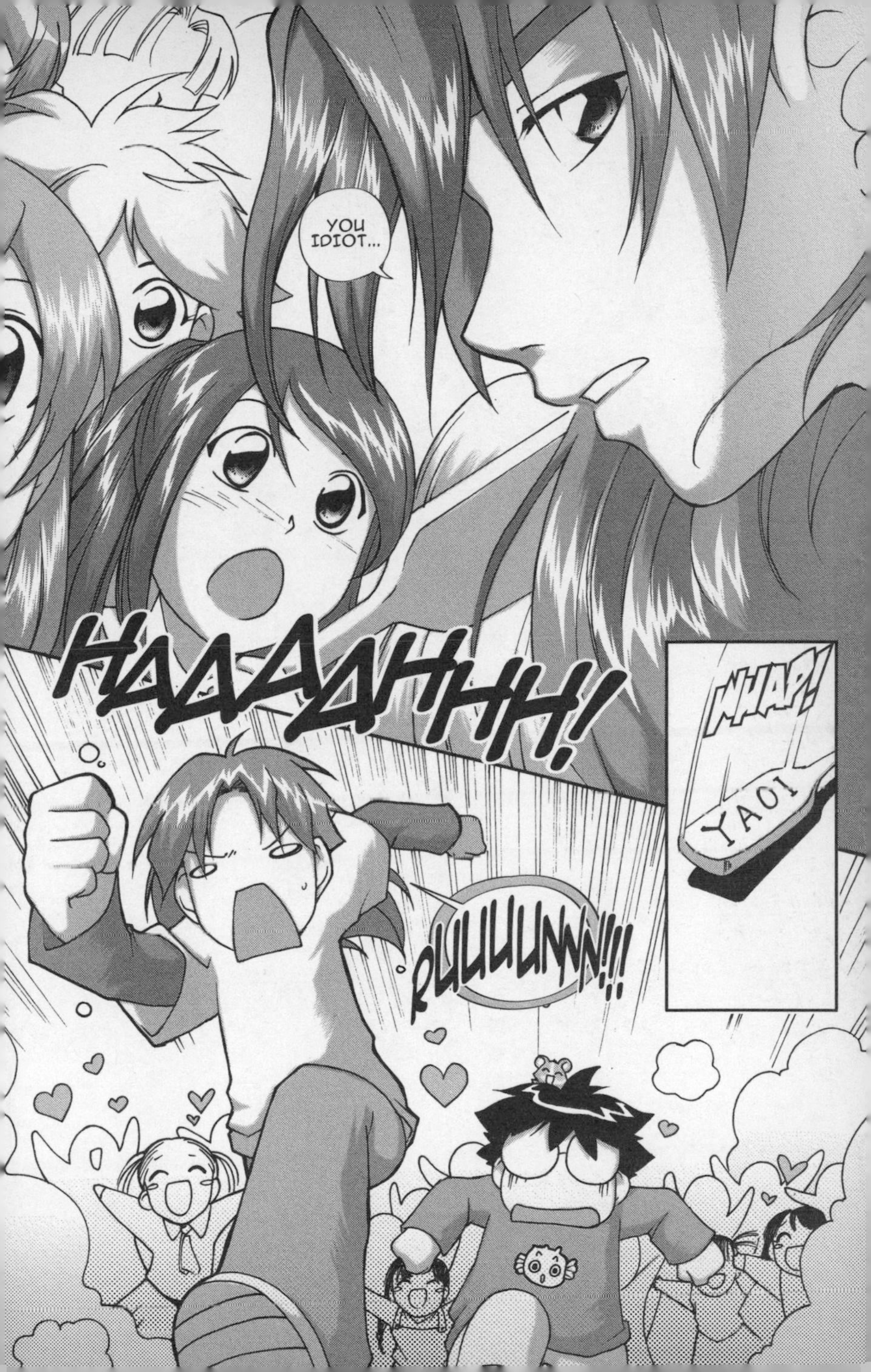
YOU IDIOT...
HAAAHHH!
WHAP!
YAOI
RUUUUNNN!!!

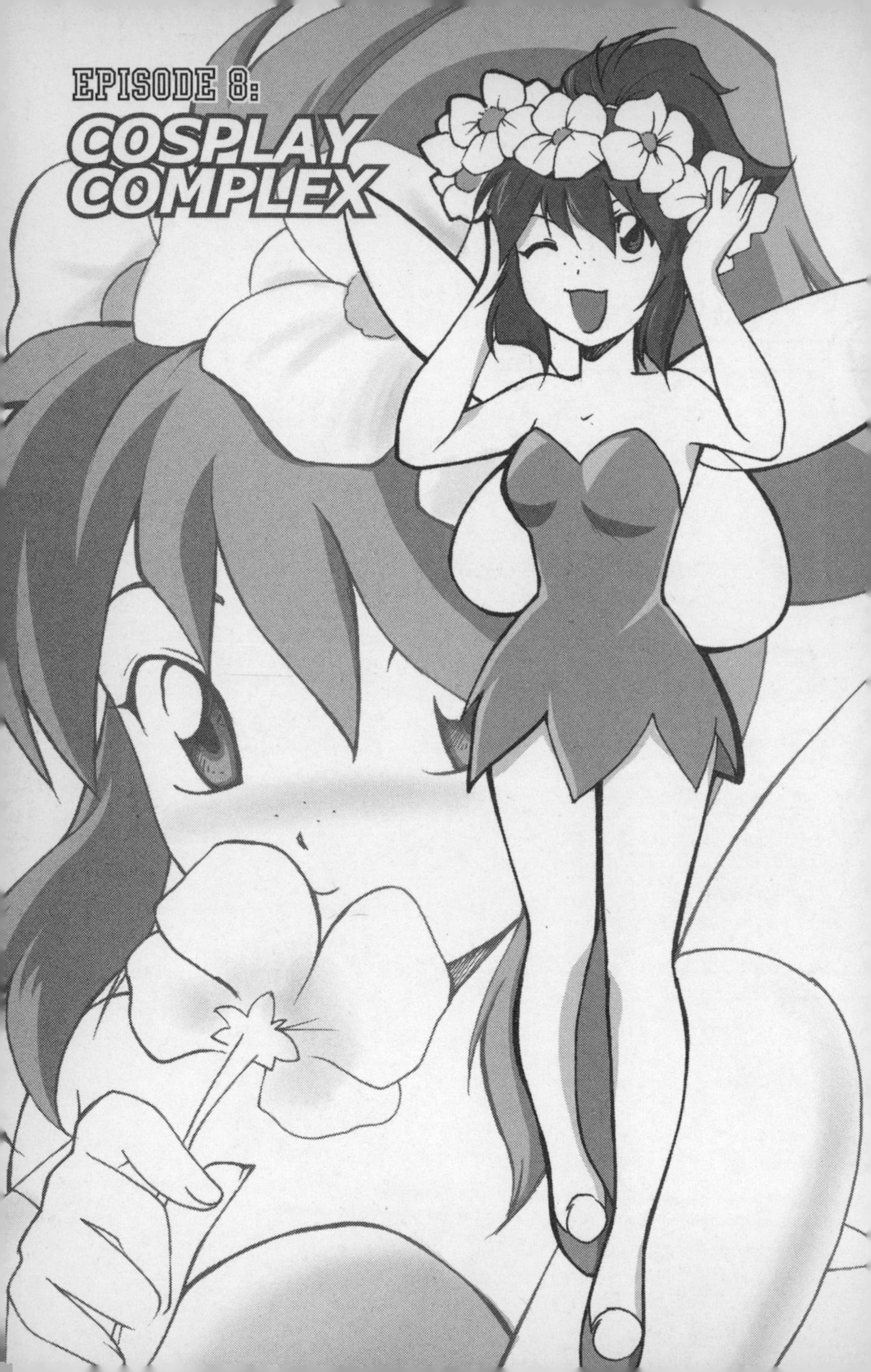
EPISODE 8:
COSPLAY COMPLEX

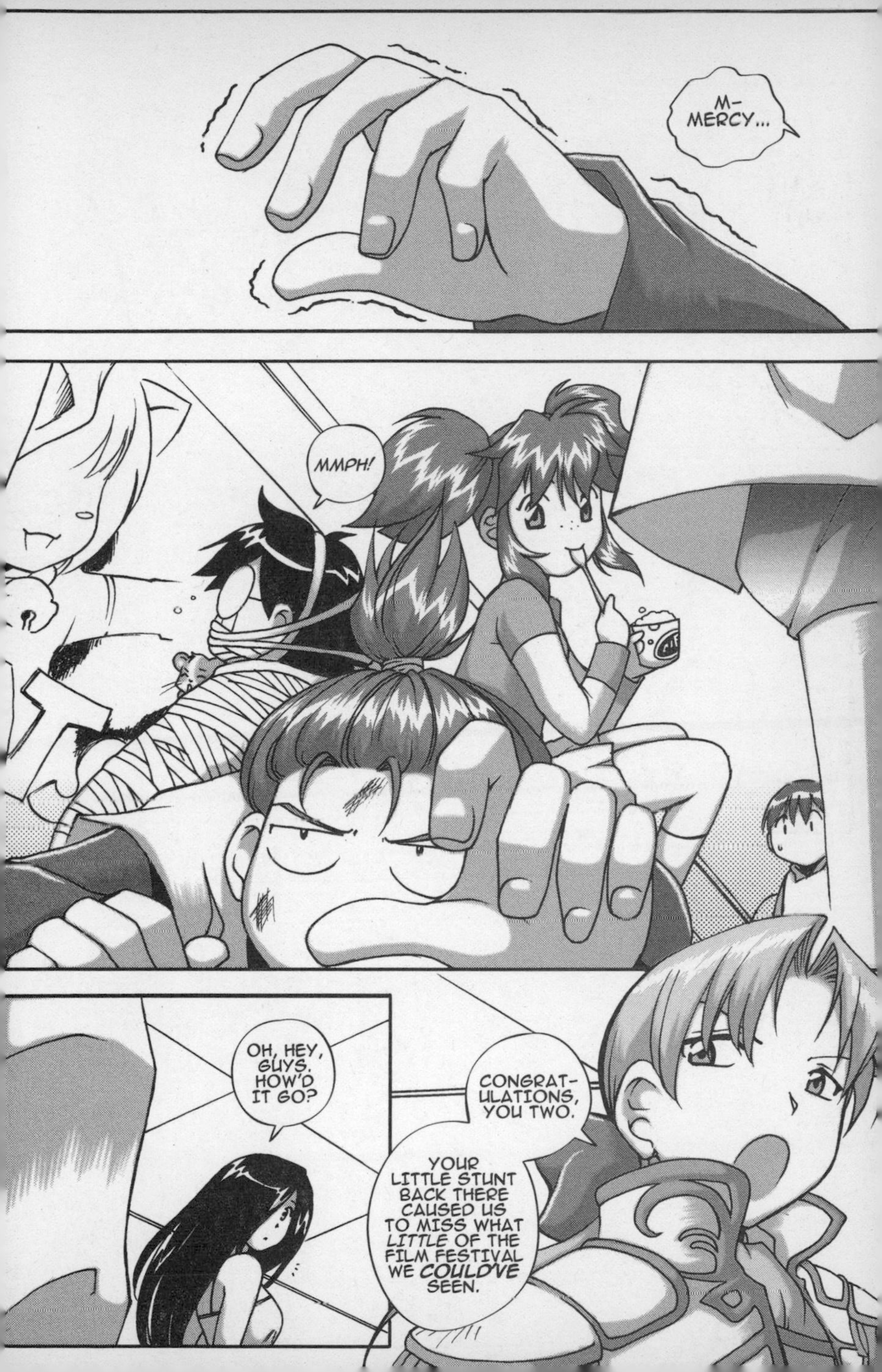
M-
MERCY...
MMPH!
CONGRAT-ULATIONS, YOU TWO.
YOUR LITTLE STUNT BACK THERE CAUSED US TO MISS WHAT *LITTLE* OF THE FILM FESTIVAL WE ***COULD'VE*** SEEN.
OH, HEY, GUYS. HOW'D IT GO?

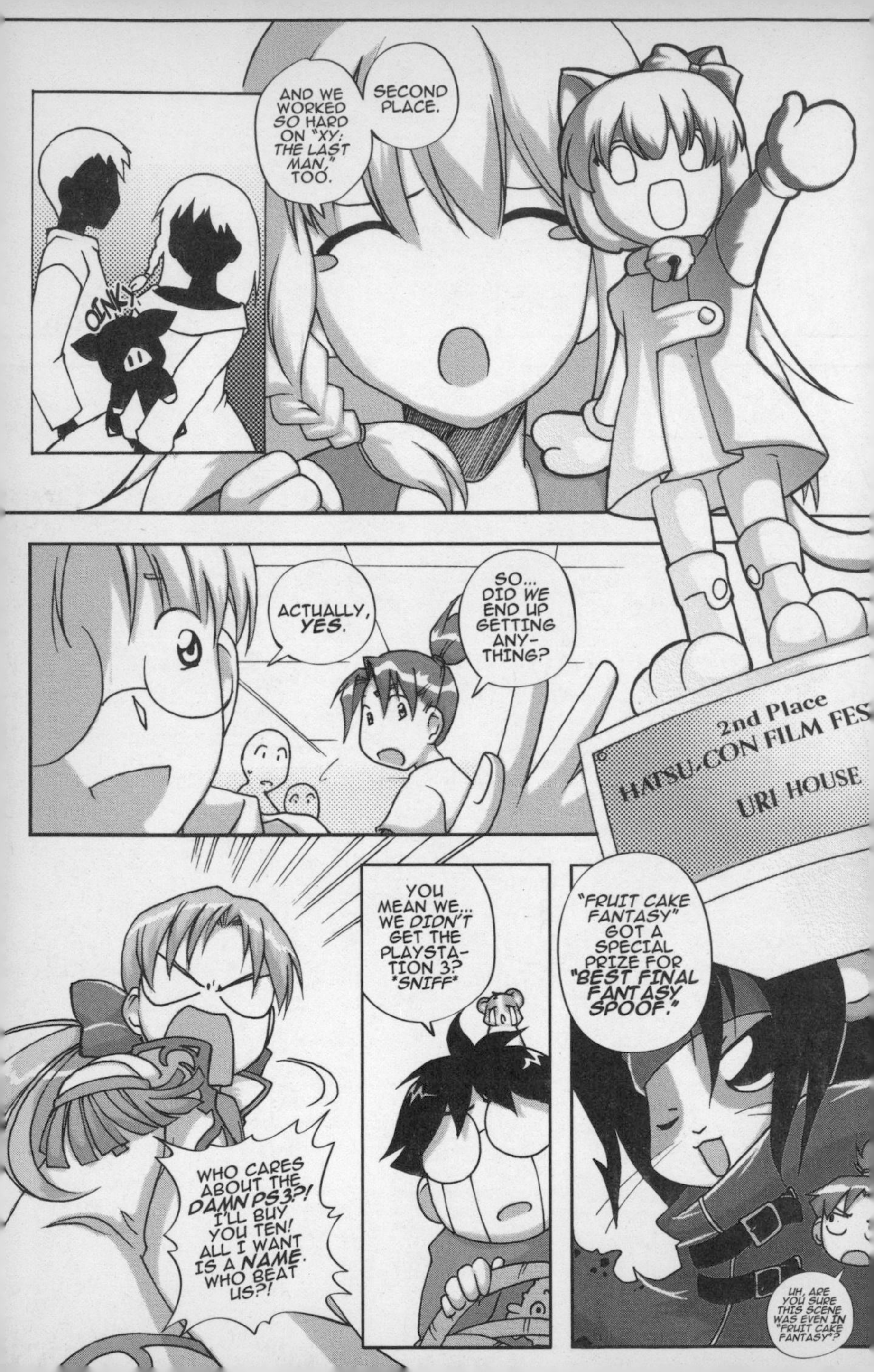
SECOND PLACE.
AND WE WORKED SO HARD ON "XY: THE LAST MAN," TOO.
OINK
2nd Place
HATSU-CON FILM FES
URI HOUSE
SO... DID WE END UP GETTING ANY-THING?
ACTUALLY, **YES**.
"FRUIT CAKE FANTASY" GOT A SPECIAL PRIZE FOR "**BEST FINAL FANTASY SPOOF.**"
UH, ARE YOU SURE THIS SCENE WAS EVEN IN "FRUIT CAKE FANTASY"?
YOU MEAN WE... WE *DIDN'T* GET THE PLAYSTA-TION 3? *SNIFF*
WHO CARES ABOUT THE ***DAMN PS3***?! I'LL BUY YOU TEN! ALL I WANT IS A ***NAME***. WHO BEAT US?!

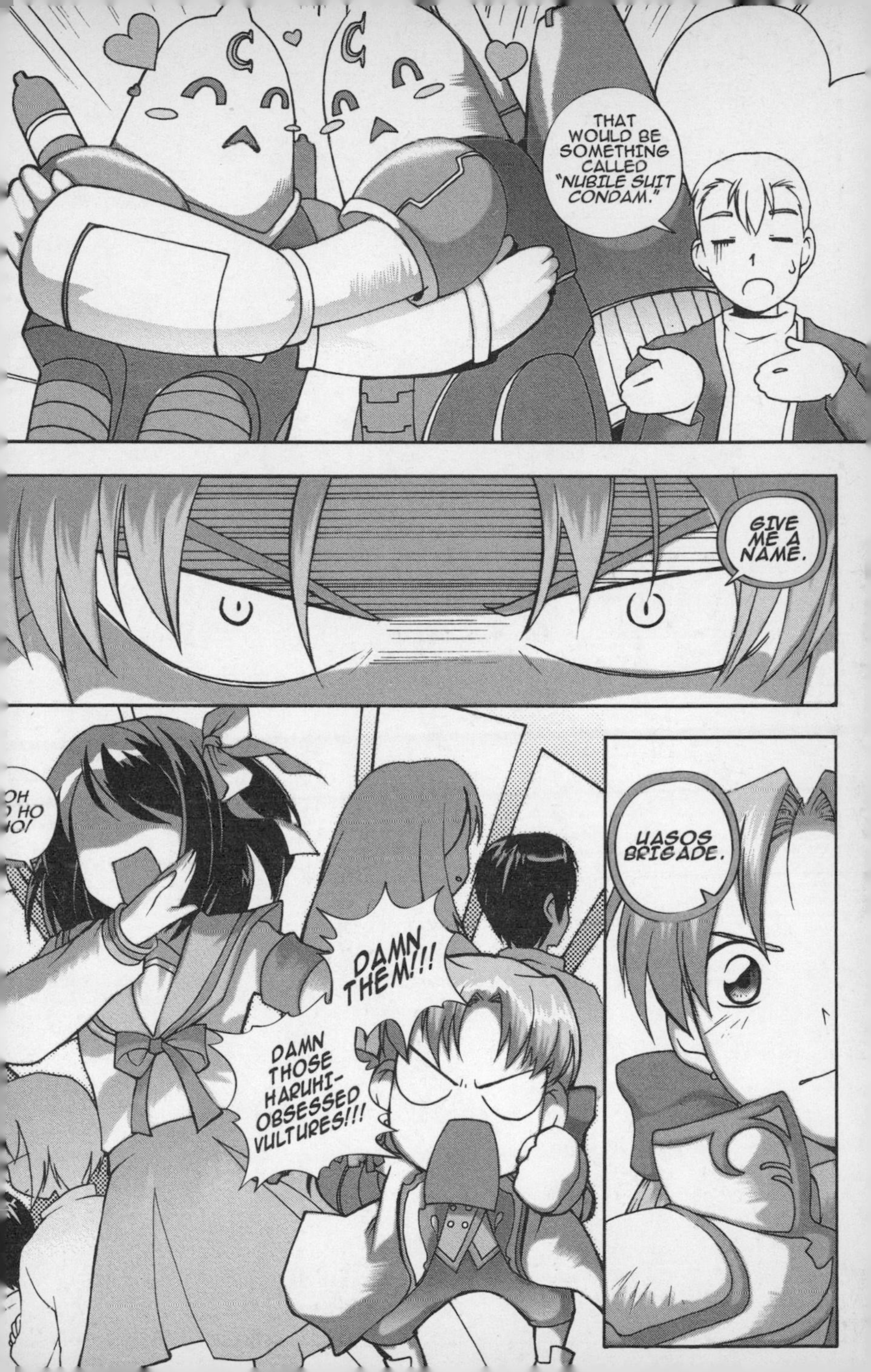

THAT WOULD BE SOMETHING CALLED "NUBILE SUIT CONDAM."
GIVE ME A NAME.
UASOS BRIGADE.
DAMN THEM!!!
DAMN THOSE HARUHI-OBSESSED VULTURES!!!

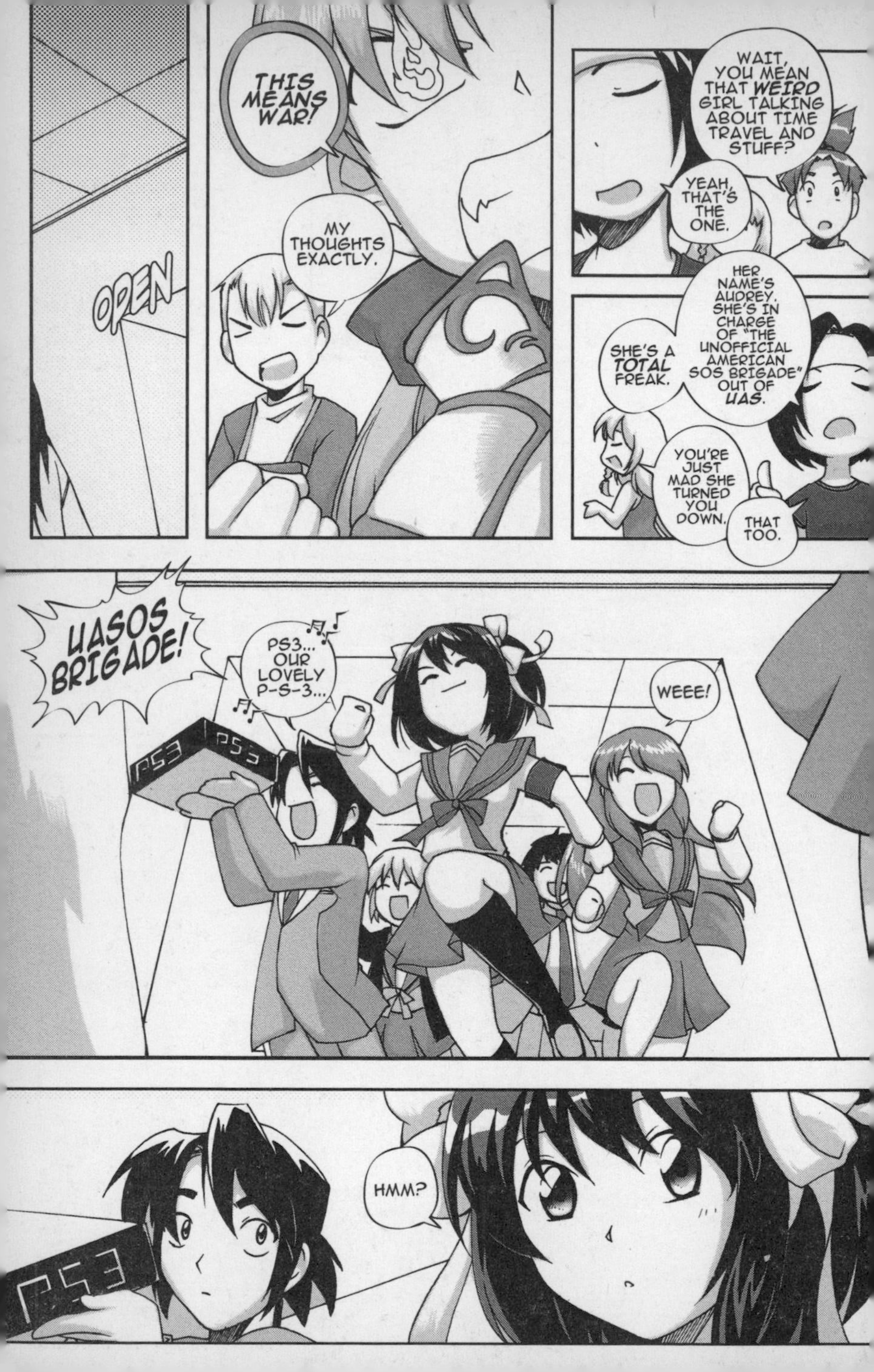
WAIT, YOU MEAN THAT WEIRD GIRL TALKING ABOUT TIME TRAVEL AND STUFF?
YEAH, THAT'S THE ONE.
HER NAME'S AUDREY. SHE'S IN CHARGE OF "THE UNOFFICIAL AMERICAN SOS BRIGADE" OUT OF UAS.
SHE'S A TOTAL FREAK.
YOU'RE JUST MAD SHE TURNED YOU DOWN.
THAT TOO.
THIS MEANS WAR!
MY THOUGHTS EXACTLY.
OPEN
UASOS BRIGADE!
PS3... OUR LOVELY P-S-3...
WEEE!
PS3
HMM?

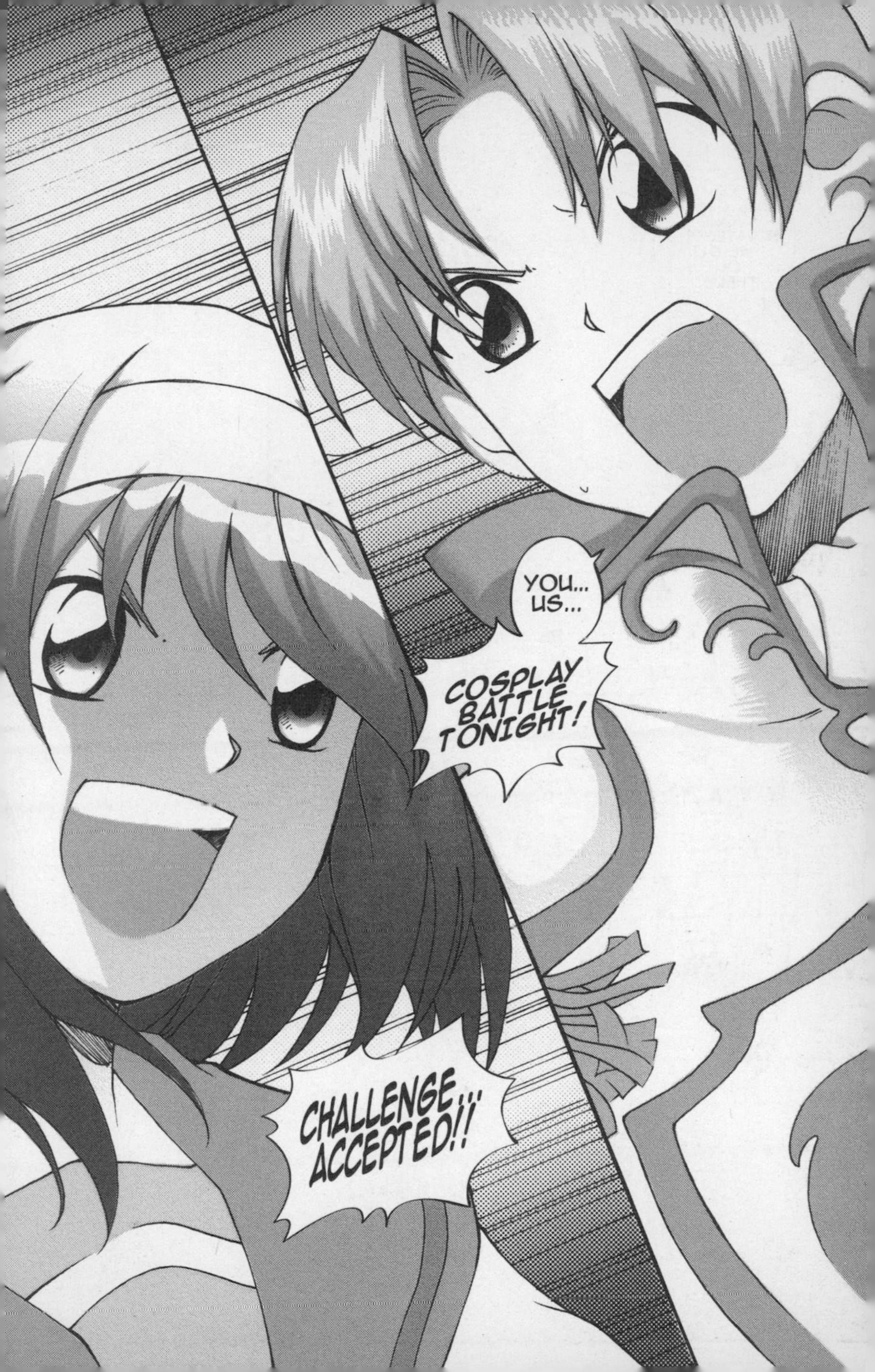
YOU... US...
COSPLAY BATTLE TONIGHT!
CHALLENGE... ACCEPTED!!

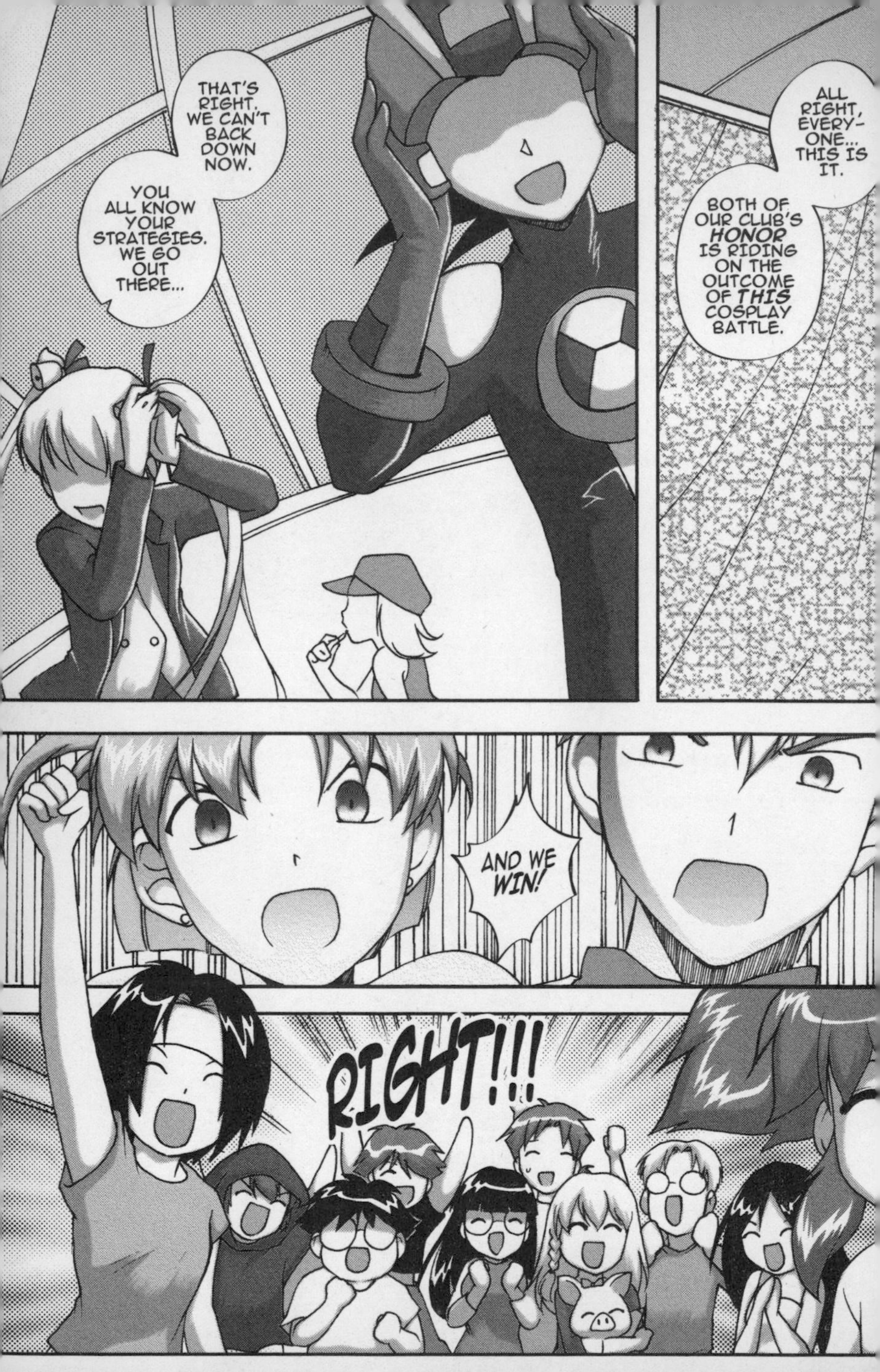
ALL RIGHT, EVERYONE... THIS IS IT.
BOTH OF OUR CLUB'S **HONOR** IS RIDING ON THE OUTCOME OF ***THIS*** COSPLAY BATTLE.
THAT'S RIGHT. WE CAN'T BACK DOWN NOW.
YOU ALL KNOW YOUR STRATEGIES. WE GO OUT THERE...
AND WE *WIN!*
RIGHT!!!

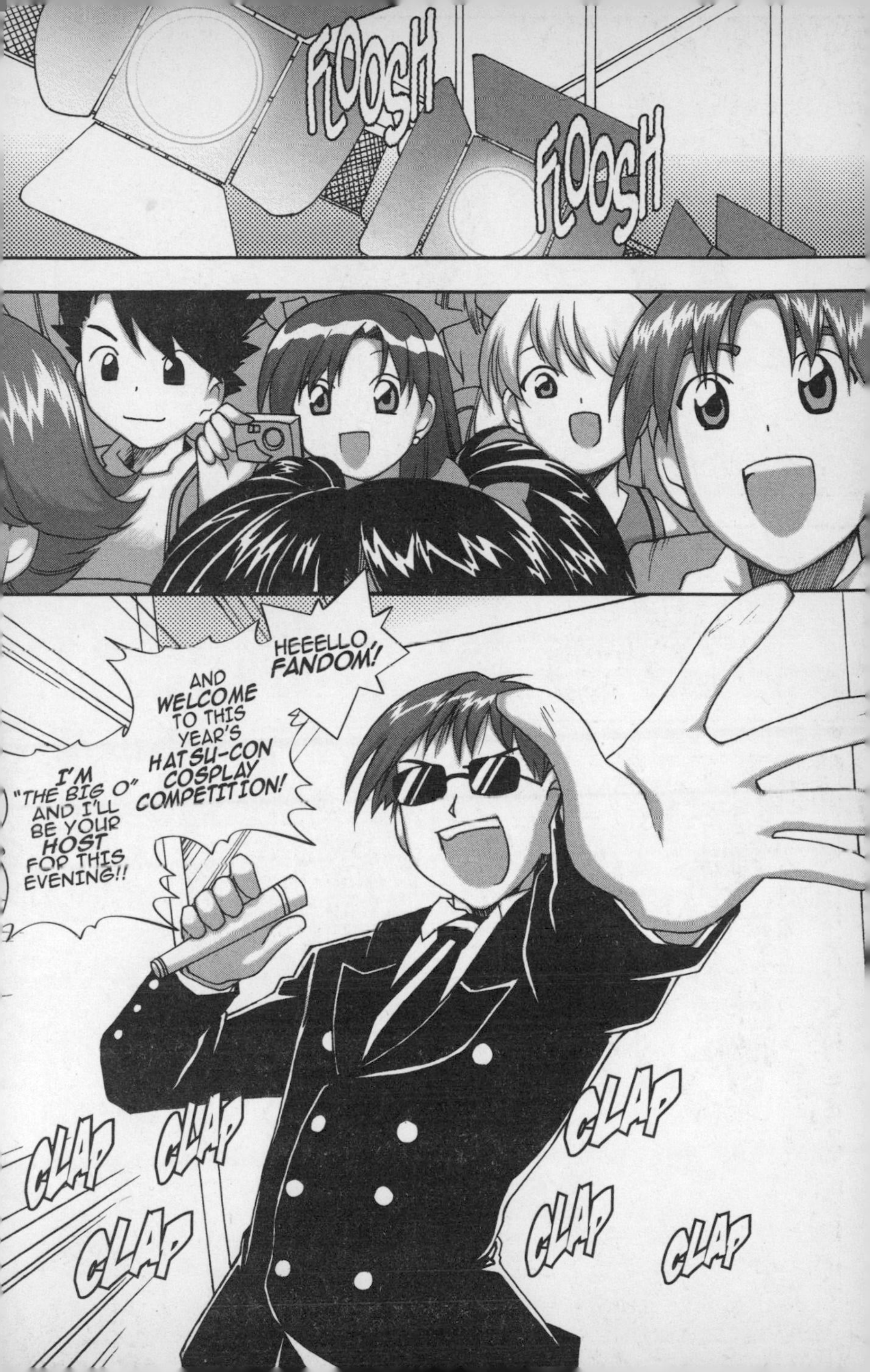
FLOOSH
FLOOSH
HEEELLO, FANDOM!
AND WELCOME TO THIS YEAR'S HATSU-CON COSPLAY COMPETITION!
I'M "THE BIG O" AND I'LL BE YOUR HOST FOP THIS EVENING!!
CLAP
CLAP
CLAP
CLAP
CLAP
CLAP

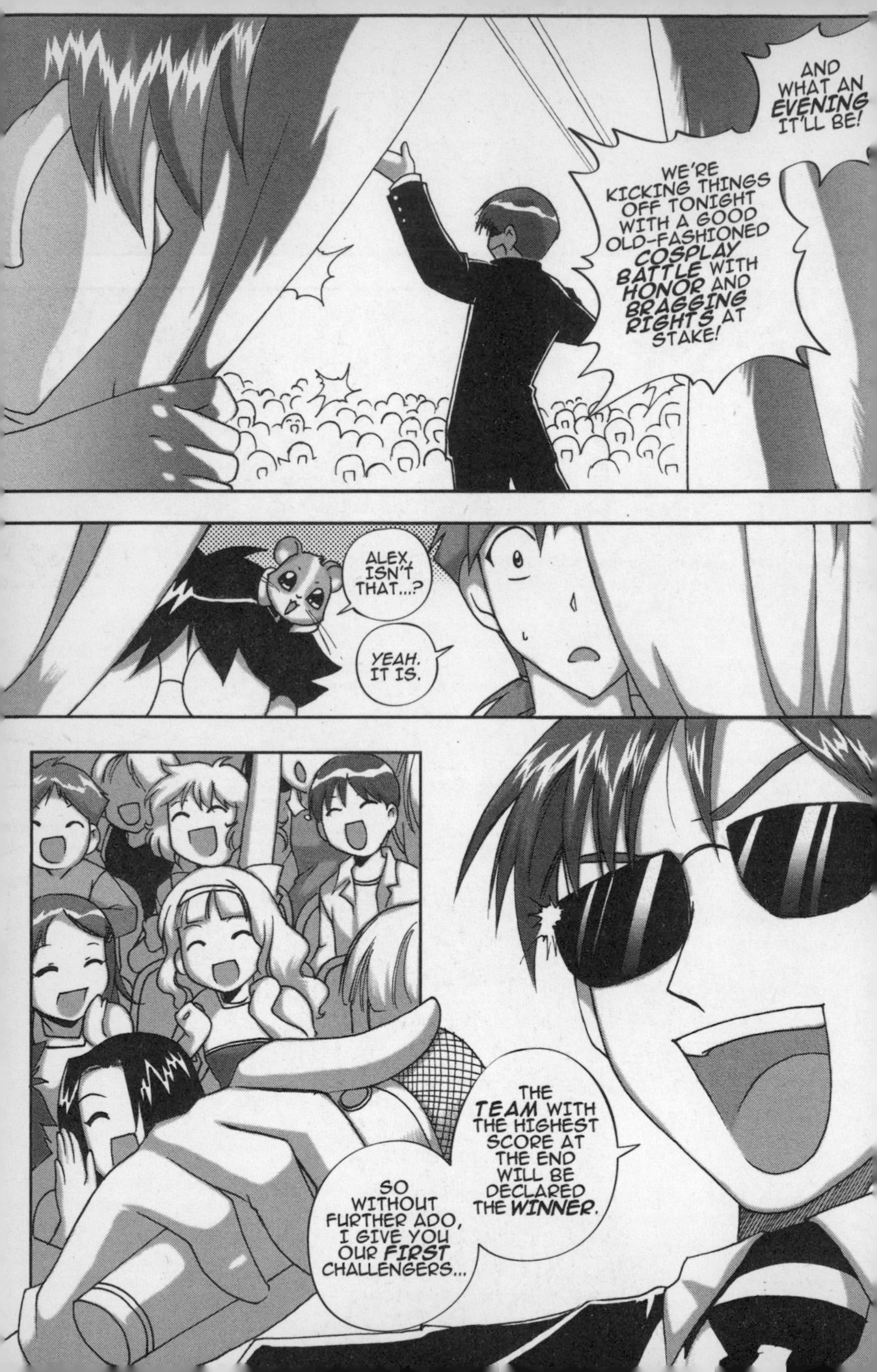
AND WHAT AN EVENING IT'LL BE!
WE'RE KICKING THINGS OFF TONIGHT WITH A GOOD OLD-FASHIONED COSPLAY BATTLE WITH HONOR AND BRAGGING RIGHTS AT STAKE!
ALEX, ISN'T THAT...?
YEAH. IT IS.
THE TEAM WITH THE HIGHEST SCORE AT THE END WILL BE DECLARED THE WINNER.
SO WITHOUT FURTHER ADO, I GIVE YOU OUR FIRST CHALLENGERS...

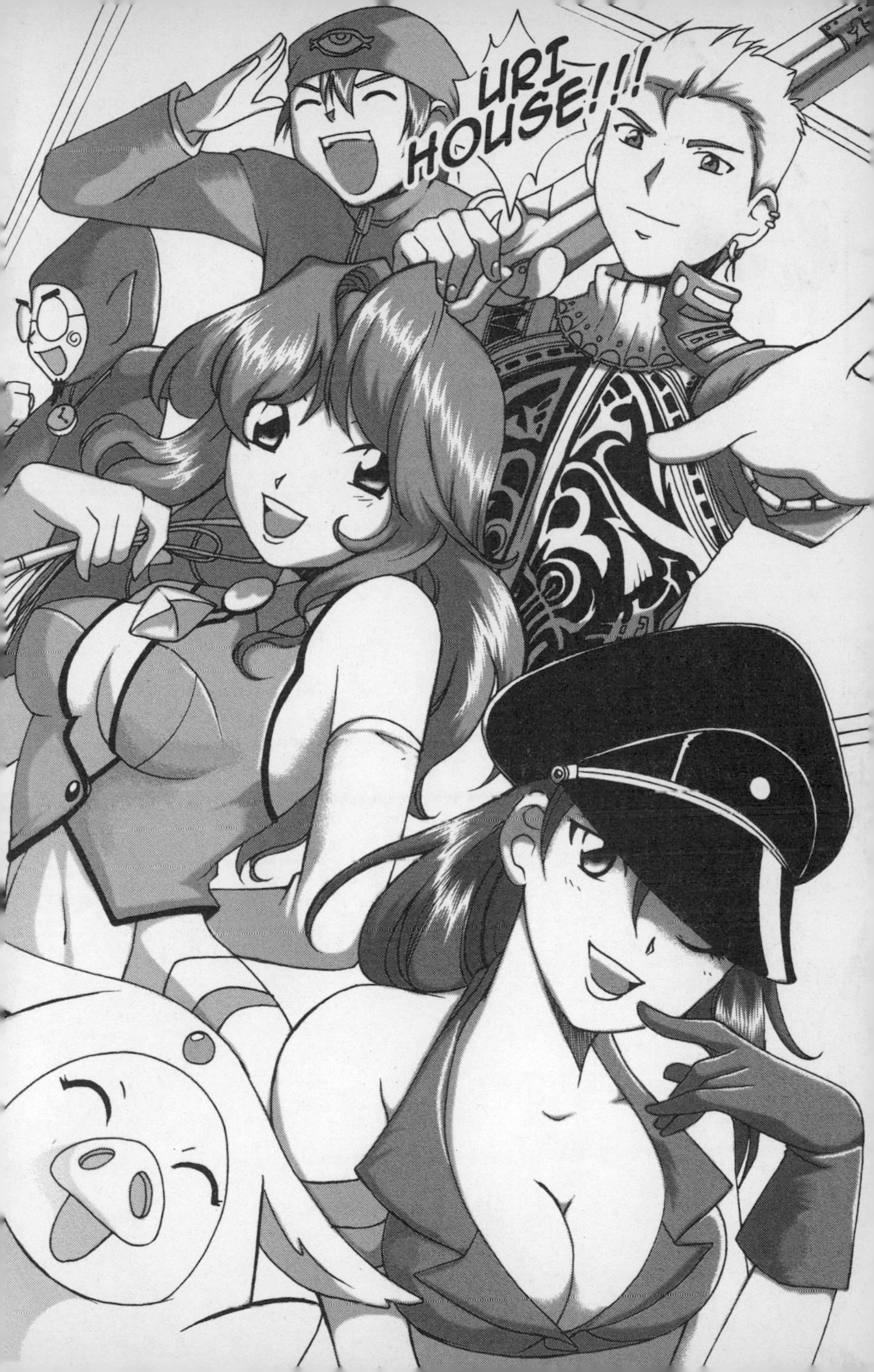
URI HOUSE!!!!

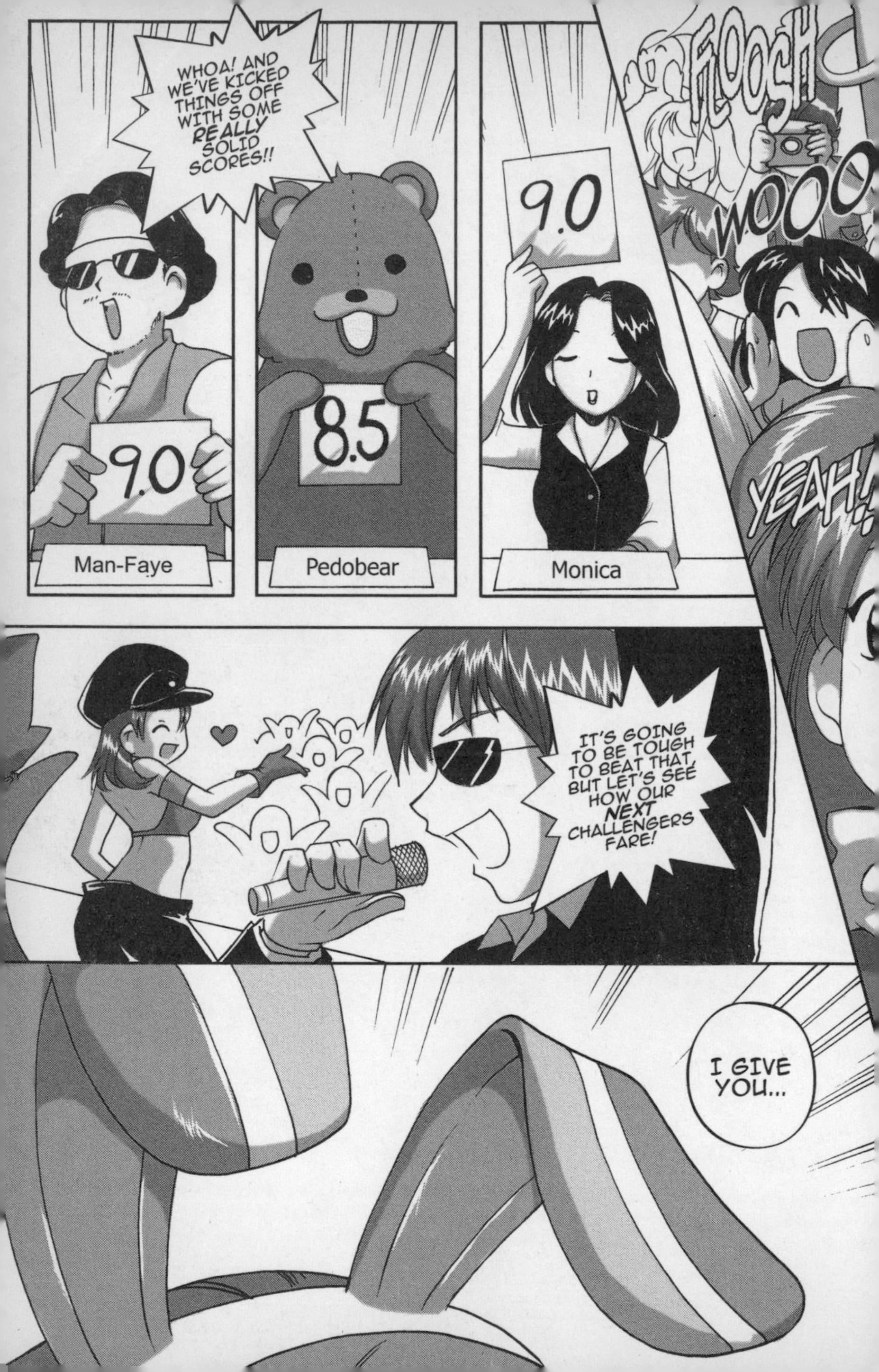
FLOOSH
WOOO
YEAH!!
9.0
Monica
8.5
Pedobear
WHOA! AND WE'VE KICKED THINGS OFF WITH SOME REALLY SOLID SCORES!!
9.0
Man-Faye
IT'S GOING TO BE TOUGH TO BEAT THAT, BUT LET'S SEE HOW OUR NEXT CHALLENGERS FARE!
I GIVE YOU...

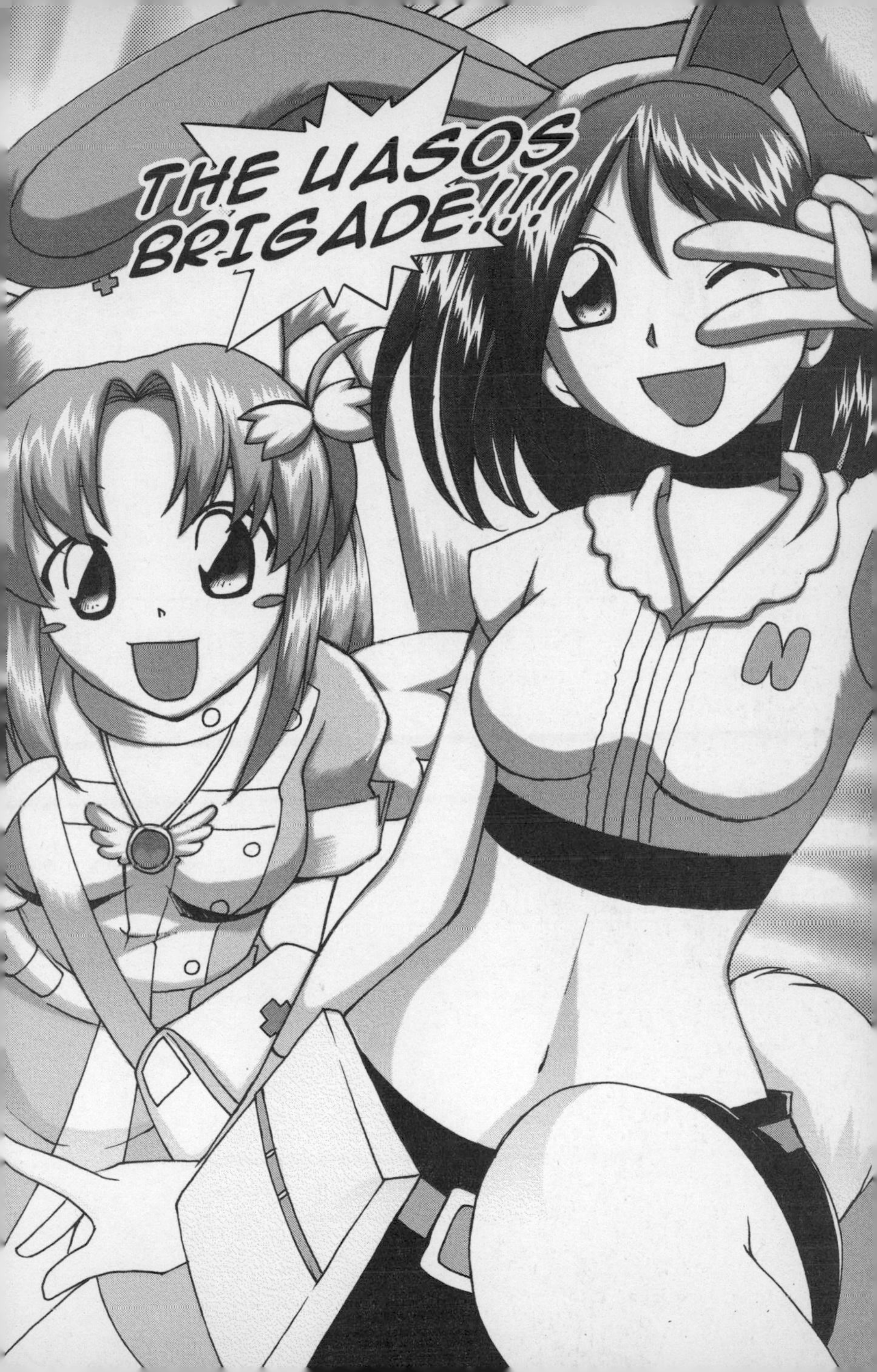
THE UASOS BRIGADE!!!!

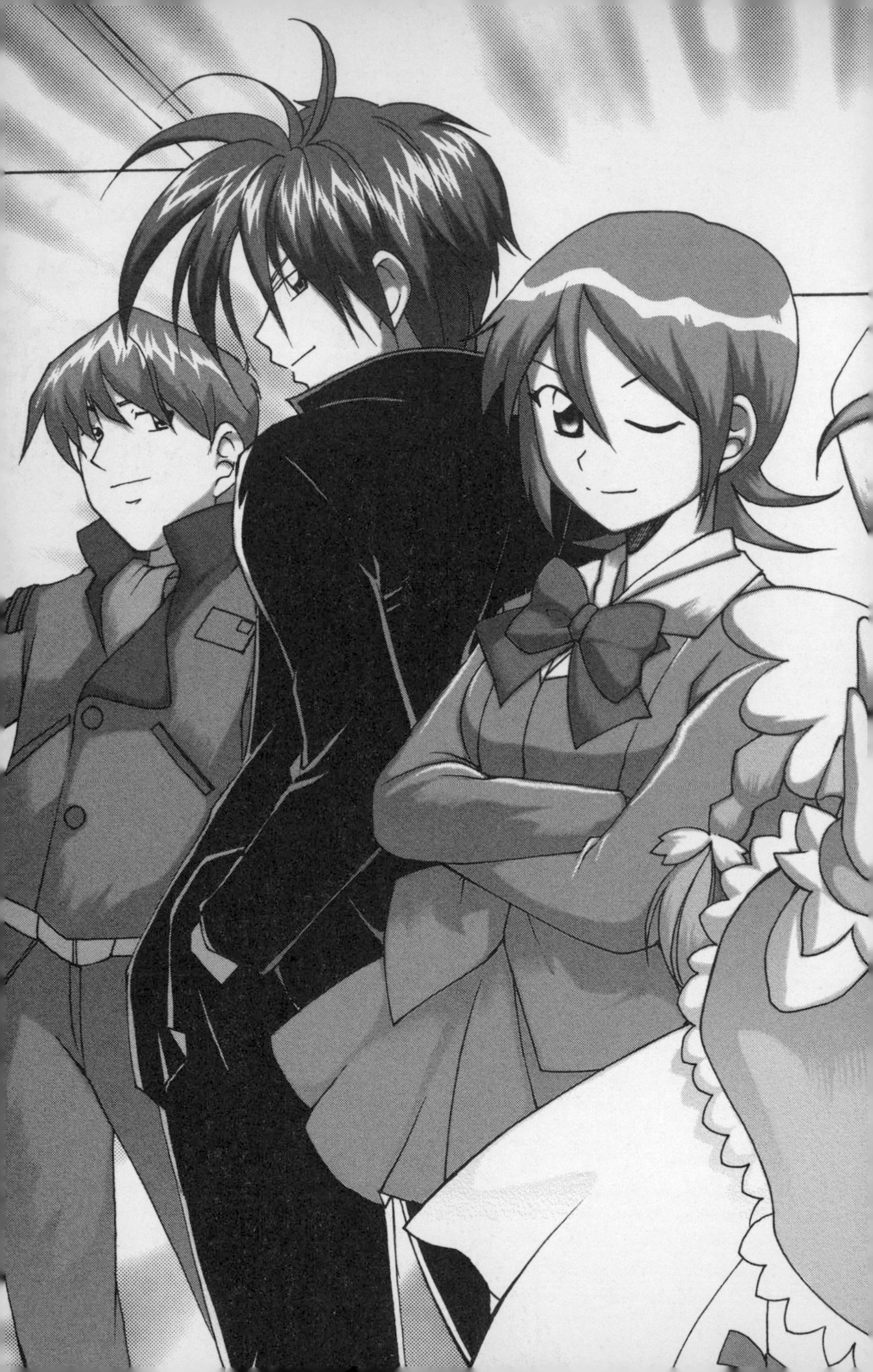

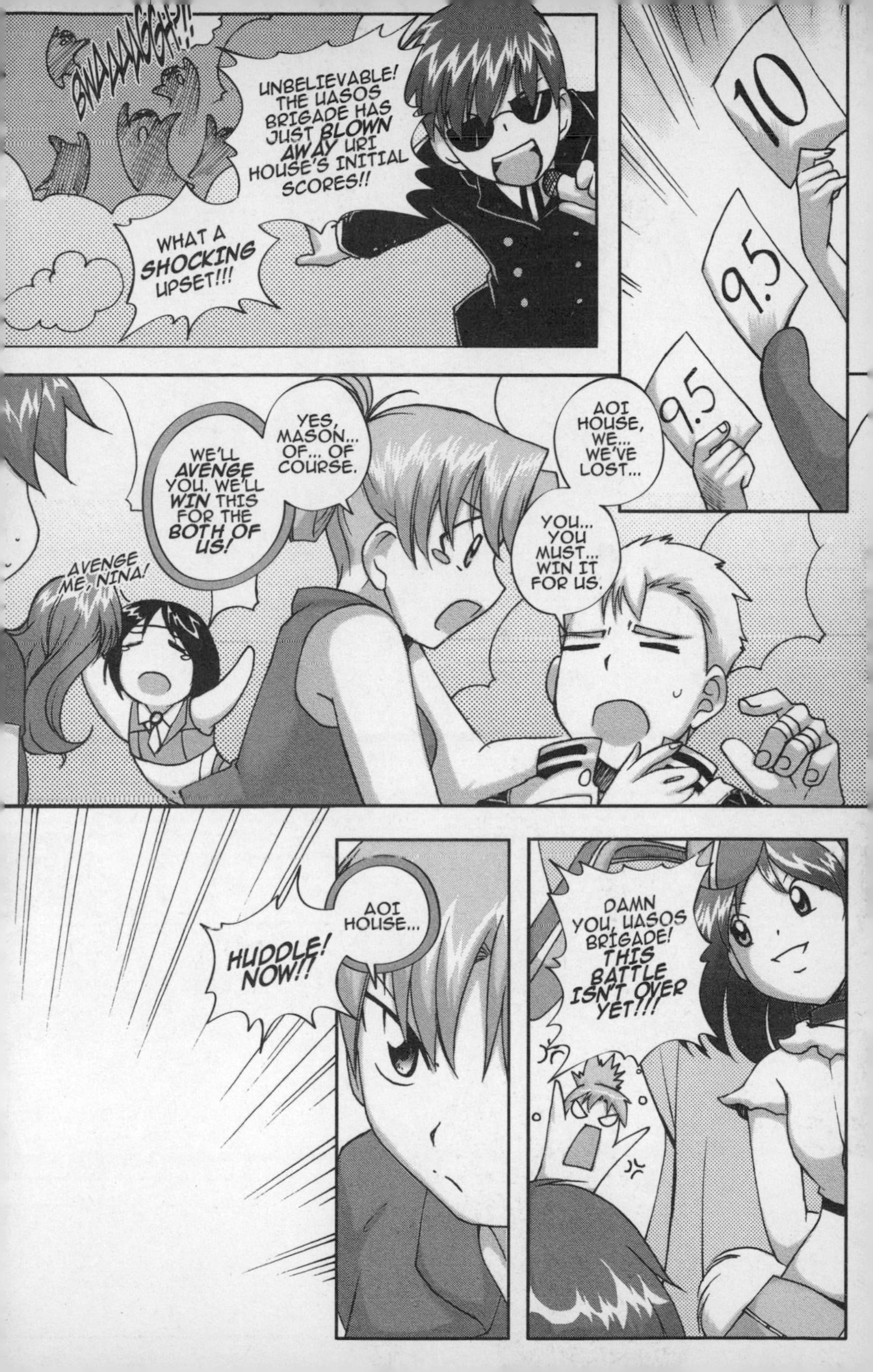
10
9.5
9.5
UNBELIEVABLE! THE UASOS BRIGADE HAS JUST BLOWN AWAY URI HOUSE'S INITIAL SCORES!!
WHAT A SHOCKING UPSET!!!
AOI HOUSE, WE... WE'VE LOST...
YOU... YOU MUST... WIN IT FOR US.
YES, MASON... OF... OF COURSE.
WE'LL AVENGE YOU. WE'LL WIN THIS FOR THE BOTH OF US!
AVENGE ME, NINA!
DAMN YOU, UASOS BRIGADE! THIS BATTLE ISN'T OVER YET!!!
AOI HOUSE...
HUDDLE! NOW!!

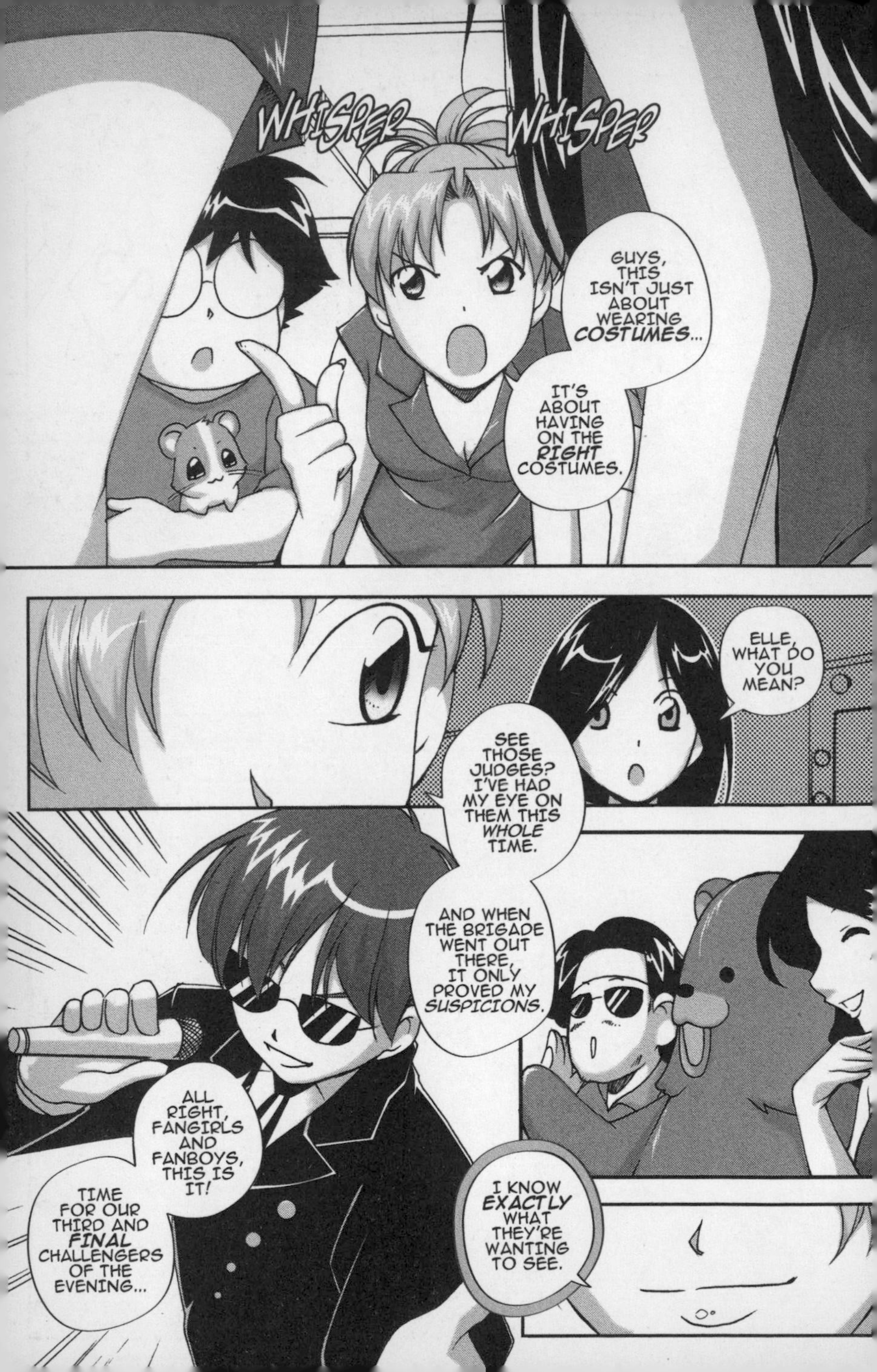
WHISPER
WHISPER
GUYS, THIS ISN'T JUST ABOUT WEARING **COSTUMES**...
IT'S ABOUT HAVING ON THE ***RIGHT*** COSTUMES.
ELLE, WHAT DO YOU MEAN?
SEE THOSE JUDGES? I'VE HAD MY EYE ON THEM THIS *WHOLE* TIME.
AND WHEN THE BRIGADE WENT OUT THERE, IT ONLY PROVED MY *SUSPICIONS*.
I KNOW ***EXACTLY*** WHAT THEY'RE WANTING TO SEE.
ALL RIGHT, FANGIRLS AND FANBOYS, THIS IS IT!
TIME FOR OUR THIRD AND ***FINAL*** CHALLENGERS OF THE EVENING...

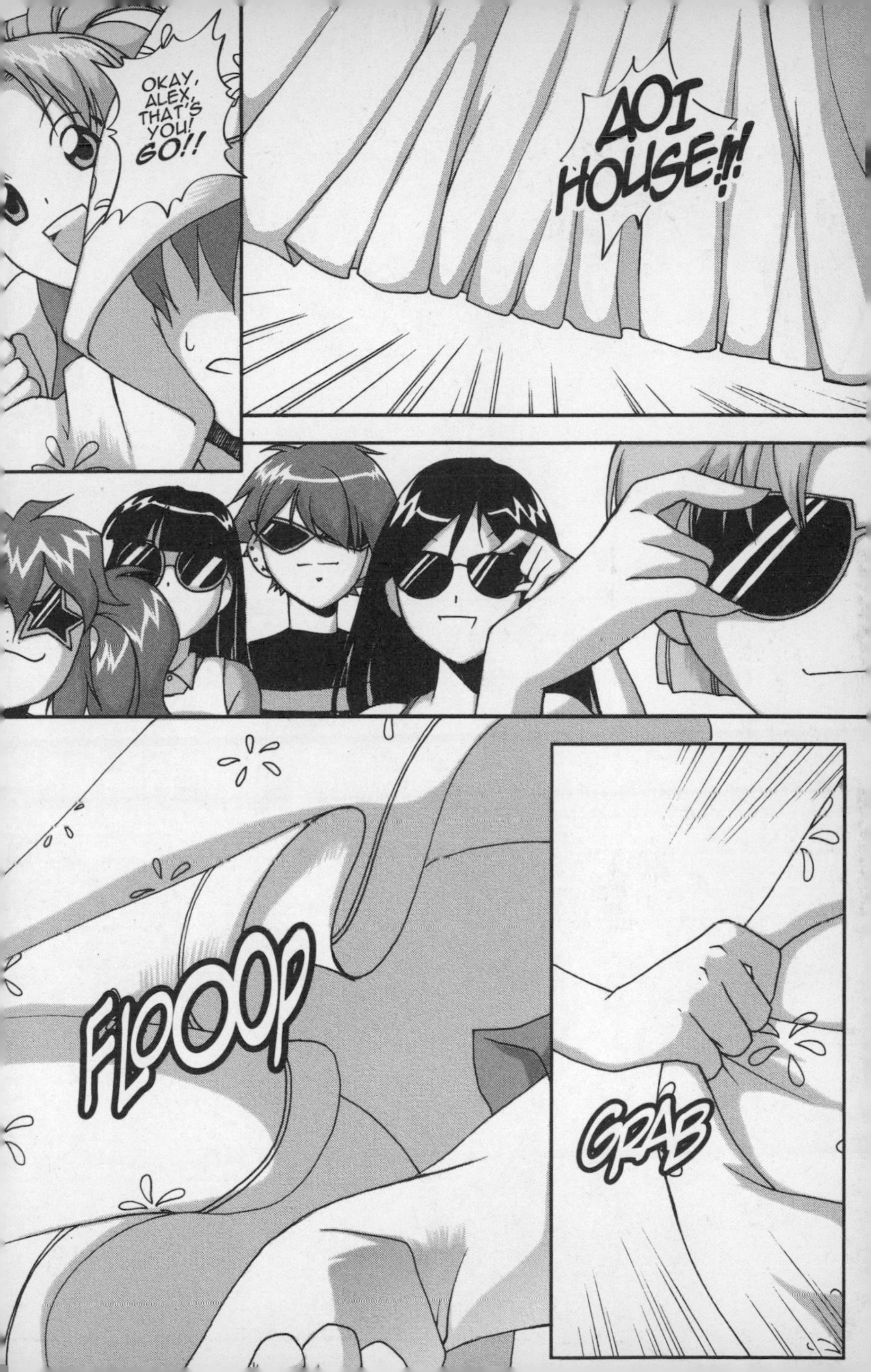
AOI HOUSE!!!
OKAY, ALEX, THAT'S YOU! GO!!
GRAB
FLOOOP

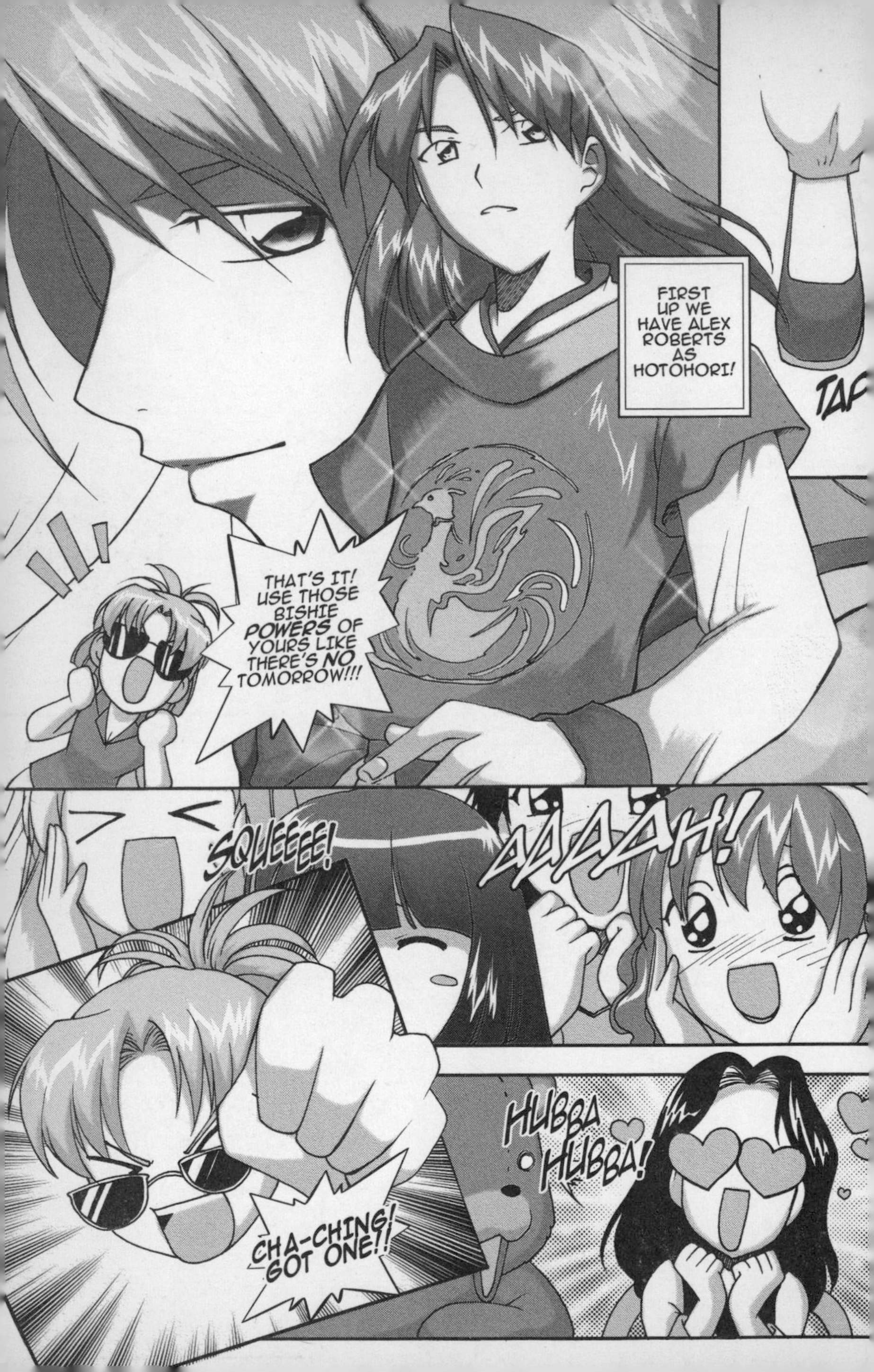
FIRST UP WE HAVE ALEX ROBERTS AS HOTOHORI!
TAP
THAT'S IT! USE THOSE BISHIE POWERS OF YOURS LIKE THERE'S NO TOMORROW!!!
AAAAH!
SQUEEEEE!
HUBBA HUBBA!
CHA-CHING! GOT ONE!!

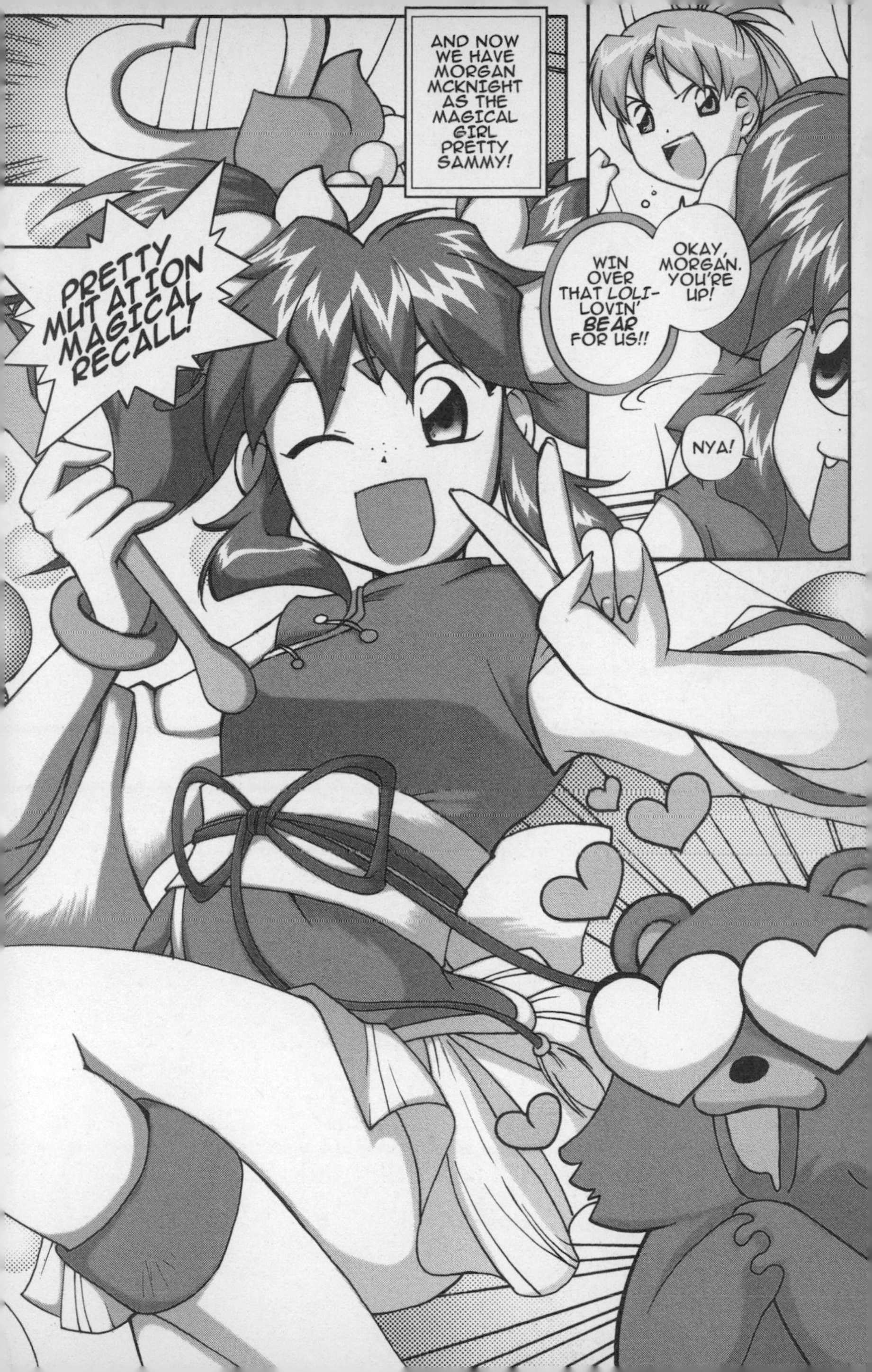
OKAY, MORGAN. YOU'RE UP!
WIN OVER THAT LOLI-LOVIN' BEAR FOR US!!
NYA!
AND NOW WE HAVE MORGAN MCKNIGHT AS THE MAGICAL GIRL PRETTY SAMMY!
PRETTY MUTATION MAGICAL RECALL!

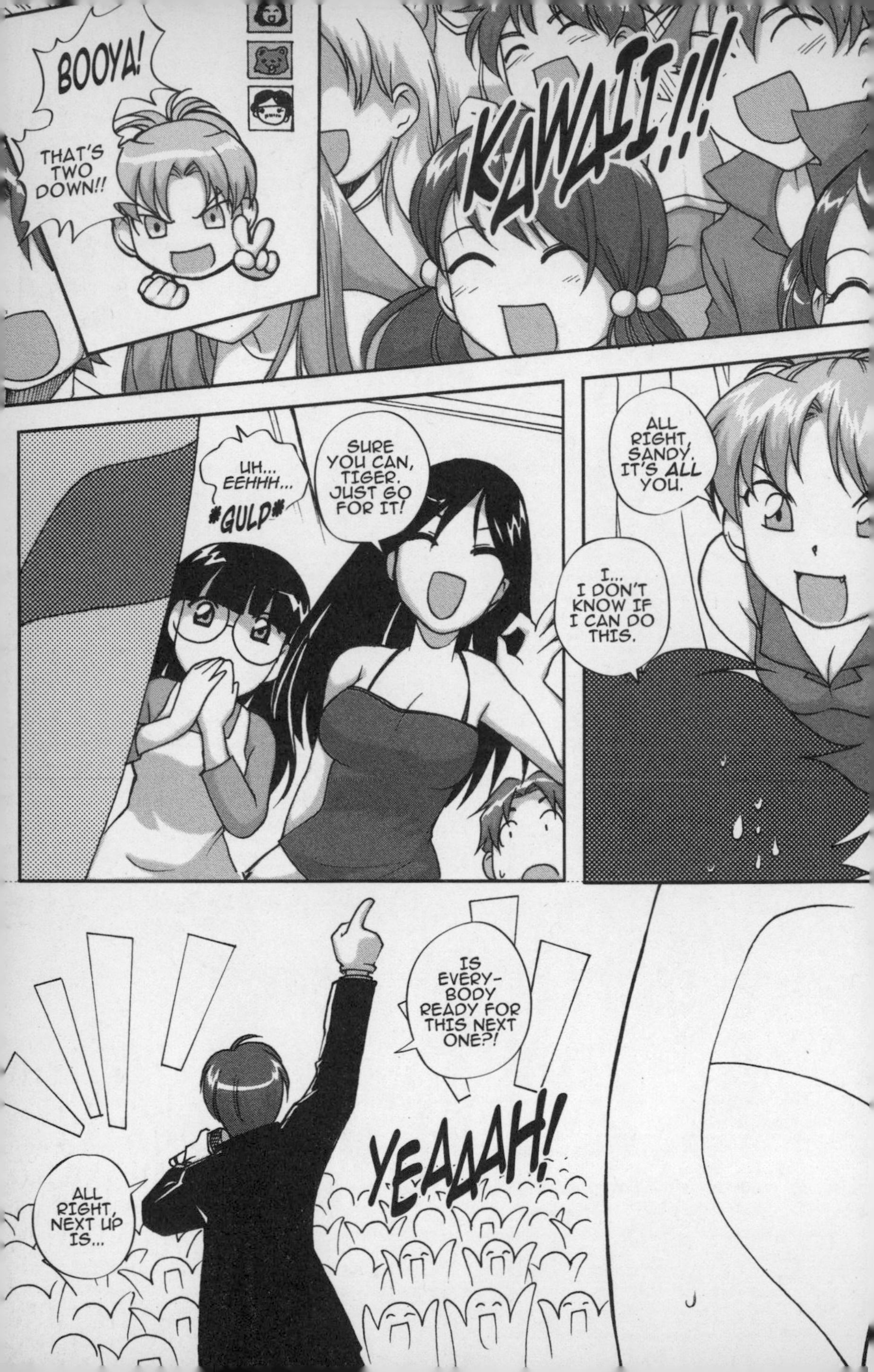
KAWAII!!!
BOOYA!
THAT'S TWO DOWN!!
ALL RIGHT, SANDY. IT'S ALL YOU.
I... I DON'T KNOW IF I CAN DO THIS.
SURE YOU CAN, TIGER. JUST GO FOR IT!
UH... EEHHH...
GULP
IS EVERY-BODY READY FOR THIS NEXT ONE?!
YEAAAH!
ALL RIGHT, NEXT UP IS...

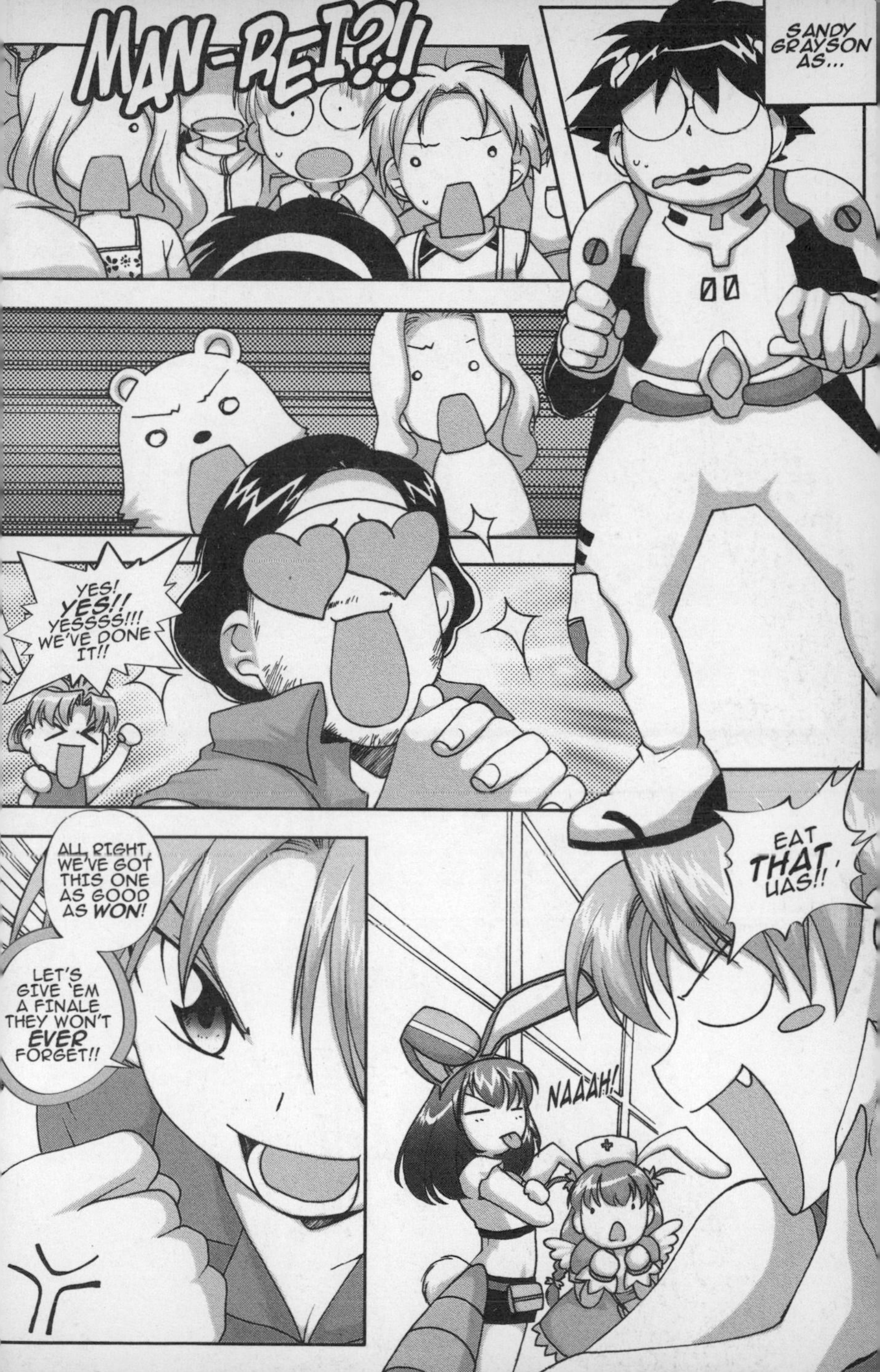
SANDY GRAYSON AS...
MAN-REI?!!
YES! YES!! YESSSS!!! WE'VE DONE IT!!
EAT THAT, UAS!!
NAAAH!
ALL RIGHT, WE'VE GOT THIS ONE AS GOOD AS WON!
LET'S GIVE 'EM A FINALE THEY WON'T EVER FORGET!!

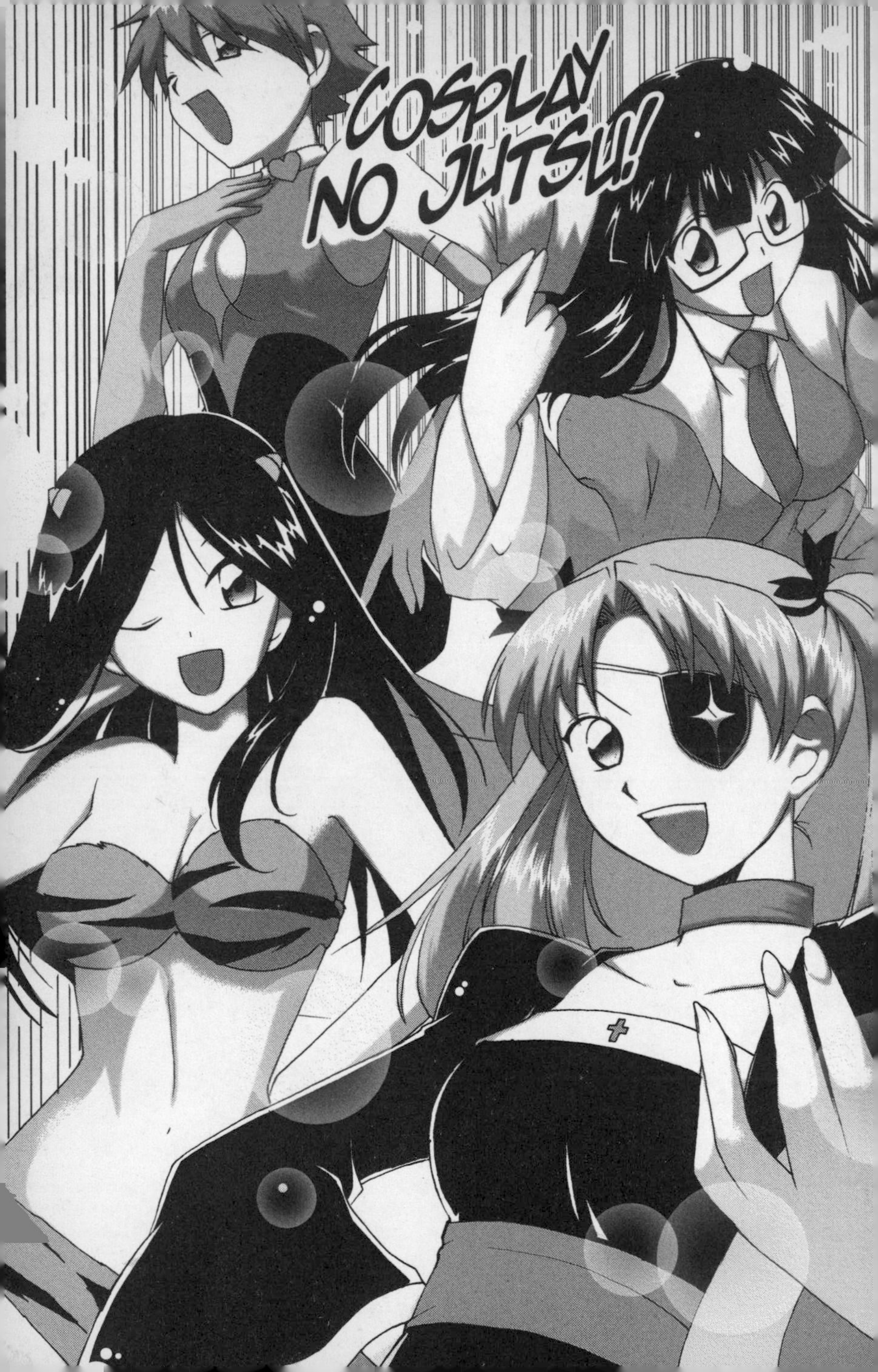
COSPLAY NO JUTSU!!

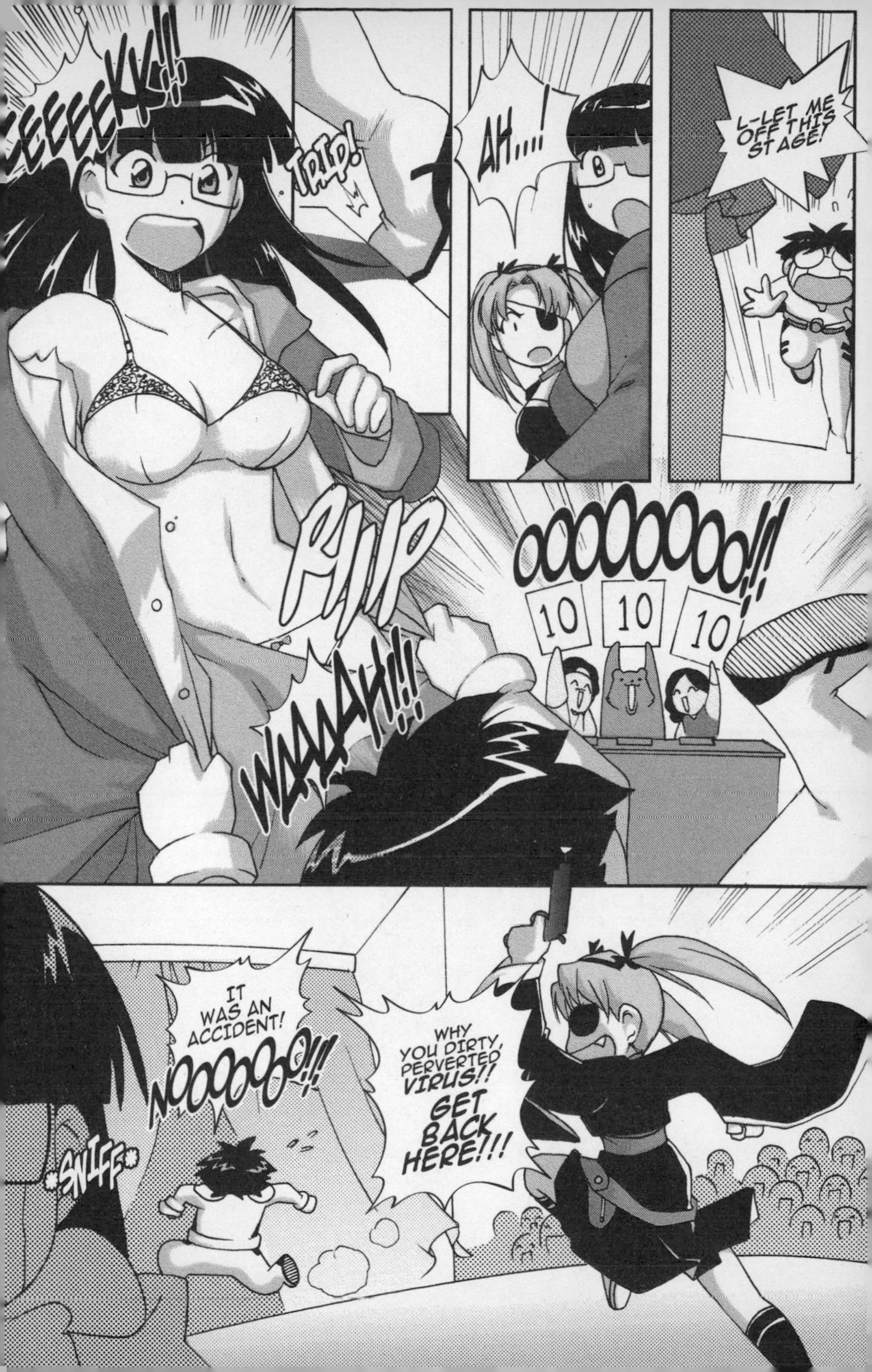
L-LET ME OFF THIS STAGE!
AH...!
TRIP!
EEEEEKK!!
OOOOOOOO!!
10
10
10
RIIP
WAAAH!!
WHY YOU DIRTY, PERVERTED VIRUS!! GET BACK HERE!!!
IT WAS AN ACCIDENT!
NOOOOOOO!!
SNIFF

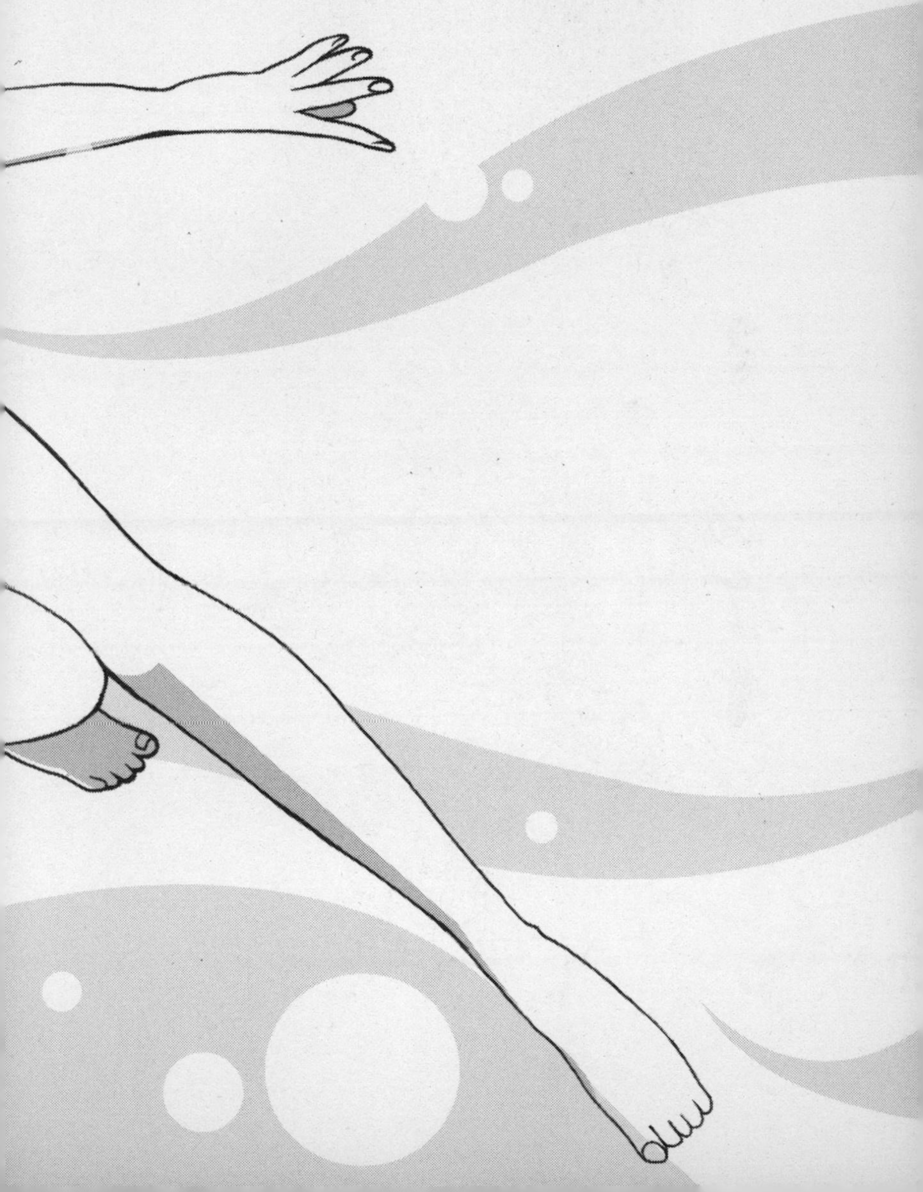

EPISODE 9:
TWILIGHT

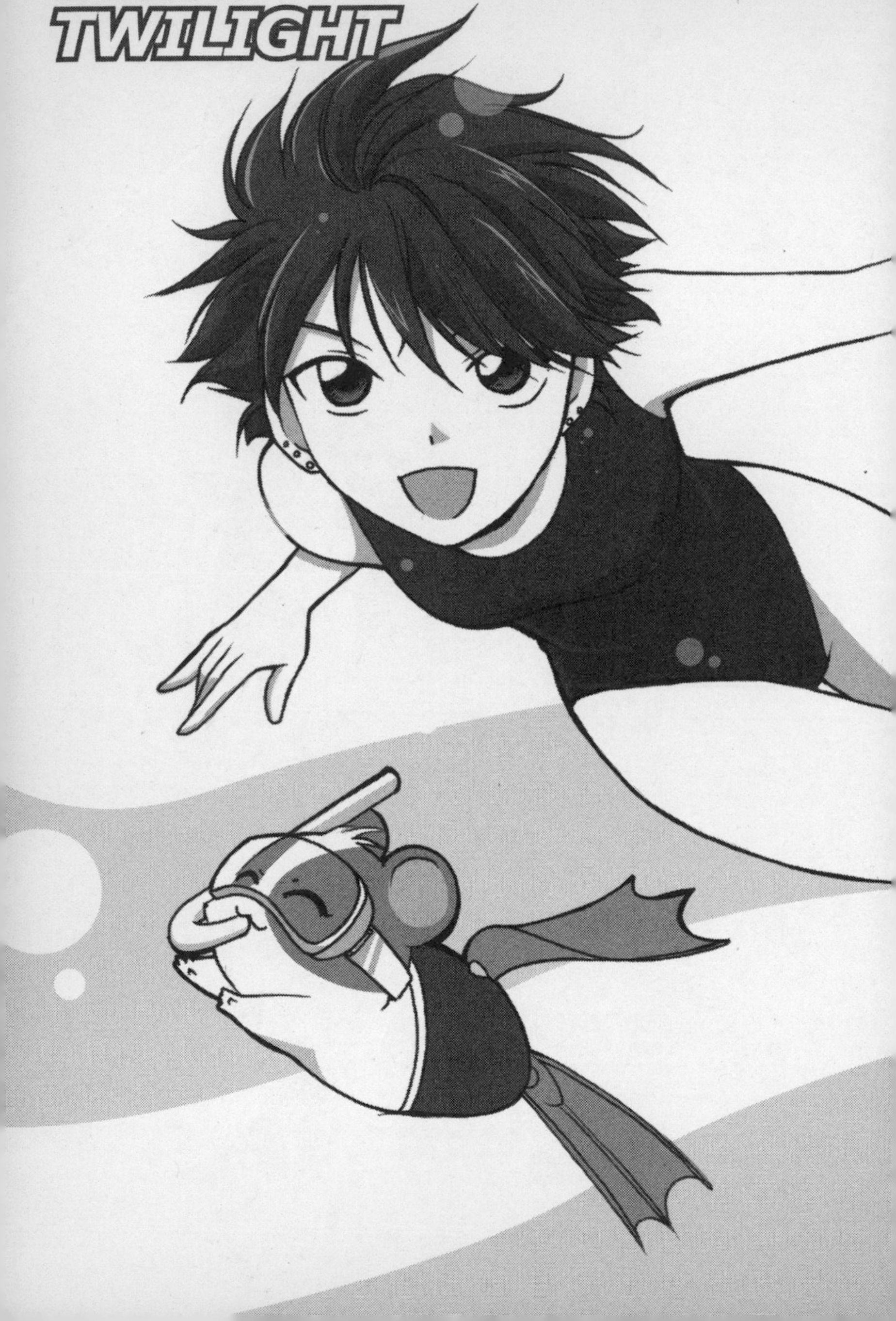

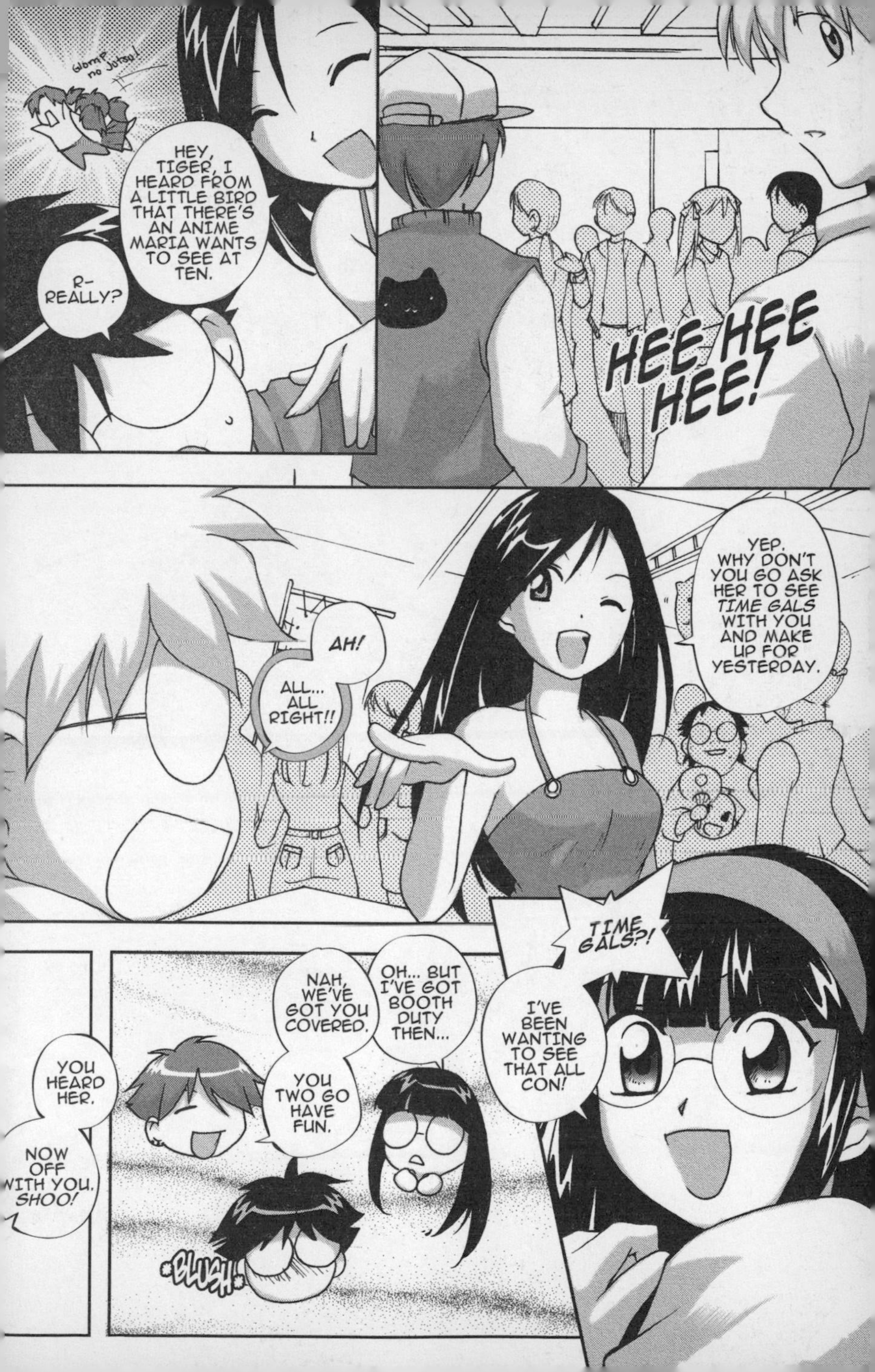
HEE HEE HEE!
Glomp no Jutsu!
HEY, TIGER, I HEARD FROM A LITTLE BIRD THAT THERE'S AN ANIME MARIA WANTS TO SEE AT TEN.
R-REALLY?
YEP. WHY DON'T YOU GO ASK HER TO SEE *TIME GALS* WITH YOU AND MAKE UP FOR YESTERDAY.
AH!
ALL... ALL RIGHT!!
TIME GALS?!
I'VE BEEN WANTING TO SEE THAT ALL CON!
OH... BUT I'VE GOT BOOTH DUTY THEN...
NAH, WE'VE GOT YOU COVERED.
YOU TWO GO HAVE FUN.
YOU HEARD HER.
NOW OFF WITH YOU. *SHOO!*
BLUSH

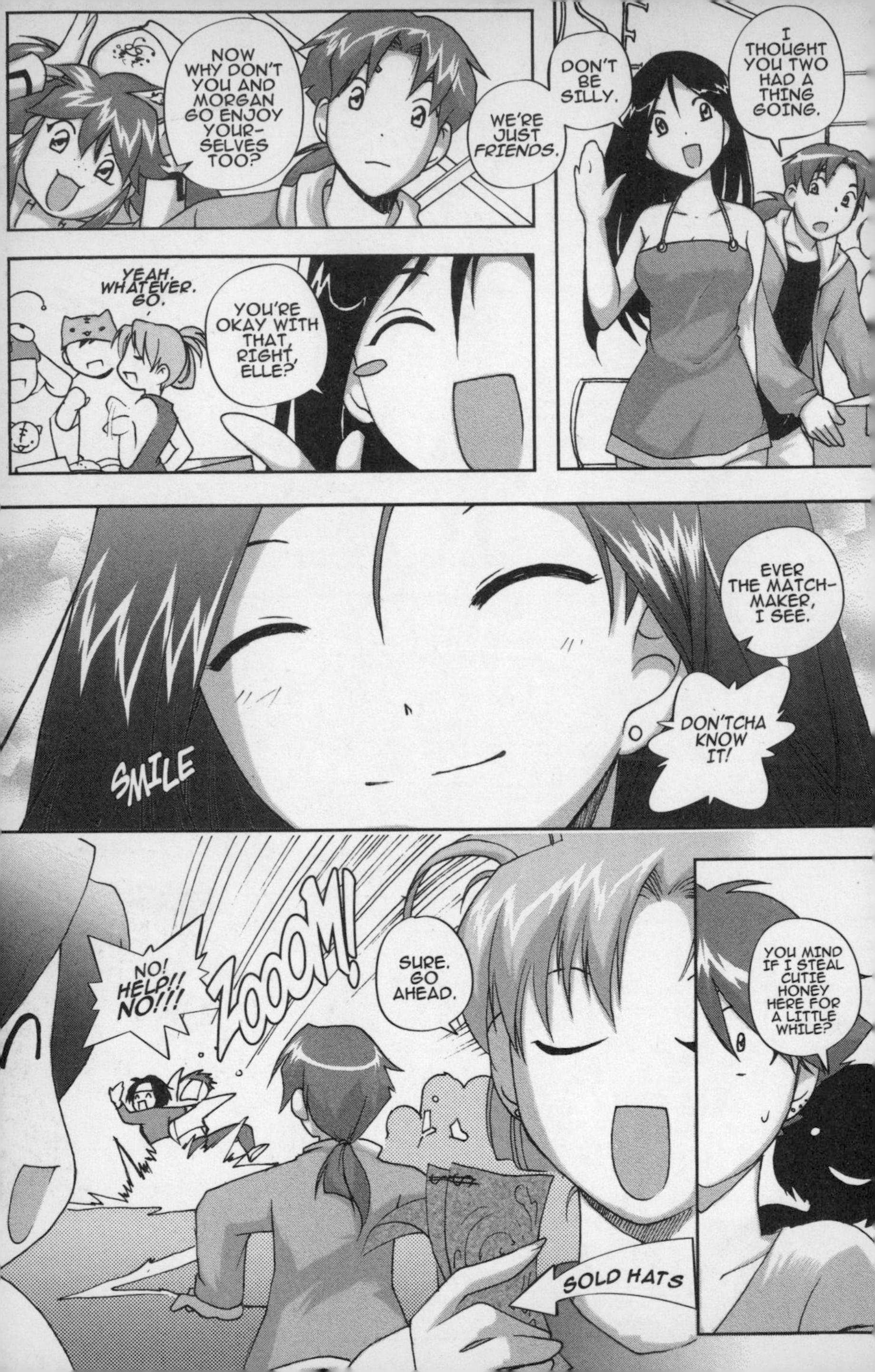
I THOUGHT YOU TWO HAD A THING GOING.
DON'T BE SILLY.
WE'RE JUST FRIENDS.
NOW WHY DON'T YOU AND MORGAN GO ENJOY YOUR-SELVES TOO?
YOU'RE OKAY WITH THAT, RIGHT, ELLE?
YEAH. WHATEVER. GO.
EVER THE MATCH-MAKER, I SEE.
DON'TCHA KNOW IT!
SMILE
YOU MIND IF I STEAL CUTIE HONEY HERE FOR A LITTLE WHILE?
SURE. GO AHEAD.
ZOOOM!
NO! HELP!! NO!!!
SOLD HATS

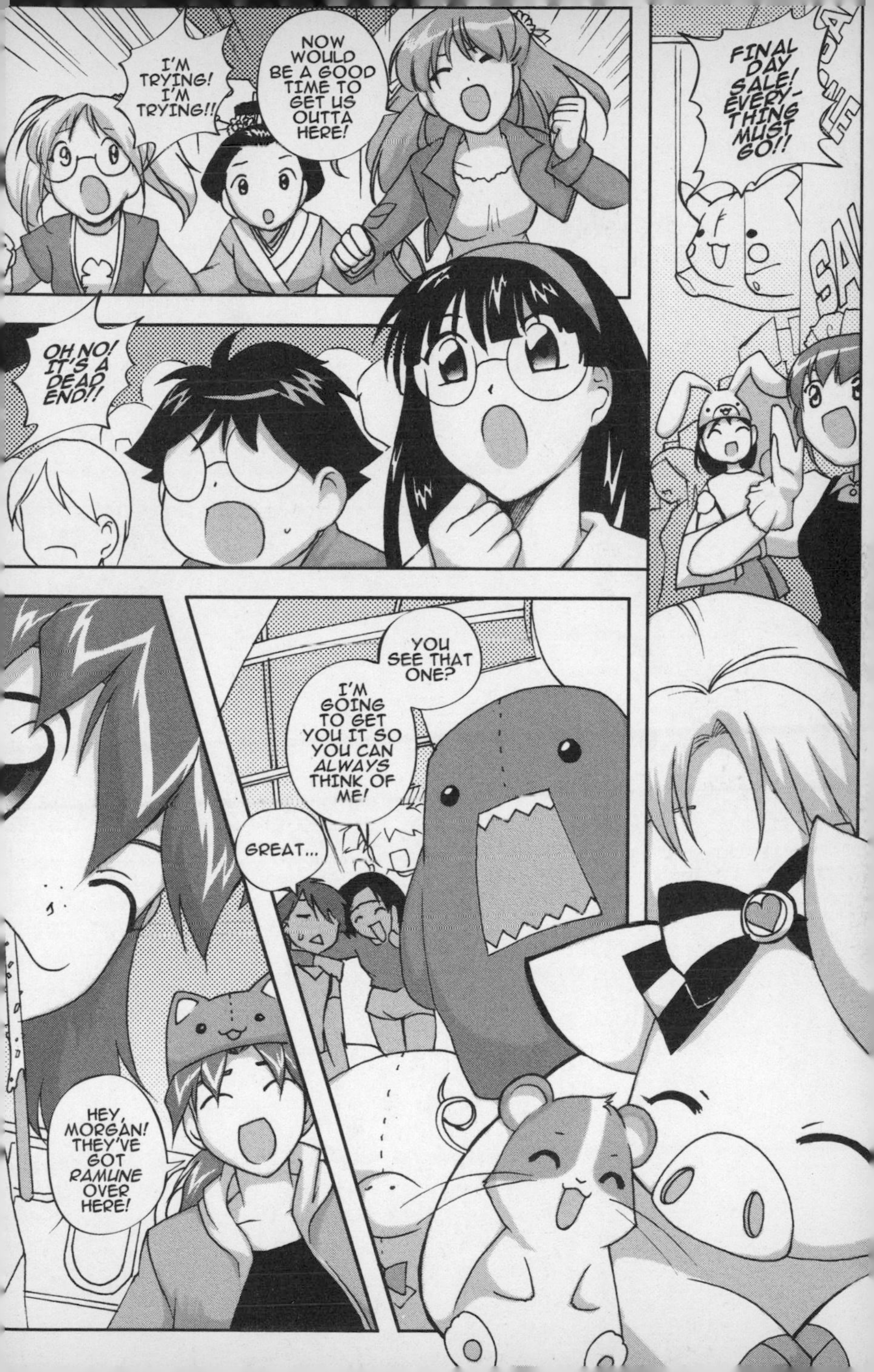
FINAL DAY SALE! EVERY-THING MUST GO!!
NOW WOULD BE A GOOD TIME TO GET US OUTTA HERE!
I'M TRYING! I'M TRYING!!
OH NO! IT'S A DEAD END!!
YOU SEE THAT ONE?
I'M GOING TO GET YOU IT SO YOU CAN *ALWAYS* THINK OF ME!
GREAT...
HEY, MORGAN! THEY'VE GOT RAMUNE OVER HERE!

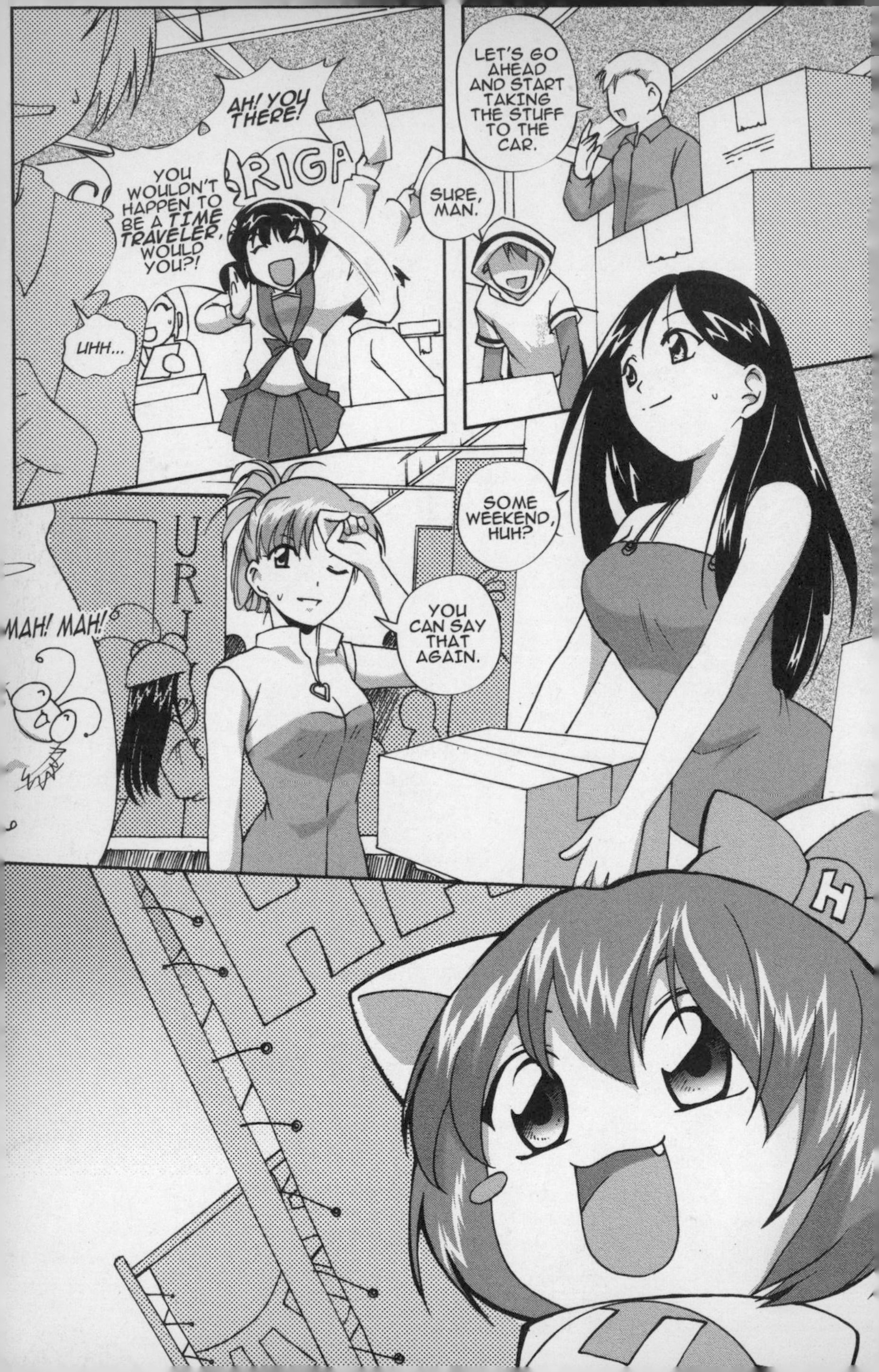
LET'S GO AHEAD AND START TAKING THE STUFF TO THE CAR.
SURE, MAN.
AH! YOU THERE!
RIGA
YOU WOULDN'T HAPPEN TO BE A TIME TRAVELER, WOULD YOU?!
UHH...
SOME WEEKEND, HUH?
YOU CAN SAY THAT AGAIN.
MAH! MAH!

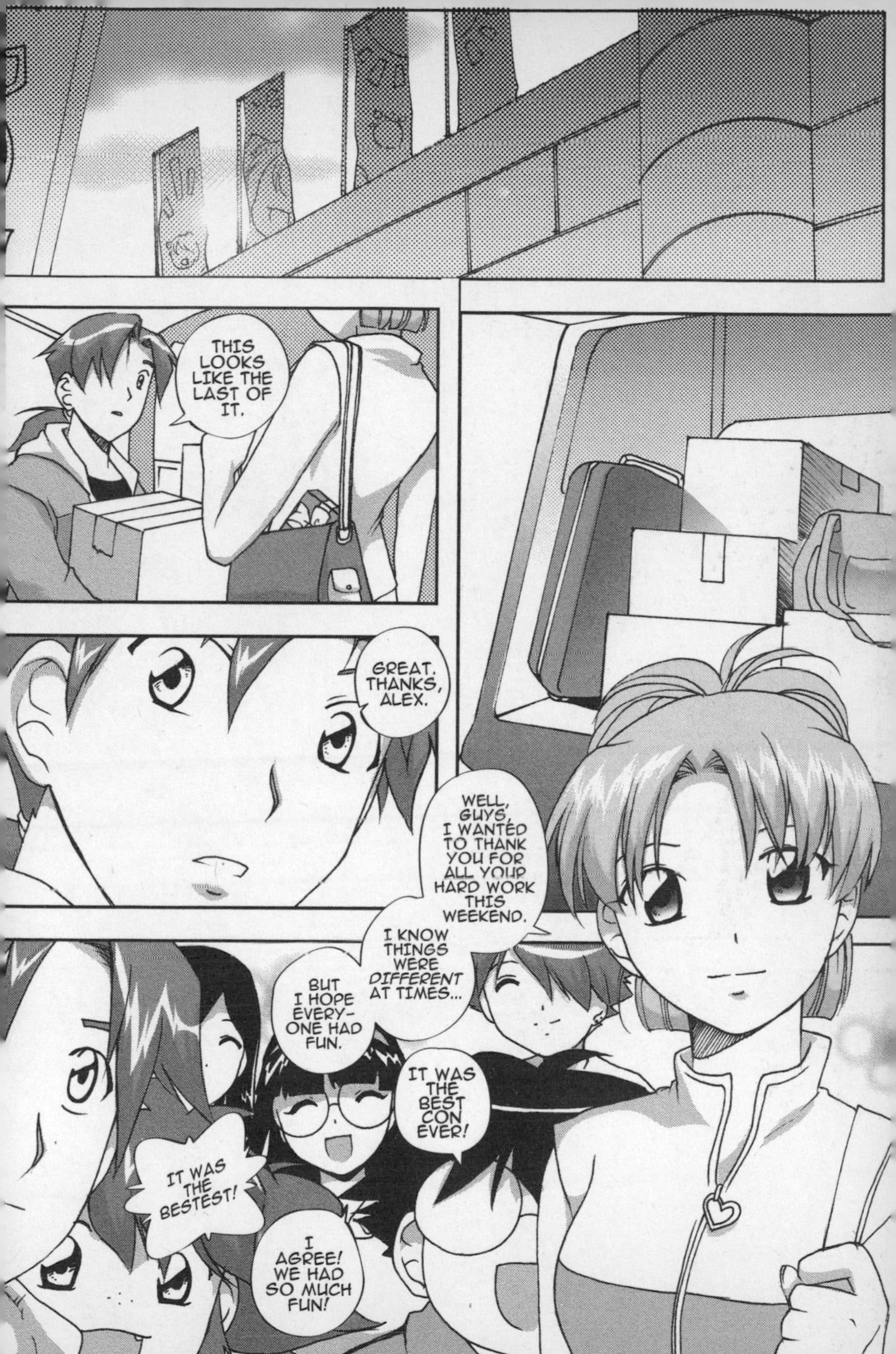

THIS LOOKS LIKE THE LAST OF IT.
GREAT. THANKS, ALEX.
WELL, GUYS, I WANTED TO THANK YOU FOR ALL YOUR HARD WORK THIS WEEKEND.
I KNOW THINGS WERE *DIFFERENT* AT TIMES...
BUT I HOPE EVERY-ONE HAD FUN.
IT WAS THE BEST CON EVER!
IT WAS THE BESTEST!
I AGREE! WE HAD SO MUCH FUN!

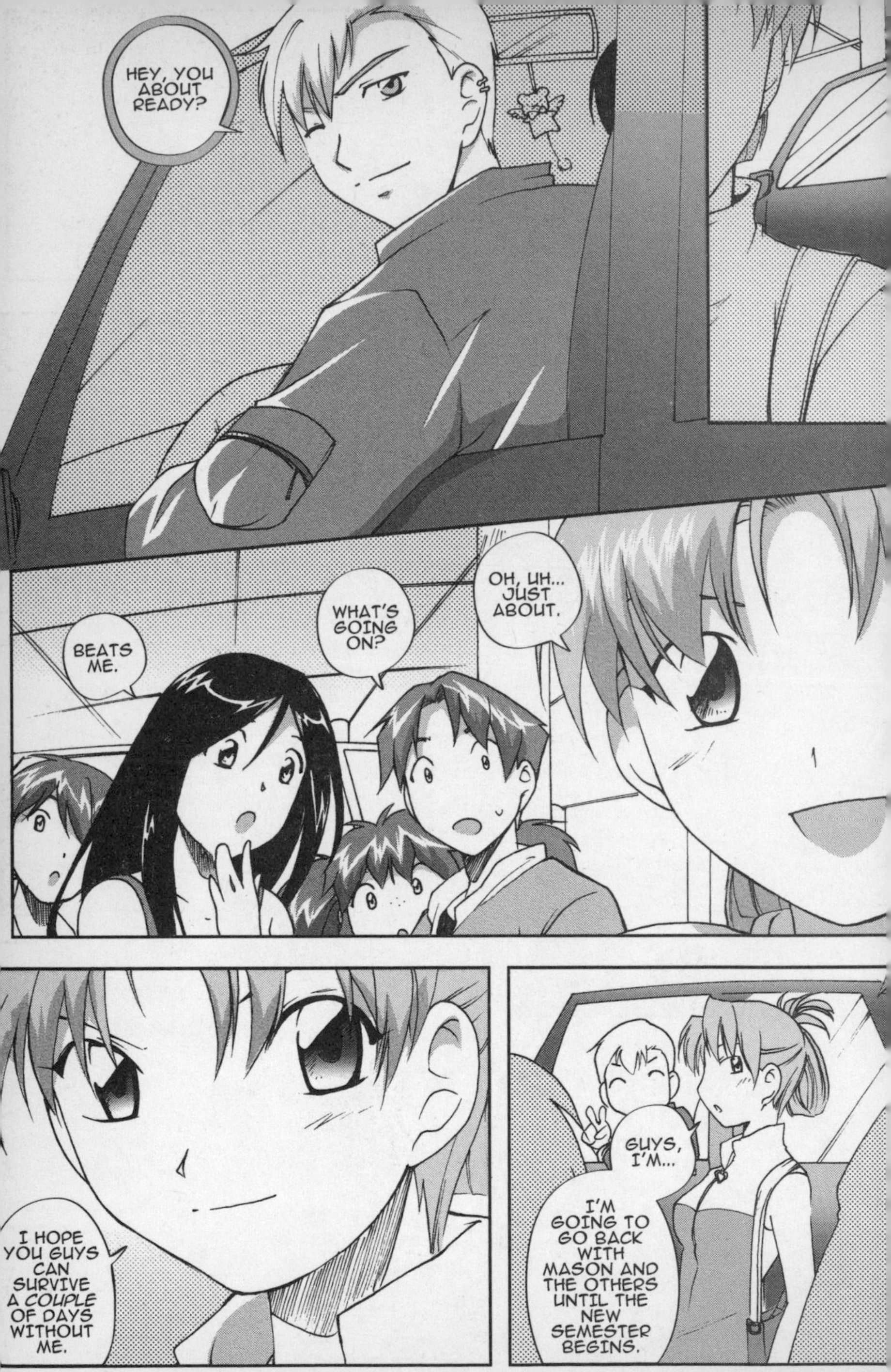
HEY, YOU ABOUT READY?
OH, UH... JUST ABOUT.
WHAT'S GOING ON?
BEATS ME.
GUYS, I'M...
I'M GOING TO GO BACK WITH MASON AND THE OTHERS UNTIL THE NEW SEMESTER BEGINS.
I HOPE YOU GUYS CAN SURVIVE A *COUPLE* OF DAYS WITHOUT ME.

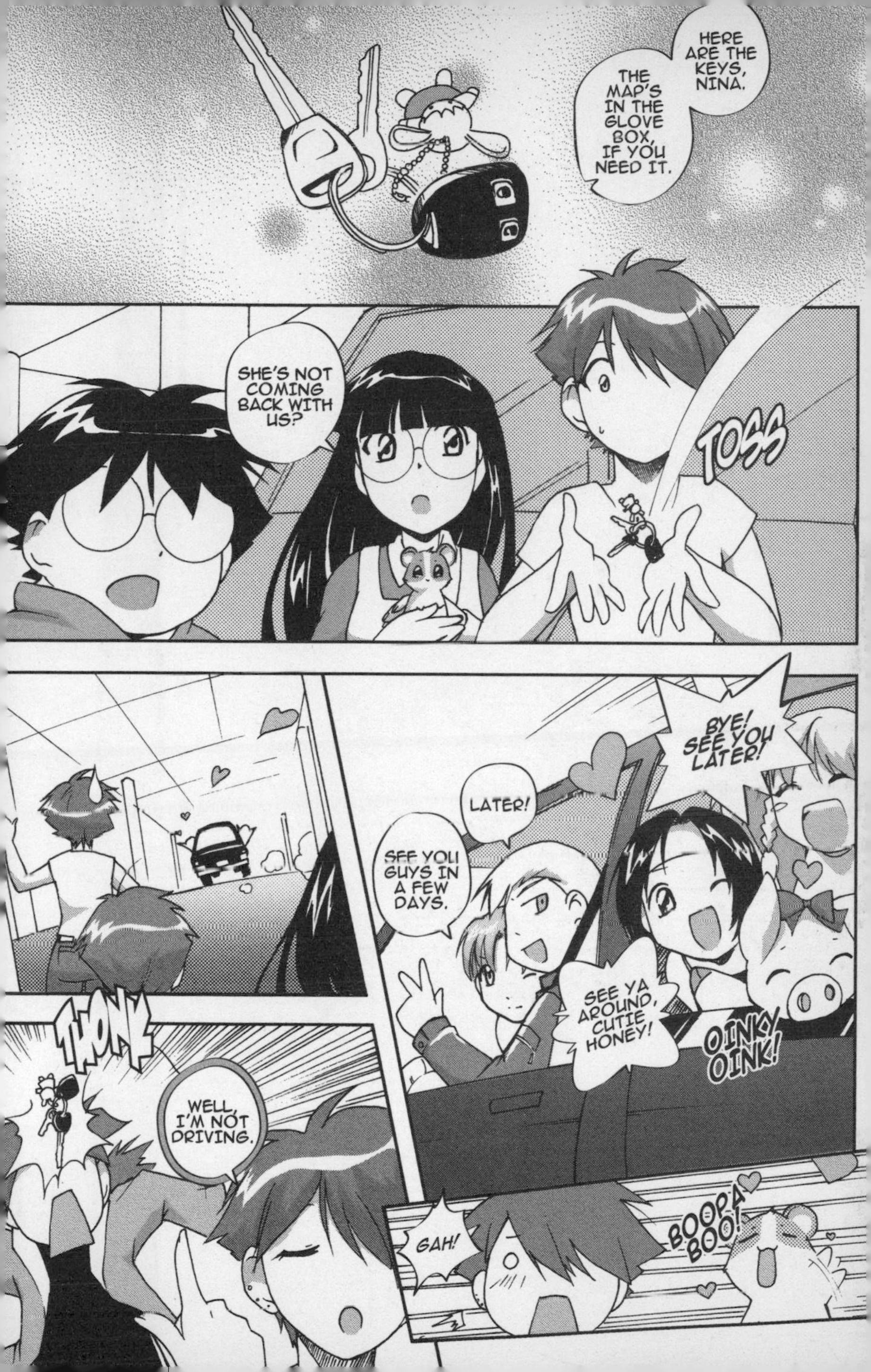
HERE ARE THE KEYS, NINA.
THE MAP'S IN THE GLOVE BOX, IF YOU NEED IT.
TOSS
SHE'S NOT COMING BACK WITH US?
BYE! SEE YOU LATER!
LATER!
SEE YOU GUYS IN A FEW DAYS.
SEE YA AROUND, CUTIE HONEY!
OINKY OINK!
BOOPA BOO!
GAH!
THONK
WELL, I'M NOT DRIVING.

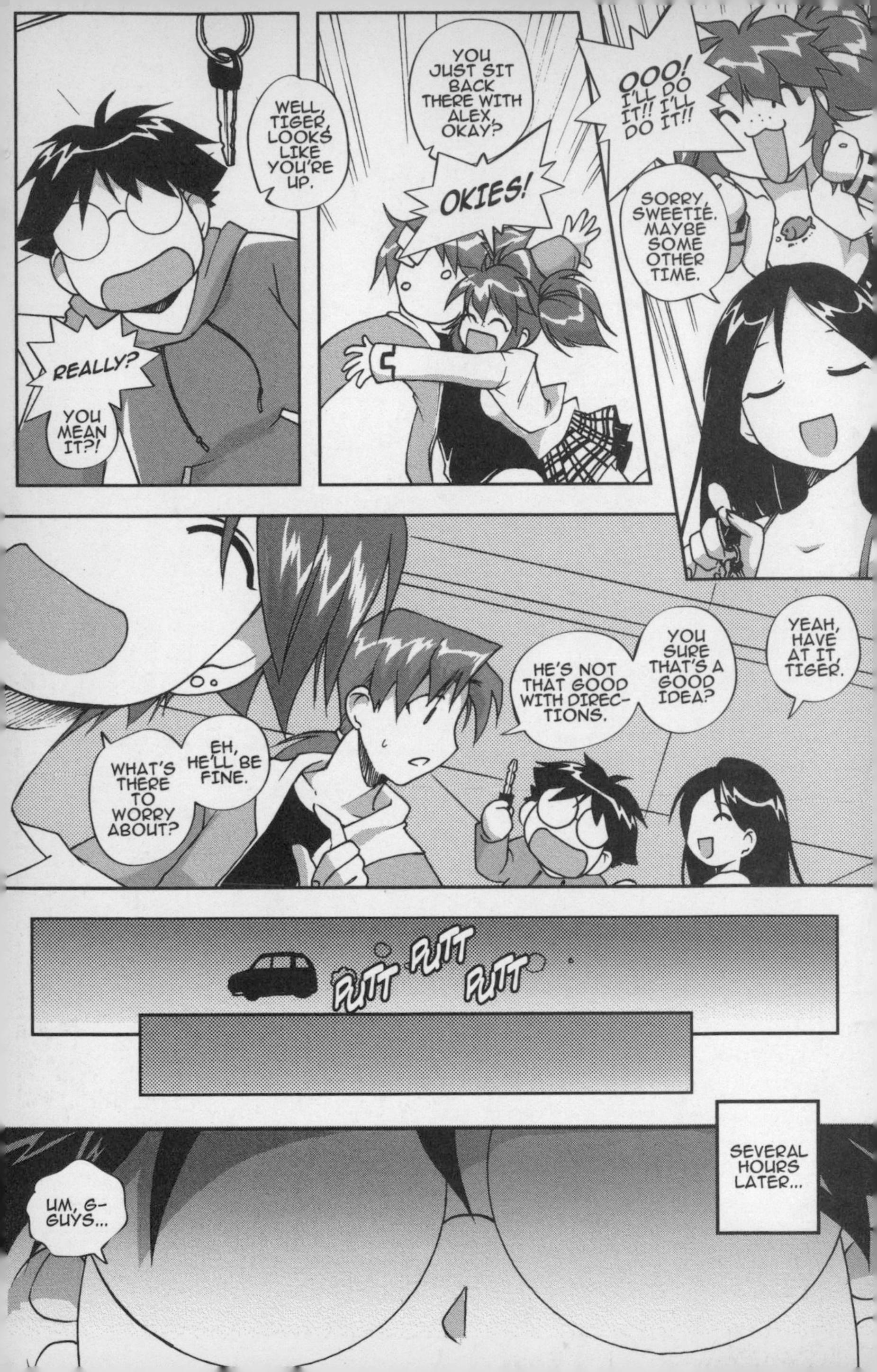
OOO! I'LL DO IT!! I'LL DO IT!!
SORRY, SWEETIE. MAYBE SOME OTHER TIME.
YOU JUST SIT BACK THERE WITH ALEX, OKAY?
OKIES!
WELL, TIGER, LOOKS LIKE YOU'RE UP.
REALLY?
YOU MEAN IT?!
YEAH, HAVE AT IT, TIGER.
YOU SURE THAT'S A GOOD IDEA?
HE'S NOT THAT GOOD WITH DIRECTIONS.
EH, HE'LL BE FINE.
WHAT'S THERE TO WORRY ABOUT?
PUTT PUTT PUTT
SEVERAL HOURS LATER...
UM, G-GUYS...

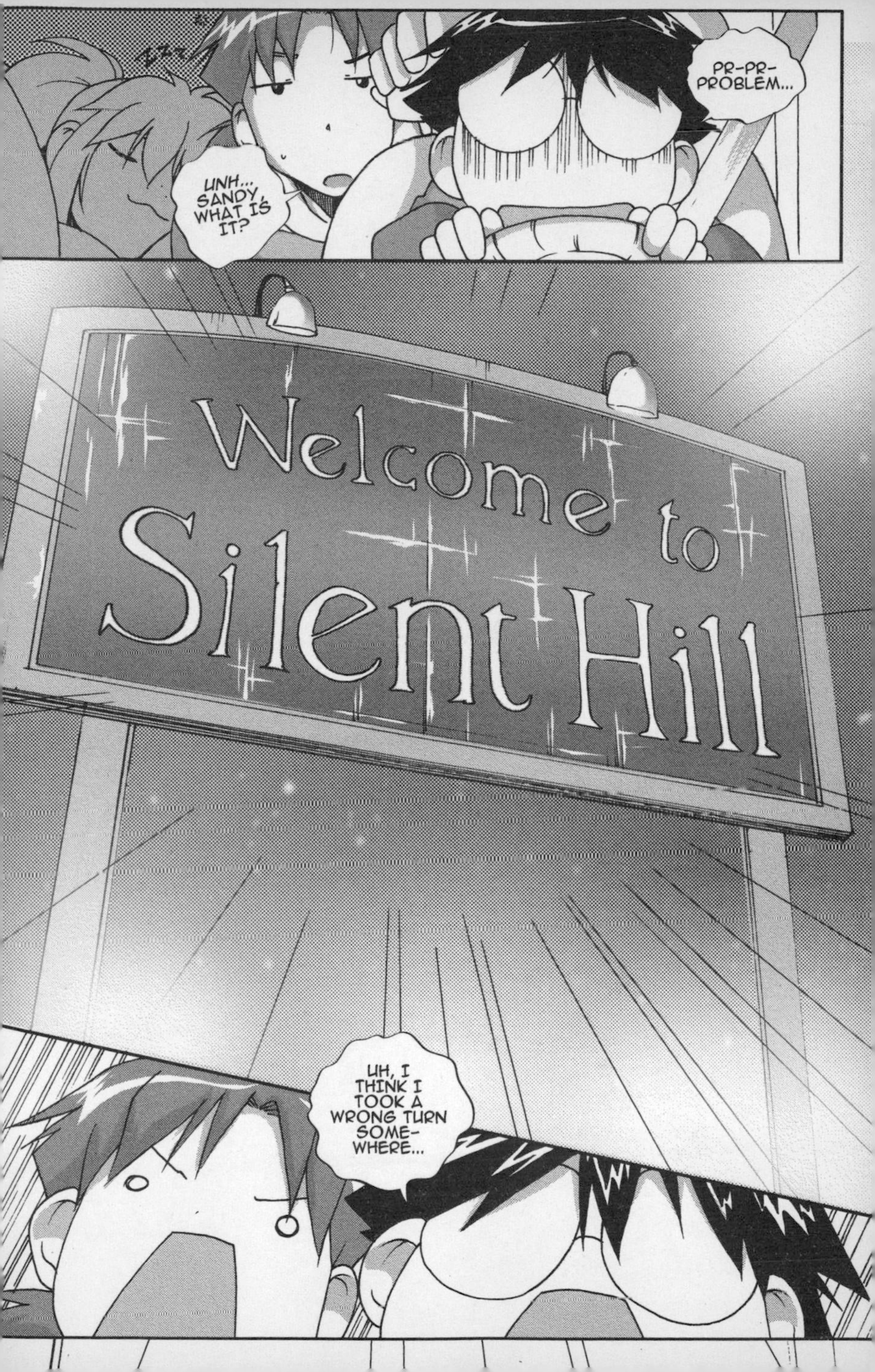
PR-PR-PROBLEM...
ZZZ
UNH... SANDY, WHAT IS IT?
Welcome to Silent Hill
UH, I THINK I TOOK A WRONG TURN SOME-WHERE...

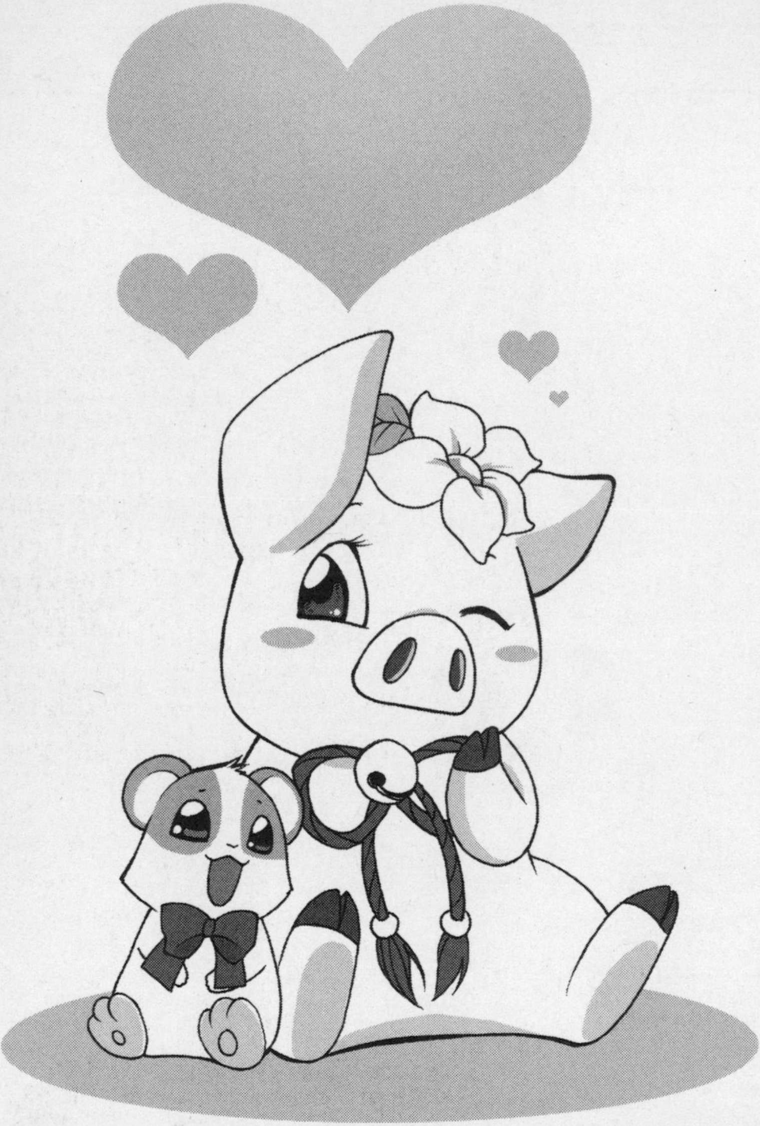

AOI NOTES

By Adam Arnold   • PRINT EDITION •   Volume 003. 2007

Line Art for this volume's cover.

Alternate Page 49

Hey, everyone, thanks for reading AOI HOUSE IN LOVE! Vol. 1!

I've gotta say, this particular volume has been a long time coming. The idea of writing a story set at a convention is one that I've wanted to do ever since I started batting around anime club concepts back in late 2004. And here it is 2007! That's two and a half years to have something brewing inside your head. I hope you enjoyed the results!

Anyway, I've got a lot of fun stuff to talk about, so let's get on with the commentary, shall we?!

Teh 'Uri House
members

▲ Original Designs of Uri House by Shiei

URI HOUSE

As you can probably tell from Shiei's original design sketch, the Uri House crew turned out quite differently in the final book than first envisioned. A big reason for this is the very nature of the story changed as I was writing it and Uri House evolved right along with it.

The initial idea for Uri House was for them to be introduced as something of a "Bizarro Aoi House" that would act as a rival anime club causing tension throughout the book. The basic thinking was that if Aoi House were this huge network TV show, then Uri House would be a rival network's rip-off... so what would happen if they met?

Back then, Uri House was going to have five boys and two girls and pretty much just be the opposite of Aoi House. That never really clicked, though. Shiei and I tossed around some ideas of there being four boys and three girls, but it just became obvious that we didn't need that many characters. Instead, I started playing with the idea that one of the Uri House girls would have a pet that Echiboo would fall in love with. I knew I wanted to use the name "Luna-P," but I didn't want the pet to be another hamster. The first thing that popped into my head was a pig, which is actually really fitting considering I subtitled this story arc "The Great Con Caper!" as an homage to the movie THE GREAT MUPPET CAPER.

Once Uri House had their own pet mascot, the personalities of individual characters started to form and I literally fell in love with the concept of Uri House. And that's where the direction of the story started to change. I no longer wanted Uri House to just appear as rivals that Aoi House would have to contend with throughout the book. I wanted them to be more like Aoi House's equals and a group of people that would be easy to get along with. And more than that, I wanted there to be some romantic chemistry between some of the characters—especially, between Mason and Elle.

MASON BLUE

I'll admit that initially Mason wasn't an easy character to get right. The problem was that I could never figure out what he was going to look like. The original sketch of the Uri House gang that Shiei did showed the president of Uri House as being this young guy with a cigarette that was kind of like Haruka from LOVE HINA.

As the story evolved, I wanted the president to be a foil for Elle and also a possible romantic interest. We both knew the original design no longer worked, but we were still drawing a blank for what we wanted Mason to look like. Then I happened upon the anime for one of my favorite manga—PARADISE KISS.

Yes, Mason's look is modeled after George from PARADISE KISS. It's the short Justin Timberlake-type hair. It just worked really well, for some reason, and gave Mason that certain something he needed to not only drive all those fangirls wild, but also be someone Elle could realistically fall for.

URI HOUSE CHARACTER DOSSIER

Mason Blue (M) –Club leader. Bit of a bad boy, but suave and charming. The perfect love interest for Elle.

Kimberly Ann Palmer (F) – Southern girl. Carries Luna-P around like a prized and pampered pet. Born February 23.

Sanae Kirishima (F) – Japanese-American girl. Bit promiscuous and playful.

Kevin Cardenas (M) – Canadian wise guy. Wears a hoody jacket, likes hitting on the ladies. Gets slapped a lot.

Dale Stevens (M) – If Sandy is a dork, then Dale is just a nerd and is therefore much cooler than Sandy. Wears glasses and is skinny. Also happens to be an artist.

Luna-P (F) - Kimberly's pet pig.

REJECTED URI IDEAS

When coming up with Uri House, a lot of ideas were thrown around and quite a few ended up on the cutting room floor. Probably the earliest (and weirdest) idea that I remember coming up with for Uri House was a result of forum speculation. I would joke with Shiei that if I ever wrote Uri House that it would be these five QUEER AS FOLK-esque guys that were into yuri.

Some of the other rejected ideas I had involved various Uri House members that never came to be. The weirdest of those was the thought of Uri House having their own version of Carlo. Shiei suggested he be kind of like Man-Faye, and I thought about what a female version of Man-Faye would be. And I came up with the concept of a "She-Spike," which is basically this really butch woman dressed like Spike from COWBOY BEBOP.

If you think that idea was bad, then try imagining an Uri House member that's obsessive compulsive and uses a lot of wet naps. Yeah, neither could I.

And that's a good place to wrap things up. Shiei and I hope you got a kick out of reading "The Great Con Caper," because we sure had a lot of fun putting it together.

Adam Arnold
May 3, 2007

UASOS BRIGADE

Since Uri House became such an integral part of the continuing Aoi House storyline, it no longer made a lot of sense for the two clubs to fight against each other past that initial jutsu-filled confrontation. However, I still had this big cosplay competition that I wanted to do for the finale, but didn't want to just make it a fan service romp without some tension. So I came up with another rival anime club that could swoop in and steal away both Aoi and Uri House's glory sparking the two clubs to have to unite against a common enemy. That enemy was the UASOS Brigade.

It should be pretty obvious that this third club is obsessed with the series THE MELANCHOLY OF HARUHI SUZUMIYA to the point that they've kinda taken the idea of simply cos-playing as the characters to a whole 'nother level and actually founded their own unofficial club devoted to the series. The members that make up the club are Audrey Mayer (F), Tessa Lass (F), Dana Hart (F), James Horne (M) and Mark Delfino (M). If you flip back to Episode 8's UASOS cosplay spread, then that's them from right-to-left.

BLADE & TIME GALS

Episode 4 opens with the guys in one of the Hatsu-Con video rooms enthralled by this new anime they're seeing. But what exactly was that series? Well, it's something that Shiei created that doesn't really have a name right now. Shiei calls it "BLADE" after the  main character and it's something that's she's been drawing off and on for quite a while now. Who knows, maybe one day Shiei'll get to do a full-fledged manga chronicling the rivalry between Blade and Roadkill. At the very least, it was fun writing them into the Aoi Universe.

Something else I had fun with was working in a little scene in Episode 9 involving a story concept of mine called "TIME GALS." I doubt we'll ever see it get made into a series, but having it as a way of helping Sandy get closer to Maria just worked nicely. Plus, it sure beats constantly paying homage to other people's stuff, right?

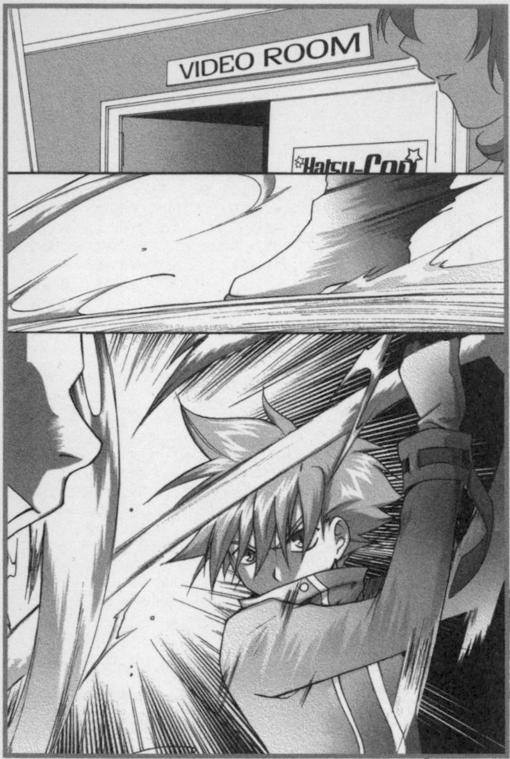
VIDEO ROOM
Hatsu-Cop

Alternate Page 64

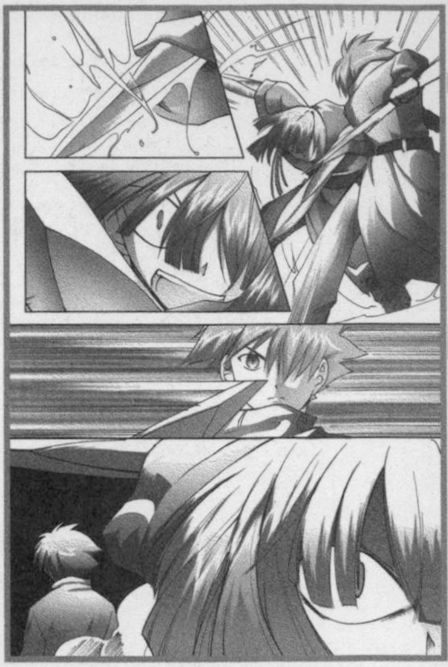

Alternate Page 65

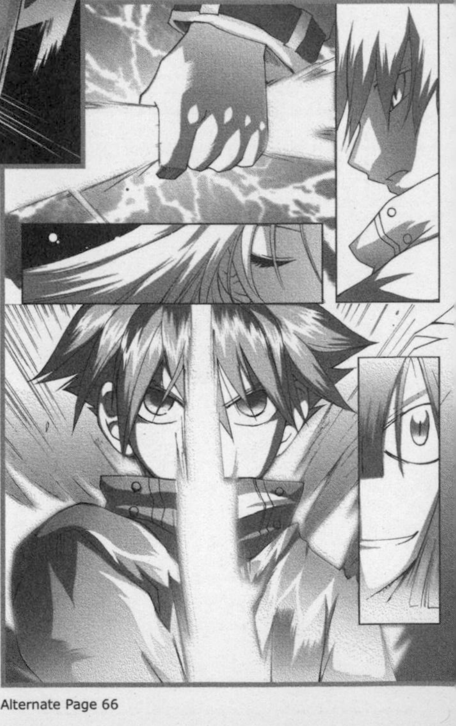

Alternate Page 66

THE ALTERNATE "BLADE" ANIME

Presented here is an alternate version of the Blade versus Roadkill anime sequence from the beginning of Episode 4. Enjoy!

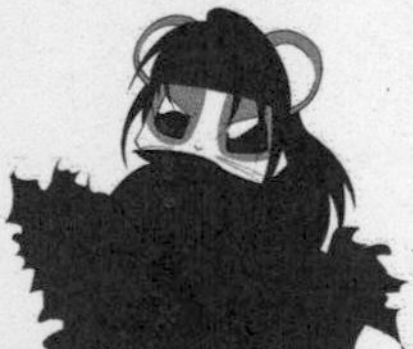

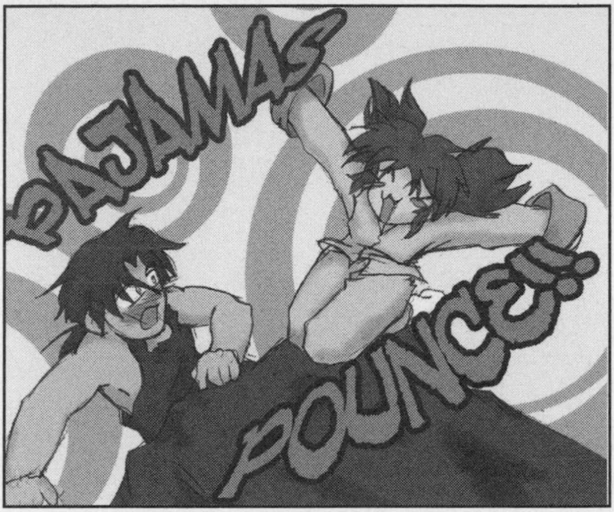
PAJAMAS
POUNCE!!!
Morgan & Alex by quarteni

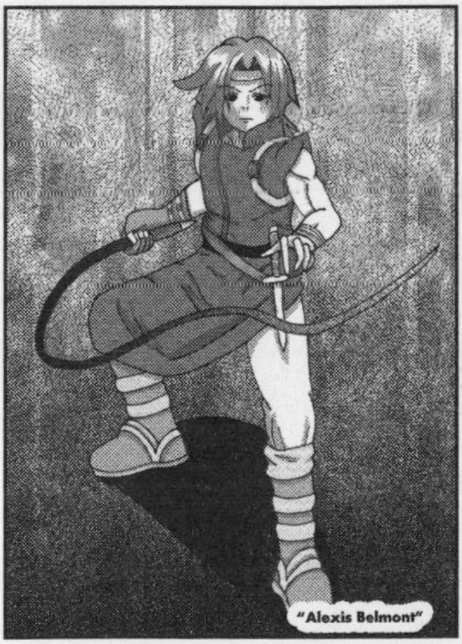
"Alexis Belmont"
Alex Belmont by Steven Kunz

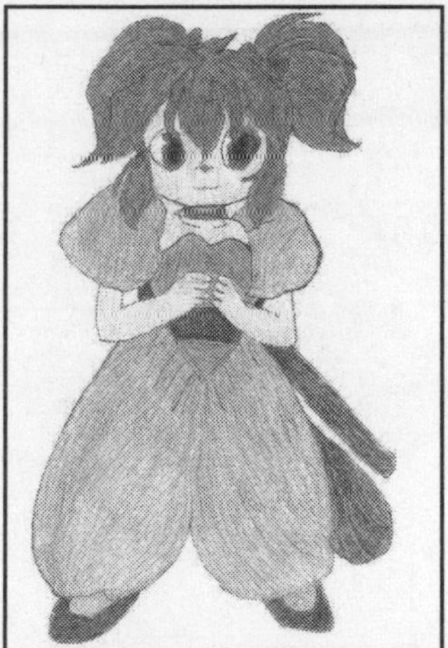
Morgan by Kadenmire

FAN ART

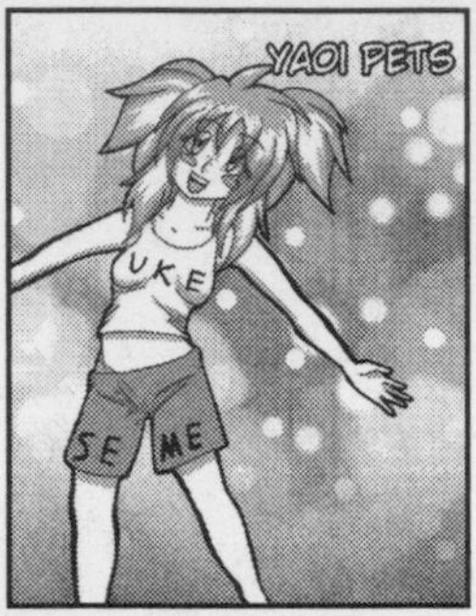
YAOI PETS
UKE
SE ME
Morgan by Steven Kunz

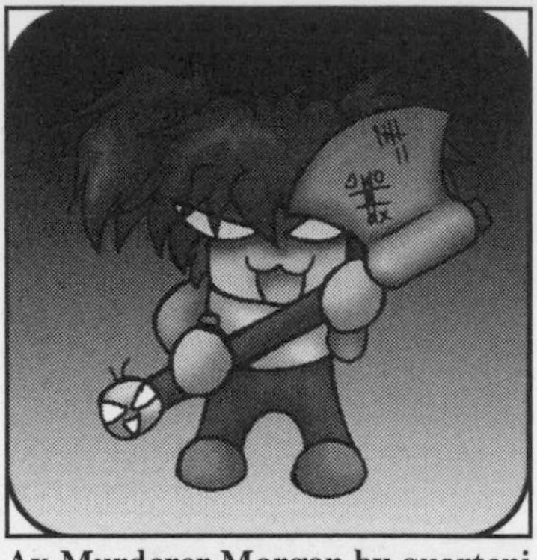
Ax Murderer Morgan by quarteni

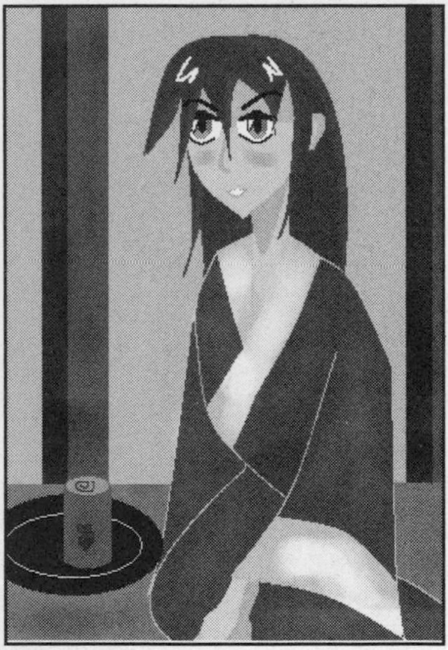
Alex by Katyasha

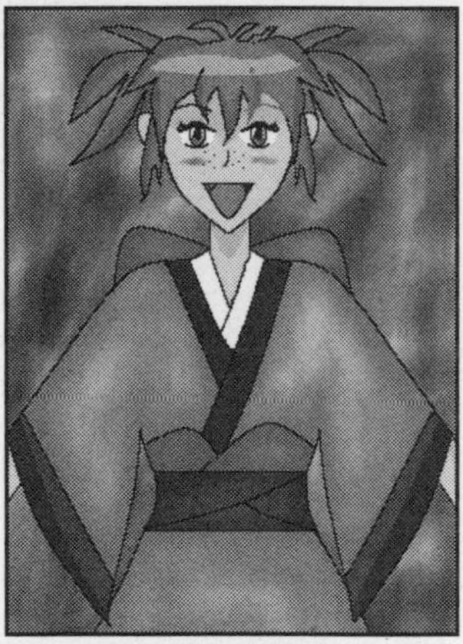
Morgan by Katyasha

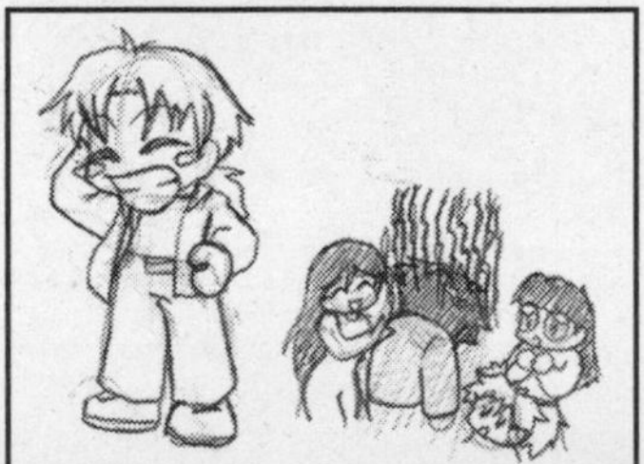
Alex is Great by quarteni

FAN ART

Aomii House by Radioactive24

Maria by dryope

Human Echiboo by Gladimus

Morgan by sleepyboi

FAN ART

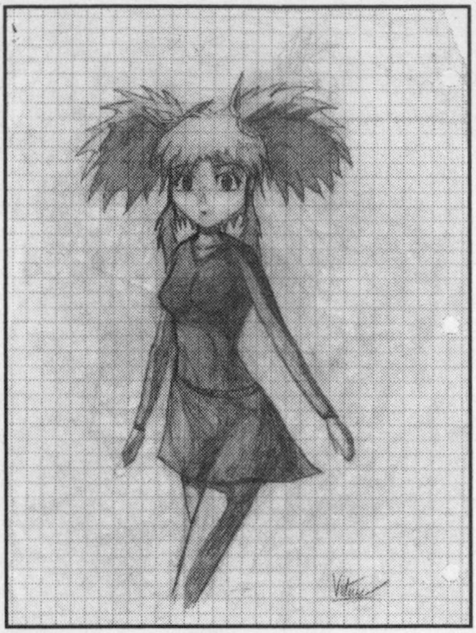

Morgan by Vitius

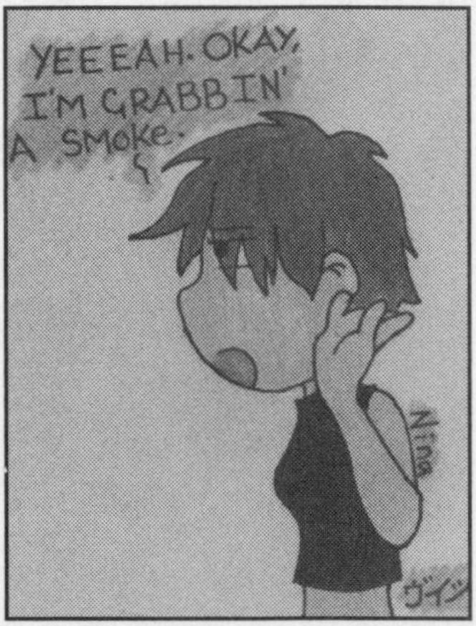
YEEEAH. OKAY, I'M GRABBIN' A SMOKE.
Nina

Nina by withxlove

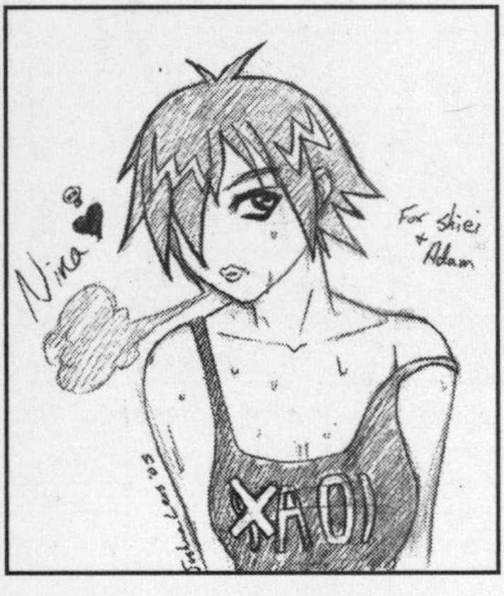
Nina
For Shiei + Adam
XAOI

Sexy Nina by Joshua Leos

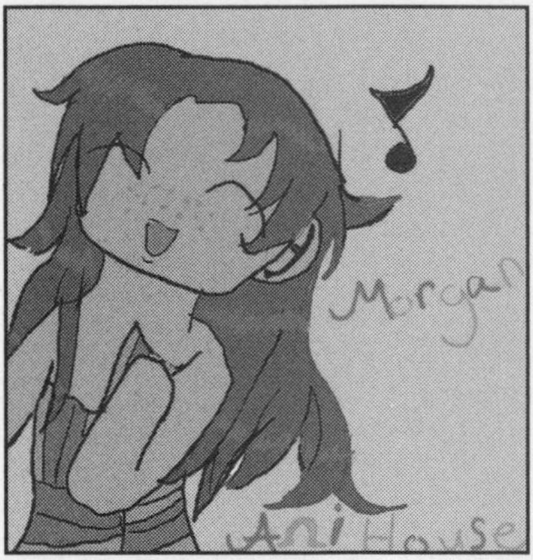
Morgan

Morgan by Chrnoskitty

FAN ART

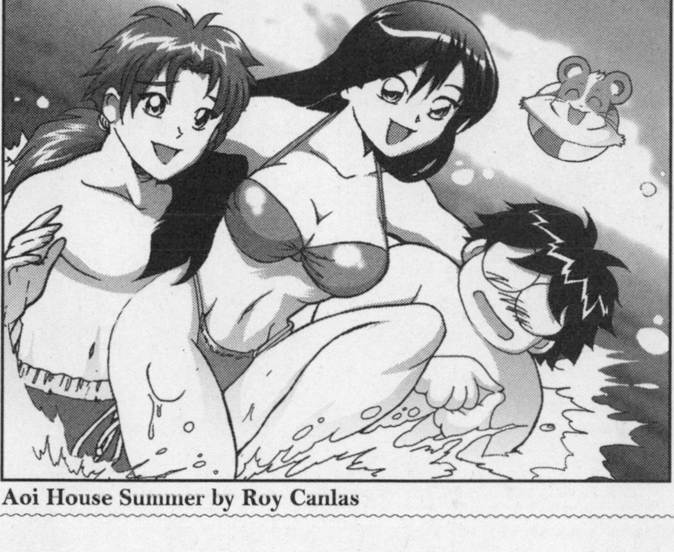

Aoi House Summer by Roy Canlas

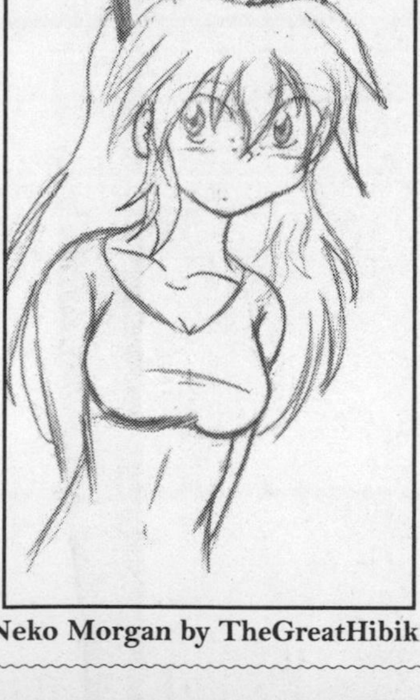

Neko Morgan by TheGreatHibiki

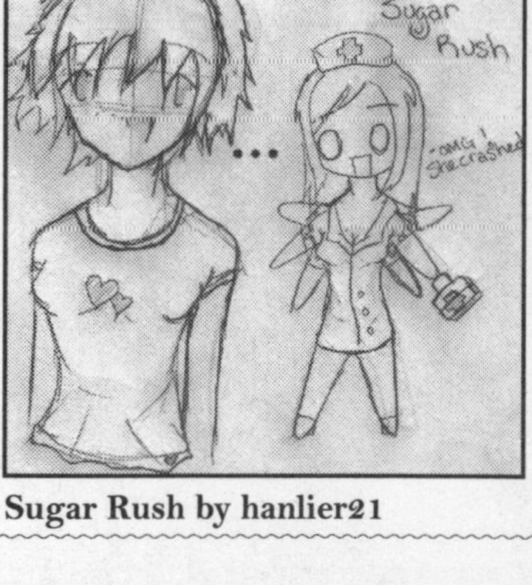
Morgan's Sugar Rush
...
-omg! she crashed

Sugar Rush by hanlier21

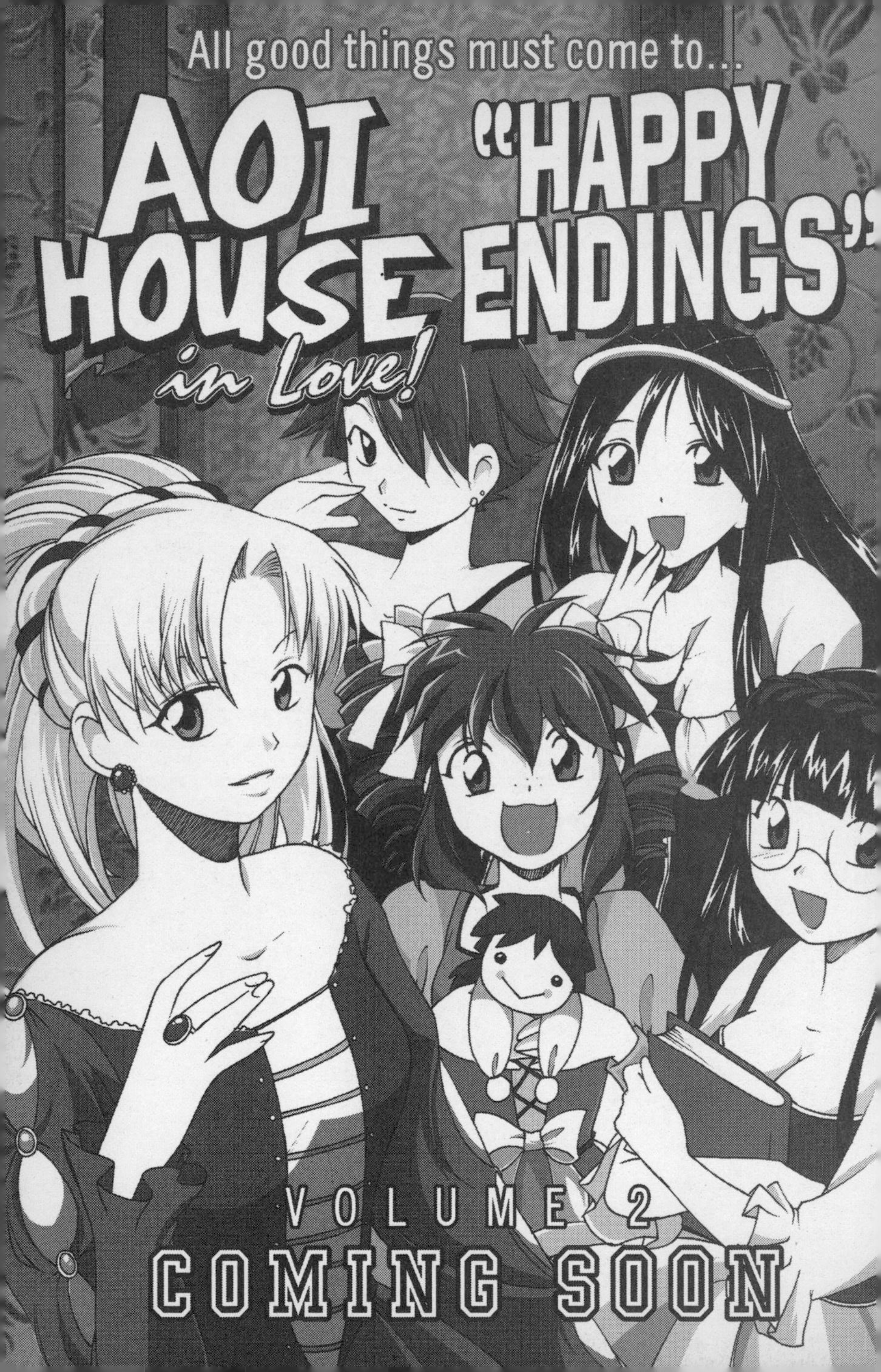
All good things must come to...
AOI HOUSE in Love!
"HAPPY ENDINGS"
VOLUME 2
COMING SOON

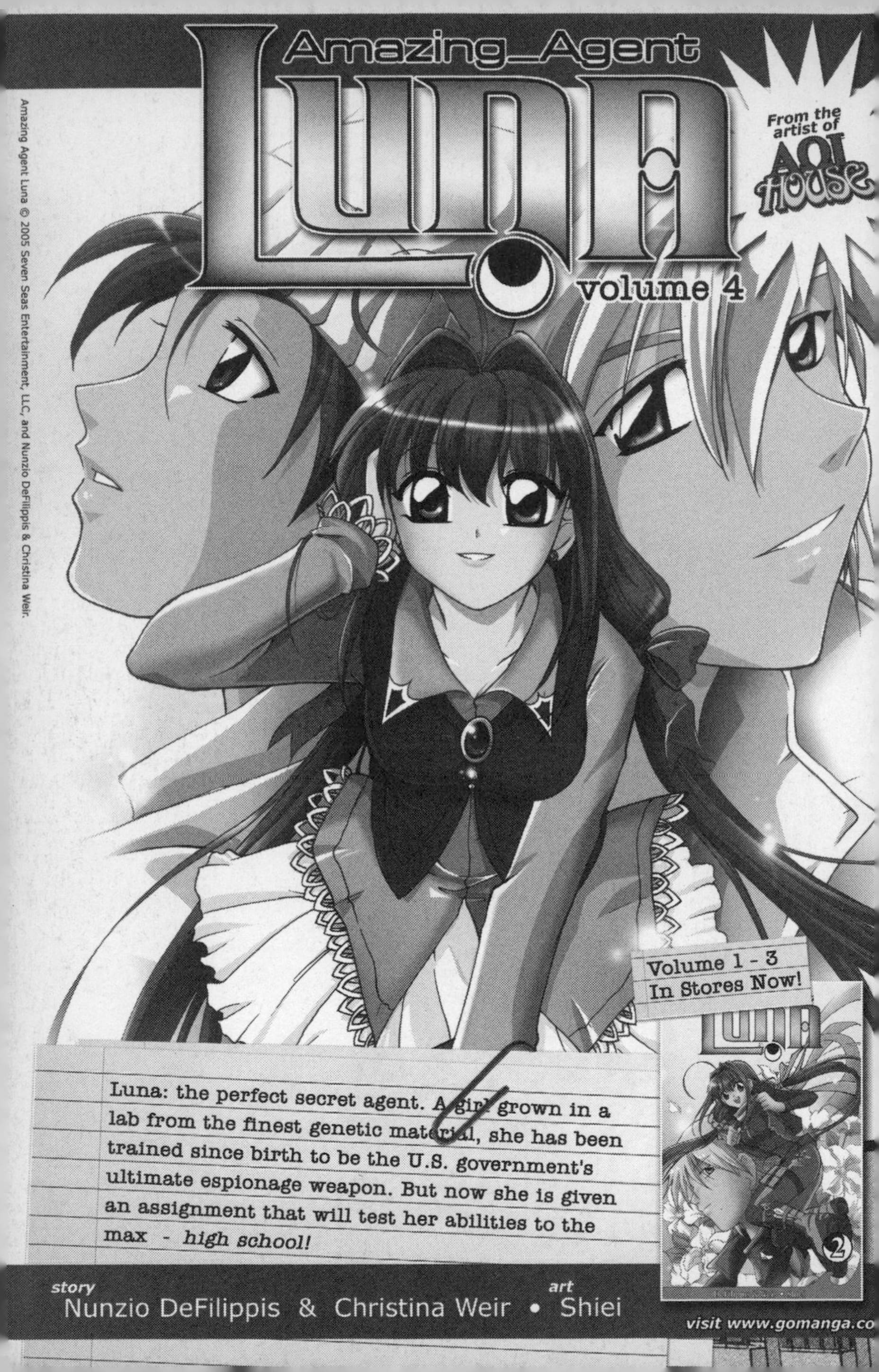
Amazing Agent
LUNA
volume 4
From the artist of
AOI HOUSE
Amazing Agent Luna © 2005 Seven Seas Entertainment, LLC, and Nunzio DeFilippis & Christina Weir.
Volume 1 - 3
In Stores Now!
LUNA
2
Luna: the perfect secret agent. A girl grown in a lab from the finest genetic material, she has been trained since birth to be the U.S. government's ultimate espionage weapon. But now she is given an assignment that will test her abilities to the max - *high school!*
story
Nunzio DeFilippis & Christina Weir
art
Shiei
visit www.gomanga.co

Every night...

I turn into a cat.

MOONLIGHT
MEOW

ON SALE NOW!

Master, how may we serve you?

HE IS MY MASTER

In Stores Now!

Fandom has never been this much fun!

I, OTAKU
STRUGGLE IN AKIHABARA

Coming October 2007

I, Otaku: Struggle in Akihabara © 2003 Jiro Suzuki

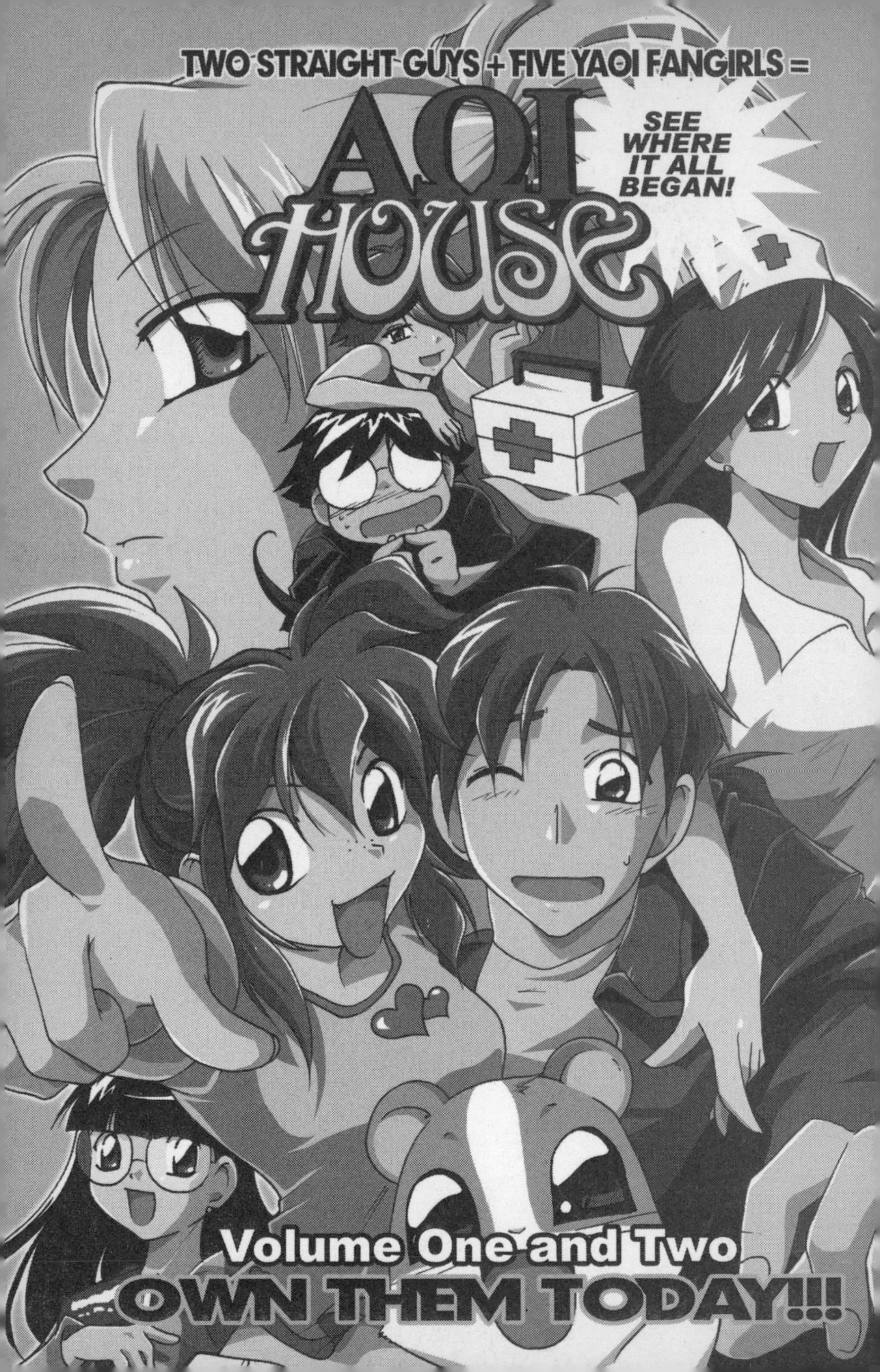

TWO STRAIGHT GUYS + FIVE YAOI FANGIRLS =
AOI HOUSE
SEE WHERE IT ALL BEGAN!
Volume One and Two
OWN THEM TODAY!!!

POCKY WARS: EPISOD

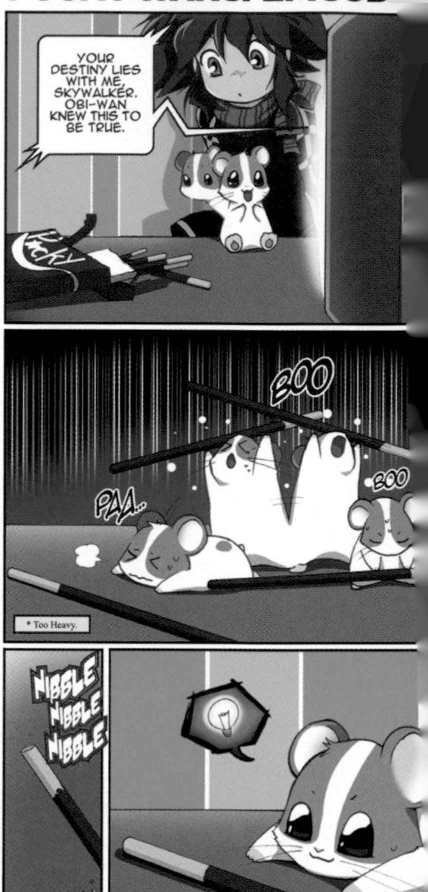
YOUR DESTINY LIES WITH ME, SKYWALKER. OBI-WAN KNEW THIS TO BE TRUE.
BOO
BOO
PAA...
* Too Heavy.
NIBBLE
NIBBLE
NIBBLE
BOOPA!
USE THE FORCE, 'BOO!

DECK THE HALLS

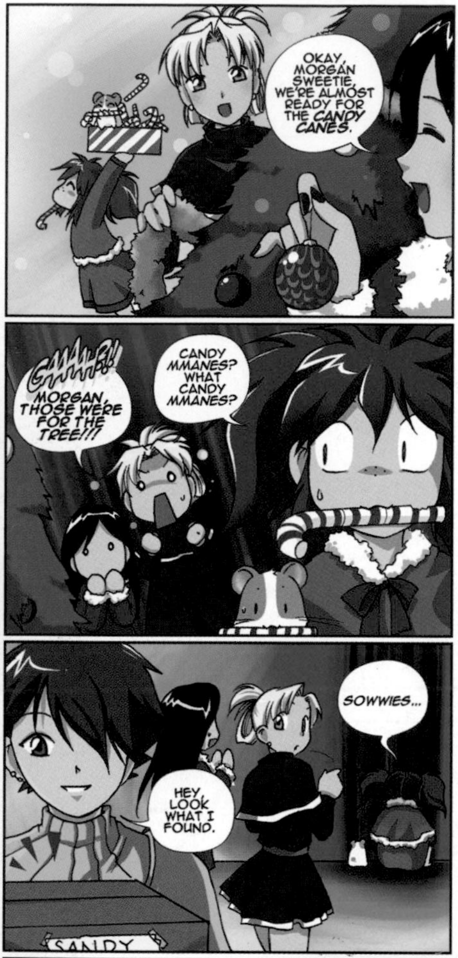
OKAY, MORGAN SWEETIE, WE'RE ALMOST READY FOR THE *CANDY CANES*.
CANDY MMANES? WHAT CANDY MMANES?
MORGAN, THOSE WERE FOR THE TREE!!!
SOWWIES...
HEY, LOOK WHAT I FOUND.
SANDY
!
MY GASHAPON COLLECTION?!!

These 4-Koma originally appeared in *Newtype USA* from January '06 ~ December '06.

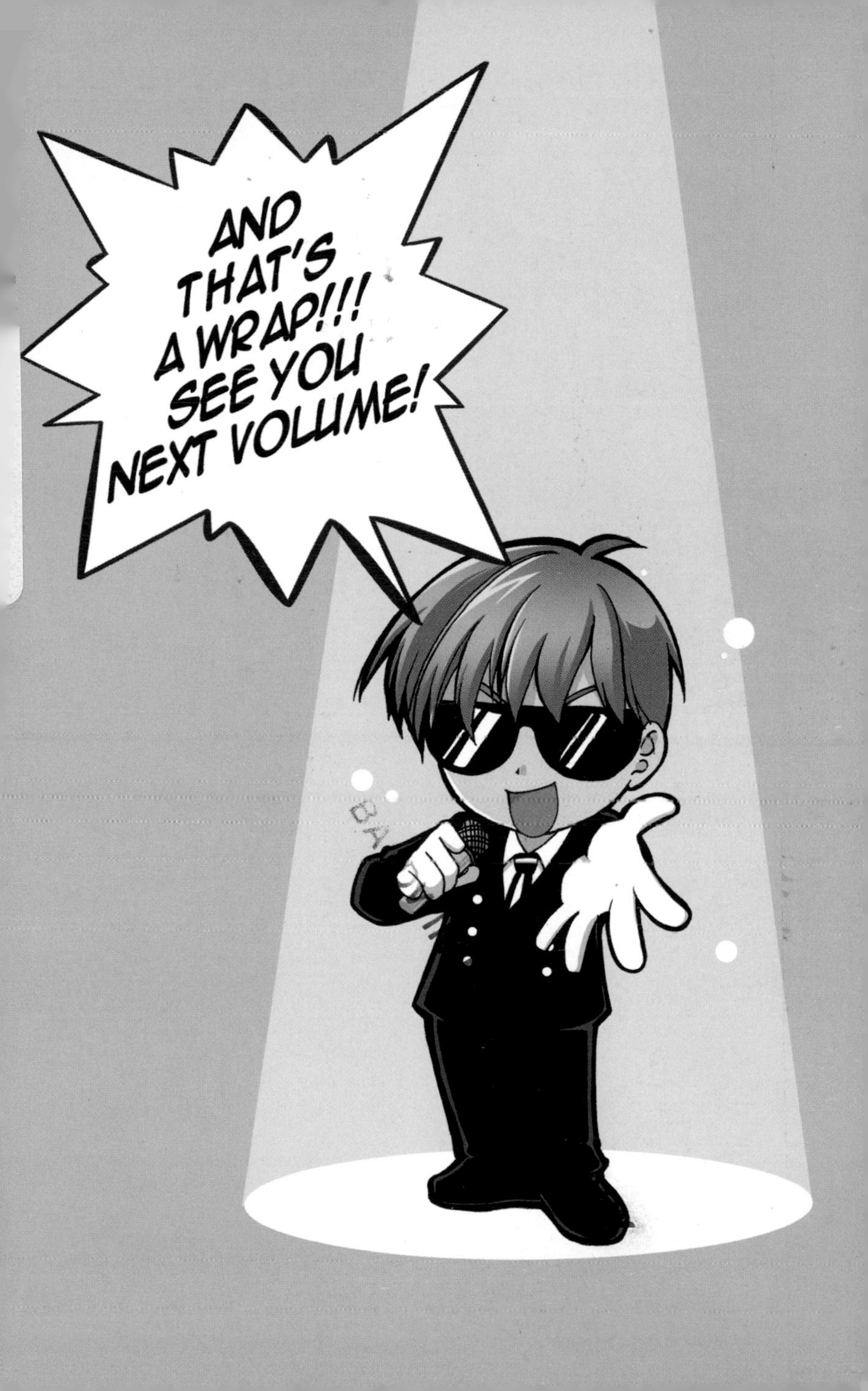
AND THAT'S A WRAP!!! SEE YOU NEXT VOLUME!
BA

DAYDREAM BELIEVER

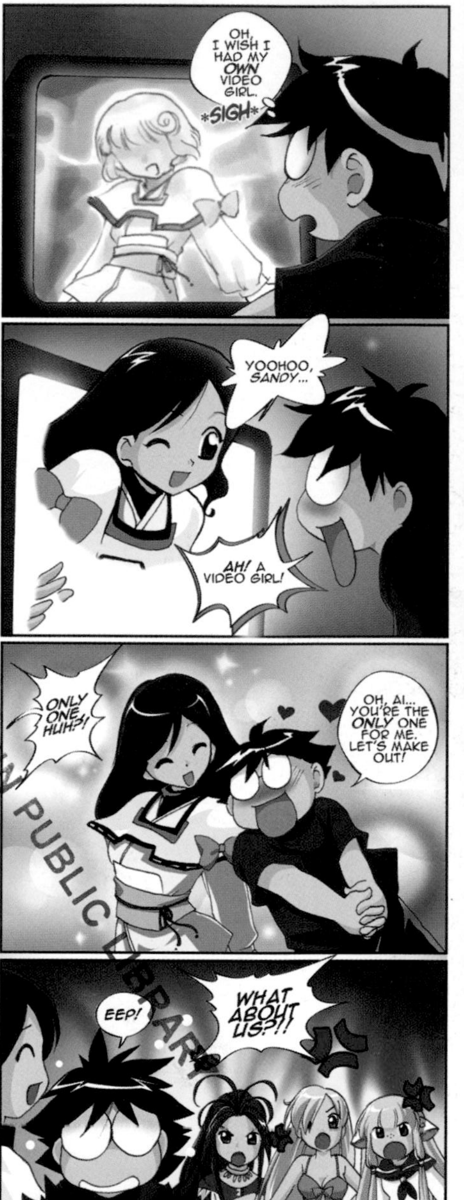
OH, I WISH I HAD MY OWN VIDEO GIRL.
SIGH
YOOHOO, SANDY...
AH! A VIDEO GIRL!
OH, AI... YOU'RE THE ONLY ONE FOR ME. LET'S MAKE OUT!
ONLY ONE, HUH?!
WHAT ABOUT US?!!
EEP!

CANDY LANE

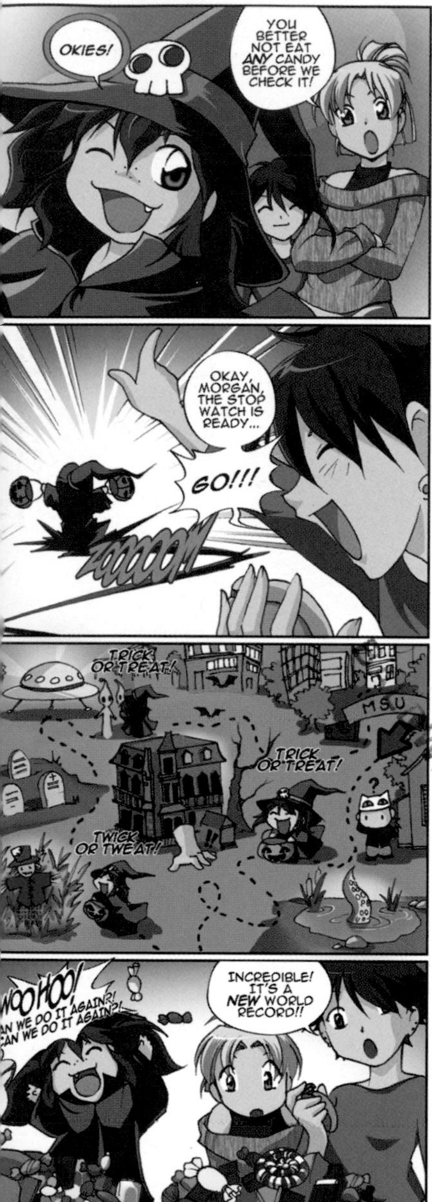
YOU BETTER NOT EAT ANY CANDY BEFORE WE CHECK IT!
OKIES!
OKAY, MORGAN, THE STOP WATCH IS READY...
GO!!!
ZOOOOOOM!
M.S.U
TRICK OR TREAT!
TRICK OR TREAT!
TWICK OR TWEAT!
INCREDIBLE! IT'S A NEW WORLD RECORD!!
WOO HOO!
AN WE DO IT AGAIN?!
CAN WE DO IT AGAIN?!

GOOD IDEA / BAD IDEA 1 (CON STYLE)

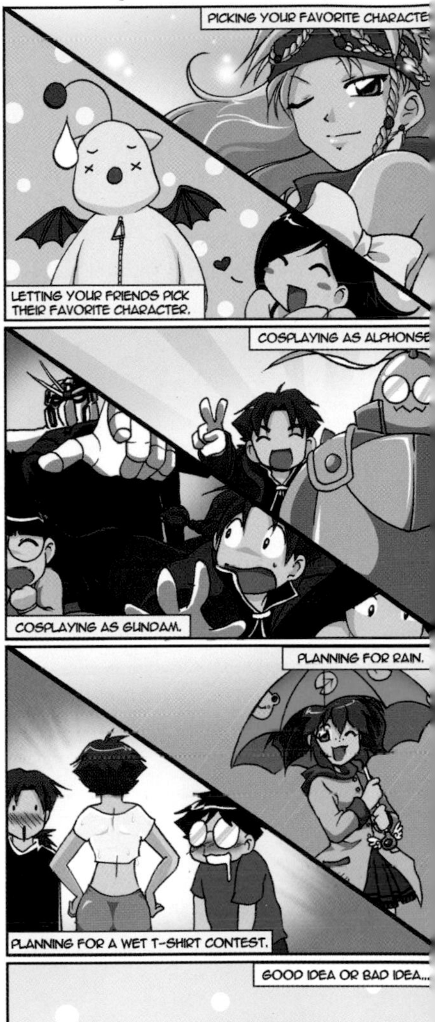
PICKING YOUR FAVORITE CHARACTER
LETTING YOUR FRIENDS PICK THEIR FAVORITE CHARACTER.
COSPLAYING AS ALPHONSE
COSPLAYING AS GUNDAM.
PLANNING FOR RAIN.
PLANNING FOR A WET T-SHIRT CONTEST.
GOOD IDEA OR BAD IDEA...
BEING A CONVENTION PANTY THIEF.

GOOD IDEA / BAD IDEA 2 (CON STYLE)

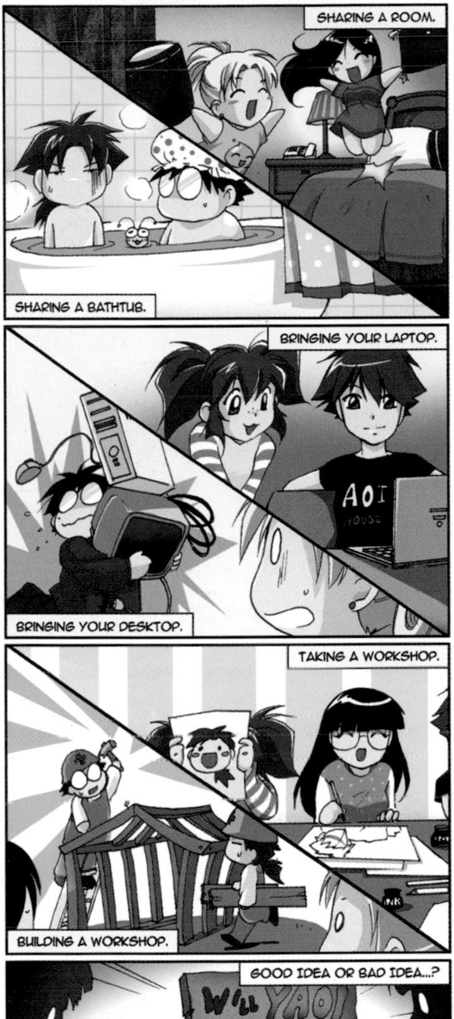
SHARING A ROOM.
SHARING A BATHTUB.
BRINGING YOUR LAPTOP.
AOI HOUSE
BRINGING YOUR DESKTOP.
TAKING A WORKSHOP.
INK
BUILDING A WORKSHOP.
GOOD IDEA OR BAD IDEA...?
WILL YAOI FOR CHANGE
YAOI-ING FOR CHANGE.

STUDY BUDDIES

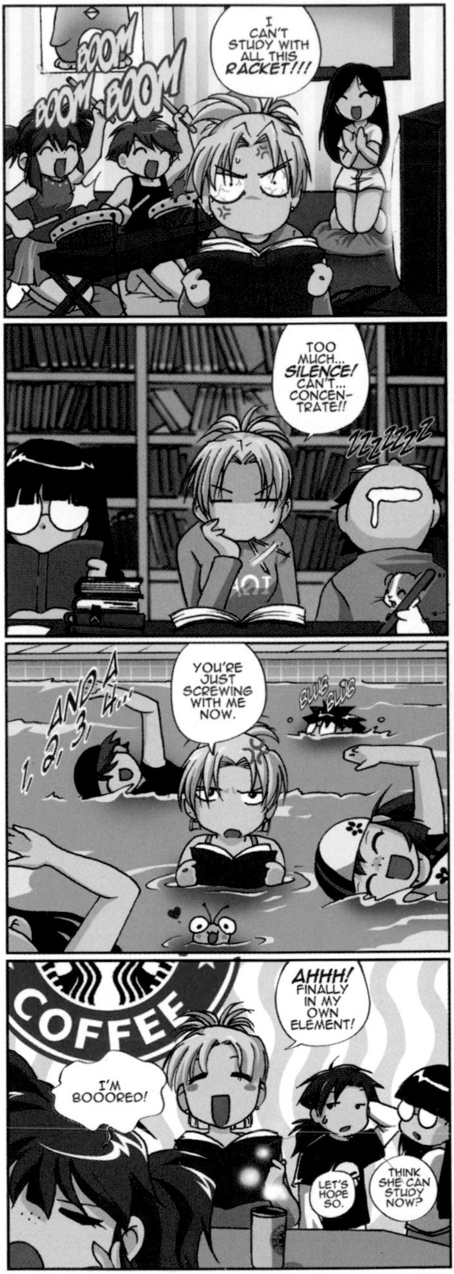
I CAN'T STUDY WITH ALL THIS RACKET!!!
BOOM BOOM
BOOM BOOM
TOO MUCH... SILENCE! CAN'T... CONCENTRATE!!
ZZZZZZZ
BLUB BLUB
YOU'RE JUST SCREWING WITH ME NOW.
AND A 1, 2, 3, 4...
AHHH! FINALLY IN MY OWN ELEMENT!
COFFEE
I'M BOOORED!
THINK SHE CAN STUDY NOW?
LET'S HOPE SO.

FUN IN THE SUN

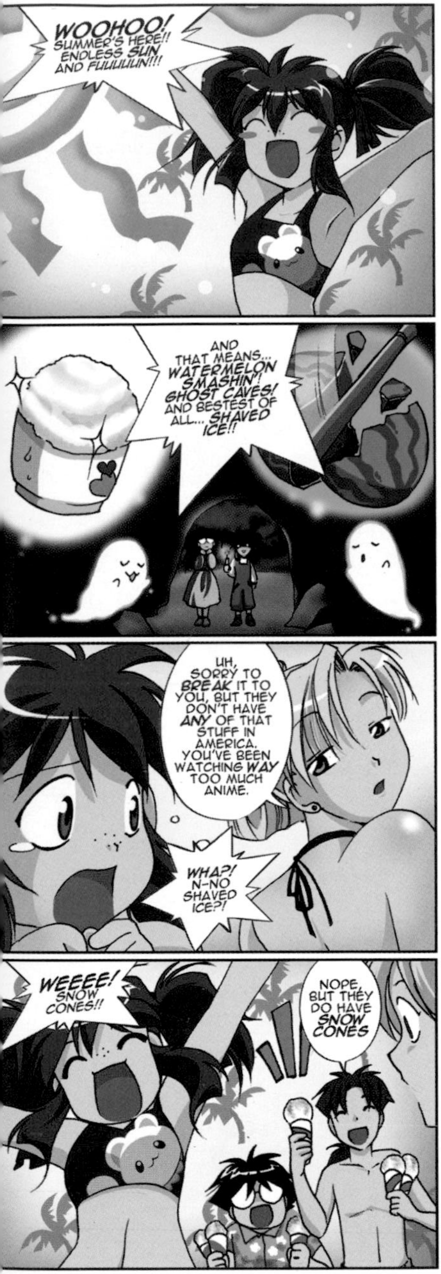
WOOHOO! SUMMER'S HERE!! ENDLESS SUN AND FUUUUUN!!!
AND THAT MEANS... WATERMELON SMASHIN'! GHOST CAVES! AND BESTEST OF ALL... SHAVED ICE!!
UH, SORRY TO BREAK IT TO YOU, BUT THEY DON'T HAVE ANY OF THAT STUFF IN AMERICA. YOU'VE BEEN WATCHING WAY TOO MUCH ANIME.
WHA?! N-NO SHAVED ICE?!
NOPE, BUT THEY DO HAVE SNOW CONES
WEEEE! SNOW CONES!!

RETURNING THE FAVOR

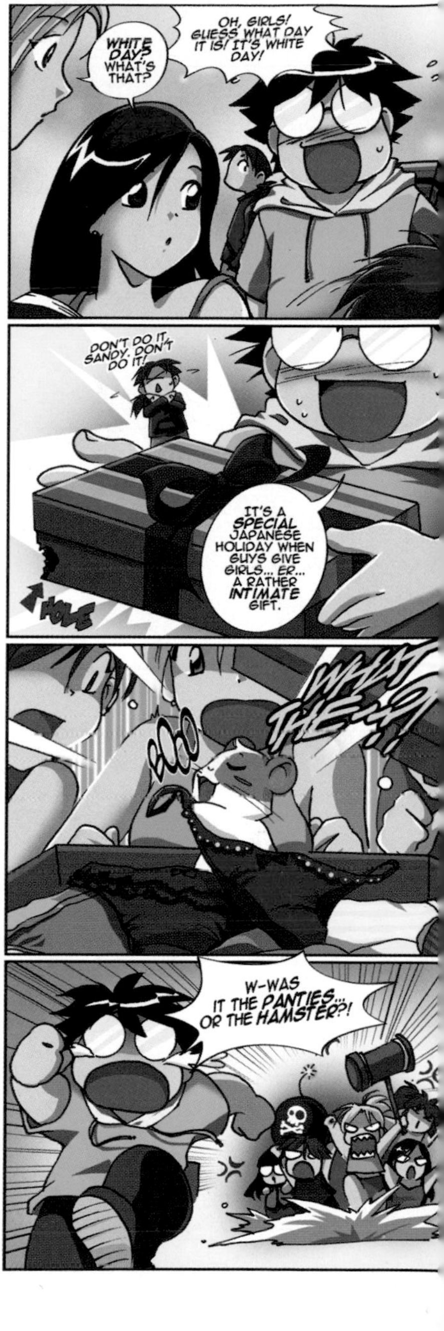
OH, GIRLS! GUESS WHAT DAY IT IS! IT'S WHITE DAY!
WHITE DAY? WHAT'S THAT?
DON'T DO IT, SANDY. DON'T DO IT!
IT'S A SPECIAL JAPANESE HOLIDAY WHEN GUYS GIVE GIRLS... ER... A RATHER INTIMATE GIFT.
HOLE
WHAT THE--?!
BOO
W-WAS IT THE PANTIES... OR THE HAMSTER?!

MANGA 101

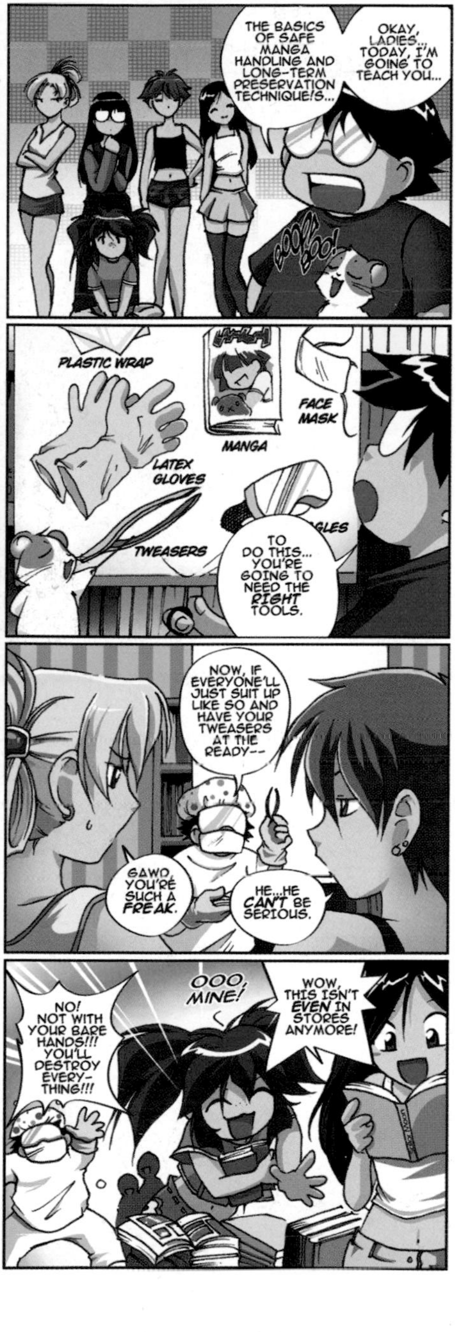
OKAY, LADIES... TODAY, I'M GOING TO TEACH YOU...
THE BASICS OF SAFE MANGA HANDLING AND LONG-TERM PRESERVATION TECHNIQUE!S...
FACE MASK
MANGA
PLASTIC WRAP
LATEX GLOVES
TWEASERS
TO DO THIS... YOU'RE GOING TO NEED THE RIGHT TOOLS.
NOW, IF EVERYONE'LL JUST SUIT UP LIKE SO AND HAVE YOUR TWEASERS AT THE READY--
HE...HE CAN'T BE SERIOUS.
GAWD, YOU'RE SUCH A FREAK.
WOW, THIS ISN'T EVEN IN STORES ANYMORE!
OOO, MINE!
NO! NOT WITH YOUR BARE HANDS!!! YOU'LL DESTROY EVERY-THING!!!

DREAM COME TRUE?

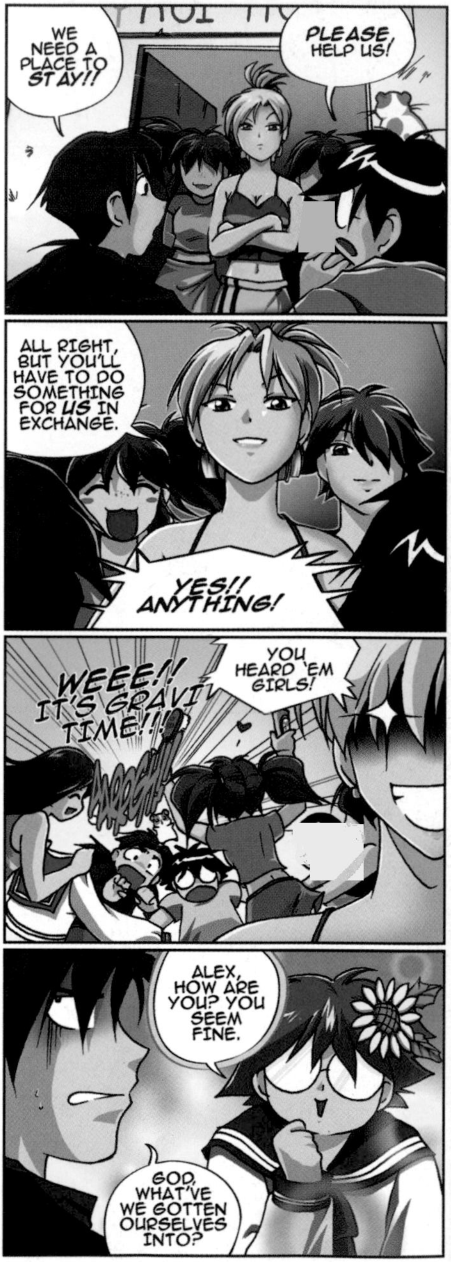
PLEASE HELP US!
WE NEED A PLACE TO STAY!!
ALL RIGHT, BUT YOU'LL HAVE TO DO SOMETHING FOR US IN EXCHANGE.
YES!! ANYTHING!
YOU HEARD 'EM GIRLS!
WEEE!! IT'S GRAVI TIME!!!
ALEX, HOW ARE YOU? YOU SEEM FINE.
GOD, WHAT'VE WE GOTTEN OURSELVES INTO?

V-DAY BLUES

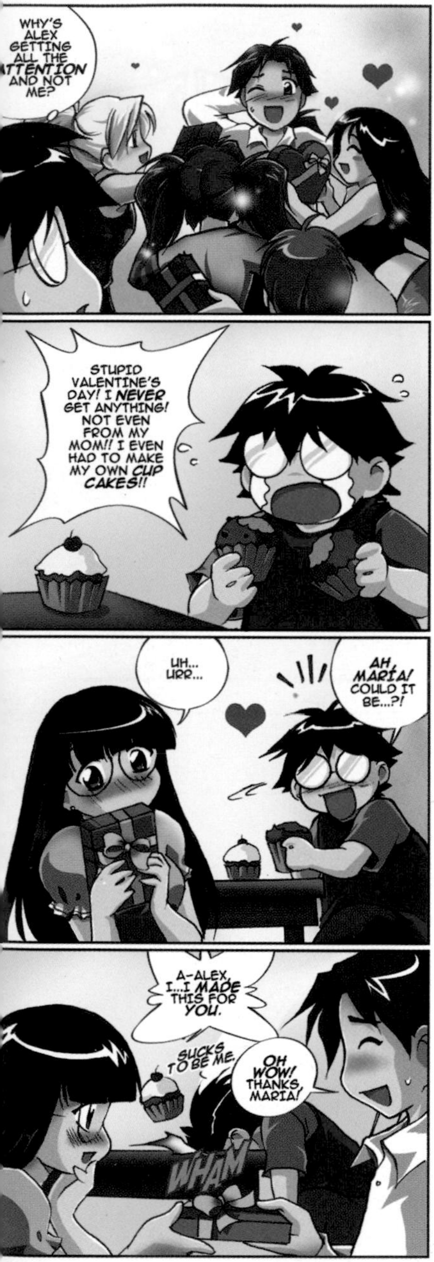
WHY'S ALEX GETTING ALL THE TTENTION AND NOT ME?
STUPID VALENTINE'S DAY! I NEVER GET ANYTHING! NOT EVEN FROM MY MOM!! I EVEN HAD TO MAKE MY OWN CUP CAKES!!
AH, MARÍA! COULD IT BE...?!
UH... URR...
A-ALEX, I...I MADE THIS FOR YOU.
OH WOW! THANKS, MARIA!
SUCKS TO BE ME.
WHAM

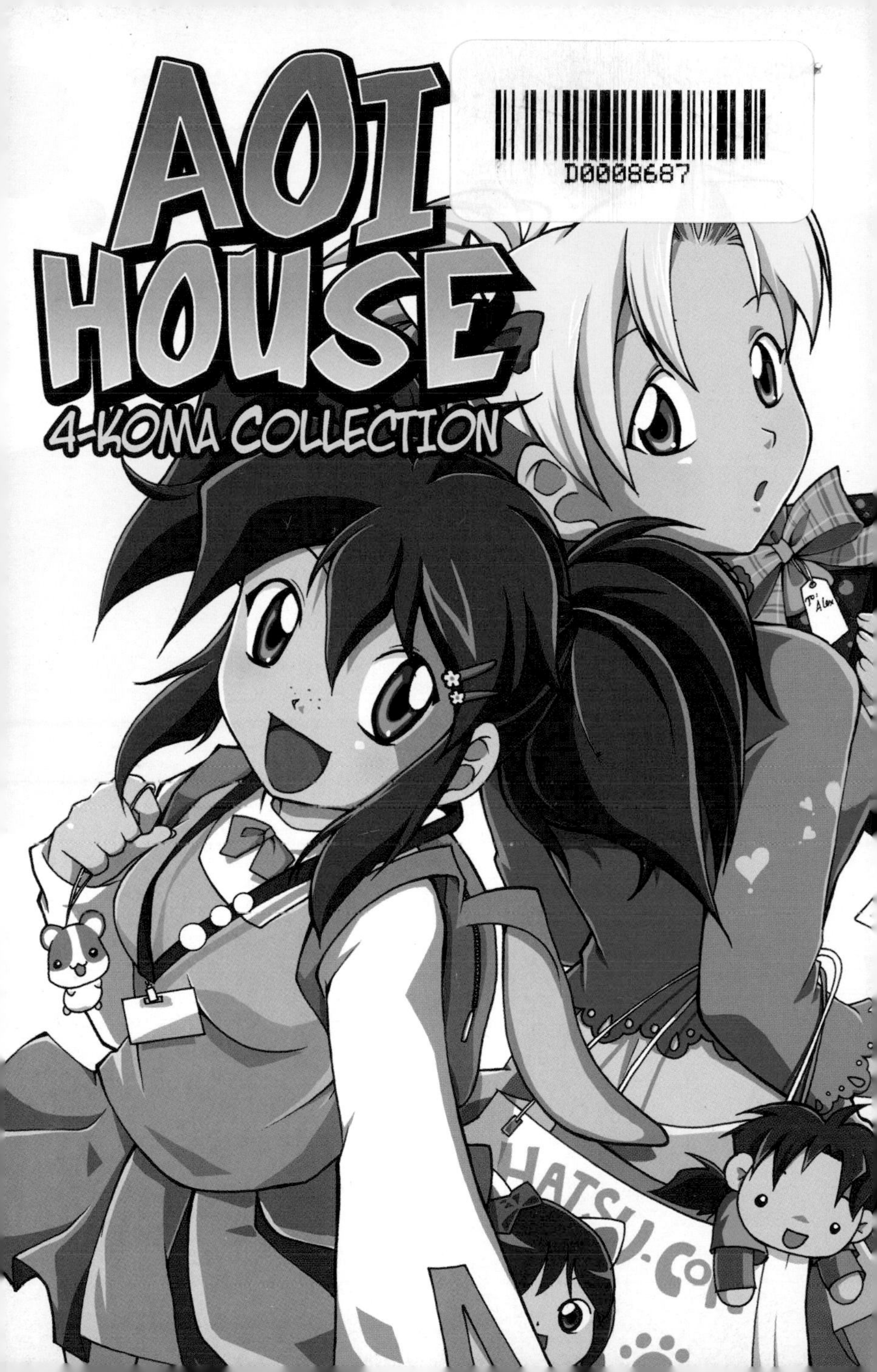
AOI HOUSE
4-KOMA COLLECTION
To: Alex